Private Charles C. Mosher, Company B, 85th N.Y. Infantry, in early 1864, before his imprisonment at Andersonville. (Wayne Mahood Collection)

CHARLIE MOSHER'S CIVIL WAR

*From Fair Oaks to Andersonville
with the Plymouth Pilgrims
(85th N.Y. Infantry)*

EDITED BY WAYNE MAHOOD

LONGSTREET HOUSE
HIGHTSTOWN, NJ
New Book No. 120
1994

©1994 by Wayne Mahood

Diary used with the permission of Louise Badgely and
Mr. and Mrs. William L. Harvey. Original copied
"from the archives of the Seneca Falls Historical
Society" and used with permission.
All rights reserved. Permission to reproduce in any form
must be secured from the author and the publisher.

Please direct all correspondence and book orders to:
LONGSTREET HOUSE
Post Office Box 730
Hightstown NJ 08520

ISBN Number 0-944413-20-X
Library of Congress Catalog Card Number 91-061412

Printed in the United States of America.

CONTENTS

List of Illustrations iv
List of Maps vii
Preface viii
Introduction xi
Acknowledgements xv
Chapter One. "I've Wanted to Enlist Since Sumter" 1
Chapter Two. The Peninsula Campaign 41
Chapter Three. "To be Gone Ten Days" 69
Chapter Four. To Plymouth, "The Queer Town" 107
Chapter Five. "The Ram is in Command: 171
The Battle of Plymouth"
Chapter Six. "Andersonville Prison: 201
Whoever Entered Here left Hope Behind"
Chapter Seven. "Out of a Filthy Hog Pen" 253
Chapter Eight. "Still Alive 285
Tears Flowed Freely"
Appendix A. Charles C. Mosher's Obituary 301
Appendix B. Company B Roster 303
Notes 309
Bibliography 358
General Index 362
Index to Members of the 85th New York 373
Author's Biography 378

LIST OF ILLUSTRATIONS

Front.	Private Charles C. Mosher in early 1864
5	Page 1 from Mosher's Original Diary
9	Postcard of Barracks No. 4 at Elmira, N.Y.
13	Lieutenant Colonel Will W. Clarke
16	Charles Mosher Soon After His Enlistment
17	The Commissary Store, Church Street, Elmira
22	Major General Silas Casey
26	Union Camp Outside Washington, D.C., January 1862
38	Transports on the Potomac
40	Major Genearl George B. McClellan
42	Fortress Monroe in 1861
50	Fort Magruder and the Confederate Defenses at Williamsburg
54	Lieutenant Amos Brunson
72	Ruins of Hampton, Va.
81	Brigadier General Henry W. Wessells
82	Winter Quarters
100	Brigadier General John J. Foster
104	James B. Robinson
111	Marcus M. Meade
130	Plymouth in 1863
154	(top) Plan of the *Albemarle*

154	(bot) Building the *Albemarle*
157	Samuel B. Adams
170	Major General Robert F. Hoke
174	Mosher's Reenlistment Paper
184	Mosher's Furlough Pass
185	Sarah Mosher
187	Charles C. Mosher, February 1864
196	The Sinking of the *Southfield*
198	The *Albemarle*
199	Fort Williams Historical Marker at Plymouth
208	The Charleston and Savannah Railroad
209	Captain Henry Wirz
211	"Fresh Fish"
216	Artist's Conception of Andersonville in 1864
220	Hounds Tearing a Prisoner
222	The So-called Hospital
224	Religious Services
226	Two Views of Andersonville in August 1864
229	Shot at the Dead Line
231	The Raiders in Action
234	Execution of the Leaders
237	Burying the Dead

239	More "Fresh Fish"
241	Infested with Maggots
244	(top) Issuing Rations at Andersonville, August 1864
244	(bot) Andersonville in August 1864
245	The Break in the Stockade Caused by the August 9, 1864 Rainstorm
247	Another Comrade Gone
249	(top) Another view of the Andersonville Stockade in August 1864
249	(bot) Andersonville Cemetery
259	Elam B. Wetmore
263	Ira N. Deyo

LIST OF MAPS

6   Diagram of Barracks No. 4 at Elmira

11   Barracks Area, Elmira, N.Y.

20   Route of the Eighty-Fifth Regiment to Washington, D.C.

39   Route of the Eighty-Fifth Regiment from Washington, D.C. to Hampton Roads

45   The Lower Peninsula

52   The Peninsular Campaign

56   Battle of Seven Pines

90   The North Carolina Coast

93   New Berne, N.C., and Defenses

95   Route Pursued in the Advance to Goldsboro

123   North Carolina in 1863

130   Plymouth in 1863

138   Plymouth, N.C., June 12th, 1863

194   Map of Plymouth and Defenses, April 17-20, 1864

213   Plan of Prison Grounds, Andersonville

221   Sketch of Andersonville Hospital

261   Plan of Florence Stockade

PREFACE

Finding this journal was serendipitous. The editor, researching the legend of the Scythe Tree near Waterloo, New York[1], was following leads seemingly all over Western New York State. The object was to learn more about the Eighty-Fifth New York Volunteer Infantry. Browsing in the Seneca Falls (New York) Historical Society, he spotted a two-volume set titled *Civil War Journal* and pulled it off the shelf. Lo and behold, it was a complete account of an enlisted man's life in the Eighty-Fifth New York Volunteers, albeit handwritten, undated and apparently unpublished.

Why was this not indexed somewhere in the voluminous sources on the Civil War? It was not even catalogued in the historical society.

How did it come about? At first there were no clues. Then late in the second volume, just prior to a printed portion, came the answer.

For almost three decades each March 1, Seneca Falls machinist, Charles Mosher, absented himself from work to celebrate with his wife his return to Union lines after his release from a Confederate prison in Florence, South Carolina, on that date in 1865. However, in 1894, at the urging of his wife, Maria, the celebration took a somewhat different tack. Mosher wrote a "short sketch" of his "last days in the Confederacy," which "took all night" and was given to his friend, Charles T. Andrews, editor of the *Seneca County Courier* in Seneca Falls, New York.[2] Publication of this sketch apparently was well received and led Andrews to encourage Mosher to "give us some more of that [prison] stuff."

Mosher had the "stuff" all right. In fact, he had kept a diary throughout almost four years of military service in the Civil War as a volunteer in Co. B, 85th N.Y. Vols. But he faced two problems. First, could he translate the prison diary that "was so faded out that I took a magnifying glass to pick it out?" The second problem--an emotional one--proved greater:

> I sat up night after night untill (sic.) 11 o'clock reading and copying it - when I would get so nervous over it - I stopped. I had to go over my life there [in Andersonville and Florence prisons] and see it all as I had lived it. My emotions overcame me to such an extent - at times that - I cried. Could not help it. After some months I finished the copying of it.

A short printed version of Mosher's prison experiences, which appeared in the *Courier*, was bound for him by Andrews. The bound volume was large enough for a full-sized book, which may have led Mosher to translate by hand his entire diary into what eventually became two volumes running to almost 600 pages.

The result is a rare treat for the reader. Most diaries read something like "Stormy-on guard-camp muddy. Camp Warren. Drew letters of the Regt." or "Pleasant-Yorktown evacuated, all of Army moving. 2 killed and 3 wounded by shell being placed in the ground with a fuse . . ."[3] Not so reticent, young Mosher.

Dec. 4.

We liked to froze last night. The boys in one of the cars built a fire on the car [boxcar] floor . . . The snow is fence high. We go over mountains, cross rivers, through tunnels, cold is no name for it.

The stations we stop at are small, but the dutch women who flock around the cars, with eadibles (sic.) to sell . . . They are very short and would roll one way as well as another. But they are so fat!

AND

March 24

We were reviewed by Genl Keyes to day (sic.) . . . Casey's [Major General Silas Casey] little boy rode with the reviewing officers. He is about 12 years old, and had on his uniform and sword like the rest of them. He rode a large gray horse and looked like a monkey mounted.

The irreverent and humorous Mosher was a faithful diarist, seldom failing to record occurrences and feelings, even during three hundred fifteen days in southern prisons, including the infamous Andersonville. Important is the fact that Mosher was a genuine diarist, respecting "the Latin meaning of *diarium* and its denial of knowledge of the future."[4] It is fresh, "real life" and spontaneous, with each day offering something new, including suspense and anxiety over what lay ahead. Only on rare occasions did he feel the need to edit.

As the editor read through the volume, he realized this was a gold mine and furiously scribbled notes on 5 x 8 index cards, but there was no way he was going to record all that was desired. So he asked Geralyn Heiser, the director of the historical society at the time, if he could borrow the journal to make a copy. Miraculously, she agreed, as did Richard Quick, Director, Milne Library, State University College, Geneseo, New York, who saw this as an addition to the library's special collection on local history.

From there it was a short step to wanting to edit and annotate Mosher's journal to make it available to a wider audience. Care has been taken to retain

Mosher's spelling, punctuation and grammar, though occasional bracketed corrections are made for readability. Footnotes were added for clarity and accuracy, and sources are noted, though Mosher was quite accurate in his recording, except for some dates of events to which he was not a party and occasional misspellings of names. For more detail in the annotation heavy reliance has been placed on research done for my regimental history.[5] Biographies of men who served in the 85th Regiment are derived from *Adjutant Generals Reports of the State of New York* (Albany: J. B. Lyon, State Printer, 1902), while biographies of generals are derived from Ezra Warner, *Generals in Gray* and *Generals in Blue* (Baton Rouge: Louisiana State University Press, 1959 and 1964). For a full account of Mosher's regiment, see my 1989 study, *The Plymouth Pilgrims: A History of the Eighty-Fifth New York Infantry in the Civil War* (Hightstown, N.J.: Longstreet House).

CHARLIE MOSHER: CIVIL WAR DIARIST

INTRODUCTION

Charles C. Mosher was a nineteen-year-old farm boy who had worked for a year as a machinist prior to enlisting. However, he seems to have come to army life naturally. His paternal grandfather, John Mosher, a 30-year-old Minute Man, took up the Revolutionary cause in 1775, leaving behind a wife and two children[1]. As a second lieutenant commissioned by Joseph Warren, grandfather John fought at Bunker Hill and in 1778 distinguished himself by sporting a bayonet against a cavalry charge. Later battles by First Lieutenant Mosher (commissioned by John Hancock) included Bemis Heights, Saratoga, and White Plains. In 1780, after five years of fighting without pay, Lieutenant Mosher returned home to tell stories about his military duty to listeners, which included his son, Charles's father, Abijah Mosher, born March 3, 1794.

Abijah carried on the tradition in 1814 serving as a sergeant at Sacketts Harbor on Lake Ontario near Watertown in the War of 1812, willingly arming and equipping himself for war. This spirit of serving one's country was reinforced by Abijah, an anti-slavery advocate, who encouraged his nineteen-year-old son to enlist in the Union Army in 1861. However, the youngest Mosher's diary suggests the spirit had waned some, for he was less than a dedicated soldier, remaining a private after almost four full years of service. Ironically, his fidelity in maintaining a diary implies a concern for posterity: he sent home a completed diary in July 1862 and then remitted his discharge and reenlistment papers just before the Battle of Plymouth in April 1864.

Not so surprising, Mosher apparently liked to read. June 20, 1863 he recorded running into a "schoolmate," Frank Chapin, with whom he had read about the Crimean War and rued the prospect that "there would be nothing for us to do when we got to be men."[2] On January 24, 1864, while foraging on a plantation in Tyrell County, North Carolina, Mosher discovered a "large room . . . filled with books" and took "a copy of Shakspere (sic.) and Youngs Night Thoughts . . ." The next day, after putting a large arm chair and a pair of antlers in a cart, he slipped into his knapsack "Two of G. P. R. James books to read on the road."

The diarist was born Charles Condit Mosher on May 8, 1842 in Waterloo, New York, to Abijah and Carlone [Condit] Mosher. He was the youngest of four children, having two brothers, David and George, and one sister, Sarah. Shortly thereafter the Moshers moved to a farm near the hamlet of Chapinville (now Chapin) just north of Canandaigua and about 15 miles northwest of Waterloo.

Mosher's reenlistment papers signed January 1, 1864, stated that he was five feet, eleven and one half inches tall with blue eyes, brown hair and light complexion.[3] They also stated that he was by occupation a mechanic. A contemporary photograph shows him to be a husky young man. (See page 16.) According to Mosher's account, on Monday, October 7, 1861,

> "Father told me that he saw that the war was turning on the question of slavery, and that he was willing that I should enlist. He is a strong Anti-Slavery man, and was a member of the executive committee of the Utica, N.Y. Anti-Slavery society in the year before I was born."

Then he recalls the military record of his father and grandfather and declares "Now it's my turn. I am going sure." The next morning, he made good his promise, and walked four miles to the recruiting station in Canandaigua to "see if I could get into Captain Clarke's company," which subsequently became Company B, 85th N.Y. Vols.[4] Undeterred by the claim that the company was full, Mosher hung around until after noon when he inquired again and was informed that "there was room for one more man." The company was to leave for the Elmira military depot at 7 p.m., so he practically ran back home to pack his clothes. Catching a ride from a neighbor, he returned in time to catch the train with the other recruits.

From Elmira the 85th N.Y. Vols. rode airy, cold boxcars to Washington, the trip in which Mosher encountered the "dutch women," preparatory to engaging in the fruitless Peninsula Campaign in spring 1862. Subsequently his detached brigade slogged through the Great Dismal Swamp of southern Virginia and northern North Carolina, engaging in a few minor skirmishes before settling in the pretty little town of New Bern to help disrupt the main rail lines between Wilmington, South Carolina and Richmond, Virginia. In mid 1863 his brigade moved northeast to the town of Plymouth, North Carolina on Albemarle Sound. Uneventful service did not seem to bother Mosher, for he reenlisted in January 1864. His reasons, though, may have been somewhat materialistic--a furlough and promise of a $750 bounty, enough to buy a small farm.

Mosher was one of the few who realized his reenlistment furlough, which was granted on February 7, 1864, because of his father's death. Furloughs for others were canceled out of fear of a Confederate attack at any time. A photograph taken while on furlough shows a healthy looking, fully-bearded, young man rather proud of his uniform. (See page 187.) Dutifully he returned to Plymouth shortly before a fateful attack by Confederate General Robert F. Hoke by land and by Commander James W. Cooke in the ironclad, *Albemarle*. On April 21, 1864, twenty-two year old Private Charles C. Mosher was one of almost 2000 Union prisoners of war who began the agonizing trip to Camp Sumter in southwest Georgia, better known simply as "Andersonville," to begin almost a year's ordeal in Southern prisons.

The last act of the soldiers before capture was to strip their company flag from its staff, tear it into pieces and distribute it among themselves. Mosher's share was "a piece of the red strip, six inches long by one inch wide."

The newly-paid, well-dressed, impudent Plymouth Pilgrims contrasted sharply with the sick, emaciated, half-alive inmates already at Andersonville. Shortly, however, the new arrivals would be indistinguishable from the others; they either traded away or were stripped of anything of value.

About 3 p.m. March 1, 1865, "tears flowed freely, couldn't help it," as Mosher reached Union lines near Wilmington, South Carolina. Helped out of a boxcar by men of the 25th Michigan, he glimpsed "our old flag and found strength" to walk toward a grove of trees under which he flopped to the ground. Coffee and hardtack, "the first I have had in nearly a year . . . was so good."

A rejuvenated Charles Mosher then recorded he was "Safe! Glory Hallelujah! This ends the three hundred and fifteenth day of prison life."

Still emaciated and badly weakened but alive, he was discharged at David's Island, New York Harbor June 27, 1865. He then slowly made his way back to Chapinville, retracing his way through Elmira and Canandaigua. Barely two months later he returned to his job as a machinist for the Steam Fire Engine Work, later the Silsby Manufacturing Co. and still later the American Fire Engine Co., in Seneca Falls, New York.

April 14, 1869 Mosher was joined in marriage with twenty-eight-year-old Maria Antoinette Badgley by the Rev. Horace C. Allen in the Town of Aurelius, Cayuga County, New York. According to a pension statement, March 19, 1915, there were no issue from the marriage.

His army experience apparently stayed with him, for he became quite active in the G.A.R. Cross Post #78 in Seneca Falls. Surprising for one who never rose above the rank of private during the war, Mosher, in turn, served as chaplain, adjutant and commander.[5] In 1906 he transferred to the Swift Post #94[6] in the city of Geneva to which he had moved in September 1899. The next year he was elected commander of that post, serving four terms, 1907-1910. A real highlight of his G.A.R. experience was a tour April 16 to May 1, 1914, to Richmond, Danville, Salisbury, Andersonville, Chickamauga and Chattanooga arranged by the Pennsylvania Railroad. The most emotional moment of the trip was on April 29 when he spent ten hours in Andersonville, Georgia, at the dedication of the monument erected by the state of New York to its soldiers who died there during the Civil War. Looking up at the twenty-one foot high monument, Mosher "was completely overcome by my emotions. I could have and would have lain down on the ground and cried. I did cry, but I stood up. I was afraid I would break down, and I did." He even recalled where his "shebang" was.

Charles Mosher retired at the age of 74 on April 1, 1916. His retirement afforded him more time to add to his journal, which at that point had become a scrapbook rapidly filling with various mementoes of his army service, including a facsimile of the Andersonville Prison Survivor's Medal pinned on him on that emotional day in 1914. He continued to add items and clarifications until shortly before his death of a cerebral hemorrhage December 30, 1920, a few months shy of his seventy-ninth birthday.

It is unlikely that this journal originally was intended for anyone else's eyes. Fortunately, it came out that way, for it is as thorough a description of Civil War army life by an enlisted man as exists. But better yet, it is good reading.

ACKNOWLEDGMENTS

Accepting the risk of all authors and editors, I thank those who helped get this diary in print. Of course, none was more important than Charles C. Mosher, a nineteen-year-old farm boy who faithfully maintained a diary for three years and seven months of his army experience, and to his wife who encouraged him to make it more widely available. Next to him I owe an immense debt of gratitude to Martha DeLavergne, who just as faithfully pressed forward with the typing of the handwritten diary and performed the kind of miracles I have come to expect of her. Nor can I forget Miss Louise Badgley, the 101-year-old niece of Charles Mosher, who with the encouragement of Mosher's grandniece and husband, Mr. & Mrs. William L. Harvey, prompted the Seneca Falls Historical Society to grant permission to edit and annotate the diary. And, of course, I want to recognize Gerry Heiser, the then director of the Historical Society who allowed me to photocopy the diary originally. Nothing could have happened without her or my friend, John E. Becker, ITFB, President of the Seneca Falls Historical Society, who stuck his neck out to vouch for my integrity.

Travel expenses were borne partly by the Geneseo Foundation (College Senate Travel Grant) and the NYS/UUP Professional Development Quality of Working Life program, for which I am grateful.

Librarians here at SUNY Geneseo have bailed me out numerous times, and Judith Bushnell as reference librarian even found the proverbial "needle in a haystack," an obscure reference that would have stumped most librarians. I am also grateful to other librarians, who did not waste time even to identify themselves at New Bern, Goldsboro, Raleigh and Plymouth, North Carolina. Alfred "Chick" Hilbert, unpaid archivist at the Chemung County Historical Society at Elmira, was of invaluable help in locating information about the barracks at Elmira, including drawings. And, my friend John Genung, helpful as always, even found an old post card of his father's showing the barracks. Craig F. Senfield of Olean, N.Y., provided a photograph of Alexander Hussey, his great-great uncle.

Last, but not least, I want to thank publicly, Dr. David G. Martin, editor, Longstreet House, who earlier risked his reputation by publishing my first attempt at Civil War history.

for

Bobbi, Bruce, Dave and Anne,

who have suffered the Civil War

with me for more than a dozen years.

CHARLIE MOSHER'S
CIVIL WAR

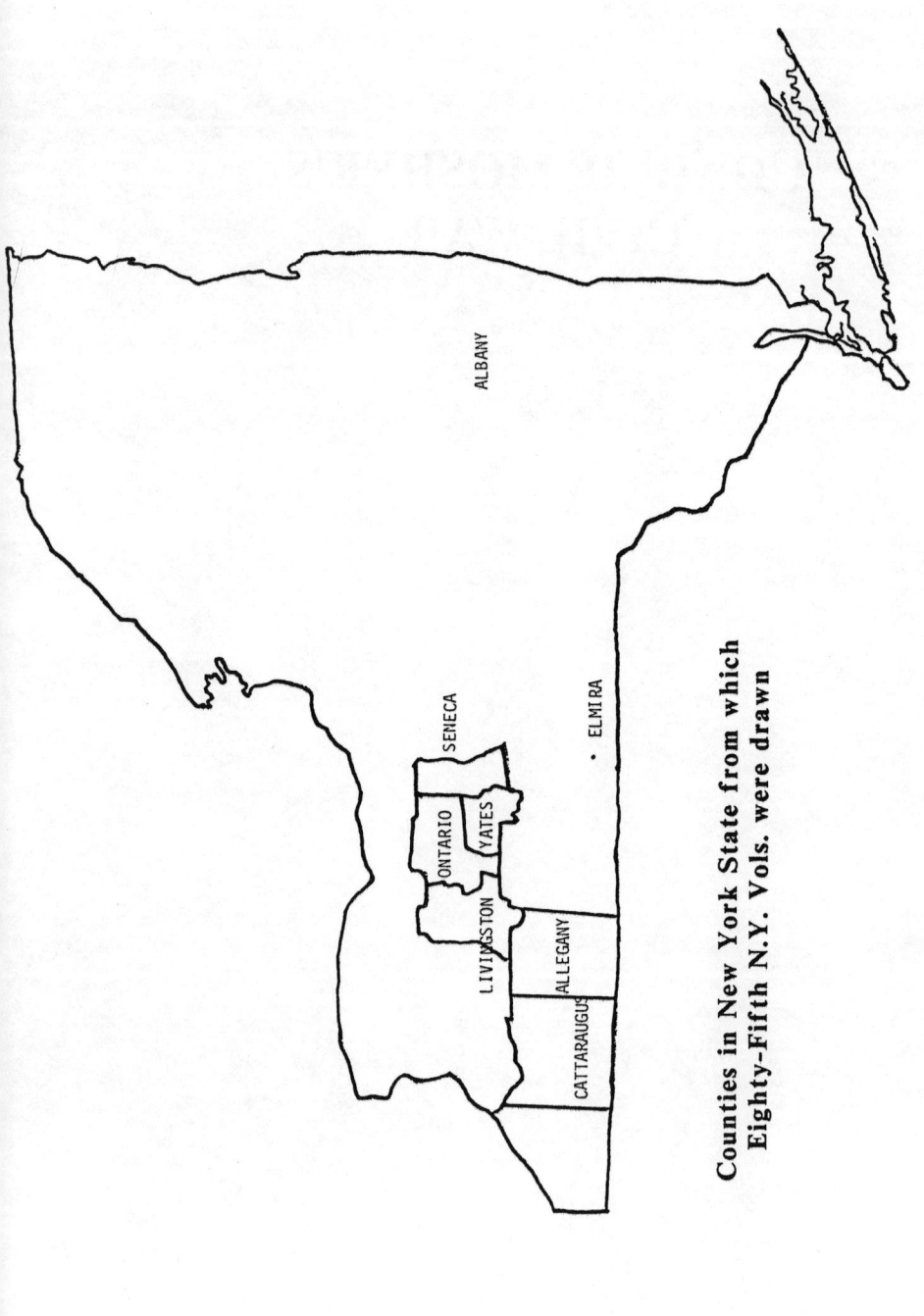

Counties in New York State from which Eighty-Fifth N.Y. Vols. were drawn

Chapter One

"I'VE WANTED TO ENLIST SINCE SUMTER"

(October 11, 1861-March 31, 1862)

With the confidence of youth and goaded by his perception of his father's and grandfather's military service, Charles Condit Mosher, a strapping nineteen-year old, felt he should enlist. No doubt his father's antislavery sentiments influenced him, though it would be inaccurate to state that he had adopted the cause. Indeed, he was still rather carefree, as is evident in his journal. Probably young Charlie Mosher enlisted out of youthful exuberance, though he did not answer Lincoln's April call for volunteers as had others from his area. Still, he distinguished himself from his two older brothers who remained civilians.

Clearly Mosher had followed events of the past year: secession, the firing on Fort Sumter, the quota of soldiers New York was to meet, the patriotic speeches being given, and the war fever gripping the North. He was a literate young man, who had read about the Crimean War and feared he would not have the opportunity to be a warrior himself.

While he acclimated rather easily to military life, Mosher was anything but a compliant recruit--he was too busy testing himself and finding ready accomplices. This seems to have come easily, possibly because of his nonchalance. His only role model was his regimental commander, Captain Will W. Clark, one of four brothers who joined the cause, and Mosher would readily take to Clark, virtually adoring him the rest of his life. Only Brigadier General Henry W. Wessells, who later would be his brigade commander, could compete for Mosher's attention and affection.

At Elmira, one of three state (later federal) depots, Mosher would be joined by other recruits from nearby counties to form the Eighty-Fifth New York Volunteers. Not surprisingly, Mosher tended to identify his friends as those coming from Ontario or Seneca counties rather than the vast majority who came from Allegany and Cattaraugus counties, though he shared the same occupation as most of them did--farming.

Because it took time to form, equip and develop at least rudimentary military readiness, the Eighty-Fifth was not formally mustered until early December. The men then headed for Washington to become part of over 100,000 soldiers of the Army of the Potomac, commanded by Major General George B. McClellan. McClellan was a favorite of many of the soldiers, but not of Mosher, who may have been influenced by General Wessells's antipathy toward "Little Mac."

December 8, 1862 found Charlie Mosher and his compatriots in the nation's capital, where military duty would take on a more serious note, especially as McClellan's plan to move down the Virginia peninsula became formed. But the youthful Mosher also found time to do his own reconnoitering (if need be, by forging passes), checking out the sights, including the Soldiers' Home, the arsenal, the Patent Office, the capitol, the newly invented gatling gun, and Kate Dean, a popular singer also from upstate New York. But he also saw death up close, for possibly the first time, when some of his fellow recruits succumbed to pneumonia. And, like others, he followed the news of the war in the west, including the capture of Fort Donelson.

In time drill weariness and boredom caused Mosher to itch for something more. Finally, after interminable delays, his outfit was on its way to war.

Chapinville Ontario County N.Y.
 Friday October 11. 1861
(My muster in date from Oct. 8.)
I have wanted to enlist for a soldier ever since Sumter was fired on. I was 19 years old on the 8th day of May. and measure five feet, and eleven and three quarter inches high.

Father told me yesterday that he saw that the war was turning on the question of slavery. and that he was willing that I should enlist. He is a strong Anti-Slavery man. and was a member of the executive committee of the Utica N.Y. Anti-Slavery society; in the years before I was born.

His father was in the war of the Revolution. a 1st Lieut. in the 8th Mass. Inf. and he was in the war of 1812. Now it's my turn. I am going. sure.

Page 1 from Mosher's original diary.
(Courtesy of Mr. & Mrs. William L. Harvey and the Seneca Falls Historical Society)

I went to Canandaigua this morning to see if I could get into Captain Clarkes company. At Mr. Howells office I was told that Clarkes company was full. Then I went to the office of the chairman of the war committee. Mr. Bull. — Bull was major of the 126th N.Y. Inft. when I was told again that Clarkes company was full. I then tried at the office of Brown + Fitzgerald who were recruiting for a Buffalo regiment. They were not in. No go.

After a while I went back to Bulls office, and was told that orderly martin of Clarkes company was just in, and that there was room for one more man. I waited untill I saw him. He told me he was to leave for Elmira at 7. P. M. with a squad of men from Bloomfield +

Chapinville, Ontario County, N.Y.

Friday, October 11, 1861. (My muster in dates from October 8.)

I have wanted to enlist for a soldier ever since Sumter was fired on. I was 19 years old on the 8th day of May and measure five feet and eleven and three-quarters inches high.

Father told me yesterday that he saw that the war was turning on the question of slavery and that he was willing that I should enlist. He is a strong anti-slavery man and was a member of the executive committee of the Utica, N.Y. Anti-Slavery Society in the years before I was born.

His father was in the war of the Revolution, a 1st Lieutenant in the 8th Mass. Inf. and he was in the War of 1812.[1] Now it's my turn. I am going, sure.

I went to Canadaigua this morning to see if I could get into Captain Clarke's Company.[2] At Mr. Howell's office I was told that Clarke's company was full. Then I went to the office of the Chairman of the War Committee--Mr. Bull--Bull was major of the 126th N.Y.[3] Later, when I was told again that Clarke's company was full, I then tried at the office of Brown and Fitzgerald, who were recruiting for a Buffalo regiment. They were not in. No go.

After a while I went back to Bull's office and was told that Orderly Martin[4] of Clarke's company was just in and that there was room for one more man. I waited until I saw him. He told me he was to leave for Elmira at 7 p.m. with a squad of men from Bloomfield and Bristol way and to get ready and go with them.

I hurried down home--Canandaigua is four miles from Chapinville. I walked both ways. Packed my satchel, bid my folks good bye and started for Canandaigua again. As I was trudging along one of the neighbors hailed me with "Where are you going Charlie?" I told him I had enlisted. Going to walk? I said yes. He told me to wait and Terry (his son) would drive up to town with me. I waited.[5]

I took supper in Canandaigua with my brother George and family.[6]

After supper I found Martin and his squad. We took the cars for Elmira a 7 p.m. There are eighteen in the squad and I am a stranger to all.

We reached Elmira in due time. The rain pouring down in torrents when we got off the cars. 1st. Lieut. C. S. Aldrich[7] met us at the station to escort us to the barracks. It was so very dark that he had to carry a lantern, then he lost his way so that we went a long way out of our way. When we reached the barracks we were wet through. Soaking wet. I slept in the Captain's room-- which is the room of Lieut. Aldrich also. The captain not being in I occupied his bunk. The Lieut. told me that I was so wet I had better take a little brandy to keep from taking cold. I thanked him and told him I was all right and did not need any, jumped into my bunk and went to sleep.

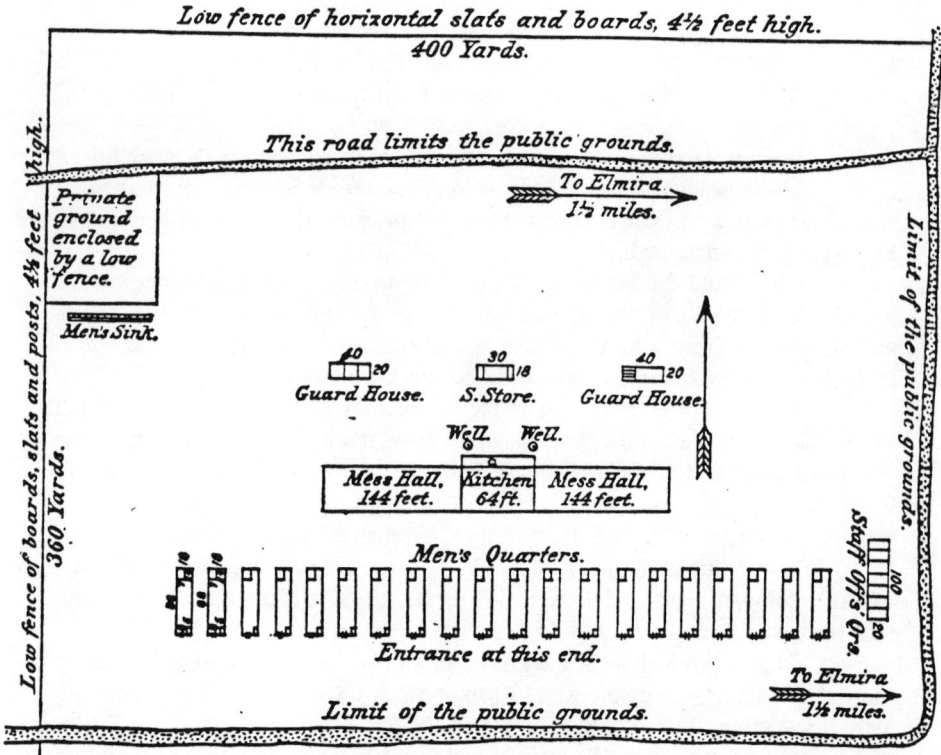

PERMANENT CAMP, KNOWN AS CAMP ROBINSON BARRACKS, AT ELMIRA, NEW YORK.

Diagram of Barracks, No. 4 at Elmira (*O.R.*, Ser. II, Vol. IV, p. 75)

October 12 [1861]. I slept good last night, if it was my first night in camp. It took me some time this morning to get my bearings. I found them in time to fall in for breakfast. A very good breakfast. Coffee, bread, potatoes, meat.

This camp is called Barracks No. 4.[8] Two regiments are being recruited here, ours, and one called the "Dickinson Guards." Each barrack is a long, one storied building and occupied by one company. There are ten companies in a regiment or will be when full. The barracks stand with the ends towards the parade ground. The interior of each barrack is fitted up with a row of bunks, three tiers high. Every bunk in ours is taken.

The entrance to them is through a narrow hallway, on one side of which is a room occupied by the Captain and First Lieut., on the other side the Second Lieut. and/orderly sergeant stay.

The cook house and mess rooms are in the rear of the barracks. The cook house is in the center with a mess room on either end.

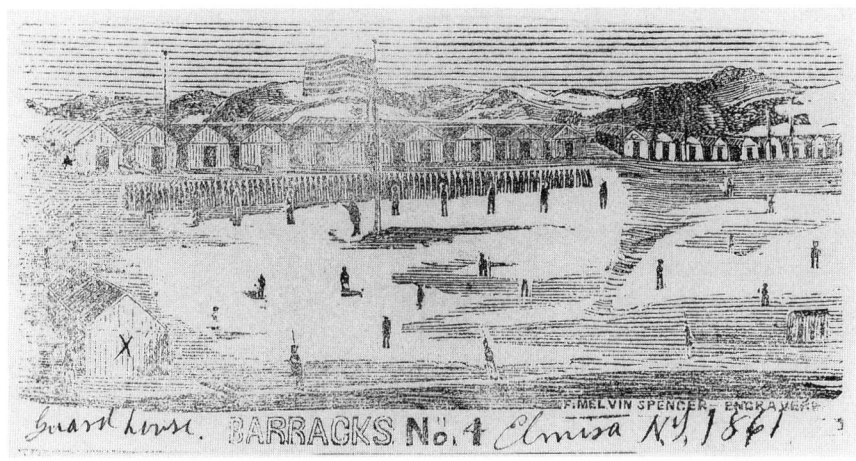

**Postcard of Barracks #4 at Elmira, N.Y.
(Courtesy of John S. Genung,
Reproduced by Ronald Pretzer)**

In each mess room are ten long tables made of boards with a bench on each side. Each table will seat one hundred men.

After breakfast this morning I found one man here that I went to school with when I was about ten years old, his name is Augustus Gregg.[9] The rest are all strangers to me.

Had my first drill in the awkward squad. I managed to get through it.

Our squad that came in last night have to get bunks up over the officer's rooms. We have placed boards over the whole place and have quite a place. Not much head room.

This afternoon I was told this company is full--all told, one hundred and one men, and there is no place for me. I am in a fix. But I am here for a soldier. This company is in the left of the regiment and Captain King's[10] Company on the right. I shall try and get into King's if I can't make a go here.

Dress parade tonight. It looks very fine. We are without uniforms and arms, but we go through the facings.

Sunday, October 13 [1861]. Roll call. Breakfast, wrote home. This afternoon Lt. Aldrich organized a bible class. This evening fifty-two of us went down to M. E. Church. We marched in church in great style and were seated in the amen pews.

October 14 [1861]. One of the squad that came down the other night has left for parts unknown which makes room for me. Hurrah!

October 15. I had my medical examination today and passed up all right. The mustering officer is here but would not muster me without a written consent from my father. Lt. Aldrich drew up a form of consent which to send to Father for him to sign. He will sign it.[11]

I am getting to like it now. Drill, drill, drill all the time. Our Captain Clarke is said to be the best drilled officer in Elmira. Correct. Our company is (B).

October 16. Brigadier General Van Valkenburg[12] and Senator Colfax of Indiana reviewed the troops here today. Drilling all the time. Our food here is very good, and plenty of it. No fault to find.

October 17. A letter from sister Sarah this morning containing my consent. Now I am all right for the mustering officer when he comes. All well at home.

October 18. On guard today for the first time. There are 25 guards around the camp and 15 pickets at night. The pickets are to pick up the men who run the guard, and try to go down town. The guards have guns and are posted a few rods apart. At night the hour is called out, after this fashion. Post No. 1 is at the guard house. He will sing out, "Post No. 1, eight o'clock and all is well." The next post No. 2 says the same, so it goes around the camp. Each guard gives his number first, then the hour. It is kept up every hour.

We stand on post two hours, then have four hours off.

I was mustered today. Now I am all right.

October 23. Our company went down to Headquarters to hold an election for 2nd Lt. Amos Brunson[13] was elected. A very good choice. I voted for Spencer Martin, our orderly sergeant. Lost my vote.

Letter from home today with a two dollar bill in it. I am going home when I get my uniform. Boiled ham for dinner today. We have mush and milk for supper quite often.

October 24. This is a nasty day. glad I am not on guard. About 60 of us went over to barracks No. 3 last night to see the artillery regiment in dress parade.

October 28. I have been promoted. I am captain of the dish washing squad.[14] Our duties are to have charge of our tables in the mess room and wash all the china.

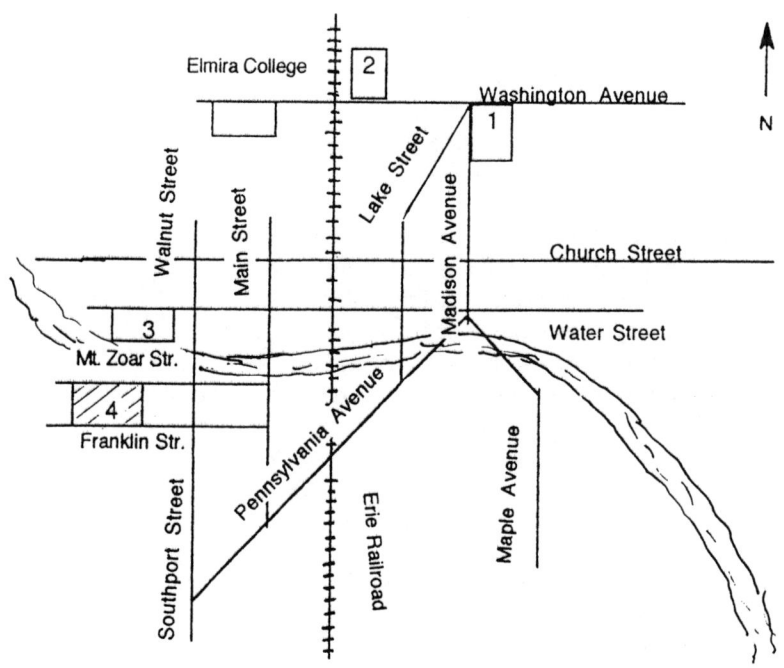

**BARRACKS AREA - ELMIRA, NEW YORK
CIVIL WAR, 1861-1865**

Our china consists mostly of tin plates and cups. A larger number of our company have gone home for a short time. I expect to go next week.[15]

The number of our regiment is 85. Our company is B.[16] In for 3 years--

[Field and Staff Officers][17]

Uriah L. Davis - Colonel
Jonathan S. Belknap - Lt. Col.
Alijah J. Wellman - Major

Wm. M. Smith - Surgeon
James D. Lewis - Asst. Surgeon
Edward Corning - Quarter Master
Horace Goodrich - Adjutant
Darwin E. Maxson - Chaplain

Company A was raised at Olean, N.Y.
Company B was raised at Canandaigua, N.Y.
Company C was raised at Friendship, N.Y.
Company D was raised at Little Genesee, N.Y.
Company E was raised at Granger, N.Y.
Company F was raised at Black Creek and Friendship, N.Y.
Company G was raised at Geneva, N.Y.
Company H was raised at Wellsville, N.Y.
Company I was raised at Richburg, N.Y.
Company K was raised at Hinsdale, N.Y.

Roster of Co. B. 85th N.Y. Vol.:
Wm. W. Clarke - Captain
Chauncey S. Aldrich - 1st Lieut.
Amos Brunson - 2nd Lieut.

Spencer Martin - 1st Sergt.
Joseph L. Cummings - 2nd Sergt.
John Buell - 3rd Sergt.
Charles McHenry - 4th Sergt.
James B. Robinson - 5th Sergt.

Chas. H. Munson - 1st Asst. (Cpl.)
Wm. H. Dillon - 2nd Asst. (Cpl.)
Chas. Humphrey - 3rd Asst. (Cpl.)
Zephaniah W. Gooding - 4th Asst. (Cpl.)
Theodore Warner - 5th Asst. (Cpl.)
James S. Carson - 6th Asst. (Cpl.)

Lieutenant Colonel Will W. Clarke of Naples, N.Y., Mosher's original company commander. (Photograph reproduced by Ronald Pretzer, from Mosher's *Civil War Journal*).

Ellicott R. Stillman - 7th Asst. (Cpl.)
Sheridan Crandall - 8th Asst. (Cpl.)
George A. Phillips - Musician
Chas. J. Simmons - Musician
Daniel Sherman - Wagoner

Privates

Ackley, Edmund
Briggs, Nathan H.
Bennett, Amos
Bancroft, Albert H.
Carpenter, Napoleon B.
Crosby, Reuben
Cone, Linus
Chamberlin, Rensaler G.
Depant, Henry
Demeritt, John
Farrar, Emory P.
Glenn, Thos. J.
Green, Stephen L.
Griffin, Henry
Gooding, Chester A.
Hussey, Alexander
Hadsell, Tobias
Ingraham, Chas. B.
Jones, Ed. R.
Kern, Clark S.
Lewis, Parmer W.
Logan, John Jr.
Mary, John J.
McNinch, Chas. B.
Mosher, Chas. C.
Purkey, Daniel
Plimpton, Wm.
Porter, Thos. W.
Phillips, Richard D.
Parks, Joel E.
Rowley, S. H.
Ross, Albert C.
Snook, Geo. A.
Such, Thos.
Steele, Edgar H.
Simmons, Henry C.

Boothe, John E.
Bentley, Edgar L.
Brogan, James
Blake, John E.
Crane, Henry
Culver, Lyman W.
Chamberlin, Oliver W.
Dunlop, James
Deyo, Ira N.
Francisco, Francis M.
Francis, John H.
Gregg, Augustus
Gilbert, Joseph
Gilbert, Wm. C.
Hart, Calvin B.
Hall, William
Ingraham, Andrew S.
Insse, Boswell
Kern, Jared
Knapp, Edwin A.
Leach, Silas
Macumber, Andrew J.
Marra, John
Morris, Lyman K.
Meade, Marcus
Peck, Benjamin W.
Purkey, Jacob, Jr.
Popple, Barber G.
Phillips, Alvah
Phillips, George A.
Reed, Daniel L.
Richardson, Wm. L.
Sheppard, Horace
Spears, James
Smith, Seymour
Seymour, Henry P.

Sage, Oscar F.
Van Wie, John S.
Wetmore, Elem. B.
Watrous, Myron G.
Wilcox, Franklin E.

Straight, John
Voad, Abram
Wheeler, Milton
Wright, Nathan
Wells, Marcellus

November 5 [1861]. My furlough came today. We all have our uniforms now--mine is a very good fit.

I left for home this morning. My old clothes I packed in a bundle and carried with me. When I reached Canandaigua I walked down on the track to Chapinville. On the way, I had the nose bleed. Reached home a little after dinner.

I am right glad to get home. My folks are happy to see me.

Had my picture taken, the first one with my uniform on. It was taken standing. For my sister.

My furlough is only for a week.

November 11. I have had a very good time but my furlough is up today and I must go back to my job.

Reached camp this afternoon. I feel very much at home here now.

November 13. Wrote home today. A letter from brother David. He says Willie has enlisted in the Infantry.[18]

This is my present address:
Co. B. 85th Regiment, N.Y. S.V.
Barracks No. 4, Elmira, N.Y.
(Care of Capt. Clarke)

November 14. The other regiment on these grounds is numbered the 89th, and is called the Dickinson Guards in honor of Daniel S. Dickinson one of the U.S. Senators from this state.

All the troops in the city paraded on our grounds to [day] and Daniel S. Dickinson made us a speach. He is a very good speaker.

November 15. David came to see me today. Had a very good visit with him. I showed him all the sights of the camp.

This afternoon we went down town. He bought me a big bowie knife. It had a buck horn handle. Now I want a revolver, then I will be in shape. Had my picture taken for "Dave."

November 16. David went home this morning. Snowed all day. Drilled one half hour. Caulked up my bunk.

Alvah Phillips[19] is my bunker, a very nice boy but short and slight.

**Charles Mosher soon after his enlistment
(Wayne Mahood Collection,
Reproduction by Ronald Pretzer)**

**The Commissary Store
Church Street, Elmira**

November 17 [1861], Sunday. Up early this morning and took a general scrub. Church service in the mess room, sermon by the chaplain. Text: part of the 4th chapter of Matthew. A good sermon.

This afternoon the Bloomfield boys invited me in the orderly room to eat lunch with them. They had recieved a barrel from home which contained cold turkey, chicken, pie, cake, cheese, bread and butter, and other knicknacks. Lt. Aldrich, Orderly Martin, our squad which bunk over head, nine of us. We had plenty, and to spare. I am counted in as one of the Bloomfield squad. I seem to be in luck every time.

Lt. Aldrich told us we were under marching orders and might leave at any time but he thought not untill next week, perhaps not then.

Some of the boys are selling their pay to the Sutler - we get $13.00 a month - they sell one month's pay for $11.00. I will wait a while.

Wrote home today.

Lt. Aldrich is a very good man but he has taught school too long to have charge of a lot of such fellows as we are. He tries to handle us as if we were a lot of school children. We bother the life out of him nights. The stove is very near his room. When we came in from guard in the night we give the old stove a shaking down so as to get warmed up a bit before we turn in. Then we generally manage to steal some bread and butter from the cook house. We toast the bread in the stove, so we have hot buttered toast for lunch. All this disturbs the Lieut. But it does us a heap of good. The weather is getting down right sharp now.

November 18 [1861]. Pork and beans for dinner, cake and cheese for supper.

November 20. Terry Caton came down to see me. He brought me a revolver and other things. (Wm. Cullistes gave me the revolver.) We went down to the theater tonight.

November 21. Saw Terry off this morning. I sold a half month's pay to day. The Capt. gave us the privilege of going home once more if we chose to. some of the boys went. It won't pay me.

November 22. Run some bullets for my revolver to day. Stood a trick on guard for P. W. Lewis[20], who is sick. When we came off the Capt. invited us in his room to eat pie, cake and cheese with him. Bully!

November 23. Down town on a pass to day. The 86th regiment leaves to day for the seat of war.[21] Good for them. Our turn soon.

November 24, Sunday. I have charge of the dishing squad again. Church in the mess room. A little darky came in our barracks to night. We gave him a lot of pennies if he would strip off and dance for us. He stripped. Some fun! Anything to drive away dull cares.

November 25. The boys came back from the furlough last night. They woke up every one in the barricks. <u>Dishwashing</u> is very monotonous work when you do the dining room work for nearly 100 men.

November 26. Took supper in the orderlys room to night with the Bloomfield boys.

November 28. Thanksgiving! Had service in the mess room by our chaplain.
Oysters in every style with pumpkin pie for dinner. That is oysters were stewed and raw. Our table service was most complete. We dealt out the oysters so generously that our squad of waiters--the dishwashing squad also have to serve at table--were short. I managed to get one cooked and three raw oysters. I never want to have charge of a Thanksgiving dinner for company B again very soon.
For supper tonight we had mush and milk. Jalap[22] in the mush. Not enough mush to go around. us waiters were short. The head cook in the cook house told us we would not suffer. After our work was done in the mess room

we went into the cook house where we had coffee and buttered toast and pumpkin pie. A great improvement on mush and milk--and jalap.

December 1 [1861], Sunday. For the last two days we have been receiving our equipments. knapsacks, haversacks and canteens first. To day we got our arms. The right, left and center companies (A is right, B is left, C is center) get Enfield rifles.[23] The others get the Belgium rifles. Enfield rifles are concidered best. Church service in the mess room.

December 2. We are having lots of fun getting in our equipments for the first time. This afternoon we pack our knapsacks[24] and sling them on our back, put on our haversacks,[25] and canteens, then our belts and cartridge boxes, then shoulder our rifles for the first time and we have battalion drill. We were tired long before we were half through. Our loads seemed to weigh nearly a ton. The weather is very cold, the ground is frozen hard but we sweat as we would in harvest.

December 3. Very tired this morning from our drill of yesterday. Marching orders at last. Hurrah! Bully for us! Hip! Hip!

Our company is numbered from right to left with the tallest man at the right. "Yankee Bill" Corporal Dillon is number 1.[26] I am number 16.

We pack our knapsacks, fill our haversacks and canteens then wait around in the cold for orders to march.

4 p.m. he long roll sounds. The order to fall in is given and the 85th Regiment N.Y.S.V. is in line for the seat of war. The band plays The Girl I Left Behind Me. We move out and off from Barracks No. 4.

We march down to the city to the railway station. Here we hang around untill seven o'clock when we got on board of box cars - cold! Small fires in any of them. The whistle blows. We are off for Washington.

December 4. We liked to froze last night. The boys in one of the cars built a fire on the car floor. We are passing through Pennsylvania now. The snow is fence high. We go over mountains, cross rivers, through tunnels, cold is no name for it.

The stations we stop at are small but the dutch women who flock around the cars with eadibles to sell are not very small. They are very short and would roll one way as well as another. But they are fat!

Baltimore, 6 p.m. Here we have a supper furnished by the people. A very good one too. We change cars. In marching to the other depot, we pass over the same ground that the 6th Mass. did on the 19th of April last.[27] Instead of brickbats we get cheers with the Stars and Stripes floating everywhere.

Our sergeant McHenry[28] was a three months man in the 13th N.Y. when they passed through. He said they had some trouble. Brickbats and other missiles.

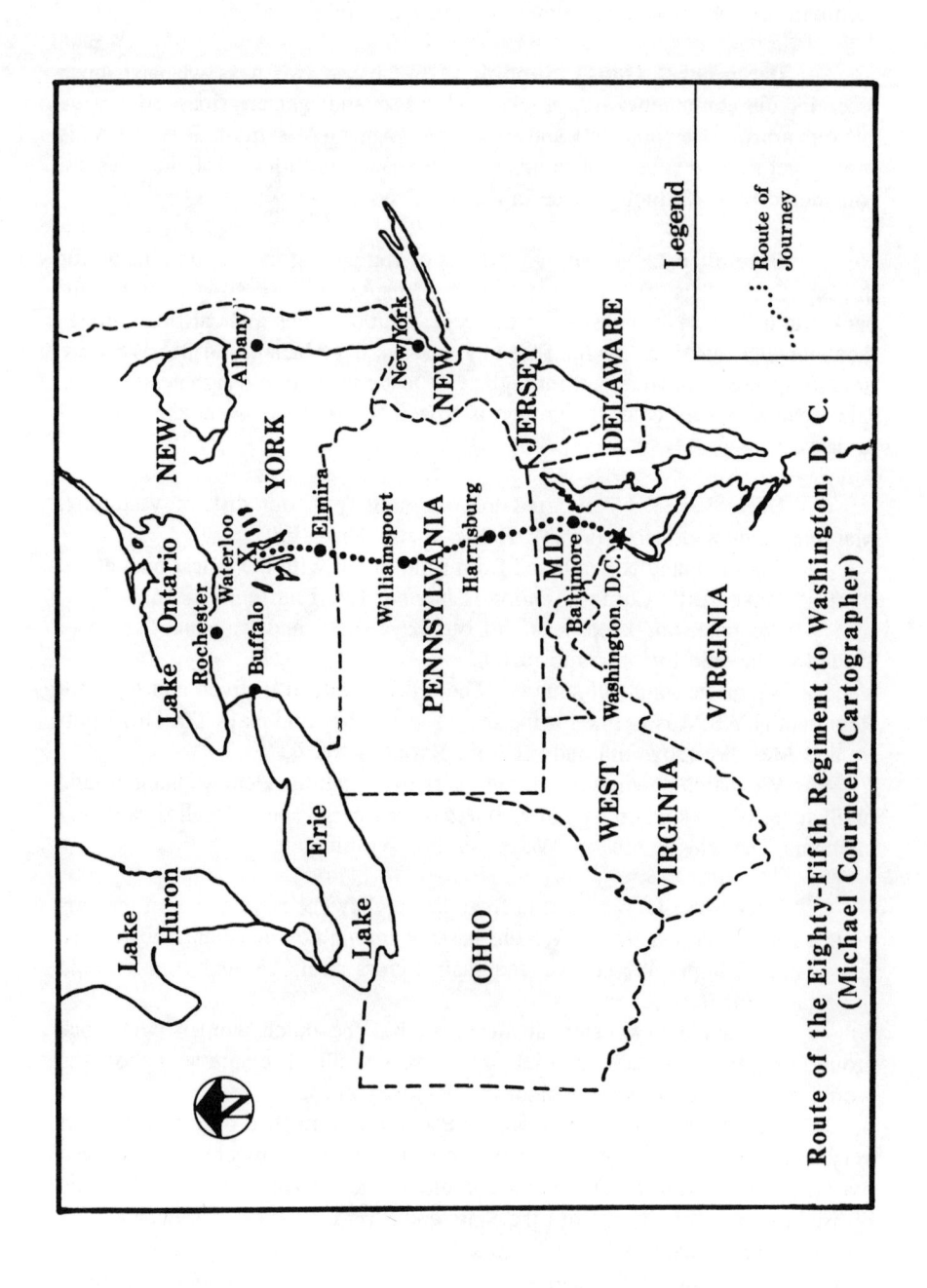

Route of the Eighty-Fifth Regiment to Washington, D. C.
(Michael Courneen, Cartographer)

December 5 [1861]. We left Baltimore last night about eight o'clock. It is not quite as cold here as it was in Pennsylvania but the cars ride just as hard. They seem to get harder.

The railroad through Maryland was well guarded. It was through a part of Pennsylvania [guarded] by the 87th Penn. Here is a regular regiment. It's a short run from Baltimore to Washington but we were a long time making it. So many stops.

Washington, D.C. We reached here about ten o'clock this morning. Tired, very.

Took dinner at the "Soldier's Retreat." It was a rare treat. Hardly! Salt-horse, or rather mule - cold at that. bread and a mixture some of the boys called coffee. Our first service in this great city. We tried to do our duty. Think we did.

After a short rest we fell in and marched to our camping ground out on the Bladensburg turnpike about 2 miles.

The weather here is much warmer than it is in New York State. We were rather warmed up by our march with our heavy load.

We are on the camp ground where General Baker's[29] brigade were camped. I am detailed for camp guard tonight. It will be rather hard.

December 6. I took my first trick on guard last night, all night. Then I turned in and forgot to wake up for my next trick. I slept until daylight. There is no more danger here than there is in father's back yard. Not a bit. We put up our tents today. They are A tents -- and will hold four men. We are getting into camp life by degrees.

We have a good view of the Capitol. All around us are troops of all branches of the service. It seems to be one vast camp as far as the eye can reach.

December 8, Sunday. A warm and very pleasant morning. Wrote home to [sister] Sarah. I sat on a bag of oats out in the open air while writing.

Our camp is called "Camp Shepherd." We are in the 3rd brigade, Casey's division, Army of the Potomac.[30]

Church service this afternoon. I saw Ed Yaw - I used to know him when I was a boy - am a man now. He is in the 1st Long Island.[31]

December 9. We are getting so now that we have things in better shape. Our company cooks are getting used to their work so we have our grub served in better style. Skirmish drill to day. Co. A and our company are the skirmish companies. Capt. Clarke gave us a long drill over the open fields and on the hill sides. It's good sport for us now. Had to bring water for the cooks which is difficult from skirmish drill.

Major General Silas Casey.
(Reproduced by Ronald Pretzer, from Luther S. Dickey,
The Story of the 85th Pennsylvania Volunteer Infantry)

December 14 [1861]. Review on Meridian Hill[32] to day by General Casey. For some reason our Co. did not go. We are drilling now every day when the weather permits.

Report says we are to cross the Potomac River soon. Hope so.

We exchanged our A tents for Sibley tent[33], a large round tent and will hold from 12 to 15 men. They are an improvement on the others. more roomy.

Camp Shepherd[34]
Washington, D.C.
Dec. 17, 1861

Dear Sister,

I think I will write to you again but think very queer you don't write to me. You don't write often enough to suit. I have not heard from you since we left Elmira.

I have just been to dinner on cold pork and bread. A very good dinner, I think it will be a good time to write you a long letter. I am on a knoll out doors roasting while I write and you are shivering over the fire, very cold.

This is a very fine day. We have been on this hill two weeks and four more regiments have encamped close by us, the 64th and 89th N.Y. (I have to get to drill.)

Wednesday morn. right after breakfast on cold beef, bread and coffee. Not I will go on with my story - 9th N.J. and the 57th Penn. There are about 5000 men on this hill. I have been over to the Catholic Cemetery. It is the nicest burial ground I ever saw. There is a little building they call the consecrated church. It is built entirely of little round sticks in the gothic style. It is very handsome.

I was out Monday afternoon and saw the artillery practice target firing. They fired both round shot and shell.[35]

We were where we could see each shot as it struck the target. How they whistled through the air.

Yesterday we had battalion drill. Lt. Col. Belknap[36] took us over about a mile to a flat and drilled over an hour on our return. Our band serenaded one of the first families of Virginia. They played the Star Spangled Banner, dixie and other tunes. The ladies came out and waved their "muffies."[37]

We have skirmish drill to day. This is the best drill you ever saw. We have the best drilled company in the regiment and the best captain[38] in the service.

The drum is beating for guard mounting. As I am on guard to day I will not go out.

I suppose you would like to know how we live here. There are ten boys in our tent. It is a large round one - Sibley. We have a good fire in the center nights so that it is comfortable.

Our rations are fresh bread, salt beef, salt pork, rice, potatoes, bread, sugar and coffee. We appoint two of the boys as cooks so we have no bother, only to eat it.

We drill four hours a day. The rest of the time we have to clean up in. We have lots of straw to sleep on. I spread my rubber blanket[39] on the straw. Two of us lay on it and have two blankets and our overcoats over us. I sleep like a log.

I got your letter last night and was glad to hear from you. I am sorry for Russ.[40]

December 20 [1861]. Up this morning at half past five. Early breakfast. Packed our knapsacks. Struck our tents. Fell into line at nine o'clock and marched for a new camp which is five miles away on the other side of the city.

We reached our new camp about noon. The mud is knee deep. This camp is called "Camp Warren" and is on Meridian Hill, back near a deep gorge.

After a short rest and dinner we pitched out tents and are living again. Oh! How muddy it is.

December 23. It has rained all day if it is Sunday. No inspection.

December 25. Christmas. Oysters for dinner.

December 26. On guard, at the cattle yard.

December 27. Washed my clothes this forenoon. Drill this afternoon.

December 28. Company drill this forenoon. Knapsack drill this afternoon. Reviewed by Genl. Casey.

December 29, Sunday. Company inspection this morning. This means lots of hard work cleaning up. This is how the inspection is conducted. We form our line, then take open order. Capt. Clarke is the inspector. He begins at the head of the line. The first man throws up his gun which the Capt. takes (he has on white glove), examines the lock, then sticks his little finger in the muzzle. if it soils his glove he is cross. then he draws the ramrod and drops it down the barrel. if it drops down without a ring he throws it back hard enough to knock one down.

Then we stack arms, unsling our knapsack, place them before us, open them up so the contents can be seen by the inspector.

Sunday is one of our hardest days. Everything has to be up and up.

December 30. I have not been feeling very well for a few days. Nothing serious. This morning reported at sick call and went up to the Surgeons. Dr. Lewis[41] is on duty. His list of questions are, How is your pulse--feels of it.

Let me see your tongue. How is your bowels? He fixed me up with a dose of castor oil with a little peppermint in it. I went down to my tent. The gripes took me. I was doubled up for half an hour like a jack knife. One of the boys gave me a little salt and water, which relieved me. I was sicker after I took the medicine than I was before.

December 31. Inspected for pay to day. Hurrah!

[1862]

January 1, 1862. New Years. No drill. We traded off a lot of our old shirts for oysters. We got enough for a good square meal.

January 2. Battalion drill.

January 3. Skirmish drill this forenoon.[42] I was detailed this afternoon to go with the wagons for brush. We went six or eight miles into the country. Had a very good time.

January 4. It was our companys turn to go on guard, but we were excused on the grounds that we were to escort the 9th N.J. on their way to join the Burnside expedition.[43] We escorted them to the depot and returned by the Capitol. My first nearby view of it. It is an immense building. It is still unfinished. The scaffolding is still up on the dome.

January 5, Sunday. Inspection at ten. Service at two. Dress parade at four. Then manual of arms by the Lt. Col. Avery. Busy day. In fact - Sunday is our busiest.

January 6. Three inches of snow on the ground this morning. No drill. Capt. Clarke came in to our tent this morning. He stumbled over a dish of water the first thing, and raised a muss pretty generally. He told us to fix up our tent better and make bunks and gave us passes to go outside and get some boards. A lot of us went about four miles, picking up a board here and there, sometimes off a fence or any place we could and not get caught. Each of us got enough, all we could carry on our back, they were mighty heavy, before we reached camp. Here we had trouble in passing the guards with our loads. We made the ripple.

January 7. Our company is on guard to day.

January 8. We raised up our tent about two feet on boards, then banked the earth around it. Inside we made our bunks on another platform to cover two thirds of the space a foot high. On this we put a thick layer of straw.

Union Camp Outside Washington, D.C., January 1862
(Battles and Leaders of the Civil War)

Over the straw we spread blankets, fastening both ends down. We have a very good place to sleep on. In the center is our stove. The rest of the space is our kitchen.

Our tent is No. 4 with fourteen men. Chas. McHenry, Z. W. Gooding, J. E. Blake, G. A. Phillips, C. J. Simmons, H. C. Simmons, C. A. Gooding, H. Crane, A. H. Bancroft, J. H. Francis, R. D. Phillips, S. A. Smith, H. P. Seymour, C. C. Mosher.[44] Bancroft and I went jayhawking boards again. Good luck. One of the boys brought in a chicken.

January 9 [1862]. It rained all night. We slept well on our new bunk. The rain did not effect us any as we were up out of the mud. Chicken for dinner.

On dress parade to night a fog rolled up so thick we could not see the Major who was in command.

January 10. We had a bit of sport with a peddler to day. He was selling medals with one side a picture of the Capitol and on the other was to be the name, Co., and regiment of the one that bought it so we could be identified in case we were lost, strayed, stolen or dead.

One of the boys was shaving me when the fellow dropped in our tent. Orderly Martin was with us also. Of course all of us wanted one. The first name he took was a fictitious one given by Francis [Francisco]. We all took the cue and gave him wrong names. As we all laughed very hard, the peddler thought the laugh was on me as I was being shaved. He thought there was not anything to shave on my face. My face was smooth and hard.

Orderly Martin's name was John Peabody, mine was Moses Peabody, his brother.[45] On guard today.

January 11. Off guard at 9 o'clock. Four men were sentenced to wear a ball and chain for getting drunk. Drill this p.m.

January 12, Sunday. Inspection. Wrote Frank Jessup.

January 13. Battalion drill this forenoon. This afternoon reviewed by Genl. Casey. Marched down to the city and back.

January 14. Snowed last night. Drill this afternoon. A letter from brother George. Three papers.

January 15. Stormed all day. Wrote to George, Sarah[,] Russ. and _____.[46] Lot of fun in our tent.

January 16. Paid today. I drew $26.90. Sent $18.00 to Father by New York draft.

Bought me a pair of boots for $4.50. Now my feet will not be wet. Shoes are bad things in wet weather.

When we were mustered for pay two of the companies were not up to the minimum number. A few men from our company and the other full one (Co. H) were transferred to them. They were paid twice.

January 19 [1862], Sunday. Raining. On guard No. 14 at the Quarter Masters department.

Bad weather most of the time now. so we are fortunate when on guard to be posted at the Q.M. as we have a tent to stand under. When my relief came off to night at 11 o'clock I saw a light in the Capt. tent and I dropped in to see what was up. Capt. and Orderly[47] sat there reading and eating crackers and cheese. I was told to take some. so I sat by the fire and munched for a while then went to the guard house.

There are nine men in the guard house to night for getting drunk. all out of Co. G. The guard house is where the guards stay when not on post. also where all prisoners are confined.

January 20. Off guard. Letters from Sarah and Terry Caton. Bought $1.00 worth of P.O. stamps. Wet and muddy. We are not drilling much now days.

January 21. Stormy today. Wrote letters home and elsewhere.

January 22. Drilled this forenoon. Letter from Sarah. All well at home.

January 23. Capt. Clarke drilled us this forenoon. This afternoon drilled in the firings.

We are having buckwheat pancakes in our tent now. I have saved two to top my boots with. Charlie Simmons, the drummer, baked one large enough for a drum head. It made a good one.

January 24. Drill. Raw pork for dinner. It rained so to night the guards were taken in. Henry Seymour is marker.

Our company from Captain down sent $3500.00 home out of our last pay day. Good for our company.

January 25. We have changed our guns. It's the Austrian rifle this time. The whole regiment have the same arm now.

January 26, Sunday. Orderly Martin was in our tent last night. He is full of the old "Harry." Man in the guard house yesterday with a ball and chain on each leg and on his hands. On guard at the Sutlers. Took dinner with him. This is a good post to be on.

January 27 [1862]. Off guard at 9 a.m. Slept in a dry goods box last night. A good bed.

Strict orders were read on dress parade tonight. They won't amount to much.

Sergeant Hays[49] of the 18th N.Y. and Jack Yaw[50] of the 1st Long Island [67th N.Y.] were here today.

January 28. Rainy as usual. No drill. Wrote home.

January 29. Out tent sent 12 letters to the office this morning. We moved our camp one half mile on the brow of Meridian Hill.

We began at ten o'clock and moved by hand and had our tent up and in good shape at four o'clock.

We have good grounds now. Gravelly and dry. The "Porter House"[51] is very near us.

The <u>Sundial</u> which is used to reckon time from - longitude[52] is on our grounds near the right of the regiment. The "Porter House" is used for a hospital. It has been very handsome in its day. A beautiful drive winds up to it with a row of evergreen trees on each side. But war has ruined nearly every thing. We have a good view of the Capitol as well as the city.

To our left are three batteries of light artillery and Rush's Penn. Lancers.[53] We see the lancers drill. each lance has a small red penant near the top. They look fine when they charge.

January 30. Stood a trick in guard for Al Bancroft. Loaded my gun for the first time today. Tom Glenn[54] stoped with us last night. He has the rheumatism very bad and his tent is not as comfortable as ours. Rainy today. Harry Seymour has left our tent. He is much too fine haired for this kind of work. Mended my stockings to night.

January 31. On police duty to day. Police duty here means to clean up the camp grounds and keep them in order. A detail for police is made every day. Battalion drill this P.M.

Adjutant Goodrich has resigned and our Lt. C. S. Aldrich has been appointed in his stead. Our company held an election to fill the vacancy caused by said appointment. Orderly Spencer Martin elected 1st Lt. jumping Second Lt. Amos Bronson [Brunson]. A trifle rough on Bronson. I voted for Martin.

Our Colonel is not much of a military man. Lt. Col. Belknap is a dandy. Brigadier General Silas Casey has reviewed us. He rides a heavy dark iron gray horse which is a pacer or racer I don't know which. The old "Man" rides so fast that his staff have to go on the gallop in order to keep in sight of him.

February 1 [1862]. Letter from Father yesterday, and answered it. No drill today.

Februry 2, Sunday. On guard at the Sutlers. We had three rounds of ball cartridges delt out to us.

February 3. Off guard this 9 A.M. We fired our guns at a mark. I hit it for a wonder and left handed. I shoot left handed. Snow today. No drill.

February 4. Battalion drill this morning. Bean soup for dinner. brought water for the cooks. This afternoon Al Bancroft and I went out side to get some poles to hang our blankets on. Queer I got no letters from home.

February 5. Bean soup for breakfast. Battalion drill. This afternoon our company went out for target practice with four rounds each. Distance forty rods. J. S. Carson[55] made the best shot and "Buz" Insse[56] next. I was no where.

February 6. Rainy and no drill. Letters from Frank Chapin and a paper from [brother] David. Sent a sheet of paper, envelope and stamp to Frank Jessup.

February 7. Drilled this forenoon in the mud knee deep. It's awful. There are a number of gunboats in the river now. Something up I reckon. A man was shot by the guard last night. Will die, I guess.

February 8. Our Col. U. S. Davis resigned today. He is trying to have Major Young[57] of Col. McQuades' 14th Brooklyn Reg. appointed in his place.
Lt. Col. Belknap is in command. Drill in the mud as usual.

February 9, Sunday. Inspection. Went to church. The text was in the 1st Corinthians 16th chapter and thirteenth verse. A good sermon. Wrote to father. Three of the 76th N.Y. came in our tent tonight. They were a lively lot. "Chape," Goff and [indecipherable] are their names.
Great rejoicing in the city over the recent victory in the west.[58]

February 10. Drill this afternoon. Target shooting this afternoon. The best shot gets a pass. Ed. Knapp[59] and I were detailed to guard a corpse to night. The officers made up their minds it would not get away so we were told to go to our quarters. We went.

February 11. My turn on guard to day. but that trick on guard last night lets me out. as well as from drill this morning, which gave me a chance to wash my clothes. Drilled in the manual of arms under Lt. Bronson this P.M.

Report says that McClellan[60] has ordered the artillery across the river. It looks like a forward movement. Hope so. perhaps we can get a chance in. Our old company B is the best on the grounds.

February 12 [1862]. Drill under Lt. Col. Belknap.
Went over to the camp of the 76 N.Y. to night. The boys scared Dunlop[61] of our company nearly to death.

February 13. The orders are to go on drill at 8 A.M. I guess we will get drill enough. I was detailed to help draw rations to day so will not have to drill.

I saw a new kind of gun to day. It was mounted on wheels and had five barrels. It was operated by a crank and was self feeding. It is called a Gatlin gun.[62] It is claimed to throw bullets like hail stones and as fast. I heard Miss Kate Dean[63] sing to night. She is a beautiful singer. It's a rare treat for us.

February 14. Valentine's Day and no valentine. We were out early this morning on the drill ground. After a short exercise the rain drove us in. Just what we wanted. This afternoon we raised a flag stall and then fired blank cartridges in honor of the event. I received four papers and some letters by to days mail.

February 15. Battalion drill this afternoon. Our company acted as skirmishers for the first time. This is a fine drill. No work this afternoon.

February 16. Oscar F. Sage of our company died this Sunday morning. His home is in East Bloomfield. This is our first loss. His body was sent home at the expense of our company.

I had a bad headache so I did not have to go out on company inspection.

February 17. Great rejoicing in the city and all through camps over the victory of Fort Donelson.[64] The men on camp guard threw down their guns and began to sing and dance. Every body is wild and half crazy over the event.

We are having quite a time over our Colonel Davis who resigned. He is working for Major Young. we want Brig. Genl. Van Valkenburg M.C. for our new colonel. He is in command of the depot at Elmira when we were there. Yesterday when on parade Lt. C. S. Aldrich, Act. Adjt. offered the following resolutions.

Whereas Uriah L. Davis, former Col. of this regiment, has made use of the most despicable political trickery, and the grossest fraud and misstatements to force upon us a colonel who is an entire stranger to us and in whom we have no reason to have confidence, and, whereas the said U. L. Davis knew that we called and were anxious to secure the leadership of Brig. Gen. Van Valkenburg and were anxious under him to show our fidelity to the union and our hatred to the rebellion.

Therefore resolved that we consider U. L. Davis unworthy the confidence of honest men and unfit on account of his demoralizing influence to be in camp and we ask the Lieut. Col.[65] to issue an order causing him to leave the grounds within an hour.

Aldrich made a speach in favor of the resolution. A vote was taken and the resolution was lost.[66]

U. L. Davis is too old to command a regiment in the field.

The rejoicing is great yet over the victory of Fort Donelson.

It has stormed so to day that we did not drill.

February 18 [1862]. I have a bad cold on hand to day so I did not go on drill.

Target practice this afternoon but I went to bed with my cold.

We heard the long roll for the first time. The occasion of it was that the 77th N.Y. were ordered to move across the river. The roads are so muddy that it took 101 mule teams to transport their baggage. If it takes 606 mules to move one regiment how many will it take to move the whole army?

The 87th N.Y. left today for Mount Vernon. We are still <u>left</u> on this hill.

A call was made by the government on our (Casey's) division for 5000 volunteers to man the western gun boats. They wanted ten from each regiment. When the order was reduced one half. then the men solicited had to draw lots. two of our boys was in it but they drew blanks. So the 85th is not represented on the western gunboats.

February 19. No drill to day. We traded coffee for onions. Wrote to Father and George. Had a letter and paper from David.

February 20. Fifteen letters went to the post office from our tent to day. Company drill under Capt. Clarke. Van Valkenburg is to be our Col. Letters from Frank Jessup and Russ Wright.

February 21. On guard today. All quiet.

February 22. Washington's birthday. fired blanks in honor of the occasion. A letter from Sarah. And sent one to her and one to "Matt."

February 23, Sunday. Inspection this morning. Went to church. Wrote David. Dress parade. All quiet.

February 24. I have broke the nipple to my gun. In order to get it repaired I had to get an order from the Lt. Col. to go to the arsenal down in the city. In order to go to the city I had to have an order from the Capt. Lots of red tape. I went by the way of Georgetown.

While they were putting in a new nipple[67], I took a stroll through the arsenal and grounds which are surrounded by a high brick wall. The arsenal is a very large brick building and is stored full of guns, placed in racks which extend from the floor to the ceiling. Distributed through the grounds were piles of cannon balls and a number of old cannon, some of which were captured at Saratoga, Yorktown, Vera Cruz. One old gun was made in 1756. When my gun was fixed I went to the Capitol. As my time was nearly up, I only strolled through the rotunda and saw some of the most beautiful paintings I ever saw. On my way to camp I passed the fruit stands. The fruit on one of them took to me so kindly that one of the largest oranges slipped into my pocket. Queer!

February 25 [1862]. Drill to day. On dress parade our company escorted the colors.

February 26. Battalion drill this forenoon. This afternoon our brigade was reviewed by Maj. Gen. Casey and staff. Two ladies accompanied the general. It was a very brilliant affair. Our first.

February 27. On guard. On dress parade to night orders were read, which our company and three others of our regiment to report to Genl. Peck[68] at Tennallytown.[69]

We struck our tents, packed our knapsacks, fell in at 6:30 and started out on our first march into the enemy's country. We had forty rounds of ball cartridges.

February 28. It was quite cold on the march last night. Our ranks kept well up for the first three or four miles. When "Al" Bancroft and I thought we could keep warmer if we walked faster, so we pushed ahead and finding an old ambulance we crawled into it so as to be out of the wind and waited for the main body to reach us. After waiting a long time they did not come. so we went back to headquarters to know why. We found that all hands were ordered back to camp. Al and I held a council of war and decided that we would not march any further, finding an empty tent we crawled in and went to sleep.

This morning it was broad daylight when we woke up, cooked our coffee and pulled out for camp. After a hard walk we reached here at 8:30 to find that the boys had our tent up and everything was ready to live again. Seventy-eight men were in line last night. The detachment was under our Maj. King[70]. There was to have been a move along the whole line last night, but as Banks[71] met with no resistance at Charlestown a halt was ordered. We would have been to Harpers Ferry in a short time if we had kept on the move.

We are just spoiling for something to turn up, so we can show our motel[72] -- or heels.

Mustered for pay today. Wrote home.

March 1 [1862]. I asked the captain for a pass to go down to the city. He gave me one and asked me to come back by the way of Georgetown and get his washing. As he is very kind to me I agreed to it. I had a good time in the city. I went through the White House grounds, the Capitol and Patent Office.

In the patent office I saw Washington's coat and small clothes, sword, belt, chairs, camp chest, treasury chest, writing case, tent and tent poles, and camp equipage. Franklin's cane, he willed to Washington, his printing press that he used when he was a journeyman printer. There was a brass plate on it on which was engraved what he told the printers in London. He said, "That it was forty years since he had worked on that press. Then he sent down and ordered up a gallon of [indecipherable]. Then all drank to the success of printers." I had a great day for me. The city is very muddy. Pennsylvania Avenue the mud is hub deep. on either side of it are large blocks of granit, which are to be used in the new treasury building.

March 2, Sunday. Inspection. Church. Dress parade. Wrote home.

March 3. Stormy. No drill. Wrote father.

March 4. It has cleared off very pleasant. Our usual drill today.

March 5. Washed my clothes this forenoon. I am getting to be quite a washer-woman. I took a long stroll over by Rock Creek untill I came to the suspension bridge. It is a very fine one. Drill this afternoon. All quiet.

March 6. Drill this forenoon. This afternoon H. C. & C. J. Simmons and myself made a pass of our own, (some of the boys call it forging a pass), and went over to the Soldiers Home. This home is for the old soldiers who have been out in the service and have no homes of their own to go to. The president's summer residence is here, a beautiful building. The main building of the home is of granit and divided off into dormitory, mess room and way up in the attic is the smoking room which has a brick floor. Here the old boys can go and have a good smoke and play their games. Some of the boys live outside the main building in little houses of their own. They're more shanty than house. Each one had a small sitting room and a bed room, and some had a small work room where they tinkered at wood work. The buildings were put up according to each individual fancy. One had a cellar under the floor about 4 ft. square and 2 ft. deep. There is a large green house which furnishes flowers for the President's home. The gardener gave me five heliotrope blossoms which I shall send to my sister. The grounds around the home contain about 500 acres and are laid out in elegant style.

We have had a good trip, and no one the worse for our forged pass and running the guards.

March 7 [1862]. On guard. The 103 Pa[73] came in today and camped near us. We helped them get their camp started.

March 8. Off guard at nine o'clock. Drilled in the bayonet exercise. The 14th regulars have camped near us.

March 9, Sunday. Inspection. Church. The regulars had a man strung up by the thumbs as a punishment. This is the how of it. They tie a strong cord around each thumb between the joints and then put the ends over the limb of a tree and draw the victim up untill his toes just touch the ground. It's a horrible punishment. It was more than our volunteer blood could stand. So we stired out our surgeon and the other surgeons and they went over and ordered the man cut down. Bully for them.

We outnumbererd Co. H on parade to night. There is quite a strife between us, who can muster the most men on parade.

The 98th and 103rd N.Y. are near us.

March 10. Six 6-gun batteries have crossed the river with McClellan's body guard. Bully for "Little Mc."

On dress parade tonight, as there was no officers in camp, our orderly sergeant Spencer Martin took command of the parade. He did it like an old hand.

March 11. Orderly Martin drilled the battalion this morning. None of the commissioned being present. Target practice this afternoon.

Ingraham is in the guard house. Companies C & H have gone out to guard an ammunition train. Last night Capt. Raines[74] took a squad and went down to the city and broke up a grog shop.

Letters from Sarah and David.

March 12. Company drill this forenoon. This afternoon two companies of us - our Co. & H. - under the command of Adjt. Aldrich went down to the city to see what could be done with a detachment of 150 of the D'Epineuil Zouaves (53 N.Y. Inf.). This regiment went out with the Burnside expedition and were shipwrecked, which demoralized them so that they refused to be reorganized but wished to be disbanded.

Before we started down we loaded with ball cartridges but did not cap. The Adjutant made a long speech to them, all to no purpose. They were an ugly looking lot of men, nearly all of them had a bowie knife or revolver in sight and they would have given us a hard fight, as we were in close quarters where we could not have used our bayonets to advantage.

March 13 [1862]. Battalion drill this forenoon. Visitors from the north this afternoon, for whom we had to fire blanks. Mrs. Wm. Hildreth of Canandaigua, N.Y. was in our tent. Wrote George, David and Frank Chapin.

March 14. Drill. I went down to Georgetown this afternoon just for a stroll. It is an old fashioned town, full of darkies. Our officers are somewhat changed now.[75] Lt. Col. Belknap is Colonel, Major Wellman is Lt. Col., Captain R. V. King of Co. A is Major. Our 1st Lt. Aldrich is Adjutant.

We had an election in our company to fill the vacancy caused by the promotion of Aldrich. Orderly sergeant Martin was elected over 2nd Lt. Amos Bronson.[76] There is a great deal of talk now about our moving. Some of the boys are afraid we will never see a battle. We are all ready for one, so we think. Perhaps.

There is something on foot now. Little Mc. is command now. Things will move.

March 15. Drill. Drill. Drill. And still it's drill. I suppose it's part of the show.

March 16, Sunday. Inspection. Church.

March 17. This morning orders came to march to Alexandria tomorrow. Each man is to take one change of under clothes and a blank only. The rest are to be packed in barrells and boxes!

March 18. We all packed up according to orders, except our tents which are still standing. Two of the regiments have their tents down.

Orders are to stay where we are. So here we are yet. There is a large fleet of vessels in the river, we may go yet. I hope so, as we are very anxious to be at the capture of Richmond.

March 21. Everything is all stired up here, and we are all unsettled, not knowing what will come next.

This afternoon Genl. Casey and staff reviewed our division.[77] Three brigades, 14 regiments in all. Our regiment is in the 3rd brigade. I. N. Palmer is our brigadier general.[78] He was promoted from a major in the 5th U.S. regular cavalry and is a fine looking officer. He rides with his bridle reins crossed on the under side. I never saw so many men together before in my life. We made a fine appearance. Our review was held on Columbia heights.

Our division is in Keyes Corps.[79] The report is that he is to review the corps tomorrow. It will be very hard work for us. There will be 45,000 men in line.

March 22 [1862]. The big review did not come off today. We are happy. It's all talk now about going in to the field. Hope we will go soon.

March 23, Sunday. Inspection. Church at eleven o'clock. The Rev. Mr. Raines of Elmira, N.Y. preached. Text was war, a good warfare. He is a very good preacher and has a son in our regiment, Capt. John Raines of Co. G. This afternoon Gooding and I went over to and through the grounds of Mr. Corcoran.[80] He is a rich banker in the city. There are over two hundred acres in his place and beautifully laid out and well kept. I picked two pine cones which I shall send home.

There are no sick in our camp - any at present. Which is good.

March 24. We were reviewed by Genl. Keyes today. 15,000 were in line, instead of 45,000 as we expected. [General] Casey's little boy rode with the reviewing officers. He is about 12 years old and had on his uniform and sword like the rest of them. He rode a large gray horse and looked like a monkey mounted.

March 28. We are still here on Meridian Hill. Orders came this morning to be in readiness to march at a moments notice. Now we are in for it sure. We struck our tents, packed up our extra baggage, which was sent down to the city to be stored. Put three days rations in our haversacks, then hung round untill nearly sundown when we fell into brigade order and marched down through the city over the Long Bridge towards Alexandria.

March 29. Alexandria, Va. We reached this sacred soil about 2 o'clock this morning. As the hotels were all filled we picked out a soft spot on the brick side walk of one of the main streets, spread down our blankets, and slept like as though we were in our feather beds. It was a little bit rocky, but thin.[81] As the transports are not ready for us this morning, we were moved out of the city about three miles when we camped down, where we made our coffee and had breakfast.

This afternoon a storm of snow and rain set in. which wet us through in a short time. It was dark before our tents came up to us, then every thing was so wet they were not much use to us. We put them up after a fashion, then cut some pine boughs in to lie on. then turned in with our wet clothes on, not to sleep, but to shiver.

March 30, Sunday. A wretched night it was last night, but we pulled through it some how.

Wrote to father this morning told him as to my whereabouts.

After breakfast we packed up and marched back into the city. After laying around a few hours we went on board the steamer Elm City. That is the right wing of our regiment and the 98th N.Y. Col. Dutton's[82] When Capt. King[83]

Transports on the Potomac
(Battles and Leaders of the Civil War)

was promoted to major our Captain Clarke became senior Captain, which gives us the right of the regiment. The post of honor. Before we were the extreme left company.

March 31 [1862]. On board steamer *Elm City* off Alexandria, Va. We slept very well last night. Gipple, Crandall & Marra[84] of our company got into Col. Dutton's state room before he did and went to sleep. so when the Col. came along he couldn't go. The boys told him that he could only use one berth, and they would sleep on the floor. He couldn't see the point and they got out. It was a joke on the Colonel.

About eight o'clock we moved down the river. As we passed Mount Vernon the bell was tolled. We were told that all vessels as they pass Washington's tomb toll their bell. An our was down[85] we passed Fort Hamilton. As we reached the Chesapeke bay we passed a Man o'war with 32 guns. The crew manned the yards and gave us three cheers. We returned the salute. We had two schooners in tour [tow].

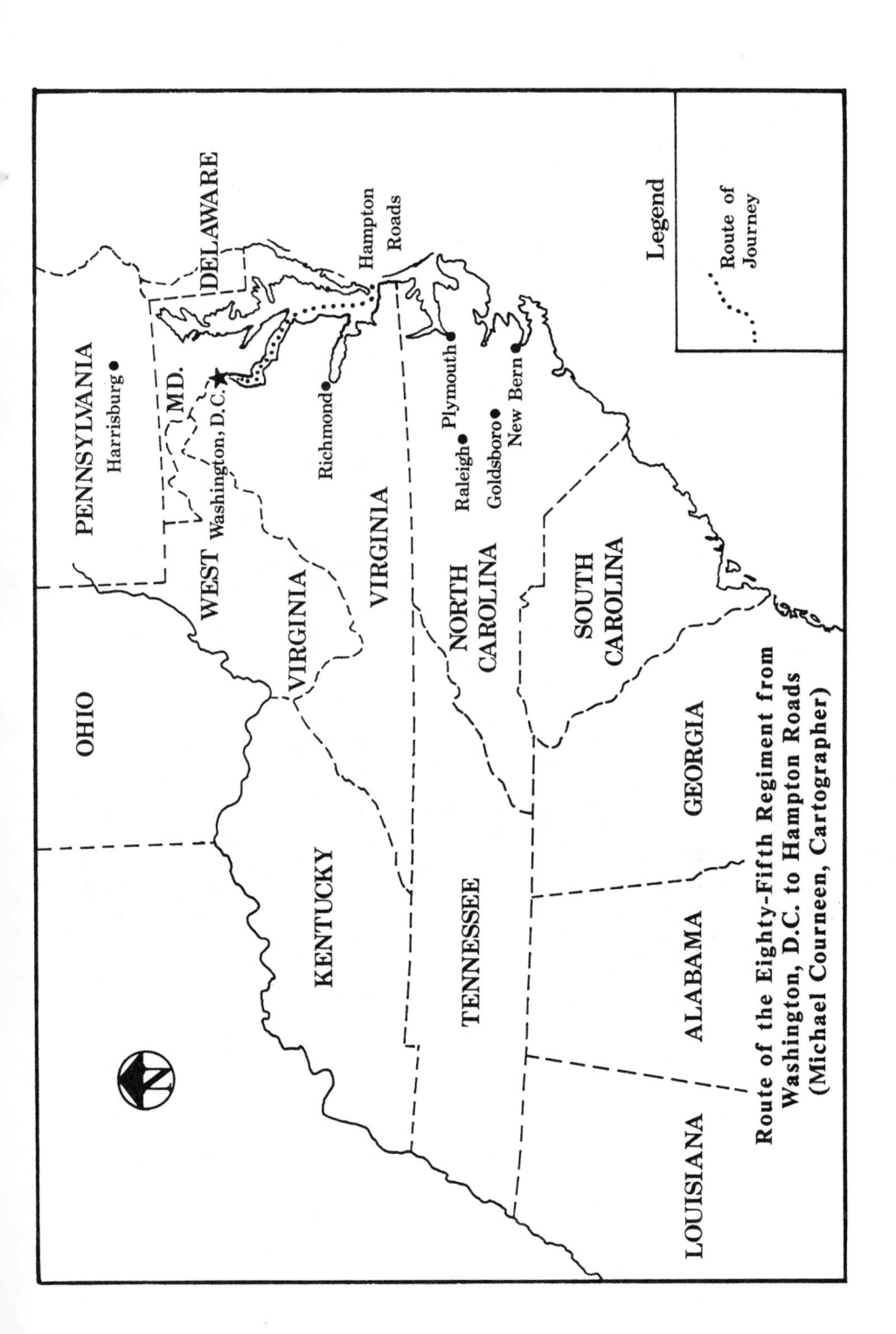

Route of the Eighty-Fifth Regiment from Washington, D.C. to Hampton Roads (Michael Courneen, Cartographer)

Major General George B. McClellan
(Battles and Leaders of the Civil War)

Chapter Two

THE PENINSULA CAMPAIGN

(April to August 1862)

The Peninsula Campaign, described by one critic as "Campaigning to No Purpose,"[1] was the brainchild of newly promoted Major General George B. McClellan, commander of the Army of the Potomac, to secure Virginia and capture the Confederate capital at Richmond. His original plan to move down to Urbanna on the James River to force the southern troops back to Richmond had to be abandoned when, on March 9, Confederate General Joseph Johnston had moved from Centreville to south of the Rappahannock, burning everything not on the road. Thus, McClellan's only choice now was to move down the Potomac on the peninsula between the York and James rivers.

Actually, McClellan had been forced into this plan by President Lincoln's General War Orders Number 2 and 3, dated March 8, 1862. Washington was made "secure" by the First and Fifth Corps, McClellan was to move approximately 100,000 men to Fort Monroe, about eight miles north of Newport News and about twenty miles, as the crow flies, from Yorktown, Virginia, where the James River dumps into Chesapeake Bay.

The Third and Fourth Corps, under Major Generals Samuel P. Heintzelman (commanded temporarily by Brigadier General Fitz John Porter) and Erasmus D. Keyes, respectively, were routed in two columns, with Heintzelman's Third Corps, the right column, heading northwest from Fort Monroe toward Yorktown. The left column (Keyes's Fourth Corps) followed the James River toward Williamsburg more than 30 miles north.

Until the battle of Fair Oaks, Mosher and his comrades in the Eighty-Fifth N.Y. Vols. were generally non-combatants, though they did experience a part of the battle of Williamsburg and its aftermath. At Fair Oaks, on May 31 and June 1, however, Mosher's regiment felt the full brunt of war, which they recalled throughout their lives. Afterward they were part of the rear guard which eventually (after the Seven Day's battle) retreated to Harrison's Landing.

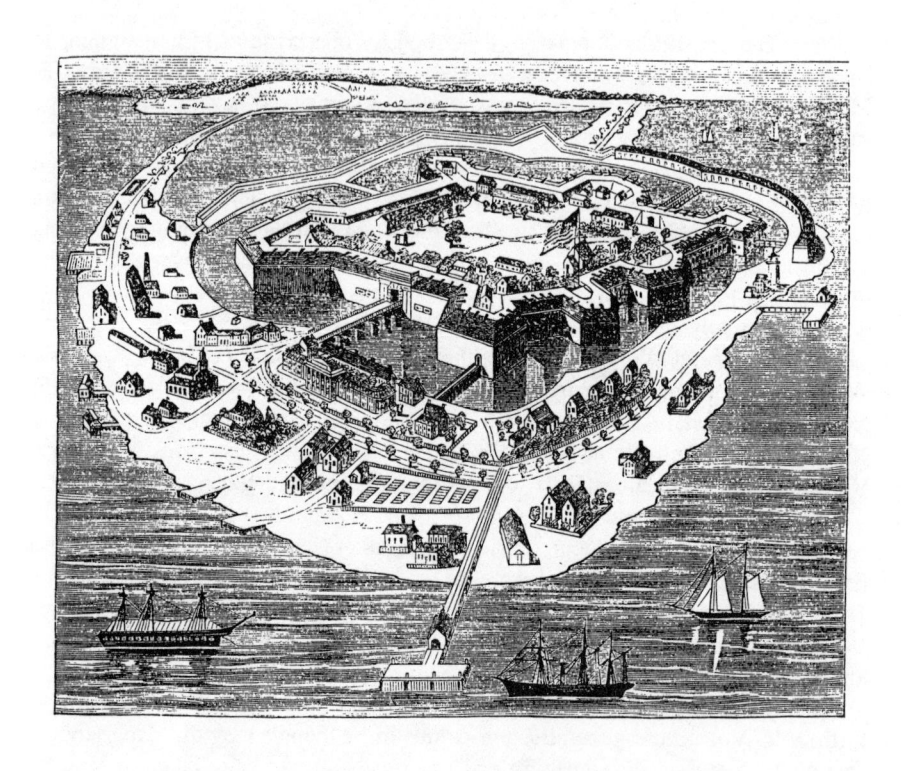

Fortress Monroe in 1861
(Lossing's *The Civil War in America*)

April 1 [1862]. Fortress Monroe, Va. We arrived here this morning at day light. We can see the little *Monitor*[2] up in the road stead among the other ships and the spars of the *Cumberland*[3] standing out of water as she was sunk by the *Merrimack*.

We went ashore about 10 o'clock this morning.

Fortress Monroe is a large post and mounted with heavy guns. In the water battery on the beach in front of the Fortress is the big gun called the Union. I can almost crawl into it. From here we can see the Rip Raps[4], Sewells Point, & Newport News.[5] Hampton Roads is full of war ships. The little *Monitor* looks for all the world like a cheese box on a raft, as the papers said it did. Some of our officers claim that they can see the *Merrimack*. I can't.

At 4 P.M. we were ordered to march out to our camp ground. We passed through Hampton, which was burned by order of rebel general Magruder.[6] It begins to look like war a trifle. After marching 4 or 5 miles the Col. ordered us to halt, and take to the woods for the night. We broke ranks, and started sure. We had begun to fix up a little when the orders were to fall in and move on farther. Drummer C. J. Simmons and I didn't. We had found a good fire, which soneone a head of us had left under a large tree. We took possession of this made our coffee, and made ready to turn in for the night. The big knife which brother David gave me in Elmira comes in all right now for cutting pines for a bed. I can lop off a pine as large as my wrist at one stroke. We are well fixed for our first night in this region.

April 2. We slept well last night. We pulled out and found our boys about one mile ahead. They were just getting breakfast, so we are all right again. There were no tents here last night except Col. Dutton's. Some of our boys stole them so the Col. had to sleep on the ground. He said Co. B. men were all fit for colonels and Captain Clarke a brigadier general. Quite a compliment for the boys. We are getting the ropes[7] in shape very readily, for new beginners. After breakfast we moved across the road and pitched our tents on a new camp ground. We have good water here and a pleasant camp.

April 4. We have moved camp again, now it is in a large peach orchard. The trees are in bloom and look very beautiful. We are within a mile of the James river, and can see the *Cumberland*'s spars, and the burnt hull of the *Congress* off Newport News. We can get a glimpse of the rebel *Merrimack*. Mornings we can [hear] the rebel bands beat the reveille, then the breakfast call, their guard mount. [A]t night we hear tattoo from their camps at Sewells Point and Craney Island.

There are plenty of rabbits here. Once and a while we manage to get one. We tried to shoot them. [But] orders were issued not to fire our guns. So we run them down.

The left wing of our regiment reached us today. Keyes corps are all here now, ready for work. The 33rd N.Y. Inf.[8] are near us. they are in our division. I was in Canandaigua when two companies from Seneca Falls passed through there on their way to Elmira.

Thirty men of our regiment are on picket to day for the first time.

There are very few houses here now, and those are occupied by darkies. They have good gardens here. The soil is a loam. It would be a fine country to live in I should think. Peas and potatoes are out of the ground ten inches. It's fine here.

April 15 [1862]. I have not kept up my diary for a few days past. When we came here the rail fences were up in good order. Now they are all burnt up. This is a part of the business. It looks rather tough. And is. I have my trick on picket.[9] There is no danger here from the rebels. they are too far away at present. We will catch up with them later. Perhaps. We do our picket dury the same as we do camp guard, relieve every two hours. I don't like it that way. It don't seem right.

April 15. Wrote to father this morning. The report is we are to advance tomorrow. Hope so.

April 16. Orders to move this morning. We pulled up our stakes, slung our knapsacks and pulled out. Sheppard, Gregg, Carson & Hart[10] are sick and have to stay here. Which is very bad for them.

It was very warm on the march to day. The road was full of blankets, overcoats & knapsacks which the boys had thrown away. Some dropped every thing but their guns. Hot was no name for it.

We passed through Youngs Mills. A small hamlet. It had been burned down. When we were about five miles this side four of us bushed and fell out. spread our blankets and went to sleep. Very tired we are.

April 17. We had a good sleep last night. Found the regiment a quarter of a mile ahead at Warwick Court House. It is called a city. We could not see it.

We are down to regular army life now. Our bread rations are 10 hard tack a day.[11] Plenty of fresh beef, salt horse [beef] and pork, good coffee. Vegetables are scarce. At our last camp some of the regiment found some leeks growing.[12] (they grow wild here) So the other regiments called us the Alleghany leek diggers.

This is a dreary place though. hen houses and fences all gone. The white folks are gone. Plenty of darkies every where.

April 21. Camp near Warwick Court House. This morning our sergeant Charlie McHenry and fifteen of us from our company were detailed for guard at G^l. Casey's headquarters.

LOWER PENINSULA.
SCALE OF MILES
1 2 3 4 5
UNION
CONFEDERATE
J. WELLS
CHESAPEAKE BAY
YORK RIVER
JAMES RIVER
HAMPTON ROADS
YORKTOWN
GLOUCESTER POINT
WILLIAMSBURG
MAY 5 1862
FT. MAGRUDER
HANCOCK
SMITH
COUCH
CASEY
HOOKER
KEARNEY
HILL
LONGSTREET
JAMESTOWN I.
HOG I.
MULBERRY PT.
MULBERRY ISLAND
DAYS PT.
BIG BETHEL
JUNE 10 1861
PEIRCE
LITTLE BETHEL
NEWPORT NEWS POINT
CAMP BUTLER
HAMPTON
OLD POINT COMFORT
FT. MONROE
SEWALLS PT.
WARWICK COURT HOUSE
LEE'S MILL
APRIL 16 1862
WARWICK R.
YOUNG'S MILL
HALF WAY HOUSE
HOWARD'S BRIDGE
COCKLETOWN
BRICK CHURCH
DR. POWERS
LEBANON CHURCH
BLOWS MILLS
MONSON HOUSE
KING'S MILL WHARF
GROVE WHARF
BURWELL'S MILL
BLACK SWAMP
PHILGATES CR.
KINGS CR.
QUEEN'S CR.
COLLEGE CR.
MOORE HOUSE
CLARKE HOUSE
TOOS PT.
POQUOSIN R.
BACK R.
NEW MARKET BRIDGE
NEW BRIDGE
BLUNT PT.
HORSE BRIDGE

We had a good tent to sleep in and not much to do. A very pleasant day for us.

When we are at our own camp we have no tents. only rubber blankets [ponchos] to cover over us.

April 22 [1862]. After we were relieved this morning, we had to remove a large quantity of ammunition. We found this hard work. Something new.

When we reached our old camp we found the regiment had moved on to the front. We found some fresh beef which they had left which we cooked for dinner. We had a good dinner, and then a smoke. when we pulled for the regiment. They were about ahead at Lees Mills when we caught up to them.

I was that used up that I asked Captain Clarke if he had any whiskey. He said yes, and gave me a smother. This is the first time I ever tasted the stuff. It braced me up some.

Our division is on the extreme left of our army before Yorktown. Heavy firing to our right now.

This is the Yorktown where Cornwallis surrendered to Washington. Historic ground.

Gooding, Humphrey, Dillon, Jared Kern and Knapp[13] were left sick at Warwick Court House. Many are sick.

As my diary is not up every day, I will copy one of my home letters.[14]]

Camp Winfield Scott
Warwick County, Va. Apr. 28/62

Dear Sister: I received your letter yesterday, and was very glad to hear from you. Last Saturday our company was on picket duty. There were 200 from our regiment. Each brigade has a certain front to picket.

Our 200 are divided into eight reliefs of 25 men each. with a commissioned officer over each 50. and into the right and left wings. Men are a rod apart.

This is some how the lines look.

left-wing		right-wing
support		support
	reserve	

To the rear of each wing is a support and in the rear of the supports is a strong reserve.

Our line is only 80 rods [approximately one-quarter mile] from the rebel line. we can catch a glimpse of them once and awhile. Part of the line is a heavy wood and part is an open lot. The rebs have a marked battery in front of the open lot.

The pickets are relieved every two hours. That night was as dark as a pocket. In order to get to some of the posts we had to cross a small stream. As the men were relieved from post, they would fall in the rear of the relief guards and go the entire rounds with them.

Two or three of the men when they were relieved were so dazed that they started for the rebel lines.

That same day a Massachusetts regiment took a rebel battery, spiked[15] the guns, but could not get them away.

Thursday we went to support a reconnoitering party under Genl. Davidson.[16] We lay on the bank of a gully in the woods face down for three hours. It was a good thing the rebs did not show them selves. We would have made it hot for them once.

This same day the Colonel & Major of the 93rd N.Y. Inf. (our brigade) deserted to the rebs.[17] They passed the pickets at three o'clock in the morning.

The pickets had orders to allow all field officers and all reconnoitering pass through their lines.

When the two men passed beyond our lines the colonel took out a white pocket handkerchief, waved it, and went inside the rebel works.

The rebs shouted as they took them in. Report says we were to open on Yorktown that day. But this move put a stop to it.

It will go hard with that Colonel and Major, if they are ever caught.

Yesterday our Colonel and some of our officers went over to the rifle pits[18] to see Berdan's sharp shooters[19] get in their work.

They said that one would take his field glass and locate a reb at one of the cannons, then tell his mate how to fire. The result would be one reb less.

They saw one reb behind the butt of a large siege gun with his musket lying on to it. the top of his head only in sight. The sharpshooters drew a bead on him and let go. The head went out of sight but came back again.

The other sharpshooter tried his hand on the reb. This time the head went out of sight. But did not come back. That's the way it is done down here.

There are 15,000 men in front of Yorktown now.[20]

You know what is going down here better than we do. You have the papers. All I know is what our regiment does. and the others close by.

I think this battle of Yorktown will close up this rebellion.

Tell mother that we have plenty to eat and wear. We are to have fresh beef and potatoes for dinner to day. No pay yet. when it comes I will send part of it up home.

I shall not write any one now but the home folks.

I am very well and in good spirits. Good bye, write soon.
          Your Brother
           Charlie

Don't worry.

April 30 [1862]. Mustered for pay to day. Four months due us now. I am detailed to go with a detachment over to McClellan's headquarters to escort the Paymaster here. We took an army wagon along to bring him and his strong box. McClellan's headquarters are on the same spot that Genl Washington's was. A large stone marks the spot.

We found that the paymaster had left for our camp. so we came back with out him.

It was a very hard, bad road. What we call corduroy. It is built of small trees laid cross wise and close together.

We were paid this afternoon. I sent $20.00 to father.

Yesterday we were out on a reconnaissance towards Lee's Mills. This is the first time our regiment was under fire. The first time we heard the minnie[21] balls whistle over our heads. It is a strange sort of feeling. We exchanged shots several times with the rebs. No harm done to us.

The Vermont boys got it bad. As they were crossing the stream, the rebs opened the flood gates at the mill[22] and flooded them. A number were drowned. It's too bad.

May 1. We advanced our picket line last night half a mile across the open lot. We got where we could see the rebel camp fires. They put a few shells into us. Hurt nothing. About midnight we fell back to our old line again. No one hurt.

To day [on] my rambles I came across a tent, near the hospital, where the surgeons were amputating a leg near the thigh. It looked like a round of beef, red and juicy like.

It looks more & more like war here. That is what we are here for.

May 3. This morning Co. H. and our Co. went over to the 93rd N.Y. and arrested one of their companies who had refused duty, and had stacked their arms. We took them to our camp. They were sent to Fortress Monroe later.

May 4, Sunday. Had orders for inspection this morning, but they were countermanded. Then the orders came to be ready to move at a moments notice, in light marching order.[23] Fall in came next. We were in line very quick. The regiment took its place in the brigade line. Forward! was the command. We moved out for three or four miles when the report came that Yorktown had been evacuated. We marched on untill we came to the deserted works of the rebs, where we cound "Old Glory"[24] floating over them. They were very good works too. Well put up for defense.

We rested by the flood gates at Lee's Mills a short time. They had things fixed here so they could have drowned a brigade in no time. This is where the Vermont boys got it.

Our march from here was very slow, as the rebs had placed a large number of torpedoes in the road.[25] One of the regiments ahead of us had one man killed, and five wounded, by the explosion of one. After marching four or five miles we encamped for the night.

May 5 [1862]. Woke up this morning to find myself in puddle of water. It had rained last night for sure. After breakfast we went back after our knapsacks, and traps.

This afternoon after we came back "Deak" Gooding[26] and I thought we would take a look at country, as there was nothing else on hand for us to do.

We must have gone two or three miles when we saw two darkies. We asked them if they could tell us where we could buy some cakes. They said yes, they would show us if we would go with them. We went to old massas house a little way further. We bought some cakes, and paid for them when the old black woman came out with a quart bottle filled with what she said was double rectified apple brandy some old massa had left. Did we want to buy it? Yes. we gave her a quarter of a dollar for it. Then started for camp.

We lost our way several times before we reached our quarters. In the meantime a heavy rain had set in. When we reached camp we found our regiment and brigade were out nearly two miles in front line of battle. We made our way to them in the mud and rain. After standing in line for over an hour all hand[s] were ordered back to camp. How it did rain. It poured. Water and mud every where. our dog tents were up as we left them. (By the way, a dog tent is made of two pieces of light canvas buttoned together on the edges, or sides. They are six feet long and four feet wide. Anything will do for poles and ridges. Two men can crawl in, and curl up quite good) Before we lay down "Deacon" and I took a taste of our apple jack. then laid down in the wet and slept.

May 6. We woke up this morning, that is "Deak" and I, bright as a whip. That stuff made a great night cap. Yesterday was the battle of Williamsburg. We were in the last line of battle last night. And did not know what was up untill this morning. Another new wrinkle in war. Be in a battle, and not know it. After breakfast, and just before we were ordered to march, I gave Lt. [Spencer] Martin a taste of our apple jack in a tin cup. He put it to his lips, tasted it, smelled of it, then drank it. In ten minutes he was the liveliest man in the regiment. The stuff is as smooth as oil. We shall keep it for night caps only. Its hard marching this morning. mud knee deep. We crossed a stream and slough where the mud was like pudding. One man was in up to his arm pits, holding his gun up over his head. He waded through. We marched untill four o'clock when we camped in a piece of woods near the rebel Fort Magruder, and near the city of Williamsburg, Va. Very tired.

Here we had a chance to pass over the battle field of yesterday. It was a hard sight. They had this place well fortified. But our men were too many for them.

James Speers is very sick.[27]

**Fort Magruder and the Confederate Defenses
at Williamsburg, May 6, 1862**
(Battles and Leaders of the Civil War)

May 7 [1862]. To day we are cleaning up every thing, and sorting out. The College of William and Mary is located here. They say it is the oldest one in the country.[28] It looks so that it might be.

May 8. I am twenty years old to day. I picked some wild flowers to day which I shall send to my sister. Our men captured a great many prisoners here.

The country round here seems to be very fine. A good place to live in.

May 9. Our regiment took the lead to day. Each regiment takes turn about leading the brigade. We led off at a great pace.

Its much easier marching at the right of the line. After marching twelve miles, we camped for the night near a large spring of pure sweet water. Its the largest spring I ever saw. The roads have been sandy so it was hard marching.

Our rations are first class and plenty. We fry our hard tack[29] in pork grease, which makes them go down better.

May 10. The road is strewed with clothing which the troops ahead of us have left. We are leaving off every thing we do not need.

Marched 10 miles to day and camped in a deep gully near McClellan's headquarters.

We do not cover much ground in a day, But it takes all day to make it.

May 11 [1862]. We are to lay here all day. Good.

Simmons and Bancroft[30] are under arrest for steeling a mule from a citizen. The Colonel has been arrested for allowing the boys to steel it.

At all the farm houses on our line of march we have to place a safe guard, so the troops will [not] plunder the people.

May 12. Our company is on picket to day. We have changed our mode of doing picket duty. Three men or three men and a non-commissioned officer are on one post together. The posts are several rods apart, or as the nature of the country admits. We all keep our eyes open during the day. At night we divide the time up between us. It's a great deal better than the old way. Our apple jack is a great thing for picket duty.

Yesterday we passed through a small hamlet, in which was an old cemetery. I saw the graves of two english officers. The gravestones were dated 1744 & 1784. The church had crumbled into ruins.

This is an old part of our country, full of ancient history. We are writing new history for it.

May 13. We were relieved early this morning. Our regiment fell into line at nine o'clock, and moved out by the road side, where we lay in the hot sun, and on the hot sand untill four o'clock. It was very hot. Scorching! When we took up the line of march again try to catch up with the rebs, Lt. Martin played out, and had to take an ambulance. A good many of the boys had to pull out by the way. I guess I would have been among the numbers if it had not been for the <u>blessed</u> whiskey. Captain Clarke stays in the rear of the regiment with his canteens of whiskey. So that when a man is nearly played out he can brace him up with a drop or two. It helps out very much.

It has been very hard marching this afternoon. Dry and dusty.

May 14. New Kent Court House, Va. We reached here at 2 o'clock this morning. used up for once. After making coffee we spread our blankets and lay down and slept untill nearly ten o'clock. I feel a trifle rested. It was a hard days work. We only marched 12 miles. It has begun to rain. This is a very large place. Court house, jail, and four other houses.

May 15. We are still here in camp and resting. It still rains, much to our discomfort.

May 16. Still here. The rain has ceased. Very pleasant now.

May 17. We are still here resting. Orders came at dark to fall in. Then out in the dark we started on the march to we don't know where. It makes no difference, if we only find the rebels, and whip them.

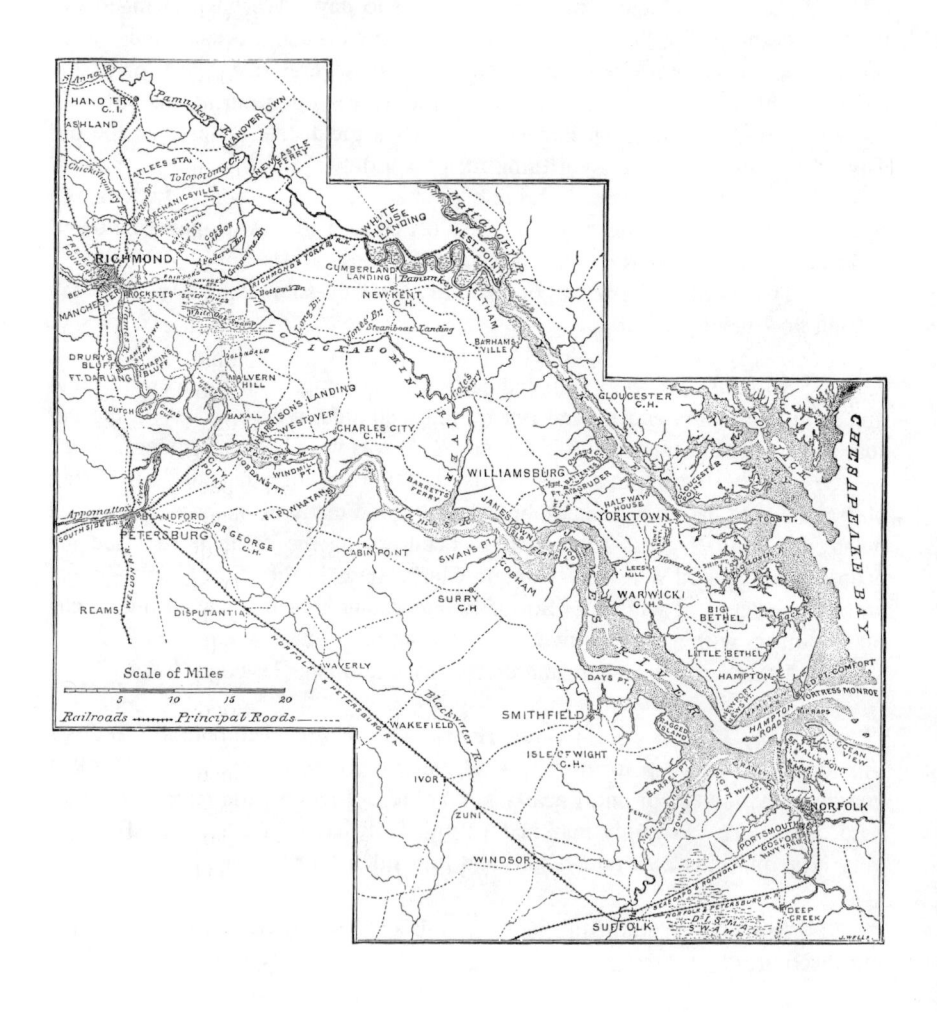

The Peninsula Campaign
(Battles and Leaders of the Civil War)

May 18 [1862], Sunday. Baltimore Cross Roads. near the White House.[31] Another all night march reaching here this 3 A.M. This night work is hard. I am on camp guard to day. Quiet. In my letter home to day I told them I was alive and well and able to eat my rations. So I am.

May 19. I had the worst dream last night I ever had in my life. I felt very well yesterday, But not so well to day. We fell in this morning before I had my coffee. I had to go just the same. We marched six miles to Royster Cottage. I am played out. Sure. Lt. Bronson is sick.[32]

May 20. Royster Cottage, Va. Brigade inspection by Genl. Palmer. I had to be excused from the ranks, I was so weak.

May 21. Advanced two miles to day. Had my knapsack carried for the first time. I am so weak I can hardly crawl. I kept up with the rest through it all.

May 22. One of the worst thunder storms to day I ever saw. Rain & hail. Hailstones as large as hens egg. We could not keep ourselves dry. I am completely used up. [Al]Most dead.

May 23. Marched three miles today. Camped early. I follow after the boys as best I can. My traps are carried.[33]

May 24. Our brigade went out on a reconnaisance[34] to day near Savage Station, and drove in the rebel pickets. Our loss one killed, one wounded. I stayed in camp.

May 25. We moved two miles to day.

May 26. We moved two miles farther to day. We seem to be crawling up closer & closer to the rebs. I am in camp every night with the boys.

May 27. Our company is on picket near White Oak Bottom Swamp. I am not able to go with them. But I am feeling better now. Will be around soon.

May 28. The rebs tried their hand at shelling us to day. No one hurt. I am no better to day.

May 29. Moved half a mile, and entrenched ourselves. We are getting very close now. I am improving I think.

**Lieutenant Amos Brunson
(USAMHI)**

May 30 [1862]. This morning began by the rebs driving in our pickets. But they were repulsed by our men. One of Co. H's men was wounded in the leg, and had to have it amputated.[35] We are at Fair Oaks or Seven Pines.[36] Our quarters are near the Seven Pine trees. I am a trifle better.

May 31. Every thing is lovely this morning. Just as we were eating our dinner, we were greeted with the music of two rebel shells whistling over our heads. We did not finish dinner. The regiment fell in promptly. I was ordered not to. C. J. Simmons - the drummer took my gun and place. I am not well.[37] But we thought it was only an attack on our picket line, as usual. We were soon convinced that it was not. Our regiment moved off to the left and went into the rifle pits. I found a seat on a log in front of the Captain's tent.[38] Where my view was good. The first thing I saw was the rebel line of battle come out of the woods in our front. Their guns were at a right shoulder shift. Just in front of me was a redoubt manned by a light battery 12 pound brass nepolitans [Napoleons] of the 1st N.Y. light artillery. They cut loose their guns, with shot and cannister, and plowed a swath through the reb lines thirty feet wide or more. The rebs never moved a gun from their shoulders, but came right on, as through they were on review. Then that battery went at them again and plowed another swath through them as before and not gun came down from their shoulders. only as the men who carried them was shot down. It was a terrible slaughter. Those rebels were heroes. The 103rd Pa went out to support our picket lines but broke at the first fire. Their colonel took them in with empty guns. It was a shame!

But those rebs in front of our battery were game, they closed their lines, and in they came as if nothing had happened. Our battery still at them. The boys never left their guns, untill the rebs drove them from their guns at the point of bayonet. Those rebs were good men. Our 85th was in the rifle pits doing good work. The rebs came on them in such shape, that they could not fire, for fear they would cross fire on themselves. Then our boys gave it to them. They too had to move out. I still sat on my log watching the <u>fun</u>, when Henry Simmons came in from the front and told [Private John] Blake and me that we had better go to the rear. Thinking that I had seen enough. I packed my traps in my knapsack, slung it on my back and dug out. Then I began to be scared. The bullets came over my head like hail stones. With a shell quite as often. How I ran, I was still very weak from my sickness. I was very afraid I would get hit in the back. My father told me never to get hit there. The men were falling fast all around me. Billy Young[39] fifer [in] Co. D. fell close by me wounded, and yelling like a loon. Still I went on untill I reached a large wood. Blake had struck off towards the wagons, so I lost him. The woods were full of our men. Our division had been driven of[f] the field. After I had rested a while, I came across Vogt and Farrar[40] of our company who helped me carry my traps. I was busted. Heintzelman's[41] corp came up, as they passed us He said, "If Casey's men did not kill these rebs, who in hell did." Just so. I kept on to the rear untill I was near Savage's house. Here I found a number of our boys.

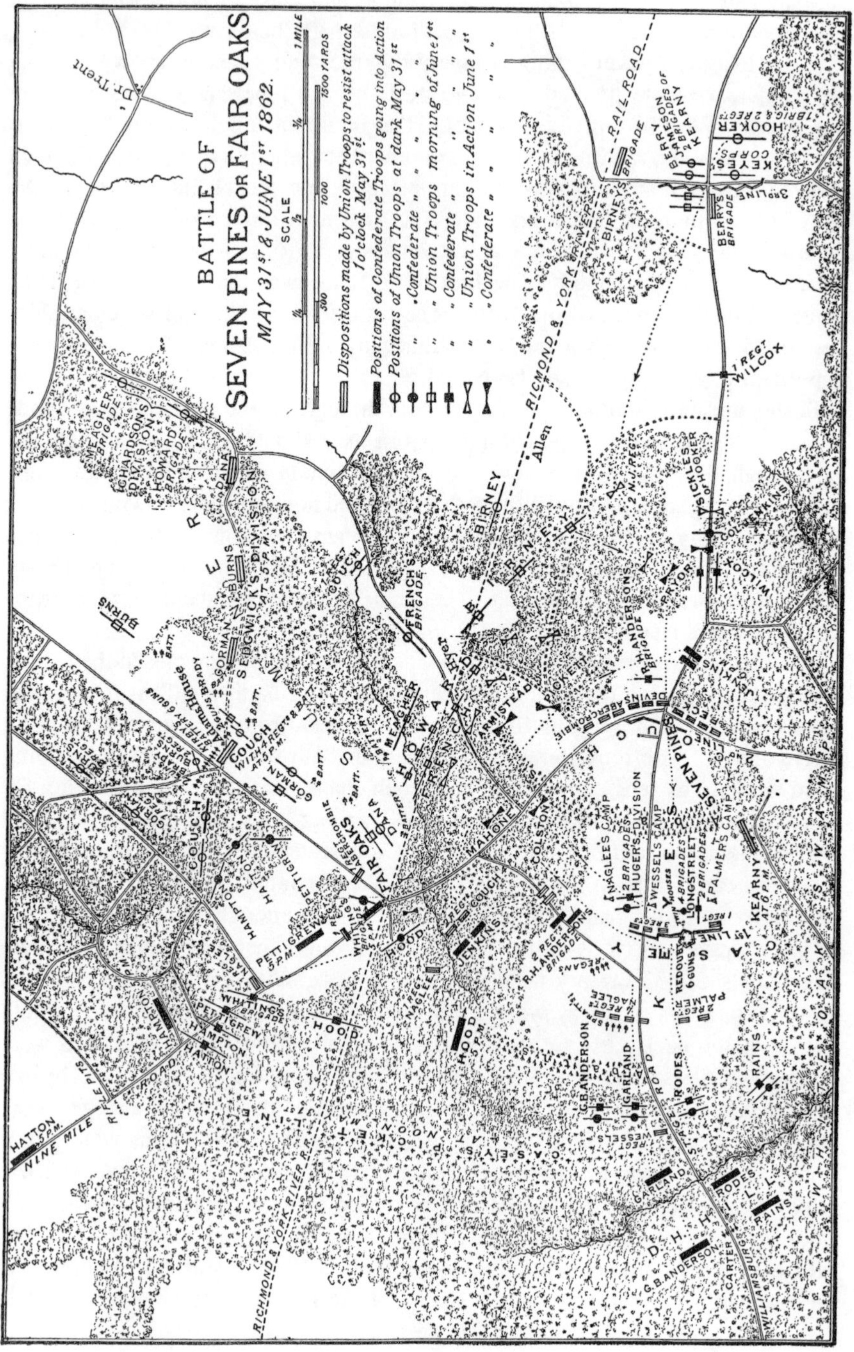
BATTLE OF
SEVEN PINES OR FAIR OAKS
MAY 31ST & JUNE 1ST 1862.
SCALE
Dispositions made by Union Troops to resist attack 1 o'clock May 31st
Positions of Confederate Troops going into Action
Positions of Union Troops at dark May 31st
" Confederate " " " "
" Union Troops morning of June 1st
" Confederate " " "
" Union Troops in Action June 1st
" Confederate " "
RICHMOND & YORK RIVER R.R.
NINE MILE ROAD
WILLIAMSBURG
Dr. Trent
Allen
RAIL ROAD

It began to rain. The fighting kept up untill after dark. As we were out of range we fixed up our blankets as best we could, and lay down for the night.

The report is Capt. Clarke is killed.[42]

June 1 [1862]. The fight is still on. I did not sleep much last night. Our men are driving the rebs. Capt. Clarke has come in with a few of our boys. There are a lot of missing. Out of our company one is killed. Crandell, Briggs, Wetmore, J. J. Mary, Alvah Phillips, Munson & Steel are prisoners. Some say Crandall is killed.[43] Quite a number are slightly wounded. A rebel prisoner told Capt. Clarke that he was in the rear with his division yesterday, and that one of their cracked brigades went into the fight in front of our 85th rifle pits and when they came back an Alabama regiment could not muster but twenty men, and two others could muster only two hundred each.[44] The reb told the captain that this was a good showing for one yankee regiment.

Lt. Col. Wellman was severely wounded in the head. He has gone north.[45] Col. Belknap is reported a prisoner.[46] But we think not. He is to big a coward, and was seen by some cavalry men making his way to the rear early in the fight. He is a bad lot.

Capt. Clarke was the man that held the regiment up. Major King is no good. Our company are getting together again. Capt. Clarke ordered Graham[47] and me to go down to Savage Station out of the way, as we are not fit for duty, and are played out completely. Here I found Buz. Insse.[48] He is wounded in the face and ankle. He was punctured with buckshot. His heel pains him a good deal. I found him a good place out of the way, on the side of the drive way where he sat nursing his heel untill a squad of rebel prisoners came in, when he went to damning them. He alternated between nursing his heel, and damning the reb prisoners. After a while I helped him on the cars to go north. That is the cars run to White House Landing, where the men are transferred to steamboats, and thence to northern hospitals. The wounded are coming in fast now. The ambulances bring in the badly wounded. Others walk in.

It's a constant stream of ambulances. one after another. some with only one in, some with two. It is horrible.

Some of the wounded are brought in on streatchers where they are so badly used up, that they can't stand the jolt and jar of the ambulance. In my wanderings I found our drummer C. J. Simmons (the one who to [I gave] my gun) with a severe wound in the face. I made him comfortable as possible, and helped him on the cars. The poor fellow was hit in the face, which is all swelled up. He can hardly talk.

Every building and out house of every discription is full of the sick and wounded. In one shed I found Co[l]. Van Wyck of the 56th N.Y.[49]

One of our boys came in and told us that our Colonel says he was captured three times and made his escape each time. He can tell that to the marines.

After Lt. Col. Wellman was wounded the command of the regiment devolved in Capt. Clarke, who is senior captain. When drummer Simmons was wounded he gave my gun to Adjt. [Chauncey] Aldrich, who leaned it against a tree, and left it. So I am out a gun. Our whole division were driven [out] of our camp ground. We lost every thing, but what we had on. This is the strangest Sunday I ever put in. The wounded are every where.

June 2 [1862]. Graham and I found a corner to bunk in last night. Not much sleep for me. At intervals through the night one poor fellow in one of the buildings called out water! water! water! It was simply awful to hear him. I skirmished around and found some grub for our breakfast. There was not of a chance to find anything [sic].

There are half a dozen amputating tents in operations here, and a large number of volunteer surgeons from the north at work. I strayed into one this forenoon, and was pressed into service as an assistant. that is, I held up the limbs while the surgeons used their tools. I held up a number of legs. It took about five minutes to a man.

The first thing they did was to give the patient a big drink of whiskey (and take one themselves) then put him under the influence of chloroform. then in a very few minutes, they would say bring in another man.

One fellow was brought in - he was able to walk - who had the flesh of his forearm torn off by a piece of shell. He was told that his arm could be saved. But he said no it had to come off. The surgeons tried to show him how that it need not be amputated but to no purpose. He was placed under chloroform. I held the sponge to his nose with one hand, and his right arm out of the way with my other. When he was thought to have been under the influence, the surgeon put his knife into the arm about half way between the shoulder and elbow. The victim jerked his right hand away from me and snatched that sponge from his face in a jiffy. The surgeons had hard work to make him give it up. I took quite a lot of scolding. He <u>threw up the sponge</u>. then had enough chloroform to put him to sleep. His arm was off and he was carried out on the grass, ready for northern shipment. Then the surgeons took their instruments and examined the amputated portion and found the elbow joint perfectly sound, and not a bone of the arm injured. It could have been saved as well as not. We came to the conclusion that the man thought if his arm was off, that he would be allowed to go home, and have no more war on his plate. He was minus an arm anyway.

I had quite an experience in the surgical business. It was sickening to say the least. One man who was in another place out doors, on whom the chloroform would not work. He had to be held down by men untill the leg was off. When he said doctor my heel aches, let me put it down on the ground. His heel was in a field with other legs and arms. How the poor fellow yelled.

June 3 [1862]. This morning Lt. Martin and Sgt. McHenry came in to see us. (last night I found Capt. Clarke and borrowed some money from him, as Graham and I were hard up for grub.) "Chet" Gooding came here to try and help out a little. Ed. Blake came in this morning. when we posted company last Saturday he struck off into the wagon road and climbed into a battery wagon and went down to Dispatch station. He came back on the cars. We thought he was dead. Martin left us some money. Blake is played out. Graham is no good. I have to be commissary for the squad.

I have made some good bargains with the sutler. That is I buy a dollars worth and take as much more. That is what a sutler is for.

When we were at Fair Oaks we were within miles[50] of Richmond. by climbing trees we could see the spires of the city.

June 5. I am feeling quite well to day. Yesterday I took care of my squad of sick. All are doing well.

All convalescents are ordered to join their respective regiments. Ours lay at White Oak Swamp about five miles from here. We started off on our own gait, and reached camp this afternoon, rather tired. We found the boys hard up. They are without tents, blankets, and a change of <u>linen</u>. Rations are scarce. Blake and I chum together. He is a growler. He is just sick enough to be cross. The first think in the morning he growls out "Mose[51] fry some pork. Mose fry some pork." then I soak some hard tack in water and fry them, which with coffee, we make our breakfast.

This is repeated morning after morning. It is a by word in camp. "Mose fry some pork." We (Blake and I) have no duty to do. I am feeling very well, but am not strong yet. I go after blackberries occasionally with good success. The regiment are out throwing up earthworks or else slashing down the trees, so our artillery can have a good sweep.

Maj. Gen. J. J. Peck is in command of our division now,[52] and Brig. Gen. H. W. Wessells is in command of our brigade.[53] We are 2nd brigade, 2nd division, 4th corps. Genl. Palmer has been assigned to another brigade.[54] Genl. Wessells was a major in the 6th U. S. Inf. There are all sorts of rumors afloat here.

June 9. We were paid to day two months pay. I sent father $15.00 by express. When I got my debts paid, I had $6.00 left, which will do me.

I am getting my strength now, so I begin to feel like myself once more. We can hear heavy firing over in the direction of Fort Darling on the James river. The first thing we hear in the morning is "Mose fry some pork."

A division sutler has set up his shop under a large tree, in the open field in front of our camp.

Yesterday we went out and sampled his stock. He had a large stock of oranges, lemons, crackers, cheese, cookies, pickles, pickled pigs feet. We had some of each. Of course he took no pay for them, because he did not know that we had bought any. And we hadn't. A sutler shop is a very handy institution in camp. Every thing is so handy and convenient for one who has long fingers. Our arms and fingers have grown wonderfully of late. It must be the climate.

June 15 [1862], Sunday. I am out of the doctors hands now. All I want is my gun. I will have to have another one, as mine was ordered on to Richmond some time since.[55]

Yesterday Capt. Clarke and Adjt. Aldrich went out into the country for a square meal. The Adjt. brought me a canteen of fresh milk, which I saved for my breakfast this morning. This morning it was thick and as sour as swill. So my breakfast was hard tack and coffee as usual. I had a bath yesterday down in the river. I changed my shirt for the first time since May 4th. Our clothing has come on, and the rest of our camp equipage, so we are in line again.

"Gust" Greeg[56] came in to day. He was left sick at Newport News. He had the mumps. Wrote home to day. This is the fourth one since the fight.

Our company is on picket to day when the mail came in. I was detailed to take it out to our boys. As I reached the last post sergeant McHenry was going down to the farm house where Lt. Martin was. As I had a letter for him I went along. They had arranged for dinner there. It was ready when we reached there. So I went in with the rest. As it was harvest time they had a good dinner. Chicken pie, fried chicken, string beans, (snaps they called them) and bacon, with plenty of fresh milk. Then to add to the interest, one of the young ladies of the house with a green bough stood opposite us, and kept the flies off the table. It seemed good to see people once more. The dinner did me good all through. It cost me a half dollar. Cheap. I stayed with the boys untill they were relieved. A few of us went back to camp another way in order to get some ripe cherries. We had all we could eat. They were luscious. Before we reached camp a heavy rain set in and we were wet through. Had a soaking.

We have whiskey rations issued to us now. It's the forty rod kind, and would kill round a corner.

June 16. Four gentlemen from Bloomfield, Ontario Co., N.Y. were here looking after the boys from that town. Lt. Bronson's brother was one. he came to have the Lts. [Bronson's] body removed to the north. He died at Royster Cottage. One of the other men had a brother captured in the fight at Fair Oaks. We get rations of potatoes, dried apples, and pickles, in addition to our regular grub. Capt. Clarke is a trifle under the weather at present. He is the best officer in the army.

June 18. Wrote to father to day. not much going on here only fatigue duty. I am all right now, but have no gun. I am ready for duty. I seem to have had a low fever, a sort of malaria.[57] With the exception of the nights at Savages Station I have kept up with the regiment right along. And haven't had to go to the hospital.

June 22 [1862]. White Oak Swamp, Va. Sunday. We are still here. There is heavy firing off to our right and over on James river. I am improving in health fast.

June 27. Every thing has been very quiet here for a few days back.

This morning we were ordered to have three days cooked rations on hand, and be ready to move at an hours notice. We are ready.

This afternoon we were ordererd out to the rifle pits, to wait for somebody, or something to come along. They did not come. We waited for 'em untill dark and went back to camp. Part of the regiment stayed in the pits.

I am all right now, as I have a gun on my shoulder and in line with the boys. H[enry] C. Simmons is sick, so I took his gun. I had the straps. It has been some time since I was out with the company.

June 28. About midnight a pontoon train passed our camp. They made a terrible racket. This morning we found they had laid a bridge across White Oak swamp. Soon after, Couch's[58] division of our corps passed by and crossed over the bridge. When the order came to fall in. Tents were struck, we fell in and moved across the bridge out on the Richmond road. We marched about eight miles, and camped in an open lot. We do not know what is up. It seems as though the whole army was on the move. There has been heavy firing over on our right.

June 29, Sunday. Early this morning we heard a racket to our left which proved to be a small body of reb cavalry that had run on to one of our marked batterie [battery]. They had it set to them in great shape.

A great many of Porter's[59] corps are stragling through here. We were ordered to guard Fishers ford. Our regiment moved on the top of a large hill in an open field. threw out our pickets and waited.

The officer in command of a cavalry force, asked our colonel to allow a company to go out and lay in ambush, while the cavalry tried to draw the rebs from their cover, so as to get a chance at them. Our company went out and lay in a piece of woods and waited for the rebs to show up.

They were not drawn out. So we lost a shot. We found a great many blackberries here of the running variety. There were as large as my thumb and very lucious.

The whole of Porters corps is pouring through and across Fisher's ford. At dark we were ordered back to the main army. When we reached Keyes headquarters we found a perfect jam. Every thing was crowded in together. Cavalry, artillery and infantry. Wagons, mules, and a large herd of beef cattle. I found the 18th N.Y. Inf. here. Capt. Farout's[60] company went from Canandaigua, in this regiment. I saw Lt. Henry Ellis & his brother George.[61] Gardner King[62] was killed the other day. He was a school mate of mine in Chapinville.

After we had our supper, and rested a while, we fell in and marched through a large piece of woods.

June 30 [1862]. We had a hard time last night. we marched only eight miles. It was march and halt, march and halt. every time we halted we dropped down on the ground to rest, then up again and move a little way, then halt, drop down by the road side, and try to catch a bit of sleep. then up and at it again. All this time we had our knapsacks on our backs. During the night there was a stampede of horses in the woods near us. We were lying down at the time, we were up in a hurry. In the excitement "Mother"[63] Hall lost his knapsack. He could not find it any where in the dark. After a long search one of the boys found it strapped on his (Hall's) back. Then we all laughed. It made sport of the rest of the night.

We did not camp untill ten o'clock this morning. A tired lot of men. After breakfast we were mustered for pay by our Colonel. We had barely time to draw our rations of hard tack and salt pork, and cook breakfast. I found time to draw a large frying pan from the hind axle of an army wagon near us. I think it belonged to some officers kit. After using it to get breakfast with, I strapped it on my knapsack for future use. We had barely time to get outside of our grub, when Fall in! Fall in! We fell in line in a hurry, for there was heavy firing in our front.

We marched out into a large wheat field. Our division formed the fourth line of battle. By getting on a rail fence we could see a little of what was going on. The roar of artillery and infantry was terrible. For a time it seemed to draw nearer and nearer. Then our gunboats on the river took a hand in the fight, then the roar of battle receded, and we felt a trifle easier. This battle goes in history of the battle of Malvern Hill.[64]

July 1. We slept on our arms[65] last night. This morning the battle was renewed in earnest. We moved around further to our right in a piece of woods. Graham and Jones[66] are sick, and were sent down to the river, and placed on board of a transport out of the way. This afternoon our company under command Lt. Martin was ordered together with a company from each regiment in our brigade. the whole under Capt. Kreutzer of the 98th N.Y. to go to the Haxells Landing on the James river and unload a schooner, which was loaded with army stores.

We reached here about six o'clock. Here we found McClellans headquarters, wagons, army wagons of every kind. Horses, mules, cattle, and a perfect mob of straglers, wounded men, rebel prisoners. We began our work and had the schooner nearly unloaded, when orders came [to] load all the stores on board the schooner and move twelve miles down the river to Harrison's Landing.[67] We placed every thing on board and went up on the bluff and got our supper. We were near a lot of rebel prisoners, under guard of our regulars. The rebs were having a good time among them selves, and were showing some pictures they had captured in battle. One was a picture of a young lady. Our Dick Phillips said that if he (the reb) had his girls picture, he would tear his heart out. Dick lost his girls picture at Fair Oaks. This job of work was rather hard on me. It was heavy work handling hard tack boxes, and barrels of pork.

After supper we turned in for the night. The whole army seemed to be around us.

July 2 [1862]. When we woke up this morning it was raining very hard. Our detachment was the ones on the ground. Every thing and every body had left sometime during the night. Not a man or beast was in sight. After breakfast we fell in and moved down the river, keeping close to [the] bank. The rain poured in torrents. Once or twice we saw the main army away off to our left. We passed through a large field of ripe wheat. The reaping machines were left in the standing grain by the farmers when our cavalry drove them out. We passed through corn and clover that would have made our northern farmers think that they had never seen such crop growing. They were the finest I ever saw any where, either up home or here.

About noon we reached the large ravine near the river, here we joined the main part of our army. There was a creek running through this ravine. The men and wagons who had passed through ahead of us had churned it and the mud into a pudding. We followed a train of heavy siege guns through. It took 11 & 12 hours to pull 'em. Smith's division[68] broke in about this time and our detachment got all mixed up with them, as we were acquainted with some of the boys. We were so mixed up that we were separated from Lt. Martin so much so when we reached high ground again "Deaken" Gooding and I were the only one[s] of our company together. We had lost all sight of our detachment. It was no use looking for them, so we pushed right down to the James river. We were wet through & our shoes were full of mud. We took off our shoes & stockings, and washed the mud out of them, then took off our pants and washed the mud out of them, and gave ourselves a good bathing. We were fortunate enough to have clean under clothing in our knapsacks which we put on when we felt better. The rain had stopped a short time before this. Then we put up our dog tent a short way from the water, and got our dinner. We had fried pork, hard tack and coffee, a very good dinner.

What we had been through for the past few days is called in history the Seven Days fight before Richmond. The army had changed its base to the James river and Richmond was not in our hands.

Our regiment had not fired a shot.

We were having a rest and a good smoke by our new quarters by the river and noticed we were getting nearer the water but paid no attention to it. perhaps the water was getting nearer to us, and it was, for it made one rush and filled our tent. The tide came in, and we did not know as there was any such thing as a tide. It was my first experience along that line.

We picked up our traps and moved up on high ground, near a battery wagon. We made no effort to find our regiment this afternoon. We rested as much as we could for we are nearly played out.

July 3 [1862]. We slept soundly last night. This morning while "Deacon" kept house I went out and tried to find some trace of our regiment or division. I found in the course of my travels a Brigadier Genl. who told me that Pecks division was on rear guard the last day in but did not know where they were now. I did not make any further search. I found the 18th N.Y. in the mud knee deep. George Ellis was wounded and taken prisoner at Gaine's Mill. Lt. Henry Ellis was cooking a mess of potatoes in a quart dish. Capt. Farrut and Lt. Green[69] were around with white collars on and looked as if they had just come out of a band box. Lt. Ellis was all the officer the company had during the past seven days fight. all the boys spoke highly of him. Good for "Hank."

Just then the firing began in front and Lt. Ellis said "boys let us get outside of the potatoes as soon as possible for we may be wanted."

This afternoon sergeant McHenry & Bancroft found us. They were trying to find the regiment. Bancroft stayed with us, and McHenry went on his search. We rested all we could untill nearly night when the battery wagons by us moved to join their respective batteries. We were left where we would be in danger of being run over by wagons and every body, so we packed up and moved a mile or so and camped under a large tree in a corn field. We put up our tents, and cut corn stalks for a bed. we are quite comfortable here.

July 4. This is the ever glorious fourth. We had a good nights rest, but we are out of rations of every kind and far away from our command.

Early this morning a Major of artillery came up and ordered us to move out, as he wished to park his guns here. We gave him some of our lip.[70] [T]hen he demanded us and said we had ought to be put to the front.

We packed up our traps and moved very quick, and learning where McClellans headquarters were, we found them. Here we found Capt. Clarke and the most of our company.

After getting something to eat we all left for our regiment. They were about two miles from the river in a thick wood. Soon an Aid[71] of Genl. Wessells came round and said we were to be reviewed in the afternoon by Maj. Genl. McClellan on our own parade ground, and that we were to present arms as he rode by, and the Genl. did not want any cheering by his men as the reviewing officers rode by. At the appointed hour McClellan reviewed us. And not a cheer. When he crossed the road and went among the Massachusetts men, they cheered him, and the mules brayed. It was hard to tell which was which. Man, or mule. Mail to day.

July 5. Wrote to father this morning. Just a line to let them know that I am all right. We have begun to fix up our camp. We took [tree] crotches and drove [them] in the ground, then lay poles across them then lay on pine boughs. Over all we put our dog tents. This gives us a good bed about 18 inches above the ground. We have the regular round of duties.

July 13 [1862]. My diary seems to have taken a jump again.[72] So I will fix it up from my home letters. I had fried meat and potatoes and green apple sauce for breakfast. We have moved our camp near a large spring of pure water. (We are a half mile from it.) It is on the opposite side of the gully and down to the bottom of it. Two streams as large as my wrist gush out of the bank. We have to take advantage of the tides being out for when it is in the spring is flooded. We have slashed the woods between us and the front so our cannon can have a good range. We have built a magazine for the 1st Conn heavy artillery. They have a battery of five rifled 32 pounders.[73] They are 13 feet long.

Our picket duty is done by companies, we have to go out about two miles. There are few houses standing around here. They were well furnished in their time. A few pieces of marble top furniture are left in one of them. Our sutler came in the other day with a wagon load of stuff. While he was putting up his tent I got into his wagon to see what belonged to me. I found a ham that looked as though it had my private mark on it. I went back to camp and tried to find one of the boys who knew my private mark. After a long search I found "Al" Bancroft who said he knew it.

We went to prove properly. I got into the wagon again. "Al" went round on the opposite side from where the sutler and his men were at work. I tumbled my ham into his hands, and he made a circuit through the woods to our tent. I stayed in the wagon nearly a half an hour then went and had a chat with the sutler. A very pleasant chat we had, as to where he had been since our last fight and so on.

Then I strolled into camp. Bancroft had the ham cut up and over the fire cooking. Boiled ham is good.

July 20. I received a letter from father this morning. all well at home. Wrote Sarah[74] to day. I was on camp guard yesterday. Off early this morning. Our colonel[75] is under arrest for cowardice before the enemy. Hope he will be court martialed and sent home.

Day before yesterday I made big bag [of] pudding - boiled - using blackberries in place of raisins. While it was cooking, I went up to the sutlers and took a can of condensed milk (The sutler allows such things to be done when he don't know it) for sauce. I made some sour sauce too. Six of us made a dinner of the pudding. All pronounced it good, the best of the season.

Capt. Clarke is in command of the regiment now.

Genl. Peck is giving us all the drill now we can stand this hot weather. Division drill takes the starch out of us. We have to carry our knapsacks on drill, which makes it much harder. Between drill, picket and fatigue we are busy. Its a part of the show.

July 28 [1862]. A letter written home on this date says we went out as a support for the picket line last Saturday and came off Sunday at Sundown. Our whole regiment was out.

My diary is resumed this date. I sent my old one home for safe keeping.

Battalion[76] drill this afternoon. and washed my clothes. Our camp is well located here.

July 29. Reported this morning to the doctors with a very sore throat. He said it was the quinsey[77]. I was excused from duty.

July 30. Excused to day. Our division was ordered in line to day, and were ordered to move. The order was countermanded.

July 31. Excused. My throat is sore. Our company is on picket. It rains.

Buell, Knapp, Van Wie, and Richardson[78] came in from the north, where they have been in hospital. They are looking well. H. C. Simmons is very sick in the hospital with inflamatory rheumatism. He is so bad that his hip joint has pulled out of its socket. He is very gritty.

August 1. Excused. The boys are in off picket.

August 2. Excused. My throat is very sore.

August 3. Excused. Saw Ed Evarts to day. He is from our place.[79] Wrote home.

August 5. Excused yesterday and to day. We are under marching orders yet. But we are not marching. All quiet.

August 6. Excused. Wrote to brother George. H. C. Simmons was taken down the boat landing to be sent to a northern hospital. He is a very sick man.[80]

August 7. Excused. Our regiment is out to support our picket line. I had rather be with them than have this sore throat.

August 8. Excused. My throat does not seem to be any better. It is badly swollen and very sore I can hardly swallow my grub. I go to the doctors every day for treatment. I use a gargle of red pepper. Deakon Gooding has gone to the landing to take care of H. C. Simmons.

Genl. Peck gives our regiment the praise of being the cleanest in his division.

August 10 [1862]. Still on the sick list. I am all over the grounds. But not strong for duty. I can't eat enough. We drew rations of cheese and red herrings. A mouthful of each. Our company is on picket. Wrote home. We have orders to move tomorrow. The report is we are to evacuate this place. We never know anything for sure here untill it happens.

August 11. I got up last night at 12 o'clock and packed up our boys knapsacks and things and help load them on wagons. My quinsey has gone down. It broke in the night. I shall feel better now. The report is that our knapsacks are to be loaded on barges and go down the river. So that we will not be bothered with them on the march. We are ordered to march at 2 P.M. Our pickets are in. Wrote home. I always write home when a move is to take place. I have not told them yet how bad my throat was.

August 12. We are still here. The surgeon has just been round and read off a list of men who are on the sick list and who are to go down the river on transports. My name is on the list but I shall not go. I am better, and have asked the captain to be detailed as wagon guard. I think I can walk or ride in the wagon easier than I can march in ranks. I do not like to be away from the regiment to go on the transports. Orderly sergeant Charlie McHenry is promoted to 2nd Lieut. Good for him.

August 13. The report is that the barges that had our knapsacks on have sunk.[81] I have been detailed as wagon guard. I am guard over the wagon containing our regimental officers baggage. Our clothing which we sent for when we were at White Oak Swamp came to day. This is the story now afloat. One dark and stormy night a short time since [ago] the guard who was on at the colonels quarters was relieved by the colonel[82] and told to go to his quarters. Of course the guard went. That night our regimental colors were stolen by some one. Now it is stated that when the colonel went home he carried them with him. He was the thief. They were the colors we carried through the Fair Oaks fight.[83]

August 14. My throat is better to day. Its nearly well. I went down to the landing for hospital stores to day. Just for fun.

**Union Soldiers on the March
(Sketch by Benedict R. Maryniak)**

Chapter Three

"TO BE GONE TEN DAYS..."

(August to December 1862)

On August 3, General McClellan was ordered to move his Army of the Potomac to Aquia Creek to confront rumored concentrations of Confederate troops before Washington again. But to the surprise and chagrin of the Fourth Corps, its commander General Keyes--and the Eighty-Fifth--the Corps was left behind, to which Keyes attributed antagonism between him and McClellan. There may be some truth to his, for Couch's division went on to fight at Antietam while Keyes languished on the Peninsula.

The Eighty-Fifth and the rest of Wessells's brigade was thus put on detached duty, which took them back to Fort Monroe and to Suffolk, Virginia where for about two months their duties consisted primarily of reconnaissance. Then on December 4, 1862, the detached brigade was made part of the Department of the South, commanded by Major General John G. Foster with orders, unknown to Mosher and to many of his fellow brigade members, to move to Albemarle Sound near the coast of North Carolina and from there is to move up the Chowan River, embarking near the village of Washington ("Little Washington"). From there they would march to Kinston, North Carolina on an expedition that would eventually lead to the taking of Goldsboro, North Carolina.

Thus, Wessells's brigade was presumably on loan to General Foster for ten days, during which they were to disrupt the Wilmington and Weldon and the North Carolina and Atlanta Railroads, among the main transportation links between Richmond and Savannah, Georgia. Indeed, "the whole North Carolina coast . . . through which all the immense supplies of one of the richest regions of the confederacy could be poured" was in danger of being in Union hands, and "therein lay the fate of the Confederacy."[1]

This move became a permanent one, for shortly after the new year the brigade was headquartered in the pretty, little coastal town of New Bern where it remained for four months as part of the Eighteenth Corps.

August 15 [1862]. Orders are to move immediately. But did not break camp untill 3:00 P.M. It took the rest of this afternoon to get the wagons in order of march. We stay inside our fortifications to night. I am to sleep in the wagon.

August 16. We were up and on the march at 3 o'clock this morning. It was easy marching for me. Had plenty of green corn on the road to day. The troops in the advance had left fires burning. Sometimes they moved before they were ready. That is they had corn in the fire roasting which they had to leave, and which fell to us. We are caught in the same fix. So it was even. The corn was just right for roasting. We kept the tail box of our wagon full to carry with us. Every time we halted we would put some in the fire. If it was roasted when we started allright; If not, the boys in our rear would get the benefit. We passed through Charles City Court House about noon. It is a very large city. Court house, jail, tavern, and a few negro quarters. A short time before sundown our division train parked their wagons in a large cornfield. We have the smallest division[2] train of the whole army. We made ten miles to day.

August 17. Up early this morning, had our breakfast and was on the road at day light. The roads are very dusty. We moved so fast that we run down our advance guard, the 96th N.Y., so we had to go slower. At noon we reached the Chickahominy river, which is a mile wide here. It had been bridged by the 50th N.Y. Eng. with a pontoon bridge. This is said to have been the longest pontoon bridge that was ever laid.

As we approached the bridge we saw Genl. McClellan and staff on a rise of ground watching the wagons cross. We had to go very slow on the bridge to keep it from swaying too much. It was a beautiful sight to see the train [of men] ahead of us. As we passed through a larger piece of woods a number of darkies were by the roadside with stuff to sell. One had two dressed chickens. I took one and told him Uncle Sam was in the rear and for him to watch out for him and he would pay for the chicken. He grinned from ear to ear and said "All right Massa, its allright." showing his ivories again. He was paid no doubt. We reached Williamsburg about 5 P.M. a tired lot. I fried my chicken for my supper. It was very good.

I had forgotten it was Sunday untill I had lain down for the night.

August 18. Had a good sleep last night. We were under way this morning at eight o'clock. The mules struck a trot which left me in the rear. I could not keep up. I put all my traps in my wagon except my gun. It was easier walking as I took my own gait. I stopped at every farm house on the way and got something to eat. One house gave me a warm biscuit and butter. Fruit was plenty, plums, peaches, pears, and other kinds. I had plenty for me. As our division train is a long way ahead of me I got mixed with Sedgwicks division[3] train. [Second division, Second corps] Our train for some reason or other took the road to our left which passes through Yorktown while Sedgwicks kept on to the right. I stayed with the later [latter]. It was a fine sight to see 400 to 500 wagons with their white covers on sweeping over the hills. I caught a glimpse of our regiment as they struck in ahead of me on the Yorktown road. By keeping with Sedgwicks train I cut a long distance from my walk.

My feet get so sore I could hardly walk. They were blistered. If I sat down to rest I could hardly get up again. So I pushed on the best I could. I caught up with our train at Big Bethel where they had stopped to feed their mules. I found Lt. Butts[4], our regimental quarter master, and told him I should have to ride in one of the wagons or stay there all night. He said he had strict orders to allow no enlisted man to ride in the wagons. I told him I must ride or I should stay there all night. He told me to crawl in and say nothing about it. I crawled in. It was not my wagon. But it proved to be better for me as I found a haversack of cookies in it. I thought the one who owned them would not miss just one if I ate it. I kept on trying just one to see how it tasted. The first thing they were inside of me and I felt the better for it. It was quite a find for me. That fellows loss was my gain.

I then went to sleep as I was tired out. I slept until we reached the pontoon bridge at Hampton creek. Here I had to get out and lead the mules across the bridge. It was midnight. We have come forty miles to day. I have had all the wagon guard I want.

August 19 [1862]. I slept rather late this morning. I am rather used up. This is my first experience as wagon guard. Hope it will be my last. I'll not ask for it again. After I got my breakfast I took a look around town. Hampton was quite a town I should think before it was burned by the rebel Magruder. All there is left is the Chesapeake hospital a large brick building and a few darkies shantys.

They are shipping artillery here for Washington. To night I found a darkey who kept an eating stand. I talked to him awhile, when he told me to sit down and take supper with him. I "took" at once. We had warm biscuit and butter. Coffee and fresh fish. I stuffed my skin.

August 20. Hampton, Va. Our wagon guards have drawn no rations since we left Harrison Landing. That is none from our "Uncle Sam."[5] And we have not starved. In looking through the wagons this morning to find some grub I found a half barrel of coffee. I filled my haversack with it and started to find the darkey with whom I supped last night. And would he trade me a breakfast for the coffee. He said yes. It was a good breakfast. So was the "dark."

This afternoon I found Joe Cummings[6] a sergeant of our company. He has charge of our division wagon guards and was out of rations. I told him of my find and would he join me in my enterprise of living on Uncle Sam. He joined me. I filled my haversack with coffee again when we started for my eating house. Warm biscuit and butter, coffee and fresh fish. What a supper we

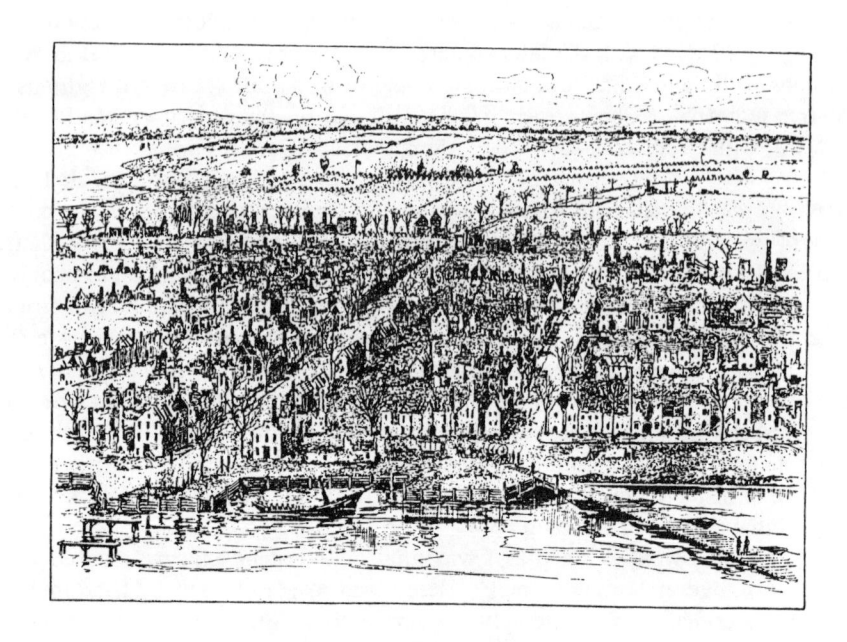

Ruins of Hampton, Va.
(Battles and Leaders of the Civil War)

made out of it. Joe was half starved. I was partly filled up by earlier efforts but I kept my end up with Joe.[7] The market price of our coffee was worth more than our eating was. We did not care. Uncle Sam paid the bill.

Orders came to night to leave here at three o'clock in the morning for Yorktown. So we turn in for a good sleep.

August 21 [1862]. We are on the road for Yorktown as per last nights orders. Plenty of forage on the road. The darkies were out with pies, cakes, and apples to sell. We helped ourselves. The darks grinned when we said Uncle Sam would pay. We would have stolen the things from them, only it would not have been right. We always like to be square.

I did a thing this afternoon which has been a regret to me all my life.[8] This is it: An old darkie by the roadside had a baked goose to sell. <u>I did not buy</u> it and let my big "Uncle" settle for it. The first man in my rear <u>bought</u> it. I was ashamed of myself for such conduct. I'll do better next time perhaps.

I saw that the train turned an angle in the road, and thinking I could save a bit of travel I cut across the fields. In doing so I passed a darkey shanty where I got a bowl of bread and milk. When I reached the yard of the "big house"[9] I saw a flock of ducks. One of them took kindly to me and was going away with me when the lady of the house told me she thought I was very mean to allow the duck to go with me. That duck went with me in spite of the lady.

I put it in my wagon, not wanting to carry it. When I went for it I was told that it had died on the way and they had thrown it away. A big lie. They stole it. Twas too bad. I wished the thing hadn't followed me off. One can't always make ducks mind.

As we neared Yorktown the country was overrun by the yankees. They were foraging. Some had a quarter of beef slung between them on a pole. others had sheep, pigs, and poultry of all kinds. As there had been no rations issued, the boys had to live. I reached my regiment at three o'clock this afternoon. very tired.

This is the second trip between this place and Hampton we have made inside of a week. The boys said that Genl. Peck swore a blue streak when he had found his division train had gone to Hampton. There was some misunderstanding between him and his Quartermaster. Us guards had a chance to see the country and get a good mess of fresh fish.

August 22 [1862]. I feel rather old this morning. Very. I lost my rubber blanket[10] and dog tent[11] on the road somewhere.

Those barges that had our knapsacks on and sunk, have been raised again. Our teams and a squad of men went down to the dock at Yorktown (We are about two miles out of the city) to get them. They had been handled so much while they were wet that they were worthless. So they came back without them. This makes the second time we had lost our baggage. This afternoon we moved our camp a short distance and laid in out in regular order, In streets. Old Peck[12] would make us to do this [even] if he knew [we] would not stay here five hours. He likes to keep us busy. A rubber blanket followed me this afternoon from an officers tent [next] to mine. I am will liked.

Battalion drill this forenoon, and company drill this afternoon. Wrote home. Our brigade has orders to march to Fortress Monroe tomorrow morning at six o'clock. Our boys have done some good foraging here. We are experts in our way. Yesterday "Marra the mule"[13] went to a house and tried to buy some milk. The lady of the house drew a revolver on him and told him she would shoot him if he did not clear out. Her revolver was a very small one. Marra pulled out an eight inch navy [gun] and said "How will you trade yours for mine." He bantered the old girl for a time. When she got to laughing and sold him all the milk he wished. John Marra is a great genius. One leg is shorter than the other. We call him the mule, because he stole one on our trip up country.[14]

August 24. We were up at two o'clock this morning and made our coffee. We fell in line at six and pulled out on the road for Fortress Monroe. A drizzling rain set in which made it hard marching for us. The soil is a kind of mud, a little wet makes it very slippery. It strains the muscles of one's legs. We reached Little Bethel at noon where we stopped an hour for coffee. When we up and at it again. We reached Fortress Monroe at 3 P.M. It still rains. We have marched 26 miles, and made good time.

A schooner loaded with boards lay at the dock, which our regiment appropriated, and put up some shanties. Genl. Wessels says our regiment beats them all for fixing up. I was on guard at the commissary a short time to night.

August 25 [1862]. We have had to drill to day just to keep us out of mischief. We are roaming the country over. Very pleasant to day.

August 26. Drill to day as usual. We are to draw new clothing in place of that which was lost on those barges.

We have orders to move tomorrow to Newport News. The rest of the brigade go to Suffolk, Va. under Peck. He is a tough one. Major King in command of the regiment.

August 27. In line at 8 o'clock this morning, and reached Newport News at one o'clock. Plenty of peaches on the march. I had a hard march (it's only six miles) as I had a touch of diarrhera. It used me up.

August 28. Newport News, Va. No drill. Fix up camp. The first thing this morning was to write home to let them know my where abouts. When we went through this part of the country last spring we lay near this place in a large peach orchard. Now the peaches are ripe. They are lucious. I ate so many this morning that my stomach aches, and I am still eating. We have a good location here for a camp. One company of the 11th Pa. cavalry and our regiment are all the troops here. Our Major King is in command of the Post and Capt. Clarke is in command of the regiment.

There are about 2000 sick in the hospitals. We have a good sea breeze. We are camped not far from the beach and can see all that is going on in Hampton Road. There is a large [?] lying in the roadstead. Men & war and transports. We have done nothing to day only fix up our quarters and eat fruit. I hope we will stay here some time. It will do us all sorts of good. This last campaign was a hard one on all hands.

August 30. I am on picket to day. We are out about a mile. Our duty is to keep the boys from going into the country. There is no enemy within miles, and miles of here. We have to keep up the form of service at all times.

August 31. Off picket early this morning. Fruit and vegetables are plenty and very cheap. Fresh fish and oysters the same. We have no money, yet we have all the good things going. They all come to us. We draw soft bread[15] here.

Sept. 1 [1862]. Our new clothing came to day. We drew every thing in place of that which was lost by the sinking of the barges. Our company has nothing to pay for this reason. Capt. Clarke offset our extra ration money against the clothing account.

Each company are [allotted] so many rations per man. If we do not draw them all, we are allowed a commutation. We are also allowed $52.00 per year for clothes. If we over draw, we have to pay up. If not, the difference is ours.

Sept. 2. Our duty here is nothing. A little fatigue and police[16] duty. Camp guard, and drill. The rest of our time is on the water, or in the water. It is a delightful place for us.

Sept. 7. Signed the pay roll to day. Sunday. After morning inspection four of us got a small boat and took and rowed out and around the Cumberland.[17] We went into her rigging. Her top masts and yards are out of water. I got a small piece of her main mast and a part of the shrouds. Just enough for a keepsake. Then we pulled around the man o'war *Galena.* She was up in the engagement at Fort Darling at Drury's Bluff. We saw how the rebel shot had dented her sides. several shot were sticking in her. Then we took a turn around the *Monitor.* Her decks are badly torn up in spots. We saw the dents made on her by the *Merrimack.* After we looked her over without going board, we went to the *Genesee,* a wooden, sidewheel steamer. Some one on board sung out to us, "come around to the other companionway and come on board." We accepted the invitation. On board we found her in the finest order. She carried a one hundred pound rifle, fore and aft, and three brass guns on each side. How every thing shone. Her brass work, her decks, and every thing glistened. While on board, the boatswain piped all hands to dinner. We were invited by the crew to join them. when we all went below to dine. The crew had on their Sunday togs (all white suits) and in order to keep them clean, before they sat down to dinner they spread their handkerchiefs on deck to sit on which seemed useless to us, as the deck was so clean.

We all sat down on the deck to eat. First we had good beef soup, then fresh beef, hard bread and pickles. We soldiers enjoyed our dinner.

After dinner we finished our inspection and thanked our sailor friends for their kindness to us. we returned to our boat and pulled to where the *Congress* lay, when she was burned by the *Merrimack.* She looked hard, Her guns were still on her and nothing had been disturbed since that fatal day. I got a small piece of her live oak side for a relic. We were back in camp in time for dress parade, having had a good time. Wrote to Father to night.

Sept. 8. We were paid two months pay. Now we will live. We lived without any money, but it will be easier for our cheek,[18] with a little money.

The weather here is very warm in the middle of the day. The mornings and evenings are delightful.

Newport News, Va.
Sept. 12, 1862[19]

Dear Sister,

I received your letter last night, and was glad to hear from you and that the folks are all well & kicking.

The sun is rather warm here now. It rained yesterday and the day before right hard. There is no news here at all now. This forenoon about a dozen of us got a large row boat and rowed around our gun boats, and the old Cumberland. Three large transports just passed up the river, with rebel prisoners on, for exchange.[20] Each vessel had a flag of truce on.

We were paid last Monday, and I will send you $15.00 in this letter. I was on picket when the rest of the boys sent theirs by express, So I will send mine this way. I want to keep a little by me, so if any thing should happen I would have some, you see. It won't be long before we are paid again. It is due us now. You can use this up in the crowd,[21] but let father have the first privilege at handling it.

I had some more of those nice peaches to day. Come down and I will give you some. Come and I'll get you up a nice dinner, So just do, Come over, do, and bring the rest of the folks. No do. But be sure and fetch along some dishes, as I have only enough for one to eat off at a time. But you might take turns untill you all got your sufficiency full and then you would have to stop or run over. Bah!

I have done lost everything I had in the shape of a needle book, So you can send just as nice a one as you please, only don't get it to large you know. You must furnish me with stamps as we can't get them here. I must write to David.[22] So good bye no more at present. My love to all, write soon.

From your Aff.
Brother Charlie

P.S. Write as soon as you get this, so I will know whether you got this money or not.

Charlie (all well)

Sept. 15. Not much duty but lots of fun. We take a five dollar greenback, and begin with the first darkey oyster shanty at dock, and call for a dish of raw which we eat with a good relish. Hand the old dark the $5.00 bill. He says "can't change that, massa. some other time, massa." Then we go to the next, and the same is repeated. Then the next & next. We have a fill of oysters and our $5.00. The darks can get more. They never get mad. It would do them no good. Fresh fish are very cheap, and very good. Sweet potatoes are in market. When we have to buy oysters, we can get them for a shilling a quart.

Dan Reed[23] and I tent together, only us two in an "A" tent. We get a loaf of soft bread, and a quart of raw oysters for a lunch. We get away with them easily.[24]

As there is not much for us to do, we have lots of spare time. Then we are in the water or in the country. In order to keep us in, the roll is called every hour. If we get picked out, we are put on police duty. Which means clean up camp, sweep the streets and all such dirty work. We have to stand it once and awhile. Because we will wander. One day a boatload of us were out on the *Cumberland*, getting the sheaves from the blacks - they are of lignum vitae[25] - to make into rings. Orderly Robinson was with us, when the hour came round for roll call. He called it in the tops of the old man o'war. We all responded. "Here!" We saved ourselves that day. For real amusement we all turn towards the darks. At night a few of us drop into their quarters, as they all sit around the big fireplace. Each of us have a small cup of flour in our hands. At a given signal we dash a small handful into the darkies faces. How they sputter, and say "Go way dar, white man." We go seeking new fields of usefulness. Something after this manner. We break off the lower end of a few cartridges, and drop them down the chimneys of their quarters, when they explode and scatter the ashes all around. Fun for us.

The 139th N.Y. of Brooklyn, N. Y. who came the other [day] have gone to Hampton for guard duty.

Sept. 24 [1862]. The *New Ironsides* just anchored in the roadstead. She is an iron clad and carries 16 heavy guns. In our boat ride yesterday, we rowed out to the frigate *Minnesota*. She is one of the old time three decked wooden ships and has both steam and sail power.

Sept. 25. Received a letter from Cousin Emily Barrows to day. She is a cousin's daughter and is attending school at Lima, N.Y. She visited us two years ago.

A large fleet is lying here. They form a line of battle nearly across the roadstead. There is a report that the rebels have a new *Merrimack* coming down the James river soon. This is why our men o'war are here. We are ready for them.

Sept. 26. We have moved our camp close in town now. Last night the long roll[26] was sounded. We all tumbled out in a hurry. But the officers were a long time in showing up.

It seems that the Major was on one of the gun boats drinking with the officers, and was bragging how soon he could get his men in line. He showed them. They all laughed at him. On funeral escort this afternoon. An officer died in the hospital. Lt. Whitney of Company A. was in charge of the escort.

He drilled us for two hours this morning in common time. At the grave we fired three vollies over it. This is my first time on this kind of service. Didn't like it.

Sept. 28 [1862]. We are having good times here. The wives of all officers and men who are hurt were ordered north a while ago. So they baked up a lot of stuff to take with them yesterday. When they were to leave. They did not go, so they sold their stuff. I bought and ate one peach pie and a quarter of another. They were baked in a long tin. I was full way up.

Sept. 30. We are drilling in bayonet exercise now a great deal. It is a fine drill, but very hard on ones arms.

This afternoon I saw the boys coming up from the steamboat landing, and each of them had a watermelon under each arm. I asked them where they found? "Down there." I followed the stream down and in the steam boat which lay at the dock. I did as the rest did, took one under each arm and marched back to camp. We asked no questions. And no one asked questions of us.

Roll was called while I was gone, so I was pricked.[27] I can stand a little police duty for two fine melons. You bet they were good.

Oct. 1. Company drill this forenoon. battallion drill this afternoon. H. Z. Shepard, C.B. Ingraham, Chet. Gooding, and C. J. Simmons came in the northern hospital this afternoon. They are all looking well. Simmons was wounded at Fair Oaks.

Oct. 2. On camp guard. Lt. Munger of Co. G. is officer of the guard.[28] He tied a man to a post, then gagged him with a bayonet, and tied that to the post. He is a mean whelp, that Munger. The officer of the day cut the man loose. Good for him.

We captured a darkie who had been smuggling whiskey into camp on the mail boat. We put him in the back room of the guard house.

Oct. 3. That "dark" we put in the guard house yesterday, dug under the floor just like a rat and got away.

Off guard early. All quiet here.

Oct. 5. Sunday. Inspection. I am detailed for picket. The report is that we are to go to Suffolk, Va. Hope not.

Oct. 6. We were relieved from picket this morning very early. Orders are to go to Suffolk. We took down our tents and packed our traps, them sat down waited. Or rather had fun with the darkies. What fun we did have, playing all sorts of jokes on them.

This 2 p.m. we marched on board the steamboat *Express*. our camp equippage was put on the steamer *Washington* and started for Norfolk, Va. We arrived here just at dark. Here we met E. B. Wetmore, J. J. Mary, N. H. Briggs, and Alvah Phillips[29] who had reached here about the same time on another boat. They were captured at the Fair Oaks fight. They were prisoners just one hundred days. They are quite heroes in our eyes, as they belonged to our company. We marched to the railroad station took the cars for Suffolk, twenty miles from here.

Oct. 7 [1862]. Suffolk, Va. We reached here last midnight. As we marched out here we passed the camps of some new troops. Who sung out to us, "You hadn't better go very far out that way, for the rebels are out there." I guess that they did not know we were. They are a lot of these $250.00 sheep and cow men, as we call them.[30] New regiments.

We camped right where we stopped last night, bout half a mile from the station.

We were up betimes this morning, as we heard last night the 148 N.Y. were here somewhere. Those of us who were acquainted with any of them, dropped our traps where we slept and started out to find them. We did not wait for our breakfast.

Their camp was not away. The first man I saw was Russ Wright. I took him by surprise. then came Frank Chapin, G. W. Caton, Dan. Redfield, Charlie Gillett, Cash Knapp, all of Co. K and all from Chapinville. How our tongues did rattle. It seemed good to see some one from home. They were more homesick than we were. Wrote home to night.

Oct. 8. On police to day, cleaning up our new camp ground. G. W. Caton was over to see me. Had a long talk over old times. A letter from home which says all well there.

Oct. 9. On camp guard to day. Frank Chapin and Cash Knapp came to see me. We were old school mates and had a very good visit. There is no one in our regiment from my home town, to talk with. It seemed to do me good to see these boys.

Oct. 10. Off guard early. Went over to the 148th N.Y. and stayed untill noon. They think this soldiering business is a hard job. After they have been into as long as we have, they will quite like it.[31]

Oct. 11. I have been in the service just one year. Have seen some very hard times, and had some pleasant ones.

On fatigue duty. The rain set in so we had to knock off.

I went down to the railroad to see the 148th N.Y. take the cars for Norfolk. They were a sorry lot of men. The rain just poured down. How they kicked. They will get the hang of things, if they [are] in the service long enough. We are old veterans beside them. Two papers from home today.

Oct. 12 [1862]. It still rains. I don't feel very well.

Oct. 13. On brigade headquarters guard to day. Genl. Wessells is about as tall as father (a short man) with a grissly beard. A trifle humped up. He wears a tall felt hat, smashed in, the rim turned up behind, and down in front. He would answer to the description of a farmer. But he is the best of men.

Oct. 14. Off guard this morning. No rain.

Oct. 15. On fatigue. Nineteen of us reported to brigade headquarters. The general told us to cut a road way through the brush, then we could go back to our quarters. We cut the road, and got back to camp at 10 a.m. This gives us the rest of the day to our selves.

Oct. 17. Nothing going yesterday. On fatigue to day. All quiet.

Oct. 18. All quiet, no news.

Oct. 19. On picket on the reserve post. Quiet.

Oct. 20. Off picket at noon.

Oct. 21. There is no excitement and we expect none.

Oct. 22. I feel as if I was going to have a touch of fever. Excused by the Doctor.

Oct. 23 to 28. On the sick list. Excused from duty.

Oct. 29. I am off the sick list. We have been putting our quarters in good shape. We took small pine trees and built up log houses about five feet high, then put our tents on top for a roof. Two bunks high on one side and a stick chimney on the other. Door in front. They make good comfortable huts. Our cook house is 20 feet square, built of logs with a shake roof. Shakes are slabs split out of straight grained pine. They are used in this region a great deal. They are kept in place by poles placed across the shakes, where they lap over one another. The ends of the poles are joined to the end rafters with pins. A large fire place on one side, with a stick chimney completes our culinary department.
Our tent is close to the cook house. Ed. Knapp is company cook. He, Francisco, Crane and I occupy it.[32]

Brigadier General Henry W. Wessells
(Reproduced by Ronald Pretzer from Luther S. Dickey,
History of The 85th Pennsylvania Infantry)

Winter Quarters
(Sketch by Benedict R. Maryniak)

I got a box from home to day. It had a chunk of butter in it, and a quantity of dried fruit and other things I needed. It came with a box of grapes for Capt. Clarke. He had about a bushel and a half. He passed them around among us boys. They were very good. Dress parade to night. I am all right again.

Oct. 30 [1862]. Have orders to move at an hours notice, three days rations. Fell into line at this 11 a.m. and moved out on the Blackwater road. There are two brigades of us under command Brigd. Genl. Terry.[33] We marched untill nine o'clock to night, when we camped out in an open field. We halted a half mile back, for a few minutes, and Len Rowley[34] said he felt like marching twenty miles further. When we turned in, Rowley was missing. It is a fine moonlight night.

Oct. 31. We were awakened this morning very early by the booming of cannon. Our batteries were playing on the village of Franklin. After they tumbled shot and shell into for a while, we fell in line and started for Suffolk about five o'clock. We found Rowley in a fence corner just where he said that he could march twenty miles. Then we gave him the laugh.

At ten o'clock we halted and made coffee. then pushed on untill noon, when we halted in an open field. Had dinner and rested. We were mustered for pay here. On our trip Knapp and I caught a chicken. After skinning and dressing it, we fried it in butter I had which came from home in my haversack. What a dinner for a soldier! We lay here untill nine o'clock to night, then started for Suffolk.

Our company is on rear guard. We had lots of fun punching up the stragglers. Plenty of forage on this trip. Knapp and I had the hind half of a sheep, and a hind quarter of a pig. We changed off in carrying it.

Reached camp at midnight.

Nov. 1 [1862]. Slept late this morning. Feel old. "Frandy"[35] had breakfast ready, with some of our mutton fried. It went good. We mustered again to day. Yesterday was only form. Letters from home, and David, all well there.

Nov. 2. Sunday. Inspection. Wrote home.

Nov. 3. A squad went into the woods, and cut some logs for Lt. Martin to build a stable with.[36] Had lots of fun.

Nov. 4. Election in New York state to day for governor. Our regiment took a vote just to see how we stood on the question. The vote showed that 27 officers and 465 enlisted men were for Wadsworth, and 27 officers and men for Seymour.[37]

On guard at brigade headquarters.

Nov. 5. Off guard early at nine o'clock. Brigade drill this afternoon. We had a good drill ground here.

Nov. 6. Rains to day, no work. Wrote home.

Nov. 7. Snow to day. All we have to do is to sit by the fire and keep warm.

Nov. 8. Pleasant to day.

Nov. 9. Sunday. Company inspection. I am reading Bayard Fugler's works.

Nov. 10. On picket. A Lt. of Co. D. is officer of the guard. He is a mean son of a gun. Had a good fire all night.

Nov. 11. Did not get in from picket untill eleven o'clock. Ate a good dinner. Went to bed and slept untill sundown.

Nov. 12 [1862]. Maj. General John A. Dix is to review all the troops here to day.

Our regiment formed its line at half past nine with knapsacks packed and moved over near Fort Dix when we went into brigade formation. There were four brigades of infantry, two regiments of cavalry and three batteries of light artillery. Our brigade is second in line. This is about the way we were formed.

Reviewing Officers

Artillery	1st Brigade	Cavalry
Artillery	2nd Brigade	
Artillery	3rd Brigade	Cavalry
Artillery	4th Brigade	

The artillery fired a salute as Genl. Dix and staff rode on the field. When he took his position in front. His adjutant general stood up in his stirrups and gave the command, At-ten-tion! Pre-pare for r-e-v-i-e-w. Then the commander of the first brigade wheeled his horse around so as to face his brigade, and repeated the command, long drawn out.

Then our old <u>Man</u> turned in his saddle and repeated the same command in a sharp quick tone. No frills on our old Man Wessells. The same command was repeated by all the other commanders.

Then came the command from the head of the line. To the rear o-p-e-n o-r-d-e-r. M-a-r-c-h. Which was repeated along the line. These orders were repeated by the regimental commanders. The commands executed, Dix and staff ride down in front of and up the rear of each regiment, in order.

As he (Dix) nears the head of each regiment the bands strike up "Hail to the chief" and play untill he turns to pass up the rear rank. It is very inspiring to see.

After he reviewed the men, he took his position on one side of the large open field when all the troops pass in review before him. Which is very hard work. In order to have all troops in motion at once, we had to march three miles or more. Every movement had to be executed in a soldierly manner. We had to have our guns at a shoulder all the time. Very hard.

Nov. 13. On fatigue at fort Union. We did not do enough work to put in your eye.

Nov. 14. A good breakfast of beef steak & c. [etc.] Brigade drill this afternoon. We formed in two lines. Our line was in command of Col. Howell[38] of the 85th Pa. The pickets have been driven twice lately by the rebs.

Suffolk, Va. Nov. 14/62

Dear Sister:

I received your last letter last Monday while I was on picket and read it by the light of a large fire. It was grand on picket that night, we had a big fire. When the moon came out, it was pleasant all night. But long towards morning it began to get cold, very. As soon as the sun came up next morning, it warmed up again. When it was my turn to lie down, I pulled the cape of my overcoat up over my head, spread my rubber blanket on the ground, lay down and slept about four hours just as well, I presume, as you did on your feather bed, and I had just as pleasant dreams as you. I drempt I was doing guard duty in Chapinville. But as I was dreaming away, one of the boys kit me a kick, and says your turn to go on "Mose." The boys all call me "Mose" or "Moses Peabody" for short. For one time in Washington last winter a peddler came in our tent to sell us some medals. He was to take our names and engrave them on the medals. The boys all gave their names wrong. Lieut. Martin was in at the time. He was Orderly then. He gave his name as John Peabody, and I as Moses Peabody. I have gone by that name ever since. But what's in a name? Hey! Tell Kate[39] I want to put in a note for her, for I want to tell her something, but I guess I won't for it won't pay. But tell her to be a good little girl and tell her that I believe you meant what you said, when you said, you had rather be some ones wife, than be ones husband. I think you are a sensible young woman for thinking so. But you be more sensible if you was ones wifey. But don't be one of those Home guards, be some good soldiers wife. There will be lots of good fellow after the war.

And I want you to speak a good word for me, in the meantime, So all I will have to do when I get home, will be to pop the question one night, and call in the Elder the next. Dont you see, <u>Aint</u> I got a long head. Can't I see a long ways. Why! I can look almost through a mill stone.

so you can tell some of those pretty young girls, that when the war is over, that I am going to lay aside the military and take up the matrimonial. (Now don't you think I am a sensible young man.)

Tell them when I get home I shall be in the market for 8 or ten years. or less. "One day I got a letter twas enough to make me sware. It said Mattie had married a Caton, and that Caton had red hair." (Spokeshave) Want it mean?[40]

Did Mother think it dreadful strange that you didn't hear from me? Well perhaps it was, but still I write as often as once a week, and more to[o].

We have no meetings now, for we have no Chaplain.[41] I have two good pair of socks, and I am going to have another pair by & by.

I got those Waverly's[42] and that box all right. Now I want you to send me some stamps. Tell Ralph Chapin's wife that I shall send her a flower as soon as I can get one. And I'll get one as soon as I can. I'll get you some moss if I find any.

If you want some cones, I will get them. Elam Beeman is in Co. G., 148th N.Y., do you want to write to him [?]

It is a nice pleasant day here. It is as warm as summer. We were reviewed day before yesterday by Genl. Dix. I will tell you about it next time for I haven't any room now.

Don't forget to send me some P. O. stamps, will you [?] for I had to borrow this one. I am well as usual, and in good spirits to[o]. Give my love to all the folks. Write by and by, no more at present. Good bye.

From your Aff Brother
Charlie

(This is a pretty long letter.)[43]

Nov. 15 [1862]. Cold. No drill. I have been cleaning up all day. Received a letter from W. L. Jessup and burned it.

Nov. 16, Sunday. On picket. The order of coming in from picket duty is changed. Each man as soon as relieved used to straggled into camp as pleased him best. Now we have to fall in the rear of the relief guard, and then all march in together. After the manner of camp guard.

Last night I went into the cook house for some pork for to days picket. There I found "Jessie" (the dark who washes for our company for $4.00 per month) and two or three of his darkey friends sitting around the fire, telling stories. Knowing that they great dancers, I asked them if they wouldn't dance a little for me. After some coaxing, they up and at it. One patted, the next danced. I could not stand by and enjoy it alone, so I went to the door, gave a yell, and told the boys to turn out and see the fun. It was fun sure.

In a short time the cook house was full of the boys, some from every company in the regiment. We kept them dancing for two hours. The best nigger show I ever saw in my life. We nearly burst with laughter. Go way with your burnt cork, and essence of Old Virginia. This was the genuine black. dyed in the wool. Sure.

Nov. 17. Last night we had orders to load our guns, and keep a good look out in front. Long about midnight we heard the report of a gun to our left. I was on post at the time.

A peculiar feeling comes over a fellow when he hears that in the dead of night. He grips his gun a trifle firmer, for fear it will get away from him. This morning we found that the shot was fired by one of the new recruits. He said he thought he saw a man with a white hat on, so be blazed away at it. It was the top of a stump. Good for him.

The Grand officer of the day has usually made the grand rounds mounted, attended by an orderly. He would ride up to a picket and give the counter sign without dismounting. Last night we thought we would make the Grand rounds do their work in a soldierly manner. (Our regiment thought so only.) Each regiment has its own line to picket. When the Grand rounds reached our part of the line, the man on post challenged him. "Halt! Who comes there!" "Grand rounds!" "Grand rounds, dismount, advance, and give the countersign." After some swearing, he dismounted and gave the countersign. He mounted and rode to the next post. The same thing was repeated. More swearing. but he had to come down. He repeated it on one more post, then gave his horse in to the keeping of his orderly, and made the rest of the trip on foot. How he did swear. And how we laughed. He said that the 85th knew how to do picket duty. Any guard has the right to make a man dismount, lay down his arms, and hold up his hands, then advance and give the countersign.

We did not get to camp from picket untill ten o'clock. We are ordered to be in line at half past twelve o'clock to go on a reconnoisance up the Blackwater country. As there was not time to cook any grub, so we took our pork, and fresh beef raw. At 2:30 p.m. we moved out. There are two brigades, one battery, and cavalry. Genl. Wessells is in command. We marched nine miles. and halted for coffee, and a short rest.

Nov. 18 [1862]. After marching all night we reached Joyners bridge[44] at daylight. Genl. Wessells, Col. Spears of the 11th Pa. Cav. and Dr. Hunt (Brigade surgeon) was on the lead last night and ran on the reb pickets who gave them a volley, but hurt nothing. The general drew his revolver and blazed away. then ordered two regiments to drive them out. Which they did after a sharp skirmish. Here at the bridge our battery opened up shelled across the river. We put a new bridge across - one we brought with us.[45] One regiment crossed over, with the cavalry. The battery could not cross. So we all moved around to the opposite of Franklin, where the battery threw shell into the town. The rebels replied with a rocket battery. We could watch the curve of the ball as it passed through the air. They did no damage.

After playing ball for a while, we marched back to the old church. Here we halted for the night. Posted our pickets. and turned in for the night.

Nov. 19. Up this morning at 3:00 o'clock, made coffee, was ready to march at five o'clock. Marched ten miles. halted and made coffee, then on again, reaching camp at two o'clock. We marched 60 miles all told, in 48 hours. I am not as a tired as I was on the other trip. Our old man Wessells can march us farther, and easier, than any other man, who has had command of us.

Letter from home.

Nov. 20. Capt. Clarke left for Albany, N.Y. He has gone to look after the drafted men. Wrote home. Rainy. All quiet.

Nov. 21. On fatigue. It was so wet we could not work building the fort.

Nov. 22 [1862]. Helped Lt. Martin built his house.[46]

Nov. 23, Sunday. Inspection. All quiet.

Nov. 24. Company drill this forenoon, and brigade drill this afternoon. Letter from home. All well there.

Nov. 25. On fatigue. Slashing,[47] so the guns of fort Nansamond[48] can have clear sweep up the Blackwater river. Capt. Chapin of Co. K in charge of us. We had lots of fun with him.

There are four large forts here. Fort Union is the largest and has 14 heavy guns mounted. There are five miles of breastworks around the town.

Nov. 26. It began to rain last night, and is still at it. Wrote home.

Knapp and I went into the woods to see about some boards for Lt. Martin's house. The darkie who was getting them out stuttered. He had a fine dog. we asked him its name. He said it was "b-b-bum bum." He was a free black, and had been all over the south. We had a long talk with him.

Nov. 27. To day is Thanksgiving, and no turkey. It cleared off in the night very cold. The sun has warmed up now. On how I would like to be up home to day. If it was as warm up there as it is here, couldn't I enjoy it. I just bet I could, right smart.

Things begin to look better now. Old Burnside[49] is driving the rebels, and we are getting ready for onward to Richmond, hip, hip hurrah. No drill for anybody to day.

Ed. Bentley[50] gave me an apple from Bloomfield, N.Y. It was right good.

Nov. 28. On picket. The orders are no fires, and two men on post all the time. No excitement on the line to day. Ed. Knapp had a box from home.

Nov. 29. Off picket at ten o'clock. Very cold last night. Lt. Martin has a twenty day furlough for home.

Nov. 30, Sunday. Inspection. Went to church. Saw some pretty girls.

Dec. 1. On fatigue at fort Union. Another reconnoisance up the Blackwater. As I am on fatigue, I can't go.

More troops came in to day.

Dec. 2. No drill to day. Heavy firing in direction of the Blackwater. The report is we have taken that rocket battery, 30 prisoners, 150 stand of arms and a number of horses.[51] Letter from home.

Dec. 3 [1862]. Rained last night. On picket, number three. It has cleared off fine.

Dec. 4. Our picket line was not relieved untill this afternoon. The 6th Mass. relieved us. Our brigade has orders to leave here tomorrow morning at four o'clock, in light marching order,[52] to be gone ten days. Those who are not able to march are to stay here. Our extra baggage is to be packed up and placed in one of the tents.

Crane[53] (in our tent) had a box from home a few days ago. He never passed any thing around among us, now he has to leave it behind. Glad of it. He is quite an old man, and was in the Mexican war. He is quite a hog. Wrote home to let them know what was up. I am all right for this trip.

Dec. 5. Up this morning at two o'clock, and had a good breakfast. It is very foggy. Our line was formed, and we marched out of here onto the Summerton road at six o'clock. We are going in a southernly direction. Where, no one knows, but the Genl.[54] It began to rain. a sort of drizzle and kept it up all day. The soil is clayey, which made the marching hard, as the road was slippery. We halted at noon for coffee. Long towards night the rain turned into snow, which added to our discomfort.

We marched about twenty three miles and camped in a large pinewood. Our company was detailed for picket. But Lt. McHenry (He is all the company officer we have with us) lied the Adjutant out of it very nicely, so he detailed Co. A. Bully for Charlie McHenry. It was our turn for picket all right enough, only the Adjt. forgot.

After many trials we got our fires going and partially dried our clothes. Every thing was wet. The ground, the pine boughs was covered with snow. A wet sticking snow. After I got warm a bit, I lay down and tried to sleep. It was no go. I got up and sat by the fire untill morning. It was a bitter night.

Dec. 6. We were up and had our coffee at six o'clock, and on the road again. Yesterday some of the Penn. men got a lot of apple jack,[55] which made them drunk. As they could not walk, some of them froze to death last night. We marched a mile south of Gatesville and camped on a high piece of ground. It has cleared off warm and pleasant. We are the first union troops that were ever in this region. The natives don't know what to make of us.

We find that Gatesville is in North Carolina and now we are not far from the Chowan river. As soon as we camped, the men scattered in all directions for forage.

Our company is detailed for picket. Now its all right. we have orders to send all foragers in under guard. Our picket line is on a ridge between the river on our left and a swamp on our right. A wide ditch was dug half way between the river and swamp. This we used for our camp fires. After our line was posted, we got our supper. Some of our pickets went outside for forage.

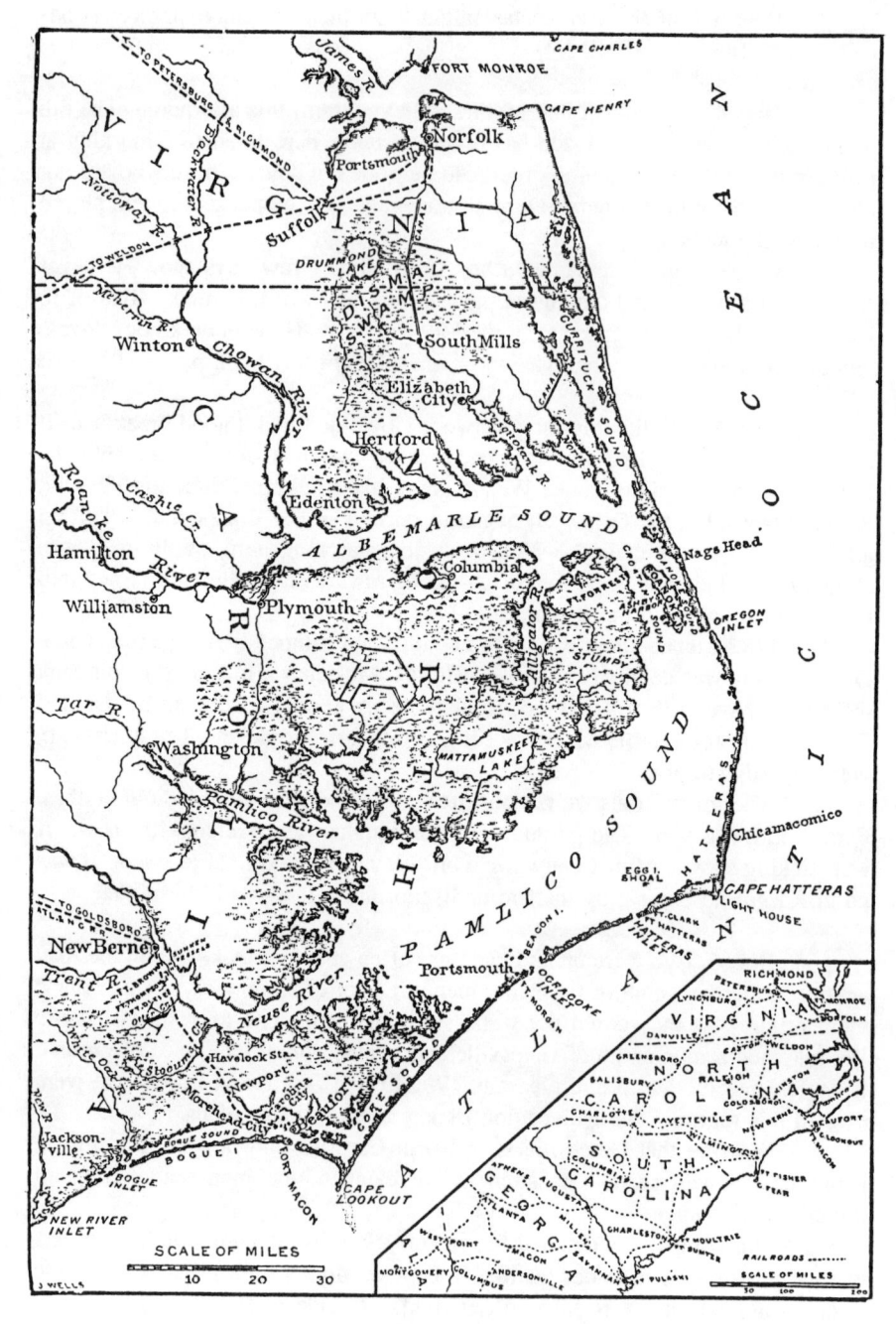

The North Carolina Coast
(Battles and Leaders of the Civil War)

A little while after dark the boys began to come in with all sorts of forage, but mostly apple jack, which we relieved them of. All men that did not belong to our regiment we sent to camp under guard. Our boys we let slip through, that is, we did not see them. It would not do. Of course our pickets partook of the apple jack freely, some more than others. The consequence was Co. B. was a bit owly before morning.

Nate Wright found that sergeant John Buell had a canteen of the stuff hung around his neck, which he was going to save for the next day. Buell had come off post, and laid down to sleep. Wright crawled in with him and sucked his canteen empty. Every body was happy. It was a memorable time for our Co. B. We captured two buckets, and 8 or 10 canteens of the fluid. Also some honey and poultry.

Dec. 7 [1862]. Saw some pretty girls. O dear!

We came off picket early. Lt. McHenry told our Lt. Col. Wellman that he did not have to send an 85th man in under guard last night. Lt. Col. Wellman is in command of our regiment, having recovered from the wound which he received at Fair Oaks. He is a good Man. To day is Sunday. It is warm and pleasant and the robins are singing. If we were up north, I would think it was spring.

After dinner, we marched about two miles to the Chowan river. The road was through a swamp about, about half the way we had to wade through the water knee deep.

Adjutant Aldrich let sergeant Stillman[56] (who was sick, as the Adjt. thought) ride his horse, and he walked. Stillman had too much apple jack last night. Not sick, but weary. Twas a good joke on Aldrich.

When we reached the landing we found a number of transports. Our regiment boarded the *Hussar.* It was a sort of gun boat and manned by a crew of what is called Marine artillery and commanded by Lieut. Doon. Its an old tub.

Our company's place was below, way forward in her bow. It was on a pile of cable chain. A soft bed. We were most asleep, when we were disturbed by the crew weighing anchor. The vessel steamed down the river, and we tried to sleep. We had a cold berth.

Dec. 8. We did not sleep much last night. Our old tub got aground two or three times. We run all day. To night we anchored at the mouth of the Neuse river. We came through the Albemarle Sound, past Roanoke Island, where Burnside had a big fight, into the Pamlico Sound here. It was very pleasant to day on deck. Every thing was new to us.

This Marine Artillery is a cross between a sailor and a soldier, and don't know as much as a land lubber.

Dec. 9 [1862]. Under weigh early this month and steamed up the Neuse river. We passed the rebels works, which Burnside captured last spring.[57] After getting aground two or three times, we came in sight of the city of New Berne, N.C.[58] We grounded again within a mile of the city for sure. A tug boat came down and tried to pull us off but couldn't. Another boat came down, which we boarded and made the dock at 4 p.m. We are mighty glad to get our feet on land once more. We have had enough of Marine Artillery. Boat and crew are no good. We marched outside the city beyond Fort Totten[59] and camped in an open field. After I had rested I took a stroll in the outskirts around the fort. Here I found Oliver Scantlin an old school mate. His battery are doing duty in fort Totten. Oliver, Geo. Phillips and I took a walk into the city. On our way back I <u>drew</u> a head of cabbage. It was attracted by me, I seem to be quite attractive to all things in the eating line. When we reached the fort, Oliver gave me a bottle of vinegar. Cole slaw for supper. It made an excelent relish for our hard tack and pork.

Dec. 10. I slept cold last night. I left my heavy blanket in Suffolk, and brought my lightest one. In light marching order we roll our blankets the long way then we tie the end together and put it over our head and on our right shoulder, and under our left arm. Horse collar fashion. Drew rations to[o]. We are to acompany an expedition from here up the country. I am detailed for rear guard to our regiment. At dress parade to night an order from Maj. Gen. J. C. Foster[60] was read in which he spoke of our past carear, and hoped we would acquit ourselves with honor in the comeing move. He gave us a general soft soaping. Genl. Foster is in command of this department. He is a fine looking man, and was a captain of engineers in fort Sumter when it was fired on. Orders were read not to fire any guns. But as we were cleaning them to night several went off. The adjutant sent round word to have it stoped. I was wiping mine, the butt on my leg and the muzzle up in the air. in cocking it my thumb slipped off the hammer, and away she went. bang! Then the adjutant was after me. I explained as well as I could, and let him talk.

We build a large fire of pine rails to night and were around singing songs, telling stories and cracking jokes untill a large hour. Nate Wright said "I wonder if you will feel as fine as this when you get back." He is always grunting and grumbling. and is never happy only when he is drunk. I think he is the hardest man in the company. Orders are to move early in the morning.

Dec. 11. Up at four o'clock, made coffee and had our breakfast. It was so foggy that we did not get under way untill eight o'clock. I am on rear guard. The 9th New Jersey took the lead. after the cavalry. (The cavalry are always in front of every thing) then a battery, then our brigade, another battery, and so on. There are 12,000 infantry, 30 pieces of artillery and several companies of the 3rd N.Y. cavalry. We started off in fine style, every man in his place. The drum corps playing "the girl I left behind me[.]" After marching a mile or so

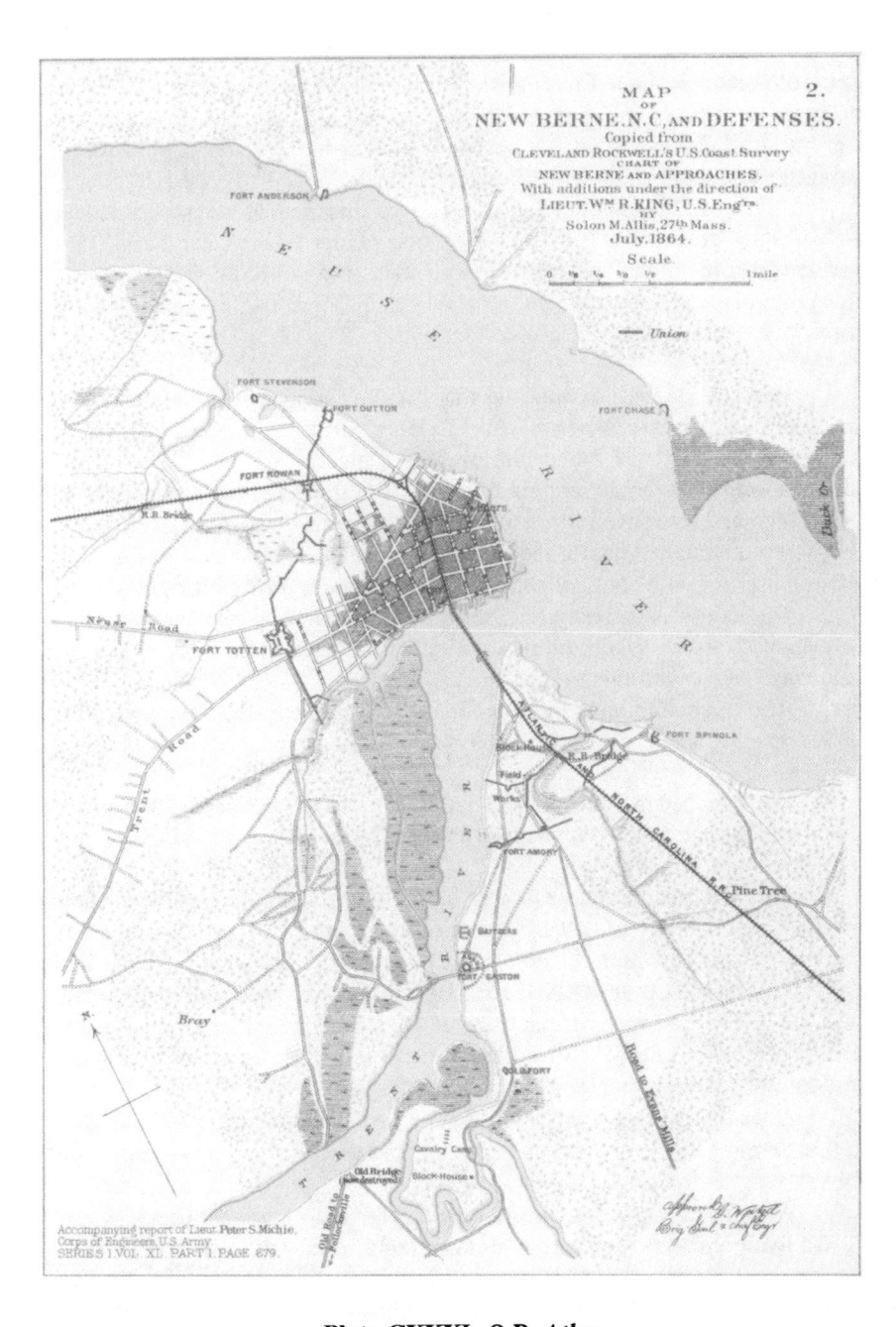

Plate CXXXI, *O.R. Atlas*

the command was "Arms at will"! Which means go as you please, and carry your gun any way. A few miles out our cavalry had a brush with the rebel pickets. cleaned them out, took three prisoners, and wounded a few. Four darkies brought a wounded man to the rear on a streacher in bad shape. His time is short. One of our men had a ball through his face, clean through just under his cheek bone. Tough. It begins to look as if there would be work for somebody very soon.

After marching about 15 miles we found that the rebs had blockaded the road by felling trees across it. Which the pioneer corps had to clear away. Here we camped for the night.[61] The officers blankets were all in the wagons which were eight miles in the rear. Lieut. McHenry said "Mose I will turn in with you tonight." We turned in at the proper time.

Dec. 12 [1862]. I woke up this morning long before daylight most froze, and found Charlie (as we all call McHenry when not on duty) had left me sometime in the night. I found him over by a big fire. He said that he had stood it as long as he could without freezing. The grass in this field was about two feet high and was covered with a heavy white frost. Twas a very cold night.

It did not take long for the sun to warm us up, as soon as it was up over the tree tops. A cup of hot coffee, hard tack and pork, put us all right.

The road was so badly blockaded that we did not get under way untill nearly eight o'clock. When the rebs cut down the trees some of them fell the wrong way. We called them union trees.

After marching eight miles we halted and made coffee. Here we got a lot of honey. It was fun to see the boys go for the hives regardless of being stung.

We marched a mile or so on this road when we struck across the country through the field. We camped to night in an old corn field.

Dec. 13. Last night, we had an alarm on the picket line. several shots were fired. Some of the boys were scared. But we were up in a hurry, all ready for anything that came along. Old Capt. Chapin of Co. K. jumped up and said "Where is my saber Lt. Peak? Where is my saber?" He had it buckled on him all the while. His boys said the old man had been drinking rather freely of apple jack, and his head was a trifle muddled. We call him "Capt. Slathers" for short. He is to old[62] for a soldier, and looks like a farmer.

After this diversion we went to sleep and slept soundly untill half past five this morning, when we got up and made coffee. Soon after we began our walk.

At eleven o'clock we came on the rebels[63] at South West Creek, where they had two guns and disputed our crossing the bridge. Our battery opened on them, and we found our way across on the mill dam a little way below. The 9th N.J. in the lead, then the 85th Pa. then our regiment. we crossed in single file. After a sharp skirmish, we drove the rebs, captured their two guns, and a few

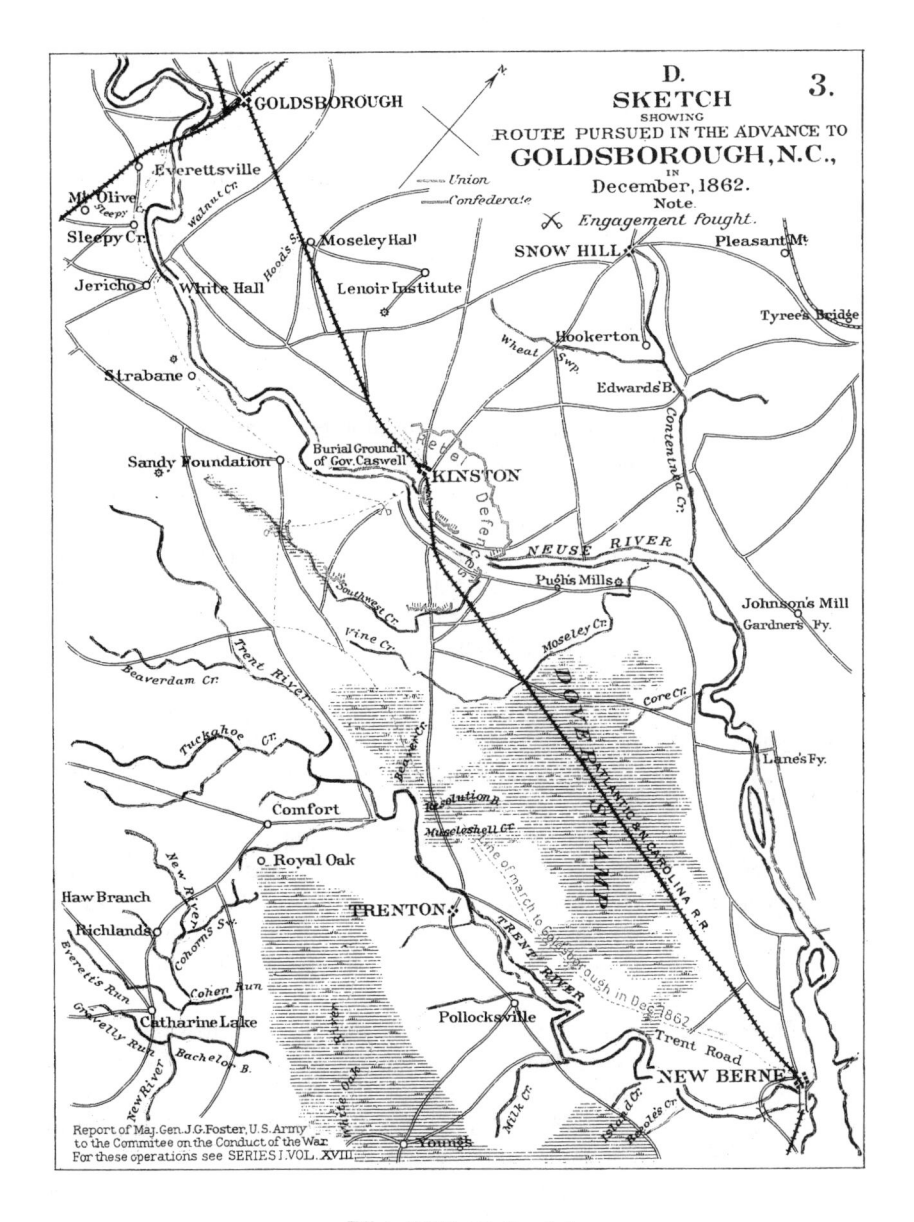

Plate XCI, *O.R. Atlas*

prisoners, besides making a few of them bite the dust. After this afair we moved a few miles, and camped for the night.

Dec. 14 [1862], Sunday. No fires were allowed last night. We found a lot of corn fodder which made us a good bed. Lt. McHenry and I sleep together. Drew three days rations.

At eight o'clock we moved out, when on our left the ball opened in earnest. We kept down the main road for a ways, when we met a section of battery B 3rd N.Y.[64] who were waiting for us. Here we had orders to support them. They struck off into a large open field and we after them. As we passed Genl. Wessells, he sung out "You New York boys don't waste your ammunition."

When the section neared the woods they unlimbered, and began to firing. They had put in two shots, when the rebs guns got range on them and drove them under their guns. We kept on untill we reached the woods. Here we took a position to the right of the 9th N.J. Col. Hickman's regiment.[65] The rebs gave us grape and cannister.[66] How we hugged mother earth, face down we were. Col. Hickmen was very cool.

All of the grape and cannister went over our heads through the tree tops. It simply hailed. We held our ground. The rebs couldn't dislodge. Clum of Co. D had his arm broke.[67] This is all the harm it did us. But our hair did stand right up for a minute.

Then we moved to the right of the line with the 96th N.Y. Col. Gray as our support.[68] Here our company was ordered to deploy as skirmishers. Tom Glenn said "I can't skirmish."[69] The first four sections of us went our first. we went through the woods to the open field beyond. We could see clear to the bridge.

On the road by the river we saw two regiments of rebs[70] moving round by our right trying to turn our right flank. Just then Maj. King started to come where we were. Lieut. McHenry told him the rebs were out there. The Maj. made for the rear. He has not got over his scare at Fair Oaks.

After discovering the rebs we fell back, and reported it. Then our whole regiment was deployed as skirmishers. The 96th N.Y. was our support. We moved through the woods, but could find nothing of those rebs. As soon as we were through we uncovered the 96th and they made a dash for the bridge. Here Col. Gray was killed. He was a brave officer, and a good man. Our regiment fanned our line on the bank of the river.

Before the 96th made for the bridge however, our men on the left, notably the 103 Pa., was knee deep in the swamp fighting for all they worth. To day they regained their good name, which they lost at Fair Oaks.[71] The rebs they were after came pouring towards the bridge and were the ones who gave it to Col. Gray. In crossing the bridge the rebs had fired it in many places. Many barrels of pitch were placed on it for that purpose. Our men put it out. We had some fun with the prisoners who fell to us. One said "I haven't fired a shot to day, just look at the nipple of my gun. I fixed so I couldn't." Sure enough he had pluged his nipple full of lead. Another one said "I am sick[.]" One of the boys said "Wouldn't the doctor excuse you." He said "no he wouldn't." We asked if he had any arms. he pulled out an old jack knife and said this is all I have. We roared.

As we were in line on the bank of the river our section of artillery came down across the open field to the bridge.

They opened on the rebs across the river, putting a few shell into a house. how the rebs swarmed out of it.

Lt. Col. Wellman lost his head here. The wound he received in his head at Fair Oaks, left him in such shape that he cannot stand excitement.

After the rebs were driven across the bridge, we marched over. There were a number of the rebel dead lying on it, whose bodies were in the fire, partly burned. It was a ghastly sight. We marched around and beyond the village of Kinston, N.C.[72] Part of us went through the place. It is a very pretty place, lying on a rise of ground. We got some good tobacco here, called the Hyco. We were out.

We camped to night in an old corn field. Our darkey boy came in with a chicken he picked up on his travels. We are a tired lot of men for once. Sergeant Gooding[73] of our company slunk out to day. He said he went to the rear with one of the 9th N.J. boys that was wounded. We think the "deacon" is a coward.

This was the battle of Kinston, N.C.
Union loss 40 killed, 120 wounded
Confed. loss 50 killed, 75 wounded

We captured 400 prisoners (who were paroled.) 15 pieces of artillery, a quantity of small arms and one stand of colors. Col. Gray was killed in trying to be the first man to plant the colors on the bridge. He took the colors from the color sergeant and made dash, a rebel gun that was on the bridge, and lay in the fire went off and the contents lead the Col. out. Chaplain [Nathan] Wardner of his regiment has gone to New Berne with the body.

Dec. 15 [1862]. We slept quite late this morning, because we were very tired last night, we had to sleep on our arms. that is we laid down with all our traps on, so if we were needed during the night we would be ready. It is always hard to sleep that way. About nine o'clock we got in line, and moved back through the town. Here we found more tobacco, candy and other stuff in one of the stores. We were merchants for a while. This brand of tobacco is the best we ever had. It is called Hyco. It's better than any we get from the north.

After we re-crossed the river, we burned the bridge, and marched up country, after leaving a detail to bury the dead. H. Z. Shepherd is the one [on the detail] from our company.[74] Plenty of forage on the road. We thought we would make an early camp to night, as we could see the light from the camp fires loom up over the tree tops, of the men were in our front, about the middle of the afternoon.

We had picked up one at a time, a drove of about fifty hogs (fresh pork is good this time of year). which we were driving ahead of us. Francisco and I had a half bushel of sweet potatoes in a backet which we were carrying. With all our marching we did not seem to get any nearer camp. The light from the camp fires in our advance seemed to be as far away. As night set in, first one hog would slip out in the woods, then another, and another, the farther we went the less hogs we had. At dark we were completely out of hogs. Maj. King saw Francisco carrying our basket of potatoes, told us to pass them up to him and he would carry them on his horse. We did so. When we reached camp he returned them to us. We carried him a good mess for his supper. We did not make camp untill nine o'clock, near a small church, in a heavy pine wood.

This afternoon the Chaplain and Surgeon of the 103rd Pa (who are just a head of us) kept falling out at every farm house we came to, and then jamming back through our ranks, to get their place again. It was very annoying as we were tired and cross.

Once the surgeon came through with a big bundle of corn stalks straped on his horse - he took a space five feet wide - singing out "make way there right and left." When he was long side of me, I drew back my old gun and gave his horse a broadside. It made his ribs rattle. He turned to me and said, "I'll let you understand who you are hitting. I'll let you know where your place is young man."

I made a few appropriate remarks, suitable to the occasion. When Lt. McHenry took a hand in, then Maj. King. [and] Capt. Webster (of Genl. Wessells staff, was riding by the side of the Major). spoke up, and said to the surgeon, "Who are you sir?" The surgeon told him, "Well sir, get into your place sir, and stay there to." [That's] One on the surgeon. We were not bothered any more by that gang.

Lt. Col. Wellman had to return to New Berne on account of his head. Lt. McHenry and I spread our blankets at the fort by a large pine tree. We had been under the blankets but a short time when Bancroft[75] crawled up to "Charlie's" head[76] and deposited a leg of pork, as a sort of peace offering. Maj. King had the same trick played on him. There is a policy in war, especially in a war on hogs. Officers never like to investigate a thing, on which they have had a square meal. It sort of reflects. We had plenty of pork, potatoes and honey here. Knapp was poking through a barn last night to see what there was in it. He opened one door and there stood a big white faced mule, with his long ears flopping. He was scared most out of his wits. Knapp not the mule.

Dec. 16 [1862]. An early start this morning. And the music began early. As our brigade took the lead at Kinston, we are in the rear now. Our batteries are playing on White Hall which is on the other side of the river. Lots of fun with the nine month's men,[77] as we march along. they are behind every stump. Some with their shoes off, looking at their feet, to see if they can find a blister. Then we blackguard them. A battery going to the rear, which had burst a gun, one of the men came along with a broken sponge stuff in his hand, his hat off, shirt neck open, and his sleeves roled up, face, arms and neck were all black with the smoke of powder. He looked fierce. his tongue was limber from too much apple jack. He said, "here is a specimen of us, there are only three of us left." We pulled out one side of the road to allow a battery to pass to the front. It was a very inspiring sight. Horses on a jump. the drivers with whip and spur urging them on faster.[78] The infantry were not engaged here. Pass more nine months men, who act as if they afraid, some of them are on the wrong side of the stump. I admit that there is a strange feeling comes over one when he is under fire for the first time. Camped in a large field early near a large stack of corn fodder. The boys were getting it to sleep on, When a staff officer rode up to Genl. Wessells and said "General do you allow those men to take those stalks." The old man turned in his saddle and replied, "I guess they are taking them," and rode off. Shortly after a guard was placed over them. We had all we needed for our beds. They make good beds. The horses were short of forage, and we are willing now for them to have their share. Bancroft and I took a stroll to see if we could find some sweet potatoes. We found them of course. When ever we saw a small stack of corn fodder, we were pretty sure of finding a pile of sweet potatoes under it. Bancroft is a good one to forage with, he seems to know how.

Dec. 17 [1862]. We were up very early this morning. The Adjutant wished this days work was done. [We were] Under motion after a deal of reconnoitering was done. Then the cavalry woke the rebs up, and the artillery began their music. Then we knew battle was opened up.

We had to pass through a large pine woods, which had been tapped for turpentine. The turpentine had dried on them to the hight of twenty feet or more. The natural thing for us to do was to put a lighted match at the foot of each tree, just to see the fire run up the trunk. It went like a streak of lightning way up. Soon the whole woods were afire.

Our brigade went through the woods to the edge of an open field, where we could see the rail road embankment.

On a knoll in the center of the field was Genl. Foster and the other Generals with their several staff officers. In a few minutes Lt. [Daniel F.] Beadle an aid-de-camp of Wessells' staff came over and ordered the 85th Pa to move out. they had gone but a short distance when the Aide came back and ordered them back into line, and our 85th N.Y. was ordered out. We marched to a position just in the rear and left of Genl. Foster and party. Here we rested on our arms. We had a commanding view of the whole field. To our right our batteries were firing over and through the woods. Directly in our front was the rail road embankment - nearly a mile of it - which extended from the extreme left to the long trestle bridge over the Neuse river. Two regiments had stacked

Brigadier General John G. Foster
(Massachusetts Comandery, Military Order of
the Loyal Legion and the U.S. Army Military History Institute)

their arms this side of the railroad and the men were tearing up the track. From fifty to one hundred would get on one side, pick it up, and end it over the other side of the embankment, then take another section. The rebs would put a few shell into them, which did no harm. Every thing was booming on both sides, when in the direction of the bridge we saw a very thin column of smoke rising. Just then Capt. Webster of Wessells staff came dashing across the field towards us. He rode up to Genl. Foster, saluted him, and said General the bridge is on fire.[79] The Capt. made a fine appearance as he dashed along on his horse. He wore a long flowing beard - at trifle red - which streamed back over his shoulders. A very inspiring sight.

The burning of this railroad bridge here at Goldsboro was the object of this expedition, as it is on the Weldon and Wilmington road, the main line from Richmond south. We burned it to cut the communication with Richmond, so that reinforcements could not be sent to Lee's army, as Genl. Burnside is attacking Fredericksburg, Va. If he does his work well as we have done ours, he has made a good job of it.[80]

After a few more rounds by our guns we move back to our brigade. This is the first time we ever had the priveledge of seeing a battle from so good a stand point. It was a fine view. In getting off the field, our brigade was in the rear of the main body. but in our rear was battery B 3rd N.Y. Art. Capt. [Joseph] Morrison in command, and the 45th Mass. Inf. a nine month regiment, as their support. We had gone a mile or so, when we heard a terrific canonaiding in our rear. Genl. Wessells came dashing back, gave the command, "Right about, forward, double quick. March!" We went back flying light. There was nothing for us to do. This was the cause of the racket. The battery had limbered and were ready to get off the field, when a brigade of South Carolinians[81] came over the railroad embankment carrying a flag of truce, which they droped after a few moments, and took their bayonets and made a charge for the battery. Capt. Morrison saw the situation at once, and that the Massachusetts men would not be of any assistance to him. He gave this command, "Give 'em hell boys, and be lively"! The boys gave them three rounds of double shotted grape and cannister (18 rounds in all) which literally wiped that brigade of rebels off the face of the earth. One of the battery boys said it was the wickedest thing he ever saw. He also said that the 45th Mass while they were under the guns, shook off the best suit of clothes Uncle Sam ever gave them.

This was the most brilliant event of this trip. We were not molested any more in getting off the field.

We were right mad to think that we had made the return on a double quick, and then to have no hand in the sport.

In going through the wood which we fired this morning, was a dangerous piece of business, as the trees had fallen across the road, and were still burning. The ammunition train had hard work to get through, without an explosion. It was a warm place for us infantry men to pick our way out. It was a grand sight to see those tall pine trees on fire from the ground to their top. To night we camped in the same field we did last night.

The Mass. men in our lead had picked up, and carried with them all the pine rails along the road, and put them in a pile near their camp, and put a man to guard them.

Of course we had to have a fire of some kind to cook our coffee, and that pile of rails was the only wood in sight, and wood we must have. In order to get them, we had to relieve that guard, which we did you upsetting him, then we had all the rails we needed. Dry pitch pine rails make a good fire. After coffee we turned in, to[o] tired to forage.

Dec. 18 [1862]. Feel rather old this morning. A late start in consequence. marched to within six miles of Kinston and camped for the night.

If we had stayed up there another night, the rebs would have made it hot for us, as they were running in troops from Wilmington to cut us off from New Berne.

We made it warm for them anyway.

Dec. 19. A foraging party went out this morning under the charge of our brigade quartermaster. Four large fat hogs and beef were brought in, for which the quartermaster [gave] a government receipt. In other words an order was given on the quarter master's department at New Berne. Where the owners will get their pay.

Stoped near Kinston for coffee. Here we found "Dad" Wessells asleep under a tree. He told one of our officers that our regiment did the best of any in his brigade in regard to straggling, firing our guns & e & e [etc., etc.]. Good for our old man Wessells.

A large house near is deserted by the family, leaving their furniture in the house. An officer rode up to the front door, led his horse into the parlor, opened the piano, up with his foot and smashed the key board in, then put corn in for his horse to eat. It was doing things up with a vengence. It was a dirty shame. From here we took the direct road to New Berne, not the one we came up on. We passed by a field where we found several dead rebel soldiers unburied, they looked gastly. It seems our advance cavalry struck this reb picket post by surprise and took them prisoners. Some of the rebs after they had surrendered, were disposed to fight more, and fired on our cavalry, who turned on them and blew their brains out to keep them quiet. They were very quiet when we found them. Peace to their bones. We are getting short of rations now.

Dec. 20. An early start this morning. Camped within 13 miles of New Berne. No rations.

Dec. 21 [1862], Sunday. Our ration this morning was one half of a hard tack for each man. A slim breakfast.

We reached our old camp ground at New Berne at noon, safe and sound, with only one man hurt. he had his arm broke at Kinston.

Plenty of grub now. Our waistbands are tight once more.

We left Suffolk, Va. the 5th [of the month]. we were to be gone ten days only. Our ten days are up, and more to.

Dec. 22. Slept this morning untill sunrise. We are completely used up and played out. The troops here call us the ragged brigade. Well we are ragged and very saucy, and once in a while a good healthy body louse thrown in to keep us lively. Officers and all have the pesky critters. One of the Mass. men, called our old man Wessells a ragmuffin general. His mouth was slapped promptly. They can blackguard us, but they must keep their mouths shut about our general.

These nine months Mass. men are a high toned lot, with their store clothes on.[82] The Mass. three years men are all right.[83] The 23rd, 24th, 25th, and 27th regiments. The 10th Conn. and 9th New Jersey are right up in every thing.

Dec. 23. Took dinner with the 3rd N.Y. Cavalry. Went down town, on my way back I took a codfish. Who says they don't like codfish?

Dec. 24. Knapp and I went down town to day. Went down by the docks. Here we found a fishing smack full of fish. As our money was very short, and could not buy fish. We each took one. They were of the variety called the drummer.[84] I told Knapp I didn't think two would be enough for our christmas dinner, and if he would hold them I would go for another, which was no trouble at all. Now we have enough. I don't think the skipper of that fishing smack, missed those three fish. "Twas the night before christmas"

Dec. 25. Christmas. Queer country this to have Christmas in. Friday so our fish just in time[85]. Knapp and I gave a Christmas dinner of fish to fifteen of the boys. We had a good time.

Dec. 26. Down town again to day. Drew tents. I am in with Lt. McHenry and Orderly Robinson.[86] We are quite a distinguished lot. It sort a looks as if we were to stay here.[87] Our ten days are way up. This is quite a city.

Dec. 27. Rainy. The orders are that we are to stay here. Our Quartermaster has gone to Suffolk for our extra baggage. Genl. Wessells is in command of a division, and Col. Hunt of the 92nd N.Y. is in command of our brigade.[88] Report says he has been promoted to a brigadier general.

James B. Robinson
(USAMHI)

Dec. 28 [1862]. It rained during the night. Cleared since. I made a good soup for dinner.

Camp near New Berne N.C.
Dec. 28, 1862

Dear Sister, I thought as to day was Sunday, I would write to you. As I have only a small piece of rebel paper an[d] an envelope, I will write only a few lines to let you know that I am alive and kicking way down in Carolina. As I haven[t much room I shall not write much. We are to stay here. Our quartermaster has gone to Suffolk for our extra baggage. When that comes I will give you all the particulars of our late tramp. It has been pleasant weather ever since we started from Suffolk. I never felt better in my life. Our regiment lost no men in this expedition. One man had his arm broke. Direct your letters as before. Every thing about this letter is rebel. Give my love to all the folks. I suppose you are anxious to hear from[?]. no more at present. I will write a gain soon. so good ye.

From your Aff. Brother
Charlie[89]

Dec. 29. Pleasant. Battalion drill.

Dec. 30. We are in the 1st brigade, 1st division, 18th corps.

Dec. 31. Mustered for pay. The mail is in, I received a pair of gloves, and three letters from home. All quiet on the Neuse.

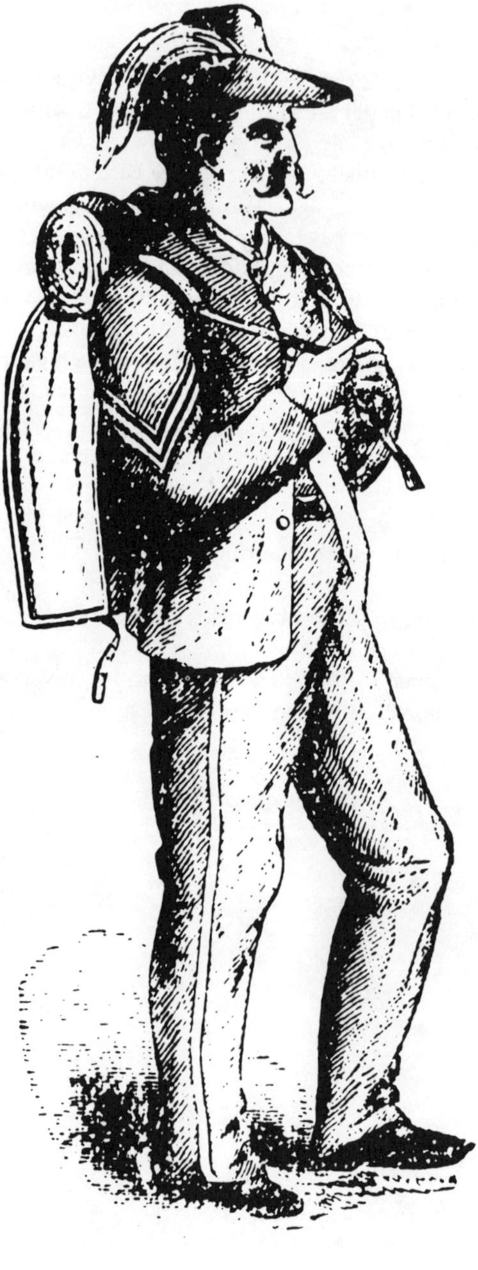

Chapter Four

TO PLYMOUTH, "THE QUEER TOWN"

(January 1 to December 31, 1863)

Beginning January 1863, the ongoing tour of coastal North Carolina by the Eighty-Fifth N.Y. Vols. took on the dull regularity of garrison duty. Their "camp life" was interrupted by occasional expeditions to control the waterways and transportation routes, and destroy Confederate stores and protect loyal Carolinians. Drills, which seemed almost daily, were employed both to keep the men in battle readiness and occupied.[1]

They were never free from threats of assault, however, for General James Longstreet, who had assumed command of the Confederacy's Department of Virginia and South Carolina, was not about to let the enemy move first. And, in fact, Lieutenant General Daniel Harvey Hill, Stonewall Jackson's brother-in-law and a known fighter, was placed in command of North Carolina troops. All Harvey Hill needed was the requisite manpower, a need Longstreet anticipated by sending 4000 men from Wilmington to bring Hill's fighting strength to 15,000. Once up to strength, New Bern was the target of a three-pronged attack by North Carolina native, Brigadier General Junius Daniel, Virginia Brigadier General Beverly H. Robertson and Carolinian Brigadier James Johnson Pettigrew.

Shortly, then, Wessells's brigade would be fully occupied at protecting New Bern. The threat seemed to disappear after a successful defense of Fort Anderson, and within five months they would be on their way to Plymouth, North Carolina, a "queer town" where the Roanoke River runs into Albemarle Sound. The importance of the town was never made entirely clear to the men, but nevertheless, entrenchments and fortifications were begun almost immediately upon disembarkation from the vessels that transported them from New Bern.

Jan. 1 [1863]. New Bern N.C. New Years and no turkey. In order to keep us out of mischief we moved camp across the Trent river. We have our tents up all right. After our tents were up we got to throwing chunks of frozen sod at one another, just for fun. I had stooped over to pick up a piece, when one took me over the eye. I saw seventeen stars. It lifted me clean off my feet. First black eye I ever had.

"Charlie" (as we call him when off duty, and Lieut. McHenry when on duty). wanted me to go down town, to the bakery to get him some fresh bread for supper. He forgot to give me a pass, so I had to run the guard. I got the bread all right, and into camp again.

Jan. 2. My pass comes to day, and I am down town. Our brigade are steeling this [town] blind. We are without money, and are ragged. We help ourselves to what we want on the sly.[2]

Down on the dock to day was a large fishing smack full of fresh fish. They were strung on up in lots of four, and were called the rock fish. 25 cents a string only. cheap. The skipper was busy selling to the boys, and some of us sat on the edge of the boat, each one with a string of fish in his hand, very familiar like, talking to the boys, and skipper, who would be selling all the time. I said come, "Capt. give my change, and I will get back to camp as it getting late." "What did you give me" he said. I told him "a half dollar." He gave me a quarter, which I took. Then I wrote an order on the baker, and signed Captain Chapin's name to it, bought a loaf of fresh bread, then bought some butter, and back to camp for a good supper. One can buy all the bread he wants at the bakery. But he must have an order, signed by some officer. This order is for the baker's voucher, that he has sold the bread. that is all. As is not always convenient to find one of our own officers. We have into the way of using Capt. Chapin's name on our own make of orders. They go with the baker every time,[3] providing the money is put up with the order. Wrote to David tonight.

Jan. 3. Our extra baggage has arrived. I am detailed to help unload it.

The line officers of our brigade are all in undress uniform and without shoulder straps.[4] We all left Suffolk, Va. as light as possible.

An officer is not required to have a pass to go down town, day or night. Last night Capt. "Charlie" King of our Company A and the Capt. of Co. B 103 PA who are great chums, were down town, when a provost guard halted them and demanded a pass.

The company B Captain, said "I'll give you a pass." He drew back his fist and passed it up the back of the guards ear, which sent the guard, with his gun, end over end into the gutter. The two captains are lovers of whiskey and were a bit full. To day an order was issued from general headquarters, that no officer should appear with out his shoulder straps on. to show his rank. That provost guard would have been in better shape to day, if that order had been issued yesterday.

Jan. 4 [1863], Sunday. Our detail reported at the back at nine o'clock to unload our extra baggage.

As the barge had not arrived we hung around untill this afternoon, when it came, and we began our work, and worked untill dark. Things are badly mixed.

Jan. 5. Finished unloading to day. I can't find my things any where yet. The rest of our tents are here. Last night I found a bag containing a half bushel of dried apples, which I appropriated, but my concience would not allow me to keep them, so I took them back to the barge this morning.

It's harder to appropriate from our own boys, than from the rebs. A concience is a quite thing for a soldier. We have them occasionally.

Jan. 6. The Lieut. and Orderly have a tent of their own now. I have taken in Knapp and Francisco in their places. We have a turf fire place with a barrel for a chimney. It works like a charm. We can broil, bake and stew on one side, and pure shiver and shake on the other.[5] There is no use talking it's grand and no mistake. I have found my needle book and portfolio.

Jan. 7. Pleasant. Reviewed by Col. Howell of the 85th Pa.[6]

Jan. 8. Cold. Reviewed by Genl. Hunt. He told us we were to be paid in six or eight days. We are six months back.

Jan. 9. Skirmish drill by company this forenoon, and skirmish by battalion this afternoon. This is the drill we enjoy most. It's fine.

Jan. 10. Down town to day. when I got back to camp, I found a great hunk of cheese under my overcoat. Queer! Our convalesents have arrived from Suffolk. They have had an easy time, while we had lots of fun.

Jan. 11, Sunday. Inspection. Warm & pleasant.

Jan. 12. Pleasant. Only drill to day.

Jan. 13. On guard. Our brigade was reviewed by Genl. Wessels. The report is that we are going to Charleston, S.C. to help Hunter take the place.[7]

Jan. 14. Have orders to be in readiness to move at twelve hours notice. Some of our brigade are getting their backs up, and say they will not go untill they are paid. Genl. Hunt has been around and asked the men to volunteer.

When Genl. Wessells heard of it, he said "I don't want any volunteering in this business. When my men get orders to go to Charleston, they are going." The old Man is right. Last night the 96th N.Y. stacked arms, and would not parade. When they woke up this morning, they saw a battery of 12 pounders trained on them then they took their arms like a lot of lambs, and went about their work. Bully for our Old Genl. Wessells.

Jan. 15 [1863]. Company drill this forenoon, and battalion this afternoon. Warner and Wilcox[8] came to day. They left us sick while we were on the peninsula, and are looking well now.

Jan. 16. Rainy to day. Letter from home. all well.

Jan. 18, Sunday. Inspection. Wrote home.

Jan. 25, Sunday. Inspection. All quiet last week. Our boys are having great times down town, and about town.

They take every thing they can reach. The stores here have very low ceilings, with the joist uncovered. In a shoe store, these joist had nails driven in them, on which hung innumerable pairs of high top boots. This is the way the boys work it. While some are buying, others are examining and trying on, at the same time talking and chaffing the clerks. After finding what they want, they will throw them on their arm, then walk and talk for half an hour. Talk with the proprietor, clerks, and all hands, untill every one familiar with them and the boots, when out they walk, with their purchase as they try to make the people think.

It works well, and every time.

Jan. 28. On fatigue throwing up a redoubt.[9] Wrote home, and recieved one from them.

Jan. 31. I went down town to day. In order to make a quick trip down, we follow the railroad track back, the cross a long trestle bridge over the Trent river.

Our "Mark" Mead[10] was down to see what there was worth picking up. He found a cap in one store, which he put under his coat out of the way.

In passing a shoe store he saw a pair of high top boots standing out in front, and nobody in sight. he embraced his opportunity and the boots at the same time and started off, when a little bell inside the boots began to tinkle, when out of the store a big darkie dashed after man and boots, when a foot race occurred in which good time was made, which resulted in Meads droping first the cap and then the boots. The dark chased him to the railroad bridge, then gave up the race, 'Twas a close call for Mead. We had the laugh on the boy for once, and always.[11]

Marcus M. Meade
(USAMHI)

Our company are on guard to day. The 103rd Pa have been paid.

Feb. 1 [1863], Sunday. on police. and get rid of inspection.

Feb. 2. Went down town for Lieut. McHenry this forenoon. signed the pay rolls for four months pay.

Feb. 3. Our brigade is developing a great knack for taking things. To day one of the boys in passing the division sutlers on Main Street. Saw a number of barrels of apples and boxes of cheese standing on the side walk. He hailed a dray cart that was passing, and told the darkie driver to roll on a barrel of apples and throw on a cheese and drive on. The darkie obeyed and took the load into the boys camp.
A good check is a good thing. All quiet on the Front.

Feb. 4. We were paid $52.00 four months pay. Sent $32.00 to father, paid all my debts and am square with the world once more.

Feb. 5. Moved to the barrack on the left bank of the Neuse river. The best quarters we have had since we left Elmira N.Y. We have taken up a subscription to buy Lt. McHenry a sword.[12]

Feb. 6. The boys were nearly all drunk last night. Report says Lt. McHenry was drunk, and put in the guard house down town. It's a shame "Charlie" will get drunk, as he is one of the best of officers, and is always looking out for our interest. He is as brave as a lion. The sword has been bought for him, but has been taken back to the store. the boys who have it in charge will not give it to him. It's too bad!

Feb. 7. Lieut. Martin is back from his furlough. He thinks it's mean the way McHenry was treated.

Feb. 8, Sunday. Adjt. Aldrich had more to do with the sword business than any one else, as he has been down on McHenry ever since the company was organized. We have but little respect for the adjutant. He is too strict for us.

Feb. 12. A few of us have made Lieut. McHenry a present of a nice pair of gauntlet gloves. Letters from home. George and David.[13]

Feb. 15, Sunday. On camp guard. It rains.

Feb. 16. Off guard at nine o'clock.

Feb. 17 [1863]. Pleasant. Company drill. Sent George and David my picture.

Feb. 18. Bayonet exercise. Rainy.

Feb. 19. Have charge of the barracks to day. cleaned my revolver, and reloaded it.[14] We have not much duty here.

Feb. 22, Sunday. Inspection. The gunboats in the river are firing salutes in honor of Washington's birth day. Grand.

Feb. 23. On picket at the railroad bridge. Cold here.

Feb. 24. Slept good last night. Relieved at three o'clock this afternoon. Lt. Martin has been dismissed [from] the service, by reason of being absent without leave. Letter from home and Boswell Insse. "Boz" was wounded at Fair Oaks, and discharged Oct. 29, 1862. At a raffle I won a watch. This is my first hand at a raffle.

Feb. 25. All the troops here were reviewed by Genl. Foster.[15] Hard work to be on review. The nine months men from Mass. are a fancy lot. The regiment from Boston have uniforms made to order, of as fine cloth and made up in the same style as the officers.

One of them was on guard at Genl. Wessell's headquarters the other day. The general stopped him as he was walking his beat. and said "What is your rank sir?" "A private." "Call your corporal to relieve you long enough to cut one button off each sleve and two off behind your coat." The poor man had to obey. Bad for the Mass. men. Enlisted men have two buttons on each sleve, and two on the back of their coats. Officers have three buttons on each sleve, and four on the back of coats. Our old Man can't stand many frills. Here is another of his drives. A number of officers were at his headquarters, one of whom wore high top boots, with big spurs on. The old Man kept him waiting untill he had finished his business with the rest, turning to him he said "Take your trousers out of your boots sir. regulations say you must wear shoes." The trousers came out. Our old Man knows how.

Feb. 26. A letter from home, saying my money is all right.

Feb. 28. It rained so yesterday we stayed inside. Mustered for pay by the Lt. Col. of the 96th N.Y.[16] Went down town and had my watch fixed. Lt. Martin goes to Washington to try and fix up his dismissal. Hope he can, for he is good officer.[17]

March 1, Sunday. On Guard. Letter from home.

March 4 [1863]. Our Colonel Belknap came in to day. We ought to tar and feather him, so we had, for he is a big coward.

March 5. Drill to day. Marra the <u>mule</u> was down town, and on his way back he got into a muss with a darkie, a provost guard interfering was knocked down without ceremony, when the Mule made for camp. The guard called his corporal and explained matters to him. When he (the corporal) took a file of men and started for the mule, who was only a short way ahead, & had turned round the barracks and run into our cook house. In a few minutes the guards were in after him. The corporal said "Have you seen a man come in here lately"? The Mule said "No. but they could look around and see if they could find anyone, if they wouldn't disturb any of the cold vituals." They couldn't find their man. He was talking to them all the while. Good for the Mule. He is a great character.

At Newport News he played off on the doctor for about four weeks.[18]

Mar. 6. On guard. first relief, post number 7.

March 7. Off guard at nine o'clock. Went down town and got my watch. No drill to day.

Newbern, N.C.[19]
March 7, 1863

Dear Father,

I recieved yours of the 21st stating that you got my package of money all right. Every thing is going along all right here. Last week a company of the 3rd N.Y. cavalry and one of the 1st N.C. Inf. (This is a regiment of loyal North Carolinians) went in scows down the river and up the sound into Hyde county looking for guerrillas, and found more than they could handle comfortably. Still they drove them back, killing their captain, and taking a lieutenant prisoner. Our cavalry had four killed and eleven wounded.[20] On their way back the lieutenant of guerrillas, who had his hand and feet tied fell over board, or some say he was pushed over, others say he jumped over, which ever way it was he was drowned. In his pockets he had a commission from Jeff. Davis, and protection from Governor Stanley (the military governor of this state) and Genl. Foster.

The 3rd N.Y. cavalry never take any prisoners if they can help it. When we were up to Goldsboro when they got after any rebs they would put the muzzle of their carbines behind their ears and blow their brains out. They are a perfect set of tigers, and the rebs are as fraid of death of them, and have nothing that can stand before them. they [are] armed with saber, carbine and revolver. They are bully boys from N.Y. More cavalry and two regiments from our brigade and going back there. As they were getting on the boats to day an old secesh was around trying to find out where they were going to and where they were to land. Our guards took after him and caught him as he was getting into his sail boat to leave. Come to find out he is an old cock who has been up to this kind of business for six months. A spy.

I guess a short piece of hemp and a dance on nothing will fix him, at least I hope so.[21] This is worst hole in all secesh, that we hold in our possession, and when Burnside took it last spring, if he had burned to the ground, all right. they ought to now just surround it and fire it in four or five places, and the first living thing that undertook to leave shoot it down, if it was nothing more than a rat. then take the ashes and make soft soap and wash out the rest of the greese spots down this way. I am getting mad as David used to say.[22] I wish we were in active service. I am getting tired of staying so long in one place. All well. Write soon and all the news, love to all, Good bye, send me stamps.

Your Aff son Chas. C. Mosher

Mar. 8 [1863], Sunday. Inspection. Went down town to the colored church and took a back seat. The service beat anything of the kind I ever saw. They were singing when I went in, and such singing I never heard. One line would last them all day. An old man was going round shaking hands and singing. when he made his trip, another one would take it up and so on. Some had the power, or something else. I reckon.

Mar. 9. Company drill this forenoon, and battalion this afternoon. Wrote home. Blake[23] says I owe him a whipping. Bah!

Mar. 10. Bayonet exercise. Down town this afternoon. I went down to the sub-marine railway and saw them at work. I saw a diver come up out of the water with his suit on. He look rather hideous with his helmet on. We have thrown in and bought George Phillips a violin. We have a stag dance most every night.

Mar. 11. On guard. It has rained most all day.

Mar. 12. Off guard at nine o'clock. Sold my watch for $12.00. A squad of us went over to the 44th Mass. barracks to night to see them in an opera. Illustrating their regiment from the time they left Boston to date. It was very good. Genl. Foster, wife and daughter were present.

Mar. 13. Capt. Clarke returned to day. He is looking well. Went to the 44th opera again tonight. Had a pleasant time. The 44th are city clerks and professional men, and are very stylish.

Mar. 14. This morning we were awakened by our gunboats firing what we supposed to be a salute, in honor of the capture of this place by Burnside one

New Bern, N.C., ca. 1863 Fort Totten is at the center
(Wayne Mahood Collection)

year ago to day. We all hurried out on the bank of the river, and found that it was a different thing than firing salutes. It was an attack of the rebel Genl. Pettigrew's[24] brigade on fort Anderson on the opposite side of the Neuse river from us. The fort is a small work, unfinished, without any cannon mounted as yet, and is manned by the 92nd N.Y. numbering less than 300 men, commanded by Lt. Col. Anderson.[25] Early this morning the rebels drove in the pickets, planted their batteries on a rise of ground in front of the post, and fired a few shot, then sent word to Col. Anderson to surrender, giving him a half hour to consider the matter. That half hour was occupied in getting word to our gunboats, and letting Genl. Foster know the situation. When the time was up the rebs sent in for the reply. The Colonel's reply was that he was there to defend the fort, therefore could not surrender. Then the rebel guns opened - (they had three batteries, 18 guns) - on the little fort. Soon our gunboats responded. It was music for sure. We were where we could see it all, but could not help in any way. About nine o'clock orders came to fall in lively men. We fell into line in short order. When [it] came. "Forward. double quick. March!" and down we went into the city to the wharf. here we got on two scows, and started for the relief of the fort, a distance of about one and half miles. There were a number of long poles on the scows which we used to pole ourselves over. The poles were all right and we made good headway untill we came to the channel, when they were so short they would not touch bottom. Now we were in a fix. The revenue cutter seeing the situation, sent two small boats who towed us untill we could use our poles again. which brought us in range of the rebel guns. The gunboats were fireing over our heads, when once in a while a shell would burst in its flight. The rebel batteries were using grape and cannister, which dropped in the water all around us. We were for once, in a place where we had to take our medicine. The bursting shell over our heads, and the grape and cannister, combined to make our situation extremely peculiar, and uninteresting. If a shot or piece of shell had struck our old scows, they would have sunk. All this made us use our poles very lively. I took a look back at the city. The whole of the people were either on the house tops, or on some other high place watching our progress. The 85th [N.Y.V.] was the center of attraction for once, too much so, for our peace of mind. As we neared the fort - our gunboats silenced the rebel guns much to our comfort - We made our landing without much formality. For a fact we were very much relieved when we put our feet on dry land, and out of range of the rebs guns. The 92nd boys gave us a hearty welcome.

But what a scene their camp presented. The tents and out buildings were completely riddled. Shot to pieces. It was the worst camp I ever saw. Two men were slightly wounded and two mules were killed, was all the real harm the rebs did in their attempt on this place.[26]

The boys had things in shape if the rebs had tried to charge the works. Every man had his place behind the words, and a number of cartridges out, and broken, into, all ready for fast loading and firing.

The rebs did not come to charge them, as they did not know what sort of people were inside.

As it was the 92nd never fired a shot, and were not in as much real danger as we were in crossing. A rebel deserter came in and said that the rebs went off swearing that the d------- yankeys would not fight and were coming back in the morning and try it again. Perhaps!

After we rested a while, we all set to work to strengthen the place in case the rebs wanted to try us on again. We built a large platform, on which we placed a twelve pound boat howitzer, which the gunboat *Hunchback* sent us. Then after dinner, Genl. Foster came over to take charge of the defense. He ordered a traverse[27] thrown up to protect us from an enfilading[28] fire. While all this was getting ready, A few of us went out side to see how things were left by the rebs. We went on our own hook, (by permission) Our gunboats shells had dug up the ground in great shape. We found a twenty pound parrot[29] that was bursted. A rebel prisoner told us this bout it. He said that the gunner swore he would have one more shot at the *Hunchback*,[30] as he was sighting his gun, a solid shot from the *Hunchback* struck the muzzle of his gun, and broke it off and burst it plowing a hole in the ground large enough to drive a two horse wagon in. The gunner went into the hole some where. all we could find of him was a bit of hair and blood.

We did not stay outside very long. When we got inside all hands were at work on the traverse. It was to be an all night job. Lt. McHenry as cute as ever, went to our Colonel and told him that a reconnoisance would have to be made in the morning, and as our company was the only one that could skirmish, we ought to have a nights rest. The Colonel agreed to the proposition, "Charlie" is a brick. We are to sleep, while the rest work. Good.

Capt. Merriman[31] of the 92nd N.Y. had a new pair of trousers in his tent, which he had never worn. A shell went through [t]he tent, an[d] cut the seat of those trousers clean out. He expressed them home to his mother, and told her he had them on during the fight. The captain is [a] very small man.

When we were crossing the river in the scows, a member of one of the new regiments in the city asked an artillery officer, "What regiment it was crossing." The officer said it was "the 85th N.Y., them devils that had rather fight than eat."

Our brigade has a good name here, and our regiment is no disgrace to it. The Old Man thinks a heep of us.[32]

Mar. 15. Our company went out on a scout this morning. Col. Belknap was with us.

We deployed, and went out on the Swift Creek road, as far as Old Gaskins[33], all we found was a darkey. Petigrew's cook. He had a large fresh fish for the general's dinner. an accident had prevented the reb from getting it. Lt. McHenry wanted to go out on this road further but the colonel who was always a coward, thought it not best, so we came back and went out by the "old fort on the glade" as it is called. the road here passes through a swamp for a mile or more. It was very narrow, and the under brush comes close to the roadway. Beyond was a large open field.

We looked through that roadway, and beyond, a good many times wondering what lay there, the rebels or what, and if we should get well into it, would they give us a charge of grape and cannister. It looked very dubious for sure. After a short rest, we deployed as much as possible, and started cautiously (but shivering) on. There was no back out, for we had to find out what was in that open field. we fairly crept through. no one spoke. The nearer we got to the field, the nearer our hearts got to our mouths. We made the field in due time, and to our great surprise, we found nothing. A great relief to us, for one dose of grape and cannister would have wiped us off the earth.

After looking around here to our satisfaction, and finding no trace of the rebels, we marched back to the "old fort" with lighter hearts than when we went out.

This "old fort" was built by the rebels to oppose Burnside's attacking Newbern from this way. They were afraid he would come this way with his gun boats some morning, on a heavy dew. A thirty two pounder had been mounted here, to defend this road against the "yanks." It was never needed. The gun had been spiked, its carriage and platform burned. A few rounds of grape, and solid shot lay around. It went by the name of the "Fort on the Glade." although there was not much of a fort, but a good place for one.

It beats all how the rebel Petigrew[34] follows our brigade. We captured him at Fair Oaks. then met him at Blackwater, on the Goldsboro raid, and here.

We crossed the river to night to our old quarters. Two letters from home. I am on guard to night.

Mar. 16 [1863]. Crossed the river this morning, and went out on a short scout, took one prisoner. We stop with the 92nd to night.

Mar. 17. Took two days rations, and started out on another scout. We go in two detachments. One in command of the Colonel takes the Swift Creek road. the other in command of the Major go out by the fort on the glade.

Our company is with the Major. We are to meet up the country at the certain point. Our detachment went six miles, and found nothing but had roads full of water.

Neither could we get any trace of the other detachment. After resting, we came back to the old fort on the glade and camped for he night.

Mar. 18. Came back to the 92nd and hung around all day. The colonel's detachment went ten miles into the country yesterday.[35] He saw what he said was a baggage wagon of the rebels, and ordered the men to charge on it. they charged, and found it was a white cow. A brave man is our colonel. It set him way up the other day, when Genl. Foster called him general. A short way from fort Anderson is a large house and barn which we occupied to night. I slept in the stable to night. Two letters & a paper from home. It rains.

Mar. 19 [1863]. It has drizzled all day. Went across to our barracks this afternoon.

Mar. 20. Rained all day. Letter from home.

Mar. 21. A rainy day. Went down town and had a shave. Our N.Y. regiments wear a short jacket as part of uniform. a very convenient coat as there is nothing in the way in the shape of coat tails.
The Pa. regiments wear the regulation U.S. coat, which has a long skirt. As there are three regiments of Pa. and three of N.Y. troops in our brigade.[36] Genl. Wessells has ordered us N.Y. boys to draw and wear the U.S. regulation uniform, so that his brigade will be alike in clothes. We draw our dress suits to day.

Mar. 22, Sunday. Pleasant. Went down town and droped into the colored church. A guard sat in the pulpit with the preacher, to keep order I suppose. They had a powerful meeting. Wrote home.

Mar. 23. Company drill this forenoon. At dress parade an order was read that we were to be in readiness to move tomorrow morning at eight o'clock, with two days rations.

Mar. 24. Reported at Foster's wharf and went on the scows and were towed across the river by the *Wheel Barrow* a small stern wheel steamer. After we landed, we broke up into detachments, and scoured the country in all directions.[37] when we came back we camped in the old "Hocker" [Hooker] house. Saw some pretty women.

Mar. 25. We hung around all day untill we were tired out. As our officers had gone back to the city, we thought we would follow, so we boarded the scows and pushed off, but owing to a strong head wind, we were a long while in getting under headway. When a short way from shore our rudder broke, then one pole after another would stick in the mud, and we would lose it. So we were in a fix. The waves run very high, every time we rode over a wave, we were afraid our old scow would break in halves. As we had neither rudder or poles, we sat down and drifted. the wind being very strong we were in danger of being swamped. Then realizing our situation, we ripped some plank up from the floor of our craft, and with an [? missing in original] we had on board we made a rudder, and sweeps and set to work in earnest and tried to make the other shore.

After a long hard struggle, we made our side of the river about sundown, a very tired lot of men, but happy.

Mar. 26 [1863]. After a good nights rest in our barracks we are all right. Orders to move with three days rations. Marched down to the wharf and boarded the steamer *Allison*. we take tents this time, and cross the river once more. After our tents are up, we go on picket. I am on post down in the swamp, where we could not get out, nor the rebs in. A company D man is on with me. Foster must expect an attack from some source, is why all of this.

Mar. 27. All quiet on picket last night. I was relieved at two o'clock this afternoon.

Mar. 28. There was a false alarm last night. We all fell out, then we all fell in again.
The report is that Jeff Davis[38] has issued a proclamation that the rebel troops shall have no pay nor clothing untill Newbern or some other seaport in North Carolina is taken. Good for Jeff, hope he will invite us to the taking. there will be fun for some body. Perhaps we have to much.

Mar. 29, Sunday. on picket to the left of the "fort on the glade"

Mar. 30. All quiet along the line last night. It rained all night. Pleasant. I was relieved at three o'clock this afternoon.

Mar. 31. This has been a hard <u>March</u> for us.

April 1. Saw a pretty girl, only she was a snuff dipper. They take a piece of sassafras root, and chew the end of it into a sort of brush, which they dip into the snuff box then daub it on their teeth, then suck the stick. Bah!
Came back to our barracks this morning. The rebel forces that attacked fort Anderson are at Little Washington[39] trying to capture that place. They have blockaded the river below the town by planting heavy batteries on either side. Genl. Foster is there.

April 2. We can hear heavy firing in the direction of Little Washington, which is about 35 miles from here. The *Hunchback* has gone up there, so report says. She is a North river ferry boat, with heavy guns on her.
Down town they are moving commissary stores on board vessels, in case there should be an attack on this place. Four companies are detailed to go to the rifle pits, a mile out. Our company goes. Things look a bit like a brush.

April 3. Slept well last night. Popple and Deyo[40] went out in a "dug out" which upset and spilled them in the water. More firing in the direction of

Little Washington. Reported that the rebs have been repulsed by our men. We had a stag dance in the barracks to night. It rains hard. Began a letter home. All quiet.

April 4 [1863]. Cleared off cold and windy. A lot of us went up the river and brought in rails, to burn in the fireplace in our barracks. The report is that Richmond[41] is in ashes, and the rebs have gone into the interior. Hope so. Some of our men from the other side of the river, are in for rations. We all feel well. Another dance to night.

April 5, Sunday. We hear an occasional gun from Little Washington way. Ordered out to the rifle pits, were out only a short time, when we were ordered in, and to be ready at the half hours notice, with three days rations, to move, for where we don't know.

The steamers are putting the cavalry across the river. The 103rd Pa. went on board a steamer, but were ordered back to camp. Report says that Genl. Foster has driven back the rebels, and has reinforcements from Suffolk, Va. so we are not to go.

All of our regiment are in from the other side of the river.

Mosher of Co. D[42] has deserted. he is none of my relation. Inspection tomorrow at ten o'clock. Wrote home.

All quiet here now.

April 6. Lt. Martin came in, he has his business all straightened out, and has been reinstated to his position.[43] Snook and Crosby[44] came back from sick leave. Had inspection, then moved out to the open field, to the place assigned us in case of an attack. The colonel is sick, and Capt. Clarke is in command of the regiment. Two companies of the 3rd Cavalry men out scouting but found nothing.

Our old brigadier general Innis N. Palmer is in command of this post now. When he came in yesterday, one of the first questions he asked, "Was the 85th N.Y. here?"

The revenue cutter has moved over by fort Anderson.

April 7. Ordered to move at a moments notice, with three days rations in our haversacks, and seven in wagons.

Fell into line at three o'clock this afternoon, marched down to the dock and boarded the *Wheel Barrow* and crossed the river, then marched out to the fort on the glade, and camped for the night.

Our Genl. Wessells is north on leave of absence. Genl. Frank B. Spinola is in command of this movement, which is to raise the siege of Little Washington. Spinola is or was a New York fireman.[45] he wears a big red shirt collar over all. He is big specimen of a man. Now we will see how much of a fighter he is.

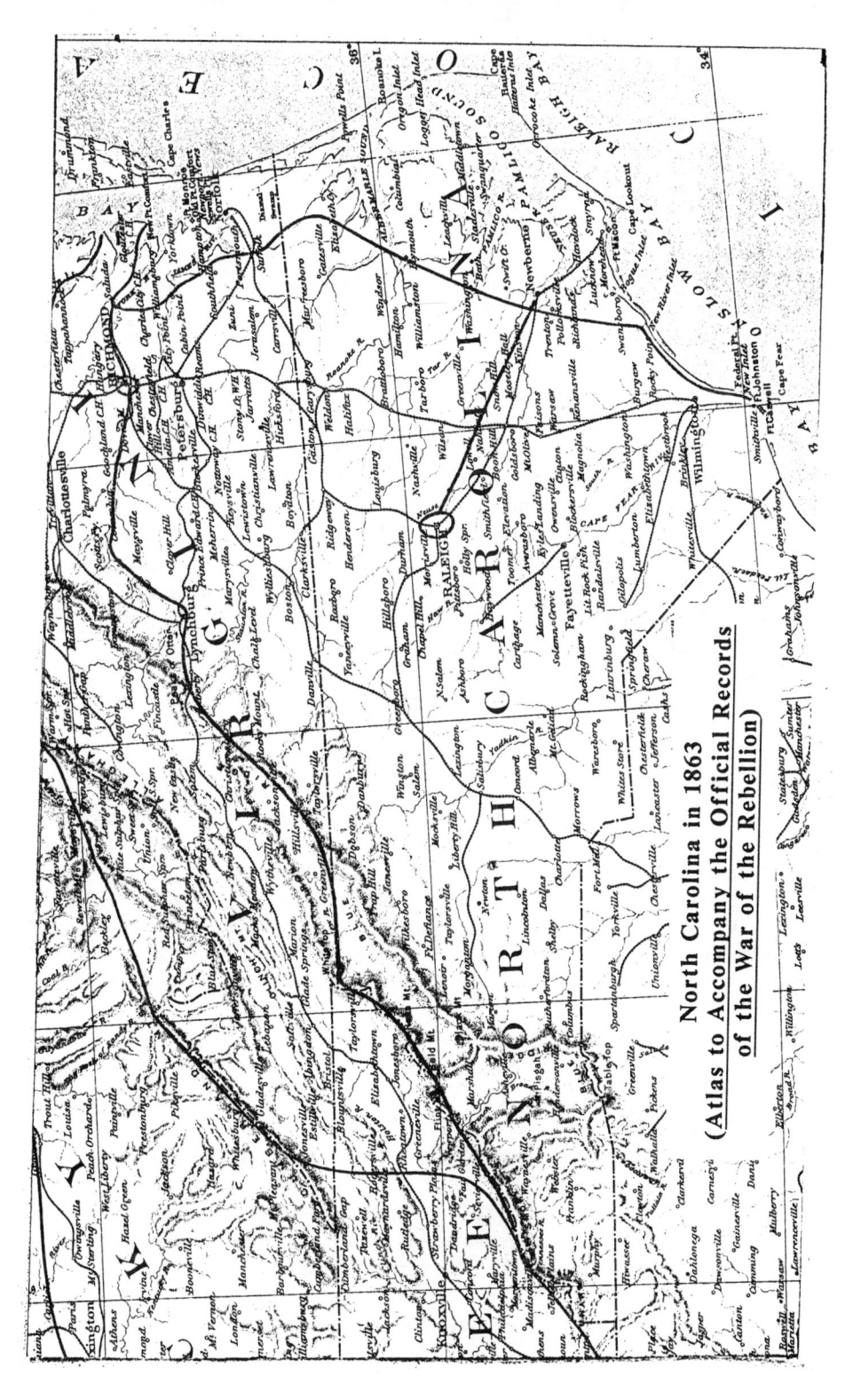

North Carolina in 1863
(Atlas to Accompany the Official Records of the War of the Rebellion)

April 8 [1863]. We hung around untill nearly noon, then fell in and marched towards Little Washington. The roads are bad, and the water is deep in places where the roads run through the swamps. Marched thirteen miles, and camped for the night. very tired.

April 9. Up early made coffee and was on the road at six o'clock. Struck the rebel pickets at Blounts Creek Mills.[46] Our brigade was in the lead, we drove the rebs across the creek, which is quite wide; and very deep here. As they crossed they took up the planks. The road here is flanked on either side by a large swamp, so we could not get near enough to do any good. our artillery shelled them a short time, the rebs returning the compliment. At their first fire they wounded Capt. Belcher of the Rhode Island battery.[47] He is Genl. Spinola's right hand man. this scared Spinola so that he gave the command "About face March"! The men in our rear were Penn. nine months men. this is their first experience. When that command was given they obeyed it very promptly and thinking that the rebs were going to cut off our retreat to Newbern, they struck a trot or rather a run, and as we were marching left in front, it made hard work for us. We made eleven and a half miles, in two and one half hours, over the worst kind of corduroy road. We marched nearly half way back to Newbern and camped at about 9 o'clock.[48] a used up lot of men, footsore and weary, with hardly life enough to make coffee.

One of the worst night marches we ever had.

April 10. Up this morning at daylight, not much rested. After coffee, we took up the line of march for Newbern again. after a good many stops we reached the banks of the Neuse river at 2 p.m. inside our picket lines. Tired does not express it. Our regiment went down by the Old Gaskins house, one company goes on picket, two to support a piece of artillery, the rest of us went out in open field to protect the troops while crossing the river to the city.

This has been one of the grandest moves on record. The New York Herald reporter who accompanied Spinola on this trip said "Frank's military qualifications are not very brilliant, but he has good horse sense." Our boys doubt the statement.

Our old man Wessells has returned. He was on the veranda of the Gaskins house, listening to our music at Blount Creek, and kept saying that he was afraid his children would get into trouble. He calls us his "children," and we call him "Dad." If he had been in command of us we would have had more than two or three hurt, before he would have left the rebels up there. Genl. Wessells is a fighter, and we have great confidence in him. After making several attempts to cross the river, as the transportation was limited, our company took the large boat of the 92nd boys, and pulled over to our own responsibility. went to our barracks and turned in a very tired crowd.

April 11 [1863]. We went to bed last night at four o'clock this morning and got up this afternoon between two and three o'clock, then got something to eat.

The man who ordered this last move, had better order one more, and then order his coffin. We went to bed very early to night.

April 12, Sunday. after inspection the captain told us that we looked a great deal better than he felt.[49] Dress Parade.

April 13. On picket up on the railroad bridge.

Sergeant Underhill of Co. E (85th)[50] has been courtmarshalled and sentenced to have one half of his head shaved, to be paraded before the regiment with a placard on his back - coward - at dress parade, and confined in fort Totten for one year.

This afternoon the sentence was executed. He was a coward at the battle of Kinston Dec. 14/62. Our sergeant Z. W. Gooding was also court marshalled for cowardice before the enemy, at the same battle, he was reduced to the ranks.

Its rather tough on the boys, but very proper. It takes all there is of one to stand up and be a man. There is no place here for cowards.

If Colonel Belknap was served a dose of court marshalled, and dismissed the service, it would be correct.

April 14. Slept nearly all night. Heavy fireing in the direction of Little Washington. Off picket at 3. p.m.

April 15. Rained last night, pleasant now. Genl. Spinola has crossed the river again. Wrote home and another letter.

Lieut. Foote,[51] a nephew of Genl. Wessells and an Aid-de-camp on his staff tells this story on the general.

The reason that the general went north was that his wife very ill and afterwards she died. after the funeral, he and some of the ladies of his family were traveling through the country, and stoped at a tavern, the ladies going into the parlor, while he stoped in the barroom by the fire, his head bowed down. The landlady saw him in that position, went out and came back with pan full of doughnuts, and handed them to him, saying "here soldier are doughnuts, help yourself, they will do you good." he put a few into his jacket and ate some, after thanking her for her kindness.

The general had on his big blue cavalry overcoat, and there was nothing to indicate his rank, and he did not inform her as to his rank.

He is a soldier and a gentleman every inch of him. We are dead in love with "Dad" Wessells.

April 16. Genl. Foster came in this morning on the steamboat *Escort* which ran the rebels batteries, on the Far river, which sent twenty shots through her hull, killed two pilots at the wheel. one was a black man. Foster having a very narrow escape, as he had just got out of his berth, as a shot went through where his head lay.

A brigade came in from Port Royal, S.C. another brigade has gone up to Bachelders creek for picket duty.

signed the half years clothing receipts.[52] I have paid $15.95 worth. Have orders to move at six o'clock tomorrow morning. Bed time.

April 17 [1863]. Company drill this forenoon. Orders to move at 3 P.M. when we fell in and moved down to the wharf, where we lay untill 11. P.M. then went on board the steamer *Allison*, and crossed the river. moved out by the Hooker house & camped.

April 18. Up this morning before sunrise, made coffee, but did not move untill 8 A.M. Our brigade is in the rear. There are two divisions, with Genl. Foster in command. Wessells has command of his own brigade. Roads are very bad.

We reached Blunt's [Blount's] Creek, and camped for the night. The rebs had a strong position here, if they had held it they could have made us trouble, as it was, they spiked their guns and left. We are going through to Little Washington, sure, this time.

April 19, Sunday. up at daylight, made coffee, and pulled out on the road, which we found to be very good. A company of 3rd N.Y. Cavalry charged 4 companies of rebel cavalry. Captured one Captain and several privates, and their regimental colors.[53] We passed a good many rebel camps, now deserted. When we reached the rebel blockade in the river (which was made by sinking old vessels in the channel) our forces split and took different roads.

Our brigade taking the direct road to Little Washington, passing rifle pits which extended for miles on either side of the road. Good works to fight behind. Camped to night at four corners, near Trinity Parochial school, and about three miles from Little Washington. Wessells used the school building for his headquarters. I am detailed for heardquarter guard. The Old Man told his Adjutant Genl. to call his boys at four o'clock in the morning, so they could have time to make coffee, before the march.

April 20. Little Washington is in our hands yet. The rebels have left for parts unknown. they must have thought we were to[o] many for them. Us headquarter guards slept in the kitchen of the big house last night, and did not wake up untill the brigade had started, but we caught up very soon. Our regiment is in the lead to day,[54] and crossed the long river bridge into the city at 8. A.M. The bridge was full of barrels of turpentine.

It was the intention to burn it, but we were too soon for them.

We marched through the city [Washington] and down to an old saw mill on the bank of the river, using the mill for our quarters. This is a pretty city for a small one, lying high on the Far river, Newbern is not to be compared to it for beauty, and location. The citizens keep very close, and those that show them selves, look kind o'sheepish.

There was a great rejoicing in here when the rebels were outside. every thing was prepared to give them a grand reception as soon as an entrance was effected. We made the grand entry first, as we hoped to.

There is a report that the colonel of the 27th Mass was going to surrender the city for a sum of money, but Genl. Foster reached here in time to stop it. that is on his first trip up.

The 27th Mass a three years regiment and the 44th Mass, a nine months regiment were all the troops in town during the seige, and three small gunboats in the river.

The 44th Mass have always said that they did not come down here to fight, but just to hold places. they have had lots of fun holding this place. How we blackguard them along that line, and they have to take it. The rebs made nothing in their attempt to take this place.

April 21 [1863]. Slept in the saw dust last night. Made a turn of the town, the boys here had good works to lay behind. Every company had a bomb proof to crawl under.[55] It is fun to hear the 27th boys blackguard the 44th fellows on their holding places.

On the opposite of the river the rebs had a battery of Whitworth[56] guns which throw a shot & shell pointed at both ends and make a terrible howling in its flight through the air. The darkies call the shells cucumbers, and its very laughable to hear them describe them as they came through the air.

Plenty of fresh fish here very cheap. On a small island in the river our men are building a water battery to command the river.[57] The island is called the Castle.

Lots of fun on the river in the dugouts, or cooners as the natives call them. They are canoes dug out of a gum tree log. they are very light, with a round bottom and sharp at both ends, which makes it very hard to ride in them, as they tip over very easy. It takes lots of practice to be able to manage them I should think. Capt. Charlie King of Co. A was a little sprung today, when he thought he could ride one. he went all right a short way when over he would go into the water, which was up to his arm pits. some of the boys right up the canoe, and help him in, when after a short way over he would go. then the crowd would yell. But Charlie was to[o] drunk to sense it. The steamers *Escort* and *Thos Collyer* are in from Newbern.

April 22. Nothing going to day but fun, and lots of it. Part of the troops have gone to Newbern. Spinola's brigade[58] are coming here, for garrison duty, and we are going to Newbern.

Peckham of Co. I.[59] is in jail, for steeling money from a "nigger" barber.

April 23 [1863]. The shed in which Co. D. 3rd Cav. kept their horses, blew down last night. A number of us went up to assist in getting them out. It was a horrible sight to see the poor horses crushed and mangled. One fine horse had his hind parts crushed under a heavy timber, which held him fast, his head and fore legs were all right, and as he stood up on his fore legs, swaying his head back and forth, and trying to pull the rest of his body from under the timber, was a most pitiable sight, one ever to be remembered. We could not release him from the timbers, and we dare not shoot him, without an order from the officer in command of the company, so this poor horse and all the others had to suffer a long time. It was cruel enough. 16 were killed outright, and a number had to be shot.

The steamer *Long Island* came in with troops. We had lots of fun on the river with the canoes.

April 24. The steamer *Phoenix* has left with troops. Company drill this morning, just to keep us out of mischief.

At 12:30, our regiment went on board the steamer *Thos. Collyer.* when we steamed down the river, we passed the rebel works, which were very formidable, and were of no avail. When we came in sight the other day, they moved out quick.

We reached the Pamlico Sound about sundown. here we found the *Phoenix* at anchor. she had broken her main shaft. Passing us a line, which we made fast, we took her in tow, which made our progress slower. When we reached the mouth of the Neuse river we anchored for the night, as our pilot was not familliar enough with the river to run at night. We have had thus far a very pleasant trip.

April 25. Bancroft and I bunked together last night, slept well. We reached Newbern at noon. On our way to the barracks, we met the pay master, who told us to hurry up & sign the rolls, and he would pay us. After dinner we signed the rolls, and drew four months rations of greenbacks.[60]

April 26, Sunday. Inspection. Went down town and had a shave. Dress parade. Letter from home, and David. Quiet.

April 27. No drill this forenoon. Battalion this afternoon. Lieut. Martin presented Captain Clarke with a handsome sword, in behalf of the company.

Sent father $25.00 to day. went down town. Good times here now.

April 28 [1863]. Rained last night, and still at it. Company drill. Wrote Sarah. Letter from home, Frank Chapin and Russ. Wright, also two papers. Tom Such[61] came in. he has been sick up north.

Dress parade.

April 29. Co. Drill this morning, and battalion this afternoon. Dress parade to night. Every thing is quiet here.

April 30. Mustered to day by Col. Lehman of the 103rd Pa.[62] Drill and dress parade.

May 1. A letter from father containing a fish line and hooks. Company and battalion drill. Orders were read on parade, to draw our baggage on board the steamer *Long Island* at six o'clock tomorrow morning, and the regiment on board at twelve o'clock, and leave for Plymouth, N.C.[63]

Went down town and bought some smoking tobacco. Had our last stag dance to night. The boys feel well. Co. B. 85th Regt. N.Y.S.V. are all right.

May 2. Steamer *Long Island* burned to the waters edge last night. The right wing of our regiment went on board of the steamer *Massasoit*, the left wing on steamer *Emille*. this morning at an early hour, when all was in readiness we steamed down the river into and up the Sound on our way to Plymouth N.C.

It was delightful riding on the water. At night I spread my blanket on the open deck near the pilot house. The water was as smooth as glass, with not a ripple on it. The sun went down a ball of fire in the water, as it were, and the moon came up out of the water round and full, a ball of fire. they seemed to balance one another, half in and half out of the water. It was a grand sight.

May 3. Slept well last night. About midnight the captain of our boat thought he would anchor and not run all night, but just then he saw the *Thos. Collyer* a head of us (she had four hours the [head] start of us) and said that "he would either run by her, or run her out of the water." So he ordered on a full head of steam and away we went, by daylight we were ahead of every thing. This boat is the fastest in these waters and this trip is one of the best I ever had. Very pleasant to day.

We arrived here in Plymouth, N.C. about noon to day. After we disembarked we went and laid in the shade untill the *Thos. Collyer* arrived with the left wing of our regiment, when we marched up into the town.

Our officers tried to get us all into an old building but we were to[o] numerous and could not see the point. Our company went into another old building by our selves. Good for us.

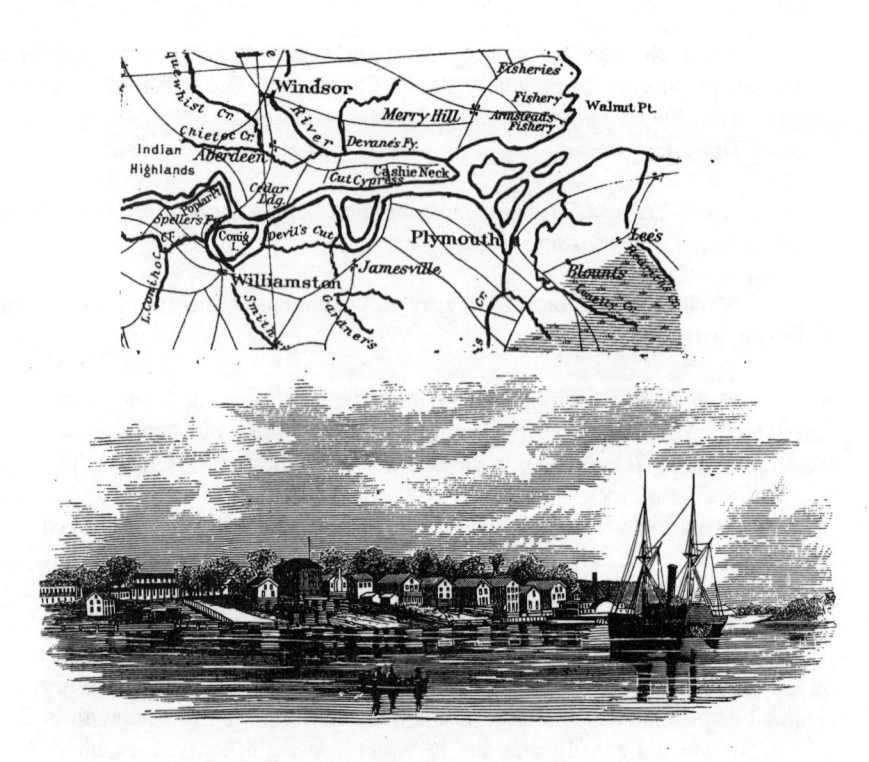

Plymouth, N.C., 1863

May 4 [1863]. This is a queer town, it was burned by the rebel cavalry last fall.[64]

It is a sea port town and a port of entry and has a custom house. the 26th, 25th and 2 Co's of the 27th Mass are on duty here, [and] are to leave soon. fish are plenty and cheap. Every body likes fish.

May 5. This morning our company was detailed for picket duty on the Washington road. I was on the last post out, at the forks of the road, two miles from town. Plenty of eggs and milk. they tasted good. At dark we were drawn in to the woods. Smith[65] and I acted as corporals so we lay down together. The rain came down in torrents and soon we were drowned out. then got up and built up a crib of rails, then covered the top with rails, spread our blankets on and went to sleep and let it rain. But we got beautifully wet, soaked. This is the first time I ever acted as a non-commissioned officer.

May 6. It has cleared off fine this morning. We went out [to] the out post again, got our breakfast. built up large fires of pine fence rails and dried out our blankets and clothes, as every thing was as wet as a rag. we were relieved at ten o'clock.

Had orders to be ready to go on a scout at midnight, but they were countermanded, but we go at eight in the morning.

May 7 [1863]. The orders of yesterday are countermanded again. This afternoon we went up and cleared off our camp ground by a small fort the 45th Mass. began. Only six companies are to be here, the best stay in town. things are working well.

May 8. I am just twenty one years old to day sometime. We went up and put up our tents. we stockaded them all four feet high and have floors in them. They are all in good shape, a fine camp. We have orders to go out scouting to night at twelve o'clock. I am not going as I am on picket tomorrow.
That is good for me, once.

May 9. the boys went out last night and I on picket this morning. I am on the Boyles Mill road near where the old mill stood. my post is on a point out in the river,[66] which I reach with canoe, all I have to do is to prevent small boats from passing up and down the river. I caught some fine fish to day.

May 10, Sunday. I was relieved this morning at nine o'clock. Slept good last night.
Wrote home. Our quarters are good.

May 11. Went to work and fixed up our tent. On fatigue this afternoon.[67] eight of us did not do enough to put in tea. We are finishing the fort,[68] we carry the earth on the parapet in or on [our own] hand barrows.[69] Went down town (its a mile) and bought some things.
Stillman, Snook and Shepherd[70] are in with me. they are the worst set I was ever in with. So taking us all together, we are not much.

May 12. Fixed up our quarters some. On fatigue this afternoon, on every day now.

May 13. On fatigue at the fort. We are getting along with it pretty well.

May 14. On camp guard first relief number four. Very hot to day. Rained this afternoon. We have fixed up awnings of evergreens in front of our tents.
Letter from home. all well there.

May 15. Came off guard at eight o'clock. Stillman and I fixed up our walk, it is brick. We have the nicest street in the battalion.

The rebels have captured two of our mail boats on the canal which runs from Norfolk, Va. to the Albemarle Sound.[71] A very bold move for them.

May 16 [1863]. On fatigue this afternoon as usual, but none this afternoon, as we have to clean up for inspection tomorrow. We are getting our fort along well. Our camp begins to look up. It beats any thing in Plymouth.[72]

May 17, Sunday. Inspection this 8 A.M. Cleaned up. Wrote home and to the 148th N.Y. boys at Norfolk, Va. Parade to night. the companies from down town were up with us.

May 18. On camp police this forenoon and fatigue this afternoon. Companies C, and I, have gone out on an expedition with the gunboats.
We don't know where.

May 19. On picket on the Columbia road three of us and Tom Porter corporal went down to the post on the river bank (Roanoke).[73] We were close to the house of an old union man, who made us go in and eat with him, but we finished nearly every thing though. The old man is a true blue and has four sons in the union army. Corporal and I were sitting in the back room by the fire (All fires here have the open fire place) for it is very cool here on the river in the evening. One of the little girls was telling us about her brothers in our army. (The 2nd loyal N.C.) how one of them was captured by the rebels, and made his escape. Porter said "he was pretty sharp, wasn't he." she said "yes he's an apt child." Very good for an eight year old.

May 20. Came off picket at ten o'clock. Have orders to be ready with three days rations to go on the gunboats *Commodore Perry* at this 7 P.M. Our full company (B) an company (E) of our regiment and one company from the 101st Pa. were there on time. The *Commodore Perry* is or had been an old North[ern] ferry boat (a double ender) and carries eight (8) nine inch shell guns and one 12 pound Napoleon (brass) which is mounted as a howitzer with a caster wheel under the tail so it has only three wheels under it to be used on the deck for quick service. Orderly Jim Robinson and I slept under one of the nine inch guns. the others found as good places to spread their blankets on gun deck, or on the hurricane deck. We do not know, nor care for <u>Where</u>.

May 21. About midnight we were routed out of a sound sleep when the boatswain whistle blew and he bawled out A-l-l h-a-n-d-s u-p a-n-c-h-o-r. The anchor up we steamed down the river into the Sound and up the Chowan river. here we joined the gunboat *Whitehead* which carried a one hundred pound parrot forward, and the *Valley City* which carries four 32 pounders and 2 12# brass pieces. We are after those two mail boats that were captured on the canal by the Reb's the other day.

The river (Chowan) leads into or rather is called the Blackwater where it leaves North Carolina and enters into Virginia. It is very crooked in places. so crooked and our boat is so long and wide that we have to take a line ashore and make fast to a tree then by the use of the capstain and pull her nose out of the bank. The sailors call it warping the corners which are so short that the boat cannot be steered around them. We anchored tonight in a dense swamp so that the guerillas could not molest us, but the musquetoes could and did. The birds are very large down this way.

Last fall when our brigade was in Suffolk, Va. we made a demonstration at Franklin, Va. This boat and others were to co-coperate with us with this in the lead. the water was low [and] the river crooked so the boat got aground. In the mean time the rebels were busy down stream and cut the trees on both banks and let them fall in the stream [with] their tops touching. This boat being a double ender did not have to turn around when her nose was out of the mud but on the way down the stream when the tree blockade was reached the rebels boarded her both bow and stern and drove the men from their guns and into the gang ways and would have had the boat in a short time but a Masters Mate - a long lanky fellow - spring to the boat howitzers and turned it on them, firing two shots of shrapnel when the rest of the crew mustered up courage, turned in & helped clear the decks, cut a passage through the trees then on down stream. That Masters Mate and three others of the crew were given bronze medals by the Secretary of the Navy. I saw one which had this inscription on "Jack Quinlan for his bravery up the Blackwater Oct. 17, 1862." His stunt was this - He swam ashore with a small line fast to him and made fast to a large hawser, which pulled ashore, made it fast to a tree, waited untill the corner was warped, then casting off the line he swam to the boat. All of this was under a heavy gun fire from the rebels, some deed, some man.

May 22 [1863]. This morning we steamed twenty or thirty miles up the river when our boat ran aground. The *Whitehead* was in the lead - then the *Valley City*. Our boat had not been aground but a short time, when the *Whitehead* came back and said that they could not go any farther up. After she pulled our boat off we all came down the river untill we came to where the Nottaway river joins the Blackwater,[74] which we ascended as far as Murfeesboo, N.C. There is a large Young Ladies Seminary here. Just before the *Whitehead* reached there, she threw a hundred pound shot over the town. Every old woman in town said that the shot went right over her head. Of course it did!

The Seminary had been turned into a hospital. Then a part of the crews of the two boats ahead went ashore, where they found large quantities of army stores, bacon, ham, lard, tobacco - various other things. among other things were two rebel flags. All of which was confiscated.

May 23. About midnight we up anchor and started down stream. In less than a mile we grounded again hard, so much so that we could not help ourselves as usual. The other gunboats had down so we had to send up rocket signals for them to <u>return</u> and help us off. In a short time they came back and both gave us a line, which broke at the first pull. several lines were broken in the attempt. We were hard aground sure and no mistake. Then the boats came along side and then passed out and over our heavy ship stores and solid shot[75] then they [still] could not pull us off. In the mean time we had placed our infantry pickets on both sides of the river. On the south side was a very high bold bluff, on the north was low meadow land. A few miles above Murfeesboro the rebels had a light battery stationed. they ahd been told of our fix. The bluff was so high, that the guns of our boats could not be elevated enough to be of any good on that bluff. While the rebels could plunge their shot and shell on us in great shape. We would have been at their mercy. Or as one of the boys expressed it "Hell would have been to pay and no pitch hot."

Us blue coats not on picket were looking around for cover in case of must. The officers of the gunboats were discussing the question of blowing our boat up. as they were talking it over, the tide came up our boat was lifted out of the mud, our picket taken on board and down the river we went. All hands were thankful for that bit of tide. Tides are good for something. Sometimes. We made good time on down trip. When we reached the Chowan river we stopped at a saw mill and took on a quantity of lumber. While here the rudder of the *Whitehead* became disabled, so that the *Valley City* had to take her in tow the rest of the trip down. When we reached a landing opposite Winfield we anchored, when the boats officers went ashore to a farm house where they were acquainted and stayed untill Sundown, then run ten miles near a fishery. Here all hands went ashore (leaving enough sailors on board to guard ship) and into the country three miles to a large farm house which we surrounded. of course the dogs were plenty here as they were in or on all the plantations. they gave us a great reception with their bark, When Capt. Flusser[76] sung out, "stop those dogs barking." they stopped as soon as the sailors got after them.

The house was entered and searched by the officers, all that was found were two old women, one an old maid who had tongue enough for fifty woman, there was not a man in sight. Our 2nd Lieut. Charlie McHenry was poking around as was his wont on such occasions when he found an officer's cap, then he kept on poking untill he poked the owner of the cap, a Lieut. of Guerillas and an irishman at that. Charlie (who is an irishman) gave him a blessing. After this three citizens were found in different parts of the house. A great find. I was on guard in the road with others. in looking around I saw a small box fastened on a high gate post, which I soon went through. It was a mail box, in it I found four Richmond, Va. papers and a letter.[77]

We nearly ready to leave, when we heard a racket in the road. We formed our line a cross the road, ready for a fight or a foot race. when the [indecipherable] came in [it] was a buggy with a man in it. He was the rebel mail carrier. all quiet, no smugglers, or smuggled goods. we began our return to the boats, taking our prisoners with us, Mail carrier and his buggy included, reaching the boats at one o'clock in the morning. Letting the mail man and his rig go on his way. The other prisoners we took back to Plymouth.[78]

May 24 [1863], Sunday. We arrived here in Old Plymouth this morning at sunrise tired and very sleepy. "Hod" Shepherd[79] brought in five pounds of smoking tobacco. Dress parade down town to night. A letter from Father, all well at home. All quiet here as usual.

May 25. We went out and brought in some evergreen trees to fix up over our street with. Nothing going on to day. The fort is finished we have named it Fort "Dad" or rather Fort Wessells. The old general calls it the 85th redoubt in honor of the builders. We think the world of the "Old Man."

May 26. On camp guard. There is a scouting party going out to night. Part of our regiment goes with it.

May 27. Off guard this morning. Wrote home and sent papers to Father. Tom Porter[80] and I went down on the river bank to see the "Old Union Man," his little girl is sick, we took her some orange jelly. Bought it from the Sutler's of course.

May 28. Pleasant to day. fixed up our tent by putting an addition on the back where two of us can sleep. the two bunks in side of tent one above the other, gives more room for the four of us.

May 29. The scouting party that went out last night found nothing but one guerilla.[81] They let him go.

May 30. On picket on the Columbia road. On post on bank of the river. Had plenty of milk and strawberries.

May 31. Just one year ago to day the battle of Fair Oaks was fought. We had hard times then. Better now. Off picket at ten o'clock this morning. Dress parade on our camp ground to night. Wrote home.

On the scouting party the other night our Col. found one old woman who wanted a doctor very bad. The doctor visited her but found nothing the matter, but he saw a large hummock at the back of the bed. He examined it and found a man in and between the ticks. The Doctor told her that he thought that a woman that could have child twenty-two years old, with his clothes and boots on, ready to walk off needed no doctoring. The child proved to be a guerilla and a son of the old woman. Quite an interesting child that.

June 1st. Went down town to day. I think I am going to be bothered with the sore throat again. The pay rolls are here.

June 2nd [1863]. signed the pay roll this morning. Chester A. Gooding and Charles B. McNinch[82] have their discharge. Gooding is all broke down. McNinch has lost his voice.

Both were good men.

June 3. On picket on the Columbia road. Our post is near the bridge on Coneby Creek, (or rather where it was, as it is now removed) The creek is quite a stream for a creek. We use a canoe as a ferry boat as occasion requires. The citizens bring in eggs and milk in plenty. We can buy all we want very cheap. The man who boards the officers of the 101st Pa. came out and engaged a quantity of [eggs and milk from] a citizen to be delivered day after tomorrow. The boys are being paid to day. All quiet on picket[.]

June 4. Off picket at ten o'clock this morning. Drew my rations of green backs from Lt. Martin. He took my pay yesterday as I was on duty. letter from Home, all well there.

June 5. Nothing doing to day. Went down town.

June 6. On picket on Columbia road as usual. Our Sergt. John Buell in charge. On at Coneby creek. I passed[83] in two pretty girls and had to escort them in to Headquarters.

That citizen with the eggs from that man came in as he agreed to. The man came in for them as he agreed. He did not get them as that would have cut us pickets out of our eggs. The Seargt. was for letting him have them. I said us pickets must have our eggs. he told me to do as I had a mind to. I did. We took the eggs much, much to the disgust of the officers man. He told me that he would remember me.[84]

Mush and milk for supper.

June 7, Sunday. A man citizen came in this morning and told us pickets that the guerillas had run him out from his home in the lower part of the county. he had been in the swamps sixteen days and said it was mean to keep a man away from his wife so long. Poor fellow. Wonder what he thought of me.

A big rain last night accompanied by terrific thunder and lightning. The rain poured. We could not see our hands before our face only as [when] a flash lightning lighted the road way and creek, we had to keep our ears open to every sound. Morning came on as it has always ever since. Last night was the worst one I was on picket. worst as to storm. Were relieved at ten o'clock. Dress parade down town.

June 8. A boat came in to day from Norfolk, Va. the first that has come through the canal, since those mail boats were captured. Five of our companies of our regiment went down to the lower part of the country on the steamer *Massasoit* (which is the general's dispatch boat). The cavalry went overland. They are going to try and clean out the guerillas down there, if they can.

June 9 [1863]. Detailed for camp guard but exchanged for picket with Z. W. Gooding (Deacon we call him). No excitement. Plenty of eggs and milk. The *Massasoit* came in to day.

June 10. Off picket this morning early. Quiet last night. Letter from home and 148th N.Y. boys.

June 11. The boys who were court martialed for neglect of duty, are out of jail. Their sentence has not been read yet.

June 12. A flag of truce from the rebels came and ordered the general to surrender and to remove the women and children by seven o'clock tomorrow morning. A big thing we can't see [doing] it.

June 13. On picket on the post to the right of the Columbia road, where there is a run way through the swamp, a nasty post. Plenty of milk, hoe cake and raspberries.

June 14. Off picket at ten this A.M. Dress parade down town.
The Colonel J. H. Belknap and the Surgeon Wm. M. Smith have resigned.

June 15. We have drawn regulation hats, much to our disgust. They are of black felt, stiff rims, one side cocked up with a brass spread eagle to keep it in place. I feel as if I was going to have the fever and ague. I feel bad all over.

June 16. No better to day.

June 17. Reported to the doctor at sick call. I surely have the fever and ague.

June 18. Feel a bit better to day.

June 19. "Shakes" again. tough.

June 20. This is my off day, no shake. A boat from Portsmouth, Va. came in by the way of the canal. With Captain Griswold of the 148 N.Y. and a detail from that regiment as guard. My old schoolmate Frank Chapin, of

Plymouth, North Carolina
June 12th, 1863

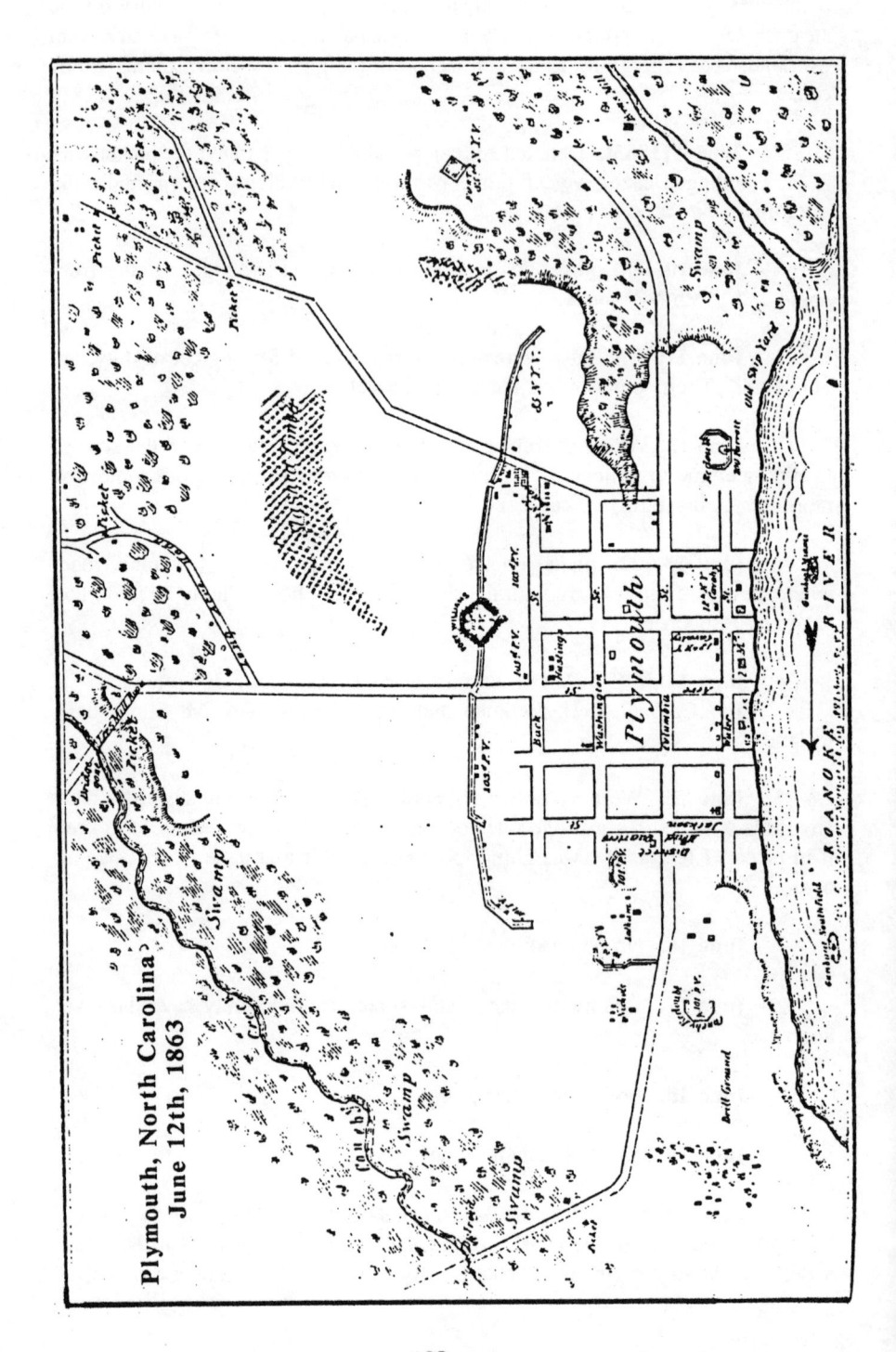

Chapinville, my home, was one of them. It did me all sorts of good to talk over old times with him. During the Crimean War,[85] we used to read about it and talk it over and said that there would be nothing for us to do when we got to be men. We have found that we have plenty to do. His visit helps out. I feel better for it. Letter from home.

June 21 [1863]. Another long visit with Frank to day. They leave this 6. P.M. Sent a letter by him to be mailed at Portsmouth, Va. for the home folks. Colonel Belknap went to day, Lieut. Whitney of A. rung the old fellows nose, just as a token of good friendship.

June 22. Rained hard last night and still at it. Feels better. My visit with Frank Chapin has done me a lot of good. One good boy.

June 23. Company drill this afternoon. Our B company and F company were together.

June 24. Company drill again this P.M.

June 25. On picket on the Washington road. First post to the right.[86]

June 26. Had a good time last night, only it rained most to[o] much. Relieved at nine A.M. Two of the 103 Pa. were leaving their post. The officers are getting to be very strict all of a sudden.
When on picket duty three men are on one post at a time. One of us keeps guard during the day and the others go into town or out beyond the picket line for forage. At night we divide into three equal parts as near as possible and each one takes a trick at it.

June 27. Rained last night. Two companies of the 12th N.Y. cavalry came in last night to relieve those who are here. Tough lot of men.

June 28, Sunday. Rained last night. Inspection this morning. Bancroft and I went out and picked some blackberries. Had parade down town to night.

June 29. On camp guard. we hae sentry boxes now to protect us from the hot sun. Rains again. Leant [lent] the orderly $5.00.

June 30. We were mustered for pay to day by Col. Morris of the 101 Pa. One year ago we were mustered during the seven days battle, where many a poor fellow was mustered out for good.[87] All quiet.

July 1. Rainy to day as usual. Received two letters and a paper. Company drill to night.

July 2 [1863]. Rained last night. Our company and company [blank] together. Capt. Clarke has been promoted to Lt. Col. Good for him.

July 3. Firing on picket this morning. The report is that the rebels shot two of our cavalry videttes.[88] Well they do not amount to much no how. I mean the 12th cavalry.

July 4. On picket on the Washington road, on the extreme right in an open field. Corporal Tom Such and I are to gether. Had hard tack, raw pork, onion, coffee and a thimble full of whiskey just enough of it to make a hot sting, it gave us a good appetite. All picketers have a whiskey ration served to them. The rebels fied on the outpost pickets this morning. A cavalry raid has gone out from Newbern, N.C. and for fear that they might be cut off from that place two signal officers have been sent here to communicate with them in case they should want to run in here.

I feasted on blackberries to day. One of the boys has just returned from downtown and said that all had drawn whiskey, and that nearly all were drunk.

Seymour Smith of our company B, was putting one of the cavalry boys through the saber exercise and gave the command Return saber! the cavalry man tried to put his saber in the scabbard the wrong way. Smith said is that the way you return saber? I'll show you how when he drew back and knocked the fellow head over heels in the gutter. So much for whiskey.

July 5, Sunday. The musketers[89] were very bad last night. Had a quart of milk for breakfast with plenty of blackberries. We were not relieved untill eleven o'clock this morning. I have had a very bad head ache all day. The whole brigade is to go out. I started with our boys and got as far as down town when I told the Lieut. That I was played out. he said all right. so I fell out and came back to camp. The rest go up the river as far as Fort Gray and start from there.[90]

July 6. I do not feel very well to day. All of us here in camp are ordered to have three days rations in our haversacks and be ready to fall into the post at a moments notice. There has been conciderable firing up the river where the brigade has gone. I stood one trick on camp guard. I liked to have shook the sentry box down. This fever and ague is wearing me down to a fine point. It's a hard thing.

July 7. Heavy firing up the river last night. Our pickets were relieved this afternoon. Co. E. came in to night. I went down town and bought four loaves of bread for the boys. I do not feel much better to day.

July 8. I feel very good this morning. The firing up the river last night was our gun boats shelling Williamston. Our regiment and the 96th N.Y. went up to Gardners bridge where they found a small force in a redoubt. they had orders not to attack, but wait for the 101st Pa and the 103rd Pa to get in there rear. as they did not get there our regiment came back to the 96th camp. This morning they went back to the bridge but found nothing. So they started back and reached here to night. They were a tired lot.

July 9 [1863]. I feel tip top this morning. The mail came in last night I had three letters and a paper. The report is that Vicksburg[91] is ours and Richmond also.[92] To[o] much news for one mail. Genl. Hooker[93] is removed from the army of the Potomac and Genl. Meade is his successor, who ever he is.[94]

July 10. Feel good to day. This afternoon our company and company H were ordered to report on board the gunboat *Valley City* at six o'clock. We were aboard all right.

When the anchor was hove up we steamed down into the sound and around to the mouth of the Chowan river where we anchored for the night.

July 11. We were up this morning at three o'clock, made our coffee (we have to have our coffee, some way or other) then the sailors began to get things in readiness for going ashore. We had the little tug *Dollie* a ship launch - (which was one of the kind of gunboats that was used in the war with Tripoli it was propelled with oars) and the cutter which belonged to our *Valley City*. us soldiers boarded the *Dollie* and the cutter. The sailors put a 12 pound boat howitzer on the launch which was manned by them. everything being ready we up anchor and steamed up to the mouth of Salmon creek, where we anchored. Then the *Dollie* took the cutter in tow. I was on the cutter, the launch manned by the sailors took the lead and we went up the creek about four miles to a landing, that was on a big plantation. Here we found a large quantity of salt, which we put on board of the *Dollie*. on the bank of the creek we found a large open shed in which was hundreds of 1/2 barrels of herring in brine, for the rebel army. This was a supply depot for stores for the rebels. We knocked in the head of the barrels and dumped the fish into the creek. The rivers and streams here abouts are full of herring. Then we found a number of horses and mules, all were branded on the shoulder C.S.A. these we shot then they were of no use to the C.S.A. After we had finished our work there we went down to the next plantation a mile or two (the boats following in the creek.) here we halted untill they reached us. Here we asked the man who owned the plantation if he had any salt, he said "a little." We found a half ton, which was put on the *Dollie*. The man had lied a bit. Then we found a quantity of ham, bacon, tobacco, snuff, cotton, and other stuff. We burned the cotton, the other things we put on the *Dollie*. In an out building we found a large quantity of new fishing seines[95] which was worth $20,000 it was estimated. They was burned by whom no one knew. Capt. Furnace of Navy said it was the soldiers, Capt. Brown of the army said it was the sailors. Guess if the truth was known the two Captains were the ones who did it. It was a good job any way.

All of the stuff we destroyed and captured was prize money for the navy. We soldiers received nothing.

All things being ready we boarded the *Dollie* and cutter and steamed down to the *Valley City* and loaded our "truck" and ourselves on board of her when up anchor, and made for Plymouth. when we arrived in sight of the town, the gunboat *Commodore Perry* did not answer our signals right. (The navy has a code of signals to let each other know if every thing is all right) then our vessel beat to quarters, the deck, her guns were run out. the fires in cooks galley were put out. the hatches were down, all hands were at their stations in less time than it takes for me to tell it. Us soldiers had to climb any where to get out of the way of the sailors.

There had been a mistake in the signals that was all. But Capt. Furnace took no chances. he said the town might have been captured during our absence. We reached the dock at 2:30 P.M. Every one of us soldiers had a ham or chicken in our hand, we made quite a parade as we marched through the town to our camp.

July 12 [1863], Sunday. On picket on the Washington road. The news is that Lee's army is all cut to pieces and that Vicksburg is taken sure. All quiet on the lines.

July 13. Off picket early. do not feel very well, did not sleep last night.

July 14. Nothing doing. Adjt. Aldrich came in today.

July 15. Monthly inspection by Lieut. Coates.[96] He is Assistant Inspector General of the District. One fine man of company H.

July 16. On picket. We have orders to keep a sharp look out for there is a large force of rebels in our front and an attack was expected. Lieut. Welch is scared.[97]

July 17. No excitement last night. Had hoe cake and milk for breakfast. When we were relieved this morning we had to report at Head Quarters, so we did not get into camp untill nearly noon. Company drill this afternoon. I did not have to go for once.

July 18. The report is that all the batteries around Charleston are taken except Sumter and Wagner, and that Genl. Meade is giving Lee all the can tend to.[98]

142

July 19 [1863], Sunday. Inspection this morning. Dress parade down town to night.

July 20. On picket on the Washington road. On the reserve with Lieut. McHenry. had a good time. plenty of eggs and milk.

July 21. Hoe cake[99] and milk for breakfast. Relieved at nine o'clock. I came in a head of the rest as I do not feel well. This picket duty uses me up for two or three days after I am off.

July 22. Nothing doing to day. Wrote home and received a letter with Sarah's photograph. Three or four riots up north.[100]

July 23. Reported to the Doctors. Had battalion drill. Our picket lines hae been drawn in nearer town because we have become so reduced by sickness that we cannot man them. It's a good thing. Wish we were out of this town as there is so many swampss around us that we have the fever and ague all the time.

July 24. Nothing doing to day.

July 25. Had hoe cake and milk for breakfast. Don't feel well.

July 26, Sunday. Inspection this morning. Received marching orders, three days rations, light marching order. We get under way about noon. Our whole brigade and a section of artillery. We took the Washington road, untill we came to the Jamesville road then we took that.[101] It was hard marching, a good many fell out, I did for once. For the first time I rode in an ambulance. We arrived at Jamesville at sundown. It was burned last fall by our cavalry so that there is nothing left but many old stacks of chimneys. Made coffee and turned in.

July 27. Slept good last night. This expedition is to draw the attention of the rebels while Genl. Foster makes a raid in another direction. He has gone up the Chowan river with a fleet of boats. We started this morning at eight o'clock and marched all day. We [Companies B. and F] went seven miles out of our way to find the rebels. We found their pickets at Fosters Mills just at dusk, drove them in, tumbled a few shells after them, burned the saw mill, then made tracks for the rear very lively with two of the cavalry men wounded in their hips. Col. Lehman of the 103 Pa. who is in command of this outfit got scared and ran us back to Jamesville, where we arrived a little after midnight. It began to rain about dark and has kept it up ever since.

I am about used up. so are all of the men for that matter.

July 28 [1863]. I feel old this morning. A good many of the men did not come in untill this morning. Part of them have gone down the river in canoes. I crawled into an old army wagon and rode into camp here at Plymouth at half past four. It has rained all day.

July 29. The General[102] with a small force went up the river on the steamer *Massasoit*. Cavalry went by land. It has rained all day.

July 30. It has rained all day. All quiet.

July 31. On picket on the Washington road. It rained this afternoon, and as soon as it stopped I had a shake of the ague, so I went into camp, when the fever came on. Its a tough proposition.

Aug. 1. Do not feel very well. Lieut. McHenry went North after conscripts.[103] good for him. All quiet.

Aug. 2. Had another twist of the fever and ague. I liked to have shook my toe nails off.

Aug. 3. Feel very good to day. The mail came in to night. Also our New Colonel[104] and Major. No mail for me, but two pairs of socks and a box of pills.

Aug. 4. Do not feel very well, but then . . .

Aug. 5. To day the same as yesterday, more so.

Aug. 6. A detail of 100 men under Lt. Col. Clark went out on the steamer *Washington Irving* for Roanoke Island.[105] Part of the 96th N.Y. have gone down to guard the canal at Currituck bridge. Orderly J. B. Robinson and Steve Green[106] have gone home on a furlough. I went down to do provost guard duty. Had to come back. Could not stand it.

Aug. 7. Reported in quarters this morning, so as not to go out in the hot sun.

Aug. 8. On camp guard. Feel well.

Aug. 9, Sunday. off guard. cleaned up. Our boys ought to be back.

Aug. 10. On camp guard as usual. We have hard work to find men enough to do duty. It is sickley [sic] here.

Aug. 11 [1863]. Came off guard early. A regiment of colored troops came in last night. They are a duskey lot of soldiers.

Aug. 12. On picket on Washington road. Mead[107] and I had plenty of green corn.

Aug. 13. The musquitoes were so bad last night we could not sleep. Relieved at nine o'clock. came in went to bed and slept untill three o'clock. Lieut. Martin has gone to Newbern.

Aug.14. Went down this morning and saw the colored troops at guard mounting. They understand their business well. They are to do two days picket duty to our one which will make it easy for us. Our boys came in this noon, and brought the mail. I had two letters from home. On the same boat was the paymaster Walter Crane.
Signed the pay roll and at two o'clock got my ration of green backs. The paymaster and his clerk are both Ontario County, N.Y. men.

Aug. 15. The colored pickets did a lot of fireing on the lines last night. went down and got a draft from the paymaster of $18.00. Monthly inspection by Lieut. Coats.

Aug. 16, Sunday. Company inspection by Sergt. Simmons.[108]
Sent my $18.00 draft to Father. Wrote David. Had parade.

Aug. 17. I have an awful head ache. Had battalion drill. I did not go out.
Our new Colonel is a good drill master. His name is Enrico Fardella, an Italian, has seen service under Victor Emanuel and was colonel of the 101st N.Y.[109] They were called the lost children and there are between twenty five and thirty nationalities in it. When the Col. comes out on parade he has three medals on his left breast which he had won in foreign service. Hope he will win as many in our service.

Aug. 18. On camp guard. This afternoon I had a shake of the ague and had to be relieved. The shake did not last long. I had no fever with it.

Aug. 19. Reported sick this morning. Feel better this afternoon.
The order came to move our camp down town. The teams came up. We had our tents down when the order came for us not to move. Good!

Aug. 20. The mail came in this morning, nothing for me. But I did have my shake as usual.

Aug. 21 [1863]. Feel well to day. The orders are to move down town. The boys have gone down to police the ground.

Aug. 22. The "darkies" (colored troops I should say) began their firing on the picket line again last night at eleven o'clock. We fell into line and lay around for an hour or more but as there was no danger we went back to our tents. The firing was kept up all night. No doubt but the "darkies" saw some body as two or three rebel cavalrymen were seen comeing down the road but turned back. Down on the Columbia road or rather to the right of it is a picket post and . . . through the swamp is a run way. The rebel cavalry have made their brags that would get a "darkie" on picket some night. It would be a good joke on the darkies. Last night the rebels tried it on. It is always [usual] to have only one man on post at a time. The "darkies" had two on. The rebel cavalryman made a dash through the swamp with uplifted saber to cut the picket down, before he knew it the second man on post put a bullet through him, and he fell off his horse. The joke was on the "reb." The colored troops are to leave to day. Adjutant Aldrich takes command of our company to day. He is figuring for the captaincy. It seems that the Adjutant made an agreement with Capt. Clark, that if he (Clark) was ever promoted Aldrich was to take his place as Capt. Clark was promoted to Lt. Col. May 1 (1863) Lieut. Martin has resigned in consequence of Aldrich prospect of being Captain.[110]

August 23, Sunday. Inspection by Aldrich to day. Our boys came in. they have been down to Columbia on a foraging expedition and brought back a lot of sheep and other forage, besides the boys brought back lots of poultry. Last week Sunday when our new Lt. Col. Clark paid us his first visit in his new uniform. I said to him "how do you like our new commanding officer." He snapped back what is that. I repeated "how do you like our new commanding officer he is a peacock." He said nothing in reply, only grinned. Those of our boys thought I was in for it. Clark knows we do not like Aldrich. we don't like him a little bit. He is an old grannie.

Aug. 24. We moved down town to day all but Companies E. & K. who stay on the old ground. Co. K. mans the redoubt or Fort "Dad" as we call it, in honor of Genl. Wessells. Our new camp is a peach. we have good shade. The back of our tents is next to the hospital. Our company street is wide with a row of tents on each side. A party of our boys under Lt. Col. Clark went out on the Washington road and lay in ambush last night. It amounted to nothing at all.

Aug. 25. Rainy. "Nate" Wright came in sick to night from picket. I had to take his place. On outpost on Washington road. Seven of our company are detailed to go on board the boat *Washington Irving* at five o'clock to morrow morning.

Aug. 26 [1863]. This morning "Hopping Jennie" came down from Capt. Hamilton's big house with a lot of cucumbers and melons which we bought. Hamilton is a rank "sesech," his two former slaves women are still with him and does his work. Hopping Jennie and Biddy. We were relieved by the 103 Pa. Had a good dinner. Bought some postage stamps.

Aug. 27. Drew fresh mutton. I took our four rations and made a pot-pie. This is the way I made it - when the meat was cooked enough I went down to the government bakery and bought two loaves of unbaked bread just ready for the oven (had to have order signed by a commissioned officer to get it [but] had to pay for it my self). This I used for dumplings. We had a good dinner, and plenty of it. Lieut. Martin went home to day. He hated to go, none of us blame him. Our company are trying to get Capt. Coats to be our Captain. That is we want him assigned to command the company. We do not like Aldrich a little bit. He is an old grannie. Wrote home.

Aug. 29. Had milk and eggs for breakfast. This is the most desirable post on the whole picket line. Capt. Hamilton's two darkeys always [bring] in something every day.

Two years ago to day our company was mustered into the U.S. service. I subscribed for a Soldiers Memorial.[111] It is to have every man's name on it.

Aug. 30, Sunday. Inspection by Aldrich. He has been to the Doctors and has got permission of him to have command of the sick and have them all come out at all roll calls and nightly inspections, and they must not leave camp. Comment is useless on this occasion. No parade.

Aug. 31. Mustered for pay by Lt. Col. Taylor of the 101 Pa. No inspection on account of rain.

Aldrich called all the non-commissioned officers of our company together in the orderly Robinson's tent. (The orderly being out of course) To see what they thought of the propriety of making Robinson first Lieut. in place of Martin resigned. That is to jump the orderly over 2nd Lieut. McHenry. Sergts Buell, Simmons and corporal Humphrey thought it would be a good thing. But the rest could not see it in that light no how. Aldrich does not like McHenry one little bit.

Our company is so reduced in numbers that if we had no Second Lieut. we could not elect one. By jumping the orderly over McHenry we could and would have a full compliment[112] of company officers. I am afraid and hope it will not work this time. Robinson is a good boy. How he would look over McHenry!

Sept. 1. On picket on Washington road outpost. Lieut. Goodrich (he is adjutant now) gave me an order for bread for we are entirely out of rations.

We got nothing to eat out here to day. to morrow we have the promise of chicken stew for breakfast. I went into camp this afternoon and got some ham. For they have drawn rations now.

Francisco bought a big pumpkin of[f] a native, who told him it was a squash. Frandy knew better and had it made into pies. Good joke on Frandy. Every thing on the lines to day.

Sept. 2 [1863]. We had a good breakfast this morning of stewed chicken. Bill $1.00. Had all we could muster, there was nearly a milk pan full of it. Then to wind up with we ate a big water melon and two dozen peaches. Quite a meal for three boys. All quiet last night. We were relieved early. Our company have a part of an old roof to cover our new cook house with. Rains now. No inspection to night. Something is wrong somewhere.

Sept. 3. Three of our cavalry men were wounded this morning as they were going out on vidette (the line). (The videttes are in advance of the regular picket line.) by a squad of the 17th North Carolina rebel regiment.[113] The cowards! They took one prisoner, but let him go for he had the fever and ague so bad they could not bother with him for they were in a hurry to get away too.

The Genl. has ordered out a large detachment to see what is going on. It is under the command of Lt. Col. [Alexander W.] Taylor of the 101 Pa. I go. We went out about ten miles, found nothing. I had a shake of the ague, so I came back by the Warwick road which leads to the 96th N.Y. at fort Gray on the river above the town. Burlingame of Co. F. (our regt.)[114] and I came in together. we stopped at a house and had some bread and milk. We rode the last two miles to fort Gray here we found a canoe and paddled down the river to camp, where we arrived an hour before the rest of the boys and less tired. I feel like death to night.

The mail came in to night. I had four letters from home.

Sept. 4. Reported sick this morning. Wrote home. Aldrich had no inspection to night. Something is the matter.

Sept. 5. On picket on Washington road, first post to the left. Every thing is quiet. Had some stewed grapes.

Sept. 6, Sunday. Relieved early this morning. Quiet last night. Had a shake with fever. Wrote to George. Dress parade to night.

Sept. 7. Feel a trifle shakey to day. Four of our company are detailed for an expedition this afternoon. received a letter from David. Battalion drill.

Sept. 8. The boys who went out yesterday came in this morning. They went on the steamer *Massasoit* and took the *Dollie* in tow. They went down the sound as far as they could with *Massasoit*, then got on the *Dollie* and run along the shore untill they were near a large house, where a large party was on for the entertainment of five rebel soldiers from Lee's army home on furlough for a visit with their friends and were having a good time generally. when our boys surrounded the house just as they were forming on the floor for a dance, they did not finish it as our boys were in a hurry to get back to camp. They brought the five rebels with them. Mean trick, wasn't it! Had a shake to day.

Sept. 9 [1863]. Feel well to day. All quiet.

Sept. 10. On camp guard, had a shake, and quit.

Sept. 11. Feel good this morning. Drew rations of ham and potatoes. They were good. Wrote to David.

Sept. 12. I finished my shake this morning. Now I feel better and all right. I am detailed for an expedition at half past two in the morning. Good!

Sept. 13, Sunday. Up this morning at half past one o'clock. Took my breakfast and reported at the quarters of Lt. Col. Clark. He is in command of this expedition. There are one hundred and fifty men from the brigade going. When we had reported we fell in and marched down to dock and on board the steamer *Col. Rucker*. There are six army wagons with their mules on board. Every thing is ready we started down the river at half past three o'clock. we run to near the mouth of the river, when we were hailed by a small boat, which reported that the gunboat *Underwriter* was aground on small island at the entrance of the Sound. The *Underwriter* was to have been our escort on this trip. We ran down into the Sound and waited for the gunboat *Southfield* to come down, she didn't come so we up anchor and put back for Plymouth here Capt. [Horace I.] Hodges - the post quartermaster - went ashore and reported to Genl. Wessells as to how things were. The orders were to go back and back we went. The Genl. and a squad of officers followed on the steamer *Washington Irving*. This time our escort is to be the *Seymour* a small steamer that belongs to the Coast Survey and carries two twelve pound brass guns. We ran the river and across the Sound to a small town called Edenton[115] where we arrived at noon in the rain. Here we disembarked [and] formed our lines. The 101. Pa. picket the town. The rest of us go into the country with the cavalry in advance, then Lieut. Andrews with twelve men.[116] I am one of them, then the wagons, with the rest of the men bringing up the rear. We went four miles to a plantation owned by one Doctor Warren, where we found a large quantity of corn. To get this corn is what we are here for. Lt. Col. Clark sent Deyo[117] and myself out into a lane to keep a lookout which we did. We looked out some very fine melons with which we stuffed our jackets. We saw no rebels. On our way back each of us bought a pair of ducks for which we paid the cash in the shape of Elisebeth City money,[118] which was better than greenbacks with the natives. which I will mention here and explain why. Some of our boys went to Elisebeth City one time not long ago. They broke into a state bank and found a quantity [of] "money" in the shape of bills which were in the whole sheets they had not been cut, signed nor numbered. The boys took them to Plymouth, cut the sheets numbered them and signed them both President and cashier, then they could buy any thing as the natives were familiar with the money of that bank. Our brigade had bank presidents and cashiers galore. we were on the high road to prosperity. I was not on that expedition but I had some of the goods. We paid cash for our ducks once. We did not steel them. After the six wagons were loaded with corn, we started back for Edenton through the mud and rain, where we arrived at five o'clock this afternoon, Wet and cold. We were wet through and through for once. When we left the boat this morning we left our overcoats and rubber blankets on board. Deyo watched our stuff while I went for them. I found my overcoat, but Deyo's blanket was gone. I took an overcoat in place of it which came in play all right as it was heavy rain and very cold. Deyo and I went around to the stern of the boat to get out of the storm. After the wagons and mules were on board, we started for Plymouth.

It was nearly dark when we started. In a short time we heard the Capt. of the *Seymour* bellow through his trumpet for our boat to stop as he was aground. Our boat paid no attention to it but kept on its course next thing a shot went across our bows for us to heave too. We did not heave, then another shot over us. We did not stop then but kept right on and soon we were out of gun shot. The Capt. of our boat said "That the *Seymour* being a gunboat had no business to tie up to a dock." The *Seymour* was afraid that the rebels might try to capture him. The storm drove Deyo and I from off the stern then we found a place in the engine room. The engines on the boat was of the oscillating kind. We were in the room just above them and the floor under us was laid out in a diamond shape pattern. the heat from below was so great that our overcoats had the diamond pattern burned itself on the coats. But we were very warm, as well as comfortable for one night.

We ran across the sound to the mouth of the Roanoke river where we anchored for the night, it being to[o] dark to find the channel. Edenton is a very fine town. The plantation where we were contains fourteen hundred acres. We saw two large field of sugar cane. The pretty girls in Edenton made [us] think of home, only it was Sunday.

Sept. 14 [1863]. We arrived here at Plymouth this morning at eight o'clock. A tired crew. Snook[119] cooked my ducks for dinner, they were good. Battalion drill this afternoon. The first I have been on.

I was all this forenoon cleaning up my gun and straps. Monthly inspection this afternoon by Capt. Coats.

Sept. 16 [1863]. On camp guard. The mail came in with two letters from home for me. A company of the 3rd N.Y. cavalry came in to relieve the 12th N.Y. Ca.

Sept. 17. Off guard at eight o'clock this morning. Wrote home. The report is that a cavalry man was shot on picket last night.

Sept. 18. Company G. of the 3rd N.Y.C. came in to day. An expedition was to have gone out to night, but it was to[o] stormy. Humphrey is a sergeant.[120]

Sept. 19. Rather stormy and chilly this morning. This afternoon I went to Capt. Aldrich's office and looked over my clothing account. I have $2.49 due me on my yearly account.

When I came back a shake began to move me, then I went down to the cook house, then I found our Parmer Lewis[121] (a nurse in the hospital) he told me to go with him the hospital store house with him and he would warm me up. I went, he took a pint cup and drew it nearly full of whiskey which poured down my throat, went to my tent and crawled under the blankets, I had no shake, but a good sleep.

Sept. 20, Sunday. Volunteered for picket this morning. The pickets had to appear on inspection. I went to the Doctors for medicine, so I did not go out. Aldrich thought I was playing off on him. I could not see him on inspection when I was detailed for duty. I am on the Washington road, on outpost. I went out to Old Hampton's grape vine and filled my haversack with grapes. He has a big grape vine on an over head trellis which covers nearly half an acre. They are of the Scuppernong variety,[122] a large white grape, with a very thick, tough skin a good grape though. Down this way they are made into wine. Another shake this afternoon.

Sept. 21. All quiet on the lines last night. A company of the 1st North Carolina Cav. came in last night from Little Washington. Had another shake when I came into camp this afternoon with a high fever attached. when the company was called out for Battalion drill I did not go, so Aldrich reported me absent with out leave. It is a big thing to report a man absent without leave, when he is sick in quarters. Aldrich is just such a man as my Mother is, No man at all. John Marra (the mule we called him) went out in the country last week and has not returned yet. The citizens say that four rebels picked him up. three was for letting him go, the fourth one could not see it in that light.

Sept. 22. An expedition went up the river this morning on the Steamer *Washington Irving*. The cavalry went by land. They went as far as Jamesville and captured three rebel soldiers and a Lt. of Guerillas. They brought in a large quantity of forage. I am excused from duty to day.

Sept. 23 [1863]. We are getting ready to put up a fireplace in our tent. Aldrich has his commmission as Captain. Bah!

Sept. 24. Put our fireplace in to day. It works well. It is made of sticks and clay. Our tents are up in good shape. they are stockaded four feet with the floor a foot from the ground. We have a leanto at the back with bunk room for two, with a swing up door the whole length, so we get plenty of air. Inside the tent proper we have two bunks one up over the other. Then over the fireplace we have a swing table on hinges so we can lift it up to the tent when not in use. We take all sorts of comfort now for soldiers. John Marra and Tom Glenn came in to night from an expedition to Currituck Sound where they destroyed a large quantity of salt and other stores for the rebel army.

Sept. 25. Fixed up around our tent. Aldrich has gone to Newbern to get mustered as Captain.

Sept. 26. Pleasant and cold. This afternoon I went out to the old Fagan house and picked up a lot of nails. They are tearing down all the out buildings here to fix up shelter for the pickets. A very good plan.

Sept. 27, Sunday. No inspection this morning. The boat came in with the mail. I recieved a paper and a package of tea from home. Orderly Robinson came in to night from the North. Had a quantity of grapes. No parade to night. Wrote home.

Sept. 28. On picket on the Washington road at the left. The lines are closed tight now. All quiet. Had a good time. Our brigade is putting up a steam saw mill on the bank of the river just below the town. the parts were picked up in many places and various parts of the country. All was ready for the circular saw. The General sent a detachment over to Edenton where they found one, which the owner was running. Our men shut the mill down took the saw off the mandril, put it on the boat, brought it here put it in place and began to saw lumber to build sheds for the cavalry horses. Queer country this.

Sept. 29. It was lovely last night. The moon shone all the while. Relieved early this morning. The rebel papers of the 24th say that our Genl. Rosecrans gave them a dressing out at Chattanoga, taking fifteen hundred prisoners with great slaughter.[123] Samuel Lindsay[124] when he came off picket shot himself through the head. He died instantly. partially deranged.

Sept. 30 [1863]. I was detailed last for an expedition to start this morning at half past six o'clock. I was up betimes for my breakfast, went on board the *Massasoit* and run down the sound seventy miles and up the Little river ten miles to a small town called Nixinton after lumber but found none. I was with the part that went ashore to picket the place. We stayed two hours. All the forage we found was a flock of geese. I managed to get one of them.

On our way here we overhauled five small sail boats, but let them go again. We left here at half past two o'clock and reached Plymouth at seven o'clock.

Nixinton [Nixonton] is a small palce with a saw mill and a gristmill, but its dead.

Oct. 1. Made a staving pot pie of my goose for dinner. There was to be an inspection at five o'clock but was countermanded on account of drill, and drill on account of so much sickness in camp. Ate a quart of grapes for lunch.

Oct. 2. Stormy last night and this morning. On picket on the Washington road, on outpost. I ate freely of ripe figs this morning. The old colored woman told me not to as they would not be good for me. I ate them all the same. Then the shakes came on, and up came those figs. I went into the Fagan house which is occupied by that old colored woman who told me about the figs. She had a fire in the fireplace and made me a bed on the floor in front of the fire. I was doing nicely for me. When about noon a man from camp came out and said I was wanted to sign the pay roll. I started for camp when I reached the reserve post I played out sure. then an ambulance was sent out for me to ride into camp. Well I am here but have not signed the rolls yet and probably will not. If I had been let alone on the picket line, I would have come out all right, but now I am not. I had rather be sick than have this miserable fever and ague.

Oct. 3. I didn't feel very well this morning. There is not a particle of medicine in the hospital at present. So us shakey fellows will have to rough it the best way we can. Signed the pay roll this morning. Dr. Page chief of the Sanitary commission at Newbern, N.C. was here to day inspecting the Post. He gave our company quarters the praise of being the best in the Post.

Oct. 4, Sunday. We drew our pay this morning. No inspection. I had a shake and fever which lasted nearly all day. The worst I ever had I think. No excitement.

Oct. 5. I have not had much of a shake to day. A very high fever in its place.

The report is that the rebel ram[125] which is being built up the river at Hamilton is coming down before long. Let her come we are ready for her.

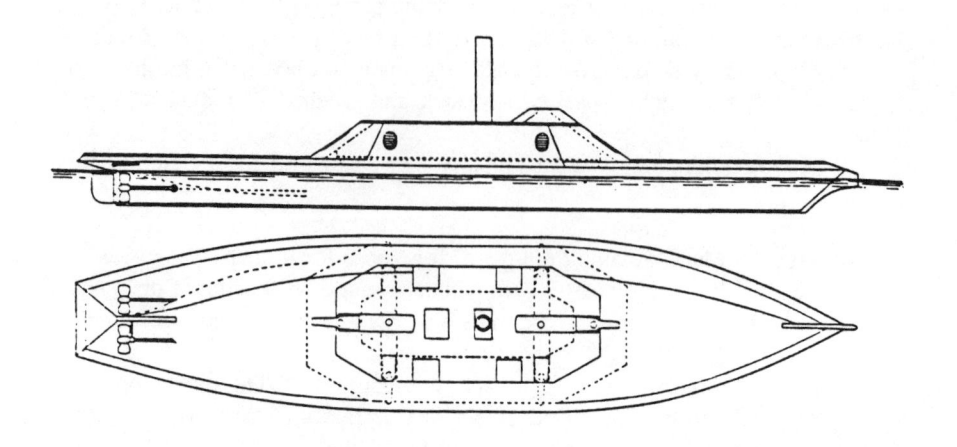

Plan of the *Albemarle*

Building the *Albemarle*

Oct. 6 [1863]. Had a fever to day that is all. Plenty.

Oct. 7. Feel pretty well this morning. This afternoon a detail came to our company for eight men and a Sergt. There was not enough well men to fill it. As I was feeling very well, I volunteered. Did not have to. we went on board the *Massasoit* at three o'clock bound for Edenton, where we arrived at five o'clock. The rebels here have been conscripting the citizens here. So they sent up to our place for help. It is the reason why we are here. Went ashore and picketed the town untill dark. It cost us fifty cents to have a pot of coffee made by one of the citizens ashore. At dark we went on board and steamed out nearly a mile and anchored along side the gunboat *Southfield* our escort. I am on duty to night at one of the gangways. I do this so I can have all day onshore to morrow. I want to know how the town looks at my leisure.

Oct. 8. All quiet last night. We went ashore again this morning. And I am at liberty to go and do as I please.
I feel a trifle shakey. We had not been ashore but a short time when the darkies began to flock in from the country and wanted to go to Plymouth. we took a load of them and put them on the *Southfield* and came back for another load. this time we took four or five white families. When all were on board it was sundown, when we made a straight wake for Plymouth, where we arrived at about eight o'clock. I have had a very good day of it. Edenton is a fine town.

Oct. 9. Every thing is quiet. Last night the pickets were nearly scared out of their wits. A couple of artillery horses broke loose and wandered out across the lines. Our Dunlop[126] was acting as corporal and was on post at the time and asleep. the horses went within two rod of him and he didn't know it. He pickets good.[127] This afternoon Francisco came in from picket sick. I had to go out and take his place. Not very lovely for me.

Oct. 10. Came off picket this morning with a severe headache. I went to bed an slept until dark but could not sleep it off no how. All quiet to day.

Oct. 11. Recieved a letter from David this morning. Feel very well. Wrote home. The rebels deserters are coming in.

Oct. 12. I haven't got "Shut" of that headache yet. I feel like sleeping all the time.
Seventeen deserters from the 17th North Carolina rebel regiment came in this morning. They say that their regiment were ordered to go to Tennessee, when they took french leave[128] and here they are. They report that the woods are full of them waiting for a chance to come in. They are a regiment that does not amount to any thing, only to shoot our men on picket.

Oct. 13 [1863]. An expedition goes out to night for Edenton. Ten from our company go. I could not get a chance in this time.

Oct. 14. On camp guard. Have a good guard house now. We have needed one.

Oct. 15. Off guard at nine o'clock this morning. Cleaned my gun. Had drill this afternoon. The whole regiment in one company under Capt. Adams.[129]

Our boys came in to night. They went down below Edenton and made a landing and when they had the town nearly surrounded one of our gunboats hove in sight and scared the rebels out on short notice. As it was they captured a Lieut. of Guerillas. A full company of rebels were in town, but got away. I am detailed for an expedition to start at half past four in the morning.

Oct. 16. Up this morning and reported to Lieut. Pitt[130] (Company E.) when we went down to the dock where the *Dollie* lay. There was no one on board but the fireman. Then it began to rain a sort of drizzle. It looked spotted for a rainy day. We were getting impatient to be off, so we blew the whistle many times and many more. When the Capt. came down rubbing his eyes. then we went aboard, took a scow in town and steamed out into the river when the *Massasoit* came along and took us all in tow. When we steamed down the river into the Sound to the mouth of Mackeys creek, where we cast off from the *Massasoit* and run up to Mackeys ferry (about two miles). Here we waited for the cavalry and wagons to come overland from Plymouth. When they came they had fourteen wagons. we ferried them all across the creek (which is quite wide) when they go into the country four miles after corn. We stay here only sixteen all told. One house and store is all there is of this place. we broke into the store and found not much. I found two singing books which I confiscated for camp use. We found a barrel of sour scuppernong wine. too sour to be good. One Capt. Dillon is the proprietor of this place and lives in the one house. We went to the house to try to get something to eat. Wetmore was spokesman for us. He asked the "lady of the house" if we could get some thing to eat. She said "no." then he said "let your girl here get it" turning to a young woman of uncertain age that stood by. she spoke up and said "I think you I am not a girl, I am a young lady." We all snickered but got nothing to eat. Then we wanted to buy some chickens of the old Man, but he would not sell any to us, then we told him that if would not sell any, we would have to take them, and we did, as many as we could catch, had to have chickens. After a while the cavalry and wagons came back loaded with corn in the ear, which we unloaded [loaded] the scow. when they started back for another load, and we boarded the *Dollie* and ran down to the *Massasoit* here we put the scow next to her and we last of all. When we started for Plymouth where we arrived at seven o'clock, or rather opposite the dock where the *Dollie* ties up - when we cast off our line from the

Samuel B. Adams. 1st Sgt., Co. C.,
September 28, 1861. 2nd Lt., July 13, 1862.
Capt., May 3, 1863. Mustered out May 1, 1865
(Courtesy of Michael Albanese)

scow and put on steam we could not move as a rope that was dragging astern of us had fouled in our propeler wheel. We blew the whistle long and loud many times for a boat to tow us back to dock. No boat came to our relief. Then we put a rope around and under the arms of the darkie fireman and lowered him over the stern into the water which was very cold - when after a long time we got out of our tangle. We had drifted away down in the swamp in the meantime, many miles. It was nine o'clock before we made our landing. Had quite a day of it considering all things.

Oct. 17 [1863]. Had chicken for dinner. It was very tough. I went down and saw the new saw mill at work. It is all right for a picked up one. Letter from home.

Oct. 18, Sunday. On picket on the left of the Washington road. Hussey[131] had a letter from John Marra (the mule) he is at the parole Camp[132] at Annapolis, Md. Sick. He was picked up outside of the picket line about the middle of Sept. and had been reported absent with out leave.

Oct. 19. Off picket rather late. Corporal Porter[133] and I went the rounds twice last night. Had monthly inspection this afternoon by Lieut. Beagle [Beadle] of Wessells staff. When our company was reached the Col.[134] said to the Maj. this is the "best Company B." His english is not any to good. [sic]

Oct. 20. Nothing going on to day. Had Ross[135] come in to night. He bunks with us. Received a letter from home, all well there.

Oct. 21. On picket on the reserve post with Lieut. Butts of company K. Our guard house here is dandy about twenty feet square of logs with a big fire place in it. We bought a peck of sweet potatoes this morning and put them in the hot embers to roast. they came out all right. Whiskey is issued to all picket and camp guard now. It is to keep the chills off. The orders are very strict on picket now.

Oct. 22. We went out with the cavalry this morning but saw nothing. I do not feel very well. I am excused from drill.
Three deserters came in from Fosters Mills. one of them is from Troy, N.Y. He said before he enlisted in the rebel service he had a friend write home to his family that he was dead, and then went and enlisted.

Oct. 23. Cleaned up my gun. I am detailed for an expedition to leave at noon. went on board of the *Massasoit*. The Genl. is with us and a lot of deserters and citizens going to Newbern, N.C. We run down to Roanoke Island, left our passengers, got the mails, coaled up and are to lay here untill morning.

Oct. 24 [1863]. We were up and moving at day light, run up the Little river to Nixonton and stayed a short time for the Genl. Wessells to look around a bit when we put back to Plymouth, where we arrived at five o'clock. A small package from home by mail.

Oct. 25, Sunday. Had inspection, the Captain is sick so Lt. Col. Clark inspected us. He said that we had not lost much since he had left us.[136]

Had a good dinner down at the cook house. The 96th N.Y. have left the canal and gone to New York City. Big riots there.[137] Wrote home. All quiet here.

Oct. 26. No stir to day. Drill this afternoon. all were put in two companies under Captain Chapin of K company. lots of fun with the old man. for instance when such a command as this, "Now then dress up there promptly men! promptly! promptly!" some of the boys would laugh. when he would say: "The first man that laughs I'll put him in the guard house, do you hear, now then promptly there men! Dress up promptly! promptly!" He is an old farmer fellow and does very well. When we were in Newbern last winter, we forged his name to our bread orders. We had to have an order from a commissioned officer when we wanted more bread.

Oct. 27. On picket on Washington road to the left. three of us and Corporal Porter. Towards night I went into camp and brought a haversack of grub and a pail of beans enough for ten men, but we managed to get outside of it before morning. It has been quiet to day and every thing passed of quiet with none to molest or make us afraid, not a rebel to be seen on the farm.

Oct. 28. Off picket early. when I got in I found a letter waiting for a reader. It did not have to wait long. Wrote home, and how I had got rid of my chills. But inside of an hour I was flat on my back chilling away and colder than Greenland's icy mountain and then came the fever, hotter than India's coral strand. I should have [been] a poet. If I had been born in the right time of the moon.

It would have been very funny.

Oct. 29. Had another chill to day. I did not drill. I am having my share of fever and ague this summer.

Oct. 30. Felt pretty well to day as usual, only more so, and not quite as much so. No chill.

Oct. 31. Two months pay due again. We were inspected and mustered by Col. Lehman of the 103 Pa. when he reached the quarters he said they were very nice. Lieut. Martin came a good one on Capt. Aldrich. It was this wise.

the capt. was in favor of promoting orderly Robinson 1st Lieut. over 2nd Lieut. McHenry, and Martin seemed to side in with him. When Martin went home he took a recommend from the Lt. Col. Clark in favor of Robinson, and one for McHenry signed by Col. Fardella, and he put them both in the war department at Albany, N.Y. of course all things being equal, Charles McHenry is our 1st Lieut.

Nov. 1 [1863], Sunday. No inspection this morning. Began a letter home. This afternoon a took a walk over to Fort Williams it is a very good work and mounts three thirty twos,[138] a ships gun mounted [indecipherable] and a brass field piece, twelve pounder.

Nov. 2. Nothing doing this morning. On police duty this afternoon, then battalion drill.

Nov. 3. On camp guard. No excitement.[139]

Nov. 4. Off guard at nine o'clock. Had and old fashioned pumpkin pie for supper.

Nov. 5. Pleasant. Nothing on this forenoon. This afternoon five men and a corporal were detailed from our company with seven days rations for an expedition with two gun boats for escort. Company drill this afternoon. Had all the officers in town out and then they could not drill us. Maj. Genl. J. J. Peck was here.

Nov. 6. On picket Washington road outpost. Had roast turkey for supper. We had quite a time with the 103 Pa. Surgeon. he came out to see Capt. Hamilton's mother is very sick and came in such a hurry that he forgot to get a pass from the Genl. but the officer of the guard passed him by the reserve post, so of course it was all right. But we remembered the surgeon of old. When we saw him coming I told the boys I was going to have some fun with him, so I took my gun and stood out in the road and hollered at him, he said "that he had forgot his pass, don't you know me." I said "no Sir we don't know anybody out here and do not want to without a pass." After I had bothered him enough I let him pass on. We have always had a grudge against him since the Kinston raid.[140]

Nov. 7. Had chicken pot pie for breakfast. The cavalry went out alone this morning. We were relieved early.

Nov. 8, Sunday. Inspection this morning. Col. Lehman 103 Pa. gave us the praise of being the best looking company mustered to day. Oh! we are it.

Nov. 9 [1863]. On picket on Washington road outpost. Saw a hard sight this morning. this is the how of it: Two white women came out here with a mullatto child, one of the white woman was the mother of it and some big darkie was the father of it. They came out to leave the child with the old colored woman who lives in the "Fagan house" who said no she would not have it, then the mother said she would leave it on the picket line. We said no to that and said it with a snap. then the old colored woman's heart warmed up and she said she would take it in. No comments on the scene just mentioned. Had a good supper after dark to night. S. Green[141] came in to day.

Nov. 10. There was only one on post last night which was all right. A heavy frost and very cold. Hopping Jennie brought us down some sweet potatoe pie and persimmon beer this morning, which was very good. Relieved early.

That expedition came in last night. They went up the Chowan river as far as Winton where they expected to meet Genl. Foster who was coming from Norfolk with a force. When an order came that Genl. Foster had been superseded by Genl. B. J. Butler.[142] then the expedition came to an end.

An expedition went out this morning at four o'clock for Columbia. Another this afternoon for Edenton. No excitement. We are having our fill of expeditions.

Nov. 11. Cold last night. Drew rations to day. I was detailed this afternoon for work at the Commissary. We had to carry four hundred boxes of hard tack up two flights of stairs. A box of hard tack weighs one hundred pounds. The consequence is I have a very severe pain in my chest, so that it just doubled me up all sorts. I am detailed for an expedition tomorrow, but can't go.

Nov. 12. I am not over that pain yet so I am excused.

Nov. 13. Excused to day. A schooner came in with Sutlers stores, she had a lot of apples that were barreled up in Old Ontario County, N.Y. They tasted like home. Good!

Nov. 14. Monthly inspection by Capt. Coats.

Nov. 15. Sergt. Simmons and I went down and saw the light battery have their inspection. we had none.

Nov. 16. Nothing but drill to day.

Nov. 17. I was detailed for picket, but got as far as Brigade guard mounting when one of my old shakes came to see me. I had to drop out, went back to my tent to entertain it, but it turned the tables on me and kept me on my back all day. Four letters from home. Sergt. Joe Cummings came in.[143]

Nov. 18 [1863]. Feel better to day. Our cooking range came to day. The boys are putting it up after this fashion. The range consists of four plates with holes in them for kettles and griddles or covers for them. the door is in a frame, we built up the sides and ends of brick, putting the door in front then at the right hight we put the plates on. at the back and over the flue we placed a section of an old boiler about three feet long bricking up one end, putting a door in the other end then we had a high oven stove such as they have up home way.
Wrote home and David.

Nov. 19. Excused to day.

Nov. 20. On camp guard. The Col. put the sergt Sam White (of Co. C.)[144] under arrest for not turning out the guard. The cavalry went on a scout and had three men wounded.

Nov. 21. Off guard at nine o'clock. Our cooking range is complete. We are having baked sweet potatoes now with our coffee for breakfast. The potatoes will bake, while the coffee is cooking. Aldrich bought the range for the company. We buy the sweet potatoes with company funds that is to say we get pay for what rations we don't draw, which goes into the company fund, which is ours to buy what we please for our comfort.

Nov. 22, Sunday. Company inspection. Maj. Genl. B. F. Butler and Maj. Genl. J. J. Peck and Admiral Lee came in this morning to inspect the post. They came on a special boat with their full staff of officers. Their ladies were with them. Genl. Butler's daughter Miss Blance was with them. She is a beauty and no mistake. Genl. Butler has one cock eye and has orderly to carry his sword and pipe after him. Both Genls. expressed themselves as well pleased with out works. Genl. Peck is a great man for fortifying. Ours pleased him. Good!

Nov. 23. On provost guard.

Nov. 24. Off guard at nine o'clock.

Nov. 25. The mail came in this morning but I got nothing. The gunboat *Bombshell* came in. She is a funny craft manned by negroes. I am on police this forenoon and a short time this afternoon, just enough to keep off from drill. Ed Knapp and Henry Crane have their discharges. Seymour Smith has his furlough. They start for the North. Good!

Nov. 26 [1863]. Thanksgiving here as well as up North. On camp guard near company C's quarters. Had oysters for dinner.[145]

Nov. 27. Off guard early. Had a good game of ball.

Nov. 28. Stormy. No drill.

Nov. 29, Sunday. On picket on the right of the Washington road. it is a terrible bad day. We managed to keep warm. It cleared off towards night.

Nov. 30. Off picket early. Pleasant but cold. letter from home. Drill this afternoon by the colonel.

Dec. 1. Cold last night. I liked to have froze up. Had a good game of ball this afternoon. Every thing is quiet.

Dec. 2. Lieut. McHenry came in last night. We were all in bed, but he woke us all up. He is looking fine. He brought me some things from home, and a twenty-five pound flour sack full of tobacco from brother George.

VOLUME II

CIVIL WAR JOURNAL

OF

CHARLES CONDIT MOSHER

Dec. 3 [1863]. Another shake to day.

Dec. 4. Nothing going on to day.

Dec. 5. On provost guard number three at the dock. This afternoon as I was looking down the river I saw two boats coming up under a full head of steam. One was the *Massasoit* and the other was the *Trumpeter* racing each other. The *Massasoit* came to dock first. She is the fastest boat in these waters. The *Trumpeter* came to relieve the *Massasoit*. Guess it won't work.

Dec. 6. Off guard early. Inspection. I am out of it.[146] Dress parade to night.

Dec. 7. Only drill to day. Company A goes to Roanoke Island to relieve Company I.[147] Lt. Col. Clarke is in command of the Island.

Dec. 8. On camp guard. We are having a change of positions in the regiment. When we came out in 1861 our company was on the extreme left, and company [A] was on the extreme right. The place of honor. When Capt. King of A was promoted to Major, our Captain Clarke being senior captain took the right of the line. We have held the right since March 1862, until Capt. Aldrich took command of us which has put us in the position of left center. We don't like it one little bit. It is a hard place to march in. When we were the right company, we had an easy place to march, being in the lead we set the pace for the regiment.

The excitement now is re-enlisting. All of those regiments whose time expires next fall are asked to re-enlist for three years or during the war. The government to give those who do, their first original bounty of $100.00. This was the part of the enlistment terms of 1861 - and a bounty of $400.00 in installments of $50.00 every six months, and in addition to this Ontario County was to give a bounty of $300.00 and the state of New York to give $50.00. So it makes quite an inducement for the men to re-enlist. A few have and more will.

Dec. 9 [1863]. The steamboat *Charleston* came in this morning with our Company I from Roanoke Island and the mails. I had a letter from home. Also a two hundred pound rifle parrot gun. It has an eight inch bore. A monster gun. It is to be placed on or in the water battery on the river. Fort Worth is the name of it. It was built to take care of that ram [ironclad], which the rebels are building up the river at Halifax.[148]

I am detailed (or rather I take Wilcox's place) for an expedition to start at half past three o'clock with three days rations. At four o'clock we are on board the steamer *Charleston* with a detail from all the regiments in the brigade. Lt. Col. Maxwell[149] of the 103 Pa. in command. A lot of darkies are on board for Roanoke Island. We run down the river into the Sound when we take the gunboat *Bombshell* in tow. We are to run all night.

Dec. 10. At two o'clock this morning we run hard and fast on a bar near the dock at Roanoke Island. It took us untill eight o'clock to get off. when we run along side of a coal schooner and coaled up. Here we put the darkies in the schooner. While this was going on Frank Wilson of Co. F[150] or the wild irishman as we called him was showing off before the darkies. his hat blew off and over board. what does he do but to get into a small boat in tow of our steamer and goes for his hat. The sound was rough and the waves running high, when Frank lost one of his oars. he had his overcoat on at the time, then he stood up to take it off and loosing his balance he fell overboard, but caught the side of the boat and hung on. There was a boats crew from the gunboat *Comodore Hull* along the side of our steamer, the officer in charge was in the cabin of our boat consulting with our captain at the time. We tried to have the boat crew go after Wilson but they would not without orders. then word was sent the officer in charge. he came out and saw the situation, and got in the boat, gave the word of command. that boat fairly flew down the sound. Wilson and his boat were a mile or more down the Sound. He was about gone when his rescuers caught him, and put him into their boat and came back with him and took him on our boat and rolled over a barrel to get the water out of him. After a lot of hard work he came to his senses and was all right. A very narrow escape for that Irishman. He is well named the wild Irishman. A good fellow. Then the crew of our boat (*Charleston*) had to take another small boat and go down and find the boat Wilson had. after a long pull they found it, then another long pull, before they got back. They were very mad, and said that they wished Wilson had drowned. At half past twelve we finished coaling. They put back after the steamer *General Berry*. She hove in sight just at sundown. she had a detachment of Company A on board and had been up to Hertford[151] a small town where they had run into a party of rebels and had a brush with them, and had three men wounded one of them badly. Then we put about and made for Roanoke Island where we arrived at eight o'clock and anchored for the night. We have to wait for the *General Berry* to go with us, where ever it is. We sleep in the hold of our boat.

Dec. 11 [1863]. Roanoke Island. This morning the steamer *Trumpeter* came in with the paymaster. A large steamer with a school in tow passed by. At nine o'clock the detail from the 101 Pa. and our regiment got on board of the *General Berry*, the rest of the command stay on board the *Charleston*. We ran down the Sound, our boat is the faster of the two. she is a stern wheeler (or a wheelbarrow) and carry one thousand men, when loaded it draws only three feet of water, and when light only one and a half feet. At five o'clock we run into Swan Quarter Bay[152] and anchored for the night.

We have run about ninety miles to day. have good quarters on this boat. The upper deck is one large room.

Dec. 12. Up this morning at sunrise and ran alongside the *Charleston*, took the 103 Pa. detail and a twelve pound brass boat howitzer on our boat, then stood out for Juniper Bay. This a beautiful sheet of water, clear as crystal, so shallow that the pilot used a pole to sound with. At nine o'clock we anchored at the mouth of the canal which connects with Mattamusket lake.[153] The canal is used by the planters to run their produce to market. Here we landed in small boats and before we had formed our line we saw several heads peering through the fence a short way ahead of us. then we deployed our line and advanced when we saw two small darkie boys, one of them piped out, "Its all right, Massa! Its all right, Massa!" It was all right, the little fellow had been sent down to spy us out. It was all right for us and them. We marched up the canal a few miles when we came to the negro quarters belonging to Judge Donelson's plantation. Here was a motley crew of old men and women and small children. (The able bodied ones had gone up the country to work.) We were the first yankey soldiers that had been seen in these parts. Such a greeting as they gave us. They shouted "Glory Hallelujah my [folks] hab come. Ise prayed for dis day. Praise de Leord my folks hab come. Bless the Lord my foks hab come." Then they would shout for all pure joy and lay down on the ground and roll, kicking up their heels. One old woman, very tall and thin, a toothless old hag she was, jumped up and threw her arms around the neck of Lieut. Pieke[154] and hugged and kissed him in good style, much to our amusement and his chagrin. Then we all shouted. Those old colored people had it in their minds that they were to be free some time, and the northern men were to free them. They were right. When conditions became normal, the Colonel told them to pack up their things and they could go to Roanoke Island with us, which they proceeded to do quite lively. Our detail went into the country farther up to the big house of Judge Donelson. In the woods here we saw a party of mounted rebels. We hung around a while but could not get a shot at them.

The darkie that lived in the rear of the "Big House" wanted to go back with us, We told him to pack up. He packed his stuff with his wife and babies into and old cart, when his "Old Missus" began to upbraid him for leaving her, telling him how she had brought him up and caring for him all these years. She used an everlasting lot of words on him, she knew how. Then his turn came.

The "Dark" was enough for her as far as words went. We started back when the "Dark" sung out "hold on Massa, hold on Massa. Ise forgot my two 'scoven' ducks and possum skin." We held on for him to get them. I bought the two scoven ducks for fifty cents. They were a fine pair of Muscovy ducks. When we got back to the quarters on the canal the darkies were packed up. Their pigs were killed and packed. Every thing but their poultry, we told them there was not room for them on board. But we boys who always liked chicken caught them and found plenty of room for them on the boat somehow. Our return to the boat was a sight. The advance guard first, then the darkies in regular order in all sorts of vehicles and traps, then the rest of the detail. A few naval officers and enough of sailors to man the boat howitzer were a long with us. On our way to the boats several large barns were burning (they looked fine). Who fired them? The naval officers said it was the soldiers. The army officers said it was the sailors. Here you have the answer in a nutshell, figure it out.

It was sundown before we had every thing and every body on board the boat, when we ran out and along side of the *Charleston* and put the darkies on board of her. There were two hundred and fifty of them all told. How they did smell, Very! Quite! Stink would express it better. Here we droped anchor and lay all night.

Dec. 13 [1863]. It was so foggy this morning that we did not get under way untill nine o'clock, reached Roanoke Island at sundown. On our way here we ran a long way out of our course. Went to Company A's quarters for supper - that is our 85th part of the detail. Here we heard that we were to go on another trip tomorrow, so we sold our poultry and bought ham, cheese, soft bread, tobacco & c [etc.] from the sutlers for the next trip. Slept on board of *Genl. Berry* to night. We have had all sorts of fun on this expedition and no mistake, We are a lively lot of lads.

Dec. 14. At six o'clock this morning we started for the Alligator river. (The Alligator river is off from the Albemarle Sound and between the counties of Dare and Tyrrell and is called the Little Dismal Swamp. Dare County is next to the Sound and is very low.) Well we run near the upper end of the river. (It is more of a bayou than a river as it is about the same width all the way from the Sound up) to Cherry Ridge Landing (not far from Gum Neck which is its Post Office) where we went ashore and up the country about three miles. all we saw was one big house with a quantity of poultry all around in the yards. The officers pointed them out to us and said "there was a lot of fine fowls, but we must not touch them." Which we proceeded to do, by going right among them and laying our hands on them and tieing their legs together so that they would not bite us. (We were afraid of chickens we were) Their owners took on badly about it. I told the old lady that I would pay for mine. I would not steel them from her, so I did, with some of that Elisebeth City money which I have mentioned in other place.[155] We took all the poultry we wanted or rather all there was and started for the boat. I had my poultry in a large round bottomed basket. When we were nearly there Lt. Col. wanted the detail from our regiment under Lieut. Butts of K company to around an other way on the road to bring in a union family who wanted to go to Plymouth with us. What would we do with our poultry as they were to heavy to carry that far. Just then some natives were going by with their carts full of corn. The Lt. Col. made one of them dump his load of corn in the road and put our poultry in take it to the boat. Which he did very reluctantly, when we went on our way. It was a long way and a long while before we found that union family. then they did not want to go as they were not ready, so we had our tramp for nothing. I had a big drink of milk and a baked sweet potato for mine. Then they told us [about] a shorter way to the boat landing. It was a run way through the swamp. The run way consisted of single logs placed about three feet above the water. It was a dark night, with a feeble moon and it was hard work to keep our balance sure. When we were about half way through we heard the steamboat whistle, (it cheered us up a bit) We responded with a yell. We made the passage through the swamp all right only one man had or got his feet wet, reaching the boat at seven o'clock tired and hungry. All hands were glad to see us. We were gone so long they thought we had fallen into a trap.

Dec. 15 [1863]. We run all night and arrived at Roanoke Island at nine o'clock. Took on the mails and made for Plymouth where we arrived at six o'clock this afternoon. We have had a very pleasant trip. No one hurt. Our poultry are in good shape.

I received a letter from home and David, also a package from cousin Elizabeth Wight of Waterloo, N.Y. by Sergt. Wyman J. Johnson who has been home on a furlough. He is a member of Co. G. our 85th N.Y. and is a good friend of mine.[156]

Dec. 16. The regiment was paid yesterday. I signed the pay roll this morning and drew rations of greenbacks $28.50. Sent a Soldiers Memorial home to Sarah and a $5.00 bill to have it framed.[157] Battalion drill this afternoon. All quiet here.

Dec. 17. Got a N.Y. Draft[158] from the paymaster Walter Crane for $20.00 which I sent to Father. On picket and it is very rainy. The report is there is a large force outside.

Dec. 18. Relieved early. It rained all night. Inspection to night.

Dec. 19. Cleaned up my gun this forenoon. Had a shake this afternoon.

Dec. 20. Had company inspection. Wrote home. Dress parade. Sunday.

Dec. 21 [1863]. Detailed for picket. Went out to brigade guard mounting, felt a shake coming on, had to retire with the loss of my breakfast. The shakes are miserable.

Dec. 22. Fell better to day. Had chicken for dinner. The Col. run horses and beat.[159]

Dec. 23. Had another shake to day. Excused from duty.

Dec. 24. Bought a pair of boots. Went on drill, but bushed.

Dec. 25. Merry Christmas. On picket, Washington road outpost. We ordered our dinner early. It came down to us at noon in this shape: roast pig, chicken, turkey, goose, sweet potato pie, fruit cake, and persimon beer, a big dinner, we lined our stomachs so that the lining touched. Fifty cents each man very cheap. There was firing on the line last night.

Dec. 26. Off picket early. Mended my pants. Cleaned up. Horse race to day, the Col. was beaten.

Dec. 27, Sunday. Letter from home. John E. Booth[160] came in last night. Chicken pie for dinner. Inspection. Dress parade.

Dec. 28. On picket Washington road outpost. Stormy. Quiet.

Dec. 29. Off picket early. All quiet last night.

Dec. 30. Drill. Sent a New Years present to Sarah. All quiet here. Very.

Dec. 31. Mustered by Col. Lehmann 103 Pa. On provost guard. It rained very hard but I have a good post out of the wet. This is the last of 1863 and all is well here in Old Plymouth.

Major General Robert F. Hoke
Victor at the Battle of Plymouth
(Battles and Leaders of the Civil War)

Chapter Five

"THE RAM IS IN COMMAND": THE BATTLE OF PLYMOUTH

(January 1 to April 21, 1864)

The new year, which started so pleasantly with games and roast goose, was to become a nightmare for Mosher and the other Eighty-Fifth New York Veteran Volunteers at Plymouth. Vague rumors of an ironclad being built near Halifax, North Carolina, presaged a momentous turn of events and a new phase of the war. The conflict would also become all-out instead of a series of disjointed campaigns, and would be fought on political and psychological as well as military terms. Like most soldiers, Mosher was unaware of this shift in strategy by Union commander Grant, but he (and they) would pay a heavy price.

While Gettysburg effectively forced the South to employ a defensive strategy thereafter, the North failed to gain additional victories. Calls for more soldiers were issued, and the war was either to be won by attrition or become a stalemate--and a political "victory" for the South.

Robert E. Lee was acutely aware of the need for the South to test the North's endurance, but to pursue politico-military objectives he had to secure the South's resources. The North Carolina coast became of particular importance, for supplies from there had to travel from Wilmington to Richmond by way of Goldsboro and Raleigh. The little bands of Union troops in Plymouth and New Bern thus were obstacles to the Confederate supply needs.

In early January Lee had informed Confederate President Jefferson Davis that, since the Army of the Potomac was in winter quarters, he could spare men to attempt to retake New Bern and capture Union gunboats on the Neuse River. While Lee suggested that North Carolinian Brigadier Robert F. Hoke take command, Major General George B. Pickett claimed seniority and took over. Shortly Pickett, concentrated near Kinston, North Carolina with 13,000 troops and fourteen navy cutters, ordered his three brigadier generals (Seth Barton, James Kemper, and Matt Ransom) to coordinate an attack with Hoke, coming from Weldon. If successful, New Bern would fall, and in its wake "Little Washington" and Plymouth. Though this specific plan proved unsuccessful, it presaged a successful, and ultimately fatal, attack on the tiny garrison at Plymouth under an alert, but unheeded, General Henry Wessells. Private Mosher was also unaware of the great events that were taking shape. For the moment his primary concerns were to stay warm and healthy and find sufficient time for foraging.

January 1, 1864. Happy New Year. Off guard early. Had a big day on the Columbia road[1] in a large field. Had a sack race, wheelbarrow race, greased pig, greased pole, & a scrub horse race. It was great sport. Horse race was the greatest fun. G. W. Snook (my tent mate) and I had a roast goose for dinner. We got away with it in good shape.

All of our men are feel well.

Jan. 2. It is very cold this morning. No wood on hand, so we waited untill the sun came out and warmed things up, when we went out and found some, not much. Wrote home, Had a sing to night. Lt. Col. Clarke and a lot of us met in Deyo's tent for a sing. We use those singing books I got up at Mackeys Ferry the other day. Lt. Col. Clarke sings base [bass], Deyo tenor. I take the soprano of course. the others chip in where they please. We have had many a good sing using those books. Clarke was our former Captain, he is at home with our company. A dandy man.

Jan. 3, Sunday. Regimental inspection by the Col. Company H and our company escorted the colors out in good shape. Quite a ceramony. Twenty four men from our Company have re-enlisted in the Veteran Corps for three years or during the war. Nearly all of the 24th N.Y. Ind. Battery have gone in. Had a good dinner of bread and raw pork. Dress parade.

Jan. 4. On provost guard, Post No. six but I traded for Post No. three on the dock, on the steamer *Massasoit*, a good post out of the wet as it rains very hard.

Jan. 5. Went on duty at three o'clock. I went on the steamer and sat by the boiler hatch, where it was warm and comfortable. Great excitement in camp about re-enlisting in the Veteran Corps. All of our company are in but eight. I still hold out. Companies I, D, G, are all in, three quarters of F. Not a man of A. as yet. The Col. has offered a bonus of $10.00 for the man that will enlist now. He is anxious 3/4 of the regiment to go in so he can hold his commission.

Jan. 6. Clear and cold. Monthly inspection by Capt. Coats at half past two, so I will have to clean up my gun and straps and get into shape. The veterans looked down in the mouth on inspection, thinking of all the inspections they will have to go through with in the next three years. The Rev. Mr. Huntington spoke to us while we were in line about the war and the duty of re-enlisting. Which was all very nice, But the Col. has his bounty up to $15.00 for the next man. Van Wie[2] of our company went to the hospital this morning and died to night, he had congestion chills. Its a nasty night, sleet and rain.

Jan. 7 [1864]. On camp guard and its very cold. Van Wie was buried this afternoon. The Col. and our Capt. have gone to Fortress Monroe. All quiet.

Jan. 8. Off guard eary. It was tedious last night.

Jan. 9. Had a slight chill this afternoon and don't feel very well my self. Great excitement among the veterans.

Jan. 10. On provost guard, post five a miserable post. Its cold and drizly.

Jan. 11. Off guard early. A nasty day this. The Veterans were reviewed by the General this afternoon. I had another old fashioned shake this afternoon. It shook all of the Veteran out of me and the patriotism as well.

Jan. 12. Excused to day. Chill.

Jan. 13. Excused.

Jan. 14. Excused. Still shakey.

Jan. 15. Feel very well to day. The Veterans were sworn in. Gooding came in from picket sick. I had to go out and take his place, on the reserve post. [Seymour] Smith came in from furlough.

Jan. 16. Off picket early. Six rebel deserters came in and brought their arms with them. Guess they are _____. [sic].

Jan. 17. Inspection. Sunday. Wrote two letters. Dress parade. I went to church this morning for the first time in a long while.

Jan. 18. It has rained all day. I have had the Veteran question in my mind as to whether I would or would not re-enlist. Mother is an invalid and Father is old and getting feeble so he can not work. Sarah is the [only] one at home. Lieut. McHenry when he was home on his furlough called on them and saw the situation, and has not urged me to. But that $750.00 looks good and it would help out a lot up home. It would build a house on the little farm on the Tree Bridge road up home. To night I took the orderly Jim Robinson by the arm and said to him, "Come with me and I will go up and enlist." He said, "good for you." So we went up to headquarters and signed the roll.

I am the last man in our company, all but three. George and Dick Phillips (brothers) and Clark N. Kern. The Phillips brothers are to be married this coming fall.[3] Fifty one of our company are in.

This is to Certify that *Charles C Mosher* of Co. B, 85th Regiment, New-York Volunteer Infantry, re-enlisted as a VETERAN Volunteer, and was duly mustered into the service of the United States January 1st, 1864, and credited on the Muster-in Rolls to the town of *Hopewell* County of *Ontario* State of New-York.

W Barstow
1st Lieut. and Acting Com. of Musters.

C. S. Aldrich
Capt. 85th N. Y. V. Infantry,
Commanding Co. B.

**Mosher's Reenlistment Paper,
Dated January 1, 1864**

Jan. 19 [1864]. On provost guard. I was examined this afternoon by Dr. Rush and sworn in by Lieut. Butts. Now I am in it for sure. I am one of them. A Veteran Volunteer. Recieved three letters from home and one of them said that father was very low and was not expected to live and wanted me to come home. On the strength of my re-enlistment I applied for a furlough. The mustering officer came in tonight. The fruits of our re-enlistment are 1st. We are to be paid in full including our original bounty of $100. 2nd a thirty days furlough home. 3rd $400.00, $50.00 every six months. the first installment of $50.00 on next pay day. 4th $300.00 from Ontario County, New York. 5th $50.00 from the state of New York. I am accredited to my old Town of Hopewell, Ontario County State of New York.[4]

Jan. 20. Off guard early. I am detailed for an expedition to leave this afternoon at seven o'clock with three days rations and fourty rounds of cartidges. Were on board the gunboat *Bombshell*, at the appointed time and run down the river into the Sound and up the Chowan river, for some where.

Jan. 21. At three o'clock this morning we landed at the Harrellville[5] landing, formed out lines and started for the village of Harrellville where we arrived between four and five o'clock. Here we found some rebel cavalry horses hitched or tied to the posts in front of the houses. In the side streets were wagons with mules attached waiting for day light so they could load them with army stores to take up country. This is a supply depot for the confederacy. A good one.

This is a very fine village situated on four corners, but we did not stop to admire it much but proceeded to business, to destroy the commissary supplies. Corporal Warner[6] and I was placed on guard over a large storehouse belonging to and adjoining the dwelling house owned and occupied by a Mr. Skull and his family. He was an old man with a young wife, whose sister lived with them. She was a good looker. The lower floor of the storehouse contained several hogshead[7] of light brown sugar and molasses, soap, lard, salt, candles. The upper floor was divided into many rooms which were furnished with beds which were for the rebel soldiers who came in town and wanted to stay over night.

We loaded what sugar we could on the wagons, the rest together with salt, soap, lard, candles, we trampled in to a mud hole in front of the storehouse. I saw a lot of good sugar being spoiled so I went to the house and asked Mrs. Skulls sister if they had a sugar box, she said "yes" and brought one that would hold a half bushel, which I took and filled, then carried it in the house and gave to the young lady. She repaid me with one of her sweetest sesesh smiles, which I should have enjoyed if I had not seen a smallish little devil lurking out the corner of her eyes. Of course the rest of the stuff was trampled in the mud. I was in and out of the house many times. I saw some very pretty shells in the parlor. I asked a darkie woman to get me one unbeknown to her "missus," which we did. On the picket line the rebels were having a hot time with our boys. When Capt. [Thomas I.] Johnson of the 2nd loyal North Carolina's "Buffaloes" the natives called them.[8] was a long with us, came up to Mrs. Skull, called her by name and bid her a hearty good morning. She asked him who he was and how did he know her. The captain told her who she was, who her first husband was, how many children she had by him, and how long she had been married to Mr. Skull. He told her more than she knew herself. Then she asked him who he was. He told her that he was Captain Johnson of the second loyal N. C. regiment. Then her tongue loosened and she congratulated him on high office and many other things. Just then the pickets began fireing rather sharp, and Capt. Johnson started on a run to see what was up. Then Mrs. Skull open[ed] on him with "run, run, Capt. Johnson, run! I hope you will get shot," she repeated it several times, When the butt of my gun went to my shoulder, with my thumb on the hammer and my finger on the trigger. I told her to shut up or I would fix her. She shut up. This is the first time I ever pulled my gun on a woman. I have felt ashamed of it ever since. One of our boys took Mrs. Skulls side saddle for one of the officers wife in Plymouth. Mrs. Skull gave me one of her pretty shells. When I was on guard over the storehouse I found a very large pipe, the bowl was as large as a coffee cup, it had a stem made of a piece of fig tree (the pit was pushed out) with a goose quill for a mouth piece. It was a dandy. And the prize of the trip.

After the warehouses that were filled with pork, bacon, whickey, were burning well and every thing done up right, Our line was formed and we began our return trip to the boat. Corporal Warner, with Perkey, Alvah Phillips and I were videtts,[9] with Warner and Perkey a rod or so in the lead. Phillips and I were chatting along about the trip, he showing a pair of shears, I my big pipe, all of the plunder we had. We had no skirmish line out on either flank. I don't know why.

We had been discussing the idea that the rebels might ambush us at that time we were abrest of a pine woods. the trees were about as big as my leg and scattering, we could see clear through them, Alvah said, nothing in there. then we came to a pine thicket, which we could not see into - no more than we could the side of a barn, Alvah said they will be in there if any where. they were and gave us a volley. a bullet went through his head. he was only a half step behind me, when he was shot. The men in the rear charged the woods and drove the rebels out leaving two or three of them dead. They excited [exited] when they fired. If they had waited untill the main body of our men came up they would have done more damage. As it was they done enough.

When the wagons came up we put Alvah's body on one of them and with out any more trouble we reached the boat. After we had loaded every thing on the boat we started for Plymouth where we arrived at six o'clock. This expedition was in command of Lt. Col. Maxwell of the 103 Pa. with one hundred and fifty men. Alvah Phillips was my bunk mate when we were in barracks at Elmira, N.Y. One good boy, and always ready for duty.[10]

General H. Wessells in his report to headquarters at Newberne N.C. reported the results of this expedition to have been the destruction of 150,000 or 200,000 pounds of pork, 270 bushels of salt, 10,000 pounds of tobacco, 32 barrels of beef and other stores, also the capture of some prisoners, horses and mules. (One good days work for us.)

Jan. 22 [1864]. I did not get up very early. We buried Alvah Phillips this morning. A very sad case for us. We were mustered into the United States Service for three years or during the war[11] by U. S. Barstow, 1st Lieut., and Acting Com. of Musters. When the roll was called every one answered here, when the name Alvah Phillips was called, no response, called again, no response, Captain Aldrich said he was shot yesterday. Lieut. Barstow said he could not muster a dead man into the service. The Captain [said] wait a few minutes untill I go and see the General. So the Lieut. waited. When the Captain came back, he said that he told the General that the man had fulfilled his part of the contract by re-enlisting and that the Government had failed in not mustering him, also that the man was the only child of his mother and she was a widow and that he was her only support. If he was mustered it would give her $750.00 a goodly sum of money for her old age. The Old General thought a moment and said, "muster the boy by all means and give my compliments to his mother." The boy was mustered. It was the first time a dead man was mustered in to the U.S. Army. We were all very happy over it.

I am detailed for an expedition and to report on the *Massasoit* at half past eleven. I reported all right. Tom Porter wanted me to let him go in my place. I told him no, he said I would get shot this time sure. I said not any. But Porter got another boys place and is with us. The detail is Corporal Bancroft, Porter, Popple, Wetmore and I. On board the *Massasoit* with two scows in tow. The gunboat *Bombshell* goes as escort with the little *Dollie* in tow. We went down into the Sound and up the Columbia river to Columbia a small town, here the *Massasoit* and *Bombshell* anchor. we board the *Dollie* with the scows in tow and go up the Scuppernong river to the mouth of the canal that goes to Lake Phelps and the Collins Plantation, where we arrived at midnight. A squad of the boys pushed on up to Lake Phelps to [twist] the flood gates and let the water in the canal and send some darkies down with an ox team to tow up the scows. The rest of us camped here for the night. Wetmore was on picket and shot a dog.

Jan. 23 [1864]. Collins Plantation on the Lake Phelps, Tyrrell Co., N.C. This morning the darkies came down with two yoke of oxen and brought up the scows. On our way up here we overhauled [overtook] an old man with a horse and cart. Quartermaster H. I. Hodges who is in command over all turned them over to me to drive and care for, for fear that the old man might go and give information to the rebels. So I ride while the rest of boys walk. Our Captain C. S. Aldrich is in command of the soldiers. We arrived up here at nine o'clock. This plantation is owned by the Collins family and contains three thousand acres and is divided into squares of one hundred acres each and each square a deep ditch about one rod wide around it with a row of trees each bank. The canal from the lake to the Scuppernong river [is] six miles long, with two rows of trees on each bank, set back far enough from each bank for yoke to go,[12] when they tow the scows down to the river loaded with farm products. This canal is the only means the planters have of getting their stuff in to the markets of the world. The soil is of a low bottom land, black and very rich and productive. It takes three hundred field hands to work the plantation, besides many others in the shop, mills and the big house. There is a saw mill, grist mill, a large shop where all kinds of tools are made to use on the plantation. The cabins for the slaves is almost a village at the foot of the lake. The big house is very large and commodius, with a big garden near by. Before this was was on it was a beautiful place. The Collins are an old english family who have been here over seventy years and were very rich. The darkies told us that it took a four horse team to move their money and had a full company of rebel soldiers for an escort. Their furniture, what they did not take with them, they put into the darkie cabins or quarters as they were called. In the overseers house we found a large box of silver plate and one of china which was confiscated by Quartermaster Hodges. To the left of this place is the mansion of Charles

Pettigrew a brother of the rebel general of the same name.[13] Our brigade have had many battles with his brigade in this war.

Jan. 24 [1864], Sunday. A squad of the 24th battery came overland from Plymouth, they came as cavalry.

To day I drove my horse and cart down to the overseer's house, (Spear is his name) here we found other carts and wagons. It is about two miles from the big house. Here the Q. M. Hodges confiscated a piano, a quantity of furniture, two large portfolios containing fine engravings. (I tried to get away with one of them, but could not make it work.) One large room was filled with books. We filled sixty large grain sacks with them. I took a copy of "Shakespere" and "Youngs Night Thoughts" for mine. Capt. Hodges put into my cart a divan (or sofa) three ottomans and a writing desk which belonged to Miss Mary Pettigrew a niece of the rebel general Pettigrew. The desk was not locked so I went through it very quick. I found some old letters, a pocket handkerchief, two silver extension pen holders, one had a gold pen in, one gold letter seal with an ivory top and one ivory paper cutter, with this inscription on, Miss Mary Pettigrew from Cousin James Badwell. Capt. Hodges put in my cart a pair of rose blankets. they were very thick and heavy. As we are to have our veteran furlough soon, I thought I would like to take one home with me. On our way back to the scows, I stoped and hid one in a fence corner, then after I had unloaded my cart I would come back and get it. When I drove down to the dock, the Capt. was there and looked my load over. when I asked him if I cuold drive the rig over land to Plymouth, he said yes patting me on the shoulder and bring that blanket back. I brought it back. The old man had the drop on me.

I was on guard last night. This morning just at day break Corporal Albert H. Bancroft came around to see how things were (he is corporal of the guard) when we heard geese quacking after they had quacked two or three times I told Bancroft to hold my gun and I would try to get one. He took my gun, (he was always to help on a trip for forage). The geese kept up their noise so I had no trouble to locate them, as it was near the overseer's house. When I opened their house I saw right big ones. I caught four, took two in each hand and carried them to near my post and put them in an out building, then went back after the other four. I got them all right and as I was near the building one of them slipped out of my hand - they were heavy - and flew off into the lake. I got seven out of the eight - a good catch. When daylight came as there was no need of a guard I retired and found a box cooped up seven geese, three turkeys and two hens quite a lot of poultry for one trip. I heard the object of this expedition up here. Last week a squad of guerrillas came this way and shot several negroes in cold blood, one they made to stand in his doorway with his arm stretched out, then shot him, leaving his family to care for the body.[14] This afternoon a number of white citizens came to see Capt. Hodges. He told them that if they did not put a stop to such works, he would make the inhabitants of Tyrrell County feel the terrors of war. A great many of the colored are getting ready to go back with us to Pymouth. One of the scows they loaded with corn, sheep and hogs. The other one is loaded with furniture, darkies and other <u>truck</u>. Every thing being ready the water was let into the canal, the ox teams hooked to them and they started for Plymouth. Bancroft goes and has charge of my boxes of poultry. The artillery officers also go by water. Porter, Popple and Wetmore are to ride their horses and help the artillery boys drive the herd of cattle overland, of course I drive my old horse and cart. There is not a commissioned officer left with us. Non Com's only.[15] We will have a lively time to night. We have had a good time.

Jan. 25 [1864]. All hands were up early this morning. We all camped up stairs last night in a building that was used by the young white men as a hunting lodge, over the big fireplace was a pair of large horns that would measure eight feet from tip to tip. They were enormous.

Before we turned in last night one of the boys suggested that we have some chickens to carry on our trip for this days trip. We were all agreeable, so four of us (I was one) paid a visit to the hen coop of the overseer. I wrenched the pad lock off the door, went in took the chickens by the head so that they would not make any noise nor bite the boys as I passed them out of the door. Their heads were wrung off. When a sufficient number were manipulated, we took them down to the lake and skinned and dressed them, then went to our room and soon had them on the fire cooking in great shape. Inside of fifteen minutes from the time chickens were mentioned they were cooking. We made very good time for once. I gave an old rooster to one Mosher[16] of the 24th battery which he cooked nearly all night then it was as blue as a whetstone. I put a large armchair in my cart, my books, a pair of dear antlers. I had two of G. P. B. James books to read on the road. The *Field of the Cloth of Gold*, and *Agincourt*, were their titles. Of course I got [them] in. After the cattle were well started on the road we took up the line of march for Plymouth. We made about nine miles then camped for the night. Had plenty of eggs on the road.

Jan. 26. We were up early this morning, got our breakfast, then on the road for <u>home</u>. I took a boy in my cart who had the ague. No adventures on the road. We arrived here in Old Plymouth this evening at eight o'clock, tired after my long ride. After putting out my horse, I went to my tent where I found some cold baked fresh pork and soft bread, which I lined by jacket very nicely. Since we have been gone, the 15th and 16th Conn. regiments have come to relieve us when we go on our Veteran furlough. Snook told me that a man strolled through the camp to day and asked where they were from. they told him from Ontario County, N.Y. then he asked if there were any Mosher's among them. they told him yes one. He said his name was Frank Mosher of the 15th Conn. The boys told me that they knew he was a Mosher, for he talked so thick and fast. After I had finished my supper I went down to their camp to hear their band play. The boys pointed out the man to me. He was on headquarter guard, on post. I passed him several times, but did not recognize him. After he was relieved I found him and made myself known. Sure enough he was Cousin Frank Mosher, Uncle Abel Mosher's son. He does talk like a Mosher sure. After a short chat I went to my tent and went to sleep. I was tired and sleepy. We had one dandy trip.

Jan. 27 [1864]. Cleaned up gun and straps. Feel somewhat old. Letter from home. My poultry came in all right and in good shape. I gave a goose to Bancroft for his trouble in caring for them on the boat.

Jan. 28. On camp guard.
Capt. Aldrich came to my tent and said Mosher! Capt. Hodges wants to know where those two silver pen holders were that were in that writing desk. I told him that I did not know anything about any silver pen holders. He said no more and went away. I simply lied to him. One pen holder I had given to Mosher of the 24th Battery. One I kept.

Jan. 29. Off guard early. Cleaned my gun and straps. This evening I went down to the Methodist Church to a concert given by the 16th Conn. band boys. Every thing was going along well with prospects of a good show, when an orderly came in and called out the regimental Adjutants. soon after the Orderly Sergeants were ordered out, then all the men were ordered out. when we reached quarters, I with others were detailed, with two days rations to report on the dock at eleven o'clock. At eleven and a half we went on the steamer *Massasoit,* run up the Roanoke river. There are one hundred and fifty in this detail with the Lt. Col. of the 16th Conn. in command.[17] Lt. Com. C. W. Flusser the commander of the fleet with a squad of sailors and a boat howitzer are with us. We had a delightful ride up the river.

Jan. 30. This morning at four o'clock we landed at Cedar Landing and began the march to Winsor, the county seat of Bertie County.[18] The gunboat *Bombshell* started for the same place and go [went] up the Cashie river that runs into the Roanoke river a few miles above Plymouth. After we landed and got every thing ready we started the sailors drawing their howitzer a short way only, as they found a horse and made it do the pulling. We reached Winsor at sunrise or rather near there and were trying to get to the rear of the place, when the sailors got in a hurry and fired a shell over the town, before we could reach the main road leading out, a company of rebel cavalry came rushing out that road and we trying to head them off, but they were too soon for us and got away. How they went, flying light. We run them out from under their saddle bags. The band lost their horns, which we picked up. I got one cavalrymans saddle bag, in it was a new shirt, several collars and a pair of home made cotton socks, all of which I appropriated. The people of Winsor expected a big time to day. The cavalry were to have a goose pull to day. This is how they do the trick.

A goose is hung by its feet to a limb of a tree, high enough so that a cavalry man standing up in his stirrups can just reach the head of the goose, then they ride around in a circle as fast as they can go and under the goose, then make a grab for its head, try to pull it off the limb. if they succeed the goose is theirs. They did not have their pull to day. A company of infantry was expected in town, every one of the towns people had a quantity of stuff cooked in honor of the great occasion. Our boys got the goods.

To get back on the job. After the cavalry had run out, we were after them hot, on the road they were on, but they had cut through the woods on to another road. we could hear their officer say "Steady men! Steady men!" they were steadying down in great shape, as their sabers jingled less and less. Steady men! Steady! Then Flusser gave his sailors the command, give them one half shell. A whole shell went out and after them. Then the rebel officer sung out to his men: "Halt! Halt! you sons of bitches! Halt! Halt! you sons of bitches!" No halting for those fellows. That officer must have been acquainted with the mothers of all of his command. How we all laughed. It was one good joke on the rebels.

After this episode we pushed through the woods to a large open field where we formed our line and waited for them. They had their eyes on us all the time. We could see them come out into the roadway, ahead of us, but not near enough for us to get a shot at them. After a while we got tired of waiting for a shot and started back for the town where we found that the *Bombshell* and crew had captured two boxes of arms a quantity of ammunition, and clothing and other stuff. Here I saw the stocks and whiping post for the first time in this south land. We had spoiled the fun for the citizens of Winsor for once. All things being ready, at one o'clock we started on our return to the landing and were on the boat at sundown and into Plymouth at nine o'clock. A tired lot of men. very tired.

Jan. 31 [1864], Sunday. They had a big fire here yesterday. Inspection this morning. Dress parade to night.

Feb. 1. Nothing but drill to day.

Feb. 2. A boat came in this morning with the report that the rebels had attacked Newbern with 15,000 men.[19] Capt.Aldrich has a letter from the War Committee of Ontario County, N.Y. that our $300.00 is ready for us at any time. All quiet here.

Feb. 3. The steamer *Thos. Collyer* came this noon from Newbern for reinforcements for that place. The rebels have drove our men inside of their works and blown up the gunboat *Underwriter* she is a double end ferryboat. The 15th Conn. goes down there to help out. That takes my cousin Frank Mosher away from here. I have had many a good visit with him. He frets to much to be a good soldier and is worrying about his wife and boy. He was at our home when I was about 10 years old.

When I was up to Lake Phelps Lt. Col. Clarke came to my tent and borrowed the big pipe I got at Harroldville.[20] (Some how he had heard about it.) He took it to the sutlers where the officers hang out nights. Capt. Hall of the Generals staff has a big pipe, Clarke wanted to match with hm. That night the Lt. Col. went in asked the sutler for a pipe of tobacco. the butler said help yourself Col. he did, then lighted up. all hands had a pull at it and when they were through, half of it was left.[21]

Feb. 4 [1864]. Monthly inspection this morning by Capt. Coats. Drill this afternoon. No news from Newbern.

Feb. 5. On camp guard. The *Massasoit* came in this morning and reported that eighteen transports were seen on their way to Newbern. So if the place isn't taken it won't be at all. Last night when the cavalry went out they reported that a rebel courier had passed up through to Weldon and told the citizens that Newbern was in their hands. (In a _____ [unreadable]). We are putting things here in shape for a siege if it comes.

Feb. 6. The regiment was out on the breastworks at three o'clock this morning. Old "Dad" Wessels is not going to be caught with his breaches down.[22] No, No, it would not look well and he an old man. No excitement.

Feb. 7, Sunday. I am not feeling very well. The *Miami* came in last night and reported that the rebels had left Newbern in a hurry. The *Miami* is the flag ship of our fleet, with Lt. Col. C. W. Flusser in command. No inspection. Had a chill this afternoon. I was detailed for picket on the gunboat *Bombshell* but could not go. Lt. Col. Clarke inspected the regiment to night.

Feb. 8. On camp guard. No excitement. The report is that the rebels are to come down on us Wednesday. Bully!

Feb. 9. Off guard early. The big gun, the two hundred pounder on Fort Worth, was fired to day and it worked well. The gunboats tried their guns and threw shells over the town. The mail came in, had a letter from home, Father is very low. Inspection tonight.

Feb. 12. The steamer *Col. Rucker* came in to night. But no Paymaster. No news.

Feb. 13. On provost guard. This afternoon the steamer *Genl. Berry* came in. Capt. Aldrich, Lieut. Fay and Sergt. Buckingham[23] go North on recrutiting service. Tonight the steamer *Pilot Boy* came in two companies of the 2nd Mass. Heavy artillery. No excitement.

Feb. 14 [1864], Sunday. Off guard early. I was around my tent about ten o'clock when the Sergt. Major E. R. Stillman[24] came and handed me furlough for 35 days. I hustled around and got my things together and just got on board the *Pilot Boy* as she was about to leave, at noon.

We reached Roanoke Island at six o'clock this afternoon whre I transfered to the boat *Genl Berry* and stayed.[25]

Feb. 15. Roanoke Island. This morning I went ashore to company A. (85th) quarters and took breakfast with Sergt. Fairbanks[26] a good breakfast. Had a visit with the boys, got my transportation for Norfolk, Va. then back to the *Genl Berry.* when the boat from Newbern, N.C. arrived with the mail we put out for the Currituck Sound and run up to the Currituck Bridge at the entrance of the canal. The Dismal Swamp canal. At two o'clock we reached the Currituck Bridge. Here we waited until the boat from Norfolk, Va. (The *Fawn* a small propeller) came in. We all transferred to her. We had 27 prisoners with us. Soon after we boarded the *Fawn* it began to rain and kept it up all night. The cabin of the *Fawn* is a very small affair. No sleeping accomodations. Had roast wild goose for supper. It was very most excellent. It was good, the first I had ever eaten.

Feb. 16. Currituck Bridge. We left here at six o'clock this morning. We passed the Stern Wheel boat *The Brothers* on her way to the camp of the 96th N.Y. Had not gone far, when the boiler pump on our boat stuck. The Capt. run the boat in shore, to hold her from drifting. When the pump was fixed and we tried to get off from the shore, couldn't. We had to wait untill the other boat came along to help pull us off. A bit of hard work but we were soon on our way. The canal runs for a long way through the Dismal Swamp. It is dismal all right.

We arrived at Norfolk, Va. at ten o'clock to night. I went to the Provost Guard quarters. (The 27th Mass. are provost guard) Here was a large room, with a coal fire in the grate. It was quite cold, so that a coal fire was very comfortable. There were many men sleeping on the floor, after I got warm I turned in on that same floor. I slept good all night.

Feb. 17. Norfolk, Va. Up quite early this morning, after breakfast with the boys I took a stroll around the city. At eleven o'clock took the boat for Fortress Monroe. Went inside for a few minutes only. I found Capt. Aldrich, Lieut. Fay and Sergt. Buckingham. We all took the five o'clock boat for Baltimore. On board the boat I found Ambrose Bucklin a former member of Company A, our regiment. He was going home on a furlough. When we were in Washington, D.C., the first winter out, he was transfered to the regular artillery.[27]

No. 1	QUARTERMASTER'S OFFICE,
	PLYMOUTH, N. C., *Feby* , 1864.

Captain of the "*Pilot Boy*" will pass *C. C. Mosher* to *Roanoke*

By order of Capt. H. I. HODGES, A. Q. M.

[signature] Clerk.

**Mosher's Furlough Pass,
February, 1864**

Feb. 18 [1864]. Batimore, MA. [sic] We arrived here at ten o'clock this morning. Had a slight chill. Then had breakfast, and took a stroll around the city. At half past nine I took the cars for Elmira, N.Y.

Feb. 19. Elmira, N.Y. Arrived here at ten o'clock this morning. Took the six o'clock train for Canandaigua, N.Y. where I arrived ten o'clock to night. I stayed at the Webster House and slept in a feather bed for the first time since November 1861. In the meantime I found my brother George and learned father died Feb. 1st. I should liked to have seen him before he passed away. But could not. I came home as soon as I could, I was too late. [*** ADDED BY MOSHER SOME TIME IN 1917. From now on untill I return to my regiment must be from memory only. It is over 52 years that my memory will have to run back. After I took breakfast with the family of my brother George, I visited with a few people I met on the street. Then I saw Mr. James Chapin of Chapinville (now Chapin) he was up in his carriage and invited me to ride down with him. I accepted the invitation. About noon I walked in my home. My Mother and sister Sarah were somewhat surprised, but very glad to see me, of course I was glad to see them, as well as to be home once more. My Mother is crippled up with the rheumatism in her feet and has to walk with a crutch, other wise her health is good. It seems mighty good to be home in God's country.

**Charles's Sister, Sarah Mosher
(Wayne Mahood Collection,
Reproduction by Ronald Pretzer)**

Father was buried in Waterloo, N.Y. Mother was not able to go to the cemetery and be at the burial.

We all talked over ways and means as to how they were to get along after I went back to my regiment. My brother David and family live in Seneca Falls, N.Y. He is married and has two children, William A. and Amelia E. David came up to see me. Before this I had been to Canandaigua and got my $300.00, Ontario County bounty. Never had so much money before. We all decided that it would be a good thing if I should go down to Seneca Falls and buy a small place there for a home where my mother and sister could live while I finished my years of service in the army. When I told them I had re-enlisted for 3 years or during the way they were not surprised at all, they rather expected that I would. I never wrote them from the army about it, which was just as well, I reckon. In a short time I went to Seneca Falls to visit David and family, when I looked the village, and settled on a small house on Troy St. I bought it through Mr. Charles L. Hoskins (a dry goods merchant) and paid $200.00 down. (The place was $600.00) knowing that my bounties when due would take care of it. After a good visit with my brother, I went back home. Of course I went to the old church and church sociables had a good time generally and saw many of my old friends and neighbors. My Sunday school teacher Mrs. James S. Manson, all were glad to see me. My mother was not only glad but proud of me. At the Town Meetings that spring the people voted on the question as to whether the men in the army should have a vote in the annual election in the fall. This is Presidential year and votes counted with both partys. I walked from Chapinville to Hopewell Center (it is more than four miles) through slush and mud to get there. Then I had to be identified as to who I was, then had to swear my vote in, all of which I did in good shape. Mr. Wm. Callister identified me and rode home with him. This was my first vote. I voted right, that the boys in the field could vote.

I met Captain Aldrich in Canandaigua many times. He had picked up a few recruits and wanted me to take charge of them when I went back. I did not want to and I did not. At a big war dinner up there on day the Capt. invited me to dine with him. I dined. It was not like dinner in camp. I paid up the small bills which had accumulated during his [Mosher's father's] sickness. By [unreadable] was the last draft I sent him had not been cashed. One day that I was in Canandaigua the 24th N.Y. Cavalry passed through. Frank Jessup is a 1st Lieut. in it. The 75th N.Y. infantry were home on their Veteran furlough and made things hum here, they broke up the colored barber shops in Canandaigua. The regiment was raised in Cayuga County, N.Y. As all things have an end so my furlough did. The time had come to say good bye. After leaving money enough with my mother and sister to move with and for their immediate use. (Before this I had my photograph taken to leave home and had bought a new diary in the pocket of which I put the photograph of my sister). Kissed my mother and sister good bye for the last time. Here I begin my new diary with this entry***.]

Portrait of Charles C. Mosher
Taken while he was on furlough, February, 1864
(Wayne Mahood Collection,
Reproduction by Ronald Pretzer)

March 16, 1864. Wednesday, Chapinville, N.Y. I left home this afternoon at two o'clock for my regiment. Sarah went with me to Canandaigua. We took supper with brother George and his family. At eight o'clock I took the train for Elmira, N.Y. where I arrived at half past eleven o'clock, went to the Washington Hotel and put up for the night.

March 17. Elmira. After breakfast I went to the Pay Masters office to get my state bounty of $50.00. I showed him my papers, he said "get out of here we have had trouble enough with you 75th men, get out of here, get out." I told him I was not a 75th man. I was a member of the 85th N.Y. He said that "the 85th was not home yet" I told him I was here all right and I wanted my state bounty of $50.00. Then he got mad and told me to get out or he would call the guard and have me run in. I got right out. I cannot get it short of Albany, N.Y. So I will have to let it go. I got my transportation for Baltimore and left here at seven o'clock.

March 18. Baltimore. Arrived here at one o'clock. Took the five o'clock boat for Fortress Monroe, got a berth, turned in and went to sleep.

March 19. Fortress Monroe. I arrived here this morning at eight o'clock and went to Adjt. Genl. Office and learned that our regiment had not left Plymouth, N.C. yet. I took boat and went over to Norfolk, Va. Here I found that the boat did not leave untill Monday. I went to the Provost Marshals head quarters and put up with the 27th Mass. I am in good hands. Took a stroll over to the Gosport Navy Yard and saw the work of destruction which the rebels did when they burned. I saw the old United States frigate, one of the three deckers of old times. Saw Paymaster Walter Crane, who told me that he had not been to Plymouth to pay our boys yet. I will be there in time for my pay. The provost guard (the 27th Mass.) furnish a guard for the theater every night. They invited me to arm and go with them, while I would have to stand I could just as well or better, without any cost on my part. I accepted their invitation. I armed and fell in line. We marched to the theater. I was posted in one of the upper galleys. I had a good view of the stage. Laura Keene and her troupe played "Our American Cousins."[28]

March 20, Sunday. Norfolk. I went to the Episcopal Church this morning. The first time I ever attended the service of that Church. Then took a talk around the city. I found an oyster house open and dropped in and ordered me a half dozen on the half shell. They were big, fat and delicious, as well as filling. After another short walk I droped in another place and ate another dozen. Then I was surely full.

March 21. Norfolk. At eight o'clock I took the steamer *Fawn* and went down the canal and reached the Currituck Bridge at half past four. Here we had to wait untill dark for the *Genl Berry*. Things begin to look familiar, home like you know. Boarded the *Genl Berry* for Roanoke Island. The Sound is very rough, with the wind blowing a gale. (I have told about this boat when on our trip to Juniper Bay.)

March 22 [1864]. Roanoke Island. We arrived here at midnight. I stayed on board and [completed] my sleep out. This morning I landed and went to the camp of our company A and took breakfast with the boys. I begin to feel at home. I am back to army life. The Sound is still very rough and the wind blowing a gale and down south. The *Genl Berry* is aground at the dock. The *Thos Collyer* is agound out near the light house and is loaded with troops. I pity the boys on her. A large sailing vessel is on the bottom of the Sound, as the wind has blown the water out from under her. She is about a half mile out. The natives here say that it is the hardest gale they have had in 25 years.

March 23. Roanoke Island. The wind has gone down some but it still blows. The *Genl Berry* has gone out and took the men off the *Thos Collyer* and gone up to Plymouth. To night the steamer *Pautuxet* from Newbern came in. She is bound for Plymouth and is anchored off the Island. Her Capt. came ashore in a small boat. When he went back I bid Company A boys good night and went with him. Lucky for once. On board the *Pautuxet*. As soon as I got aboard, the steward wanted me to help him clean some shad, of course I helped. They cleaned so hard, we put them in a tub of water to soak. We went below, where the steward and I ate a big pie, then went back and tried the fish again, but no go, so he gave one of the deck hands 50¢ to clean them in time for breakfast. We went below and turned in for the night.

March 24. Plymouth, N.C. When I woke up this morning at five o'clock I myself here and only two days over time, which are easily accounted for, owing to the gale. I went up to camp and finding the boys asleep, I went back to the boat and had breakfast. Here I found Lieut. Elam Beeman. I did not see him last night. He is an Ontario County man and in 1861 he was a member of the 44th N.Y. Elsworth Avengers they were called, his home is on the west side of Canandaigua Lake. I came very near of going in his regiment in 1861. Now he is an officer of colored troops. Quite a brag. He said that in the first battle he was going to be a live Captain or a dead Lieut. He did not know what he was talking about. He lied. He came out as he went in. He wanted me to apply for a commission in the colored troops. I had rather be a high private in Cmopany A, 85th N.Y. than be an officer of a lot of darkeys. I did accept his invitation to take dinner with him on this boat just the same. After a long chat with him I went back to camp. All the boys were glad to see me. I have not been reported absent with out leave, so I am all right. I stand a good chance of going home again when the regiment goes on their Veteran furlough. Part of the troops are here to relieve us. The 15th Conn. have left, but the 16th Conn. are here. Wrote home.

March 25 [1864]. Drew my commutation money this morning $6.00. When we are on furlough we get pay for our [uneaten] rations, twenty-five cents per day. The boys asked me how I voted at the town meeting when I was home, on the question of the soldiers in the field voting next fall at the Presidential Election. I told 'em that I walked four miles through mud and slush to the poles [polls] and voted yes that we all might vote in the field next fall and that I had to swear my vote in after I had been identified by a friend. They gave me three cheers. The report is there is 10,000 rebels at Lees Mills. Must be a mistake.

March 26. The cavalry went out to Lees Mills and found only one rebel and brought him in. We are expecting a fight before long.[29] We are getting ready.

March 27, Sunday. Inspection by Lieut. Jones.[30] Lieut. McHenry is sick. We thought the rebels were coming down on us last night. Sure. The gunboats *Miami* and *Southfield* are lashed together in expectation of the rebel ram. They are spread by a spar twenty feet long and then heavy cables hold them together. The plan is to let the ram run between the boats and under the spar and cables, when they will plunge the shot into her and sink her. Hope it will work.

March 28. On picket Washington road outpost. Black Biddy brought us our dinner down.[31] The rebels were down on the cavalry videttes last night. I have a big head ache. I feel not very well.

March 29. I did not stand on post last night. Was not well enough. We were relieved by the 16th Conn. Rained this afternoon and to night it blows a hurricane. That rebel ram up the river at Rainbow, sure pop![32]

March 30. The steamer *Lancer* came in to night with our new arms. They are the Springfield rifle, made at Colts armery. The paymaster came in this afternoon. The same boat brought in two large guns for the gunboat *Southfield*.

March 31. We drew our new guns and equipments. We had quite a time in finding enough equipments to turn in with out loss. This is the why of it. Captain Aldrich is home on recruiting service. 1st Lieut. Charlie McHenry is in command of the company and is responsible for the complete outfit we are to turn in. During the past years of service of course we are shy of many parts of our outfit especially the straps. We skirmish around in our own quarters, as well as the quarters of other companies to make good. Which we did. Now

Lieut. McHenry won't have to put up any good money out of his own pocket. In 1861 Charlie McHenry went out with us as fourth sergeant. (He was a member of the old thirteenth New York from Rochester, N.Y.) Then he jumped over both the 2nd and 3rd sergeants to orderly sergeant. then when 2nd Lieut. Amos Bronson died in 1862 he was promoted to 2nd Lieut. A good officer and likes his whiskey. Capt. Aldrich did not like him a little bit.

We signed the pay roll this afternoon. The steamer *Col. Rucker* came in and took 125 men of the 16th Conn. north, so they could vote for a Republican Governor. That is the report.

April 1 [1864]. On picket on the [unreadable] road in the swamp. I am in command of the post. At eleven o'clock 3 of the Company I boys came out to relieve us so we could go in and get our pay. I received $200.00 in full up to February 1st. Back on picket towards night. It is raining quite hard. My check is for $150.00. I have paid all my little debts, so I am square with the world.

April 3, Sunday. Inspection by Lieut. McHenry. Last night the gunboat *Whitehead* was up the river on picket and saw a small boat with two lights on coming down and makeing soundings. The *Whitehead* hailed her, when she put about and started up stream. It created quite a sensation. That ram is there. Sure!

I was down town this afternoon with my old clothes on and my sailor cap on when I met our Col. Fardella. I saluted him he returned the salute and asked me "what you belong." I told him the 85th, he said is it possible? ha! ha! ha! I not know you! He is a gay old coon. An expedition went out on the steamer *Massasoit*, 2 days rations. one sergeant and 4 men from our company. Then *Genl. Berry* came in. Wrote to David.

April 4. I woke up this morning shaking with the ague and a very sore throat. I feel miserable. I reported to the doctor's he gave me a dover powder,[33] feel a little easy to night.

April 5. Feel rather old this morning. Lieut. McHenry came to see me. he is afraid that I was going to have a sore throat such as he had a short time since and told me I must go to the hospital (It is only a few rods there) I told him I would not, then he said "dam you if you won't go, I'll have the men carry you over." As it is cold and wet I concluded to go. Here I am in our regimental hospital for the first time in my life. I must own that is a very comfortable after all, only the name of being in the hospital, I detest above all things.

April 6. I feel very well to day. only my throat is badly swollen and very painful. I will come out all right yet I reckon. Only I had rather be with the boys. It is quiet here.

April 7 [1864]. In the hospital yet. Warm and pleasant. A boat came in last night with those [16th] Conn. men, they had been home to vote for governor, but went to Hatteras on a court martial. When I was home on my furlough I bought a watch. All the boys are trading watches all the time and I traded. Guess I got beat. "Gus" Gregg[34] got in the guard house yesterday for wearing his over coat on at guard mounting. He is out again to day. Monthly inspection by Capt. Coats.

April 8. Warm and pleasant. Have been in my room nearly all day, reading and writing. I have a copy of George Crabb's poems. They are fine. John Buell came in the hospital to day he is on the sick list. Brigade drill is the order of the day now in camp. The boys say that Col. Fardella does not know any thing about it. Lt. Col. Clarke is ordered to take command of Roanoke Island, Co. A. of our 85th is there now. Major Crandall[35] fell from his horse and is badly hurt. The *Massasoit* came in with a small mail.

April 9. The weather is lousy this morning. Drizzling this afternoon which turned into rain and kept it up untill night. Genl Butler has ordered the paymaster here to pay us. The reason we have [not] gone on our veteran furloughs is because the exingencies of the service would not admit of it and that our furloughs shall be extended in proporition to our stay here. Good for Butler. A letter from Sarah says Mother is at Georges and she is in Geneva. They have moved their things down to Seneca Falls, N.Y. and they are going to visit a while before they go down. Good!

April 10, Sunday. Rained all night. Pleasant this morning. All quiet here.

April 11. Pleasant to day. The boys have brigade drill every day.

April 12. Pleasant this forenoon and rainy this afternoon. Wrote home. Had a letter from George. All well there.

April 13. Pleasant. All quiet.

April 14. Quiet. I spoke to the Doctor to night about my going back to my company. He said if I was well enough I might. I am well enough and did not want to come here. Guess it has been for he best for me to come.

April 15. Reported for duty this morning to my company. I have been in the hospital ten days. Capt. Aldrich of our company Lieut Fay of F Co. and Capt. Cartwright[36] of Company I came in from recruiting service and in nearly 100 new men.[37] I feel sorry for them, they are so green.

April 16 [1864]. No drill to day. The gunboat *Tacoma* came in. she mounts 12 guns. Her commander had a dispute as to senority with Lt. Com. C. W. Flusser of the *Miami*. Flusser won out. The *Tacoma* put back for Newbern.

April 17, 1864, Sunday. The 16th Conn. band gave us a concert last night, they play fine. Had regimental inspection this morning by the Col. Fardella. Our company escorted the colors to its quarters. One company of the 16th Conn. left for Roanoke Island to day.

About half past four o'clock, on my return from Black Biddy's with warm biscuit for supper (She is the colored woman who bakes for us sometimes) I met a squad of cavalrymen holding their Lieut. on his horse. I asked what was wrong. They said a squadron of rebel cavalry charged down on them and drove them in. The Lieut. was wounded at the first volley.[38] I rushed back to quarters and reported to the orderly J. B. Robinson. He blew his whistle and the command "fall in! fall in!" rung out. We were soon in line. The general orders here are for each regimental command to form at the place assigned them at the fortifications. Our regiment was to form on our parade ground and await orders. Our regiment is divided up a follows:[39] Co. A. Roanoke Island, Co's C. & H, up the river at Fort Gray. Co. K. in the 85th redoubt - or more proper Fort Wessells. Our other six companies are here in town. Our six companies were formed in our companys streets before our officers knew what was going on. They very soon found out however. That rebel cavalry not only drove in our cavalry out post but our infantry pickets on the outpost Washington road are captured. Our Lieut. McHenry has always said that he wanted to be on picket when the rebels came down on us. He was on all right.

Our garrison consists of the following commands, with Brigadier General Henry W. Wessells in command.

    101st. Pa. Vet. Vol. Lt. Col. A. W. Taylor, 300 men
    103rd. Pa. Vet. Vol. Col. Theodore F. Lehmann, 400 men
    16th. Conn. Vet. Vol. Col. Francis Beach, 400 men
    85th N.Y. Vet. Vol. Col. Enrico Fardella, 450 men
    24th N.Y. Ind. Battery Capt. Lester Cady
    Detachment from companies A and F 12. N.Y. cavalry, Capt. Roach[;]
    Two companies of the 2nd Mass. heavy artillery, Capt. Sampson

Captains [Thomas I.] Johnson and [Calvin] Haggard of the 2nd Loyal North Carolina were recruiting for that regiment. (Buffalos they were called) each had a small detachment. Capt. Marvin (our 85th former Sergt. Major)[40] and Lieut. Bascom were recruiting for U.S. Colored Troops. The morning reports show that 1800 were reported for duty.

Our town in full of excitement now. The officers have discovered that there is fun ahead. The mail steamer leaves soon for Roanoke Island. The officers wives go there. I sent my discharge paper and certificate of re-enlistment to my brother David for safe keeping. I closed the letter with this, "We expect some from here." We have been spoiling for a fight here for months. We will have it.

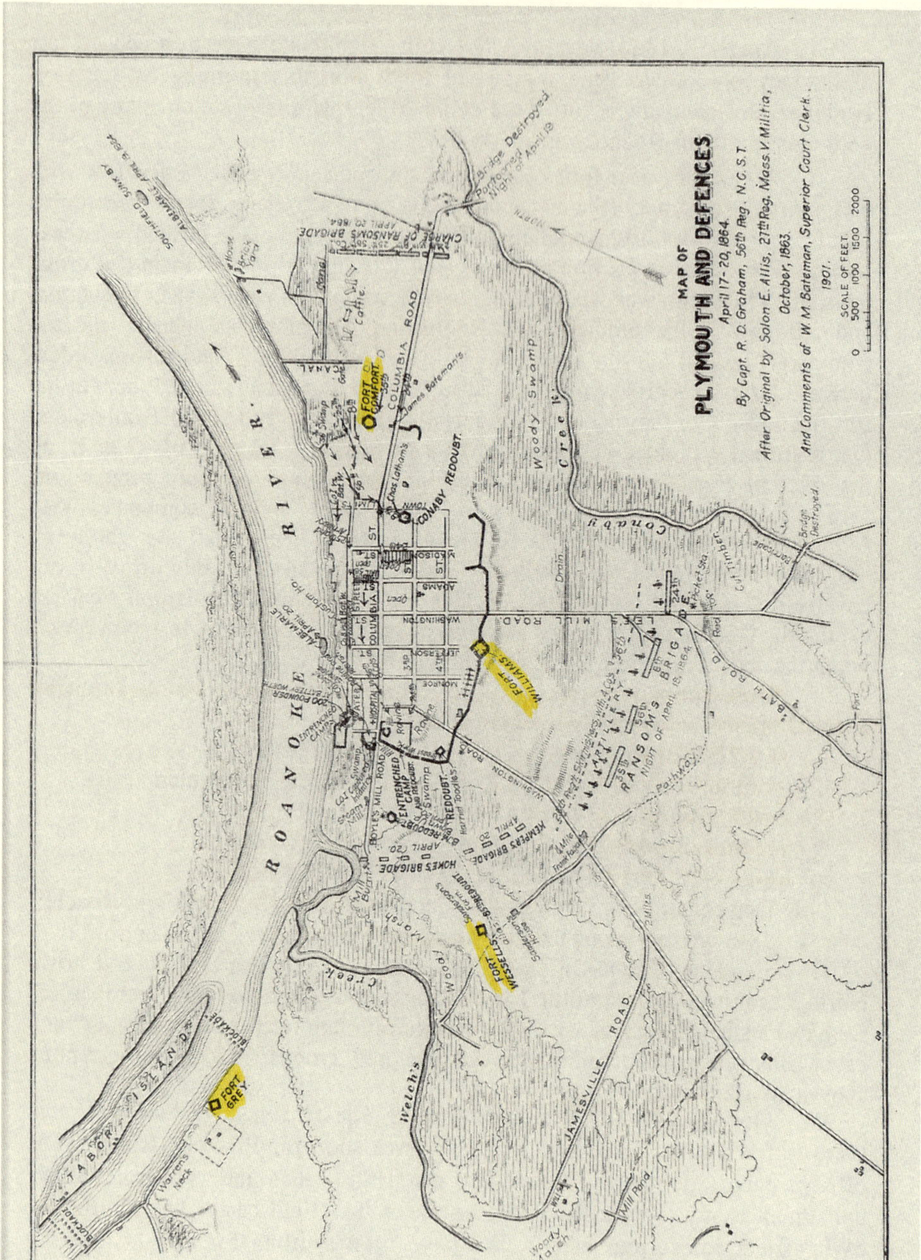
MAP OF
PLYMOUTH AND DEFENCES
April 17-20, 1864.
By Capt. R. D. Graham, 56th Reg. N.C.S.T.
After Original by Solon E. Allis, 27th Reg. Mass. V. Militia,
October, 1863.
And Comments of W. M. Bateman, Superior Court Clerk.
1901.
SCALE OF FEET.
0 500 1000 1500 2000
NORTH
ROANOKE RIVER
FORT COMFORT
FORT WILLIAMS
FORT WESSELLS
FORT GREY
CONABY REDOUBT.
COLUMBIA ROAD
WASHINGTON ROAD
LEE'S MILL ROAD
JAMESVILLE ROAD
BATH ROAD
BOYLE'S MILL ROAD
HOKE'S BRIGADE
KEMPER'S BRIGADE
RANSOM'S BRIGADE
CHARGE OF RANSOM'S BRIGADE
ENTRENCHED CAMP
TABOR ISLAND
Woody Swamp
Conaby Creek
Welch's Creek
Warren's Neck
Mill Pond
Woody Marsh
CANAL
Bridge Destroyed
SOUTHFIELD SUNK BY ALBEMARLE APRIL 19, 1864
200 POUNDER
Custom Ho.

The Battle of Plymouth, N.C. is on.[41] Heavy firing up the river at Fort Gray. [See map page 138.] Our fortifications are fort Williams at the front and center, battery Worth on the right and on the river front, and to the right and font on, or in, an open field is fort Wessells seperated from the town by a half mile and man works by a wide morass. To the left [looking from river] of fort Williams and Cempher and Coneby[42] redoubts, a line of rifle pits or breast works manned all together except Forts Wessells and Gray.

The gunboats *Miami* and *Southfield* are shackled together to get that ram.[43] We have orders to sleep on our arms to night, ready for any emergency. It means to sleep with all of our clothes and accoutrements on and our guns by our side.

April 18 [1864], Monday. Heavy fireing up at fort Gray last night. The boys on duty up there last night saw small boats in the river with lights on making soundings for that ram. Battery Worth on the river front with her hundred pound parrot gun is waiting for her.

We were up at three o'clock this morning and stood in line untill day light. I was detailed for picket this morning. Lieut. Fay[44] of Co. F. is officer of the guard. Seven of us are on the ridge of sand between fort Wessells and that morass.[45] We have a good view of the whole field and woods in our front. The picket line has been drawn in half way between our old picket line and the works, in the slashing. We can see clear through the woods where the rebels are planting a battery. A shell from the 32 pounder in fort Wessells goes right after it and makes it change its position very quick. When a shell from a 32 pounder explodes it kicks up a big dust. You bet. A heavy skirmish line from the rebels make a drive across the open field. Our boys get after them and rush them back in a hurry. This is done many times. On the picket line to the right of fort Wessells I saw one of our men crawl out over the open field to near the woods where the rebels opened fire on him when he run back to our lines. I don't know who he was, or what he was after. He was a brave and a bold fellow. Out on the picket line (our old picket line) near the reserve post stands a large pine tree. behind of it was a rebel soldier. Before this I had made me a cob house of pieces of rails to rest my gun on, as I lay down prone. Then when I saw that rebel away from his big tree, I banged away at him, how near I came to him I don't know. Then he discovered my whereabouts and returned the compliment. We had quite a duel there for a half hour more or less. He droped a bullet about eight feet or so in front of me. He had a dead bead on me. It made me feel creepy. How near I got to him, can't say. Orders came for the pickets to case fireing. We stoped. It was quite sport. About dusk the rebels cut loose all their guns on the town, 30 in number and in different positions. Our picket line had orders to fall back. Most of the boys went by the Boyles Mills road.[46] I went through the morass. I knew of a run way of single logs through it which I took. I had not gone a rod when a shell plunged in the mud near me (so it seemed then) I run faster, then another shell was after me. Of

The Sinking of the *Southfield*
(Battles and Leaders of the Civil War)

course the rebel gunner did not see me there. His shell was looking for me just the same, which answered every purpose. If I had by any means made a misstep or a shell had disabled me, I surely would have been in a fix. Those shells chased me clean through that morass. When I was through I was directly in front of our regimental lines. I ran up on our Col. [Fardella] he said stop here. I said no I will go to my company. I found them. During the afternoon I had been in after more amunition, so I knew their position at the works. The rebel artillery fire was so sharp and heavy that the gunboats *Miami* & *Southfield* had to unshackle in order to be able to use their guns on the rebels, which they did with good effect. Between nine o'clock and ten o'clock the rebels captured fort Wessells[47] and turned the guns of fort on the town.

April 19 [1864]. Tuesday. This morning just before day light. The rebel ram *Albemarle* came down the river and hit or ramed the (our) gunboat *Southfield* and sunk her the first crack. Her hurricane deck was out of water and the crew had their 12 pound boat howitzer up there. Jack Quinlan (a sailor) and his mate had charge of it (the gun) so Jack not being able to depress its muzzle enough to reach that ram took hold of the button (casable)[48] at the butt of the

196

gun with his hands and gives it the proper angle, then his mate pulls the langard, both were knocked down by the recoil of the gun, but they got up and fired another shot or shell and it went through the ram's open port hole and set her on fire. (Jack Quinlan is the sailor who received the medal from the Navy Dept. for bravery up the Blackwater river in 1862) Lt. Com. C. W. Flusser, commander of the navy, who was on board of the *Miami* was killed. When the ram came down past fort Worth (with its hundred pound rifled parrot gun) the ram was so close to the fort, our men could hear the rebels talking on her.[49] The gunman in charge of that big gun, sung out, "number one are you ready." "Yes" was the response. Then the Captain asked what have you got her trained on boys? "Why, the ram of course," was the reply. Then the Captain gave the command not to fire, as that would draw the fire from the ram. That was what that fort was built there for. Just that ram and nothing else. Hard luck! The 2nd Mass. heavy artillery had the full charge of that fort and its big gun. the enlisted men of that company were all right. The Captain had no sand.[50] Last night when the rebels captured fort Wessells a full rebel brigade charged it four times before they took it. The commandant of the fort, Captain Chapin, was killed. He had sand, plenty.

The fort had a deep ditch and a row of abbatis[51] around it. Our Co. K. boys used hand grenades with good effect, they had more rebel prisoners in the fort than there were of themselves. After the ram had done her work, she run down the river between the swamps and lay there barring any reinforcements from getting up to help us out.

Last night Barber G. Poppel and Seymour Smith[52] of our company B. was killed. Both were good men.

Yesterday while I was on picket our men threw a line of breastwork between us and the river and paralel to the main line in our front and about twenty feet from it. Between each company was built - or thrown up - a traverse, so that the ram could not enfilade us with her guns. Each company had built a bombproof[53] in one corner of our own compartment, if you please to call it by that name. We are in good shape for a fight. Waiting for the rebels to come out after us.

We go down town when we want to and buy stuff from the sutler. Pay later. To night I am detailed for guard on the parapet. Every body is happy and singing to suit their fancy. "We sang of love and not of fame

"Forgot was Columbias Glory.

"Each heart recalled a different name

"But all sang Anna Laura."[54]

April 20 [1864]. Wednesday. Early this morning[55] the rebels opened in good style. All I had to guard last night was own front and watch the fire of the Ram. I would look down the river for the flash of her gun, then get down off the works out of the way. There was no need of my dodgeing, as her shells went away up and over every thing. The rebels began to close in on us. We

The *Albemarle*

were all inside the works in town. The rebels were bringing a gun up to batter in the rear gates of fort Williams. All of us opened on her with our rifles. we piled men and horses up in a heep. They had to go for another gun. About that time our Captain Aldrich sung out "Company B fall in (only twenty-five of us to fall in) forward march." He in the lead. down we went to the main street and out on it untill we came to an angle in it. Turning it we met a full regiment of rebels on a grand charge up the street. We were so close to them we could look into their eyes. On they came. We changed ends with ourselves, or in other words we showed them our heels and started back for our place in the works. Just as we turned to run, the rebels gave us a volley. Jake Perkey got his one and droped down.[56] We kept right on and into our hole. We had good shooting all the morning after this as the rebels swarmed the town. It was like shooting into a flock of black birds. Mighty good shooting for a while. Then we got it, as the rebels in order to reach us had to climb the trees, they began on our right. When they made it too hot for the first company the "yanks" held up a white rag drop their guns, climb out of their holes, run along the top of the works to get out of the range of rebel fire, so were prisoners of war. About this time our color guard stripped our colors from its staff and divided among the boys. My part was a piece of the red stripe, six inches long and one inch wide.[57] The rebels did not get our regimental colors only by pieces. Then they had to get the "yank" that had one of them.

Fort Williams Historical Marker at Plymouth

It did not take the rebels long after to get this place. Soon our company had to climb out of our hole with a white cloth in our hands. As we run along out on top of the works those rebels kept up their fireing on us. None of Company B got hit. When I got out into the open, I passed by a well and droped my revolver in to it for safe keeping. I did not want the rebels to take it away from me. I could have kept it, as we were not searched at all.[58] About noon this 20th day April 1864 when every thing and every one had been captured except fort Williams and its garrison.[59] Brigadier General Henry W. Wessells, surrendered. the Flag was lowered to the ground and Plymouth N.C. was in the hands of Rebels.

We were treated very kindly. Not one of us insulted, nor molested. A few of our men, and only a few, had a cap or haversack taken. All of us were well clothed, each had his overcoat and blanket or blankets.[60] Our boys thought so much of general Wessells that fifty of us clubed together and sent the money north to his home city for his photograph. This was only a few weeks before this. We never recieved them.[61]

After our surrender and we were out in an open field, I heard two rebel officers talking. One said to the other "We have had 1,700 killed and wounded in this fight."[62]

[Added by Mosher sometimes after 1916]
"Headquarters, Dept. of North Carolina
Newbern, N.C., April 22, 1864
General Order[63]

With feelings of deepest sorrow, the Commanding General announces the fall of Plymouth, N.C., and the capture of its Gallant Commander Brigadier General H. W. Wessells, and his command. This result, however, did not obtain untill after the most gallant and determined resistance had been made. Five times the enemy stormed the lines of the General and as many times were repulsed with great slaughter, and but for the powerful assistance of the ironclad ram Albemarle, and the floating sharpshooter battery the Cotton Plant, Plymouth would still have been in our hands.

For their noble defence the gallant General Wessells and his brave band have and deserve the warmest thanks of the whole country, while all will sympathise with them in their misfortune.

To the officers and men of the navy the commanding general tenders his thanks for their hearty cooperations with the army and the bravery, determination, and coolness that marked their part of the unequal contest.

With sorrow he records the death of the noble sailor and gallant patriot Lieut. Commander C. W. Flusser, U. S. Navy who in the heat of battle fell dead on the deck of his ship with the lanyard of his gun in his hand.

The commanding general believes that these misfortunes will tend not to discourage, but to nerve the army of North Carolina to equal deeds of bravery and gallantry hereafter.

By command of Maj. Gen.
John J. Peck
J. A. Hudson
Asst. Adjt. Gen."

This is the way the Confederate congress served it up to Hoke (army) and Cooke (navy):[64]

"Resolved by the Congress of the Confederate States of America, that the thanks of Congress and the country are due and are tendered to Maj. Gen. Robert F. Hoke and commander James W. Cooke, and the officers and men under their command, for the brilliant victory over the enemy at Plymouth, N.C. Approved May 17, 1864."[65]

Chapter Six

"ANDERSONVILLE PRISON: WHO EVER ENTERED HERE LEFT HOPE BEHIND"

(April 20 - September 10, 1864)

Initially, not even their approach to Andersonville Prison, albeit under guard, would extinguish the impudence of the "Plymouth Pilgrims"--an impudence which propelled commandant Henry Wirz into a frenzy. They were, according to John McElroy, "attired in stylish new uniforms, with fancy hats and shoes, the snuggest, nattiest lot of soldiers" the western soldiers had ever seen.[1] But once inside "the Gates of Hell," despite their relative health and wealth, only some indefinable inner strength saved any from the prolonged, agonizing deaths that visited one hundred seventy-five members of the Eighty-fifth Veteran Volunteers.

Remote, infamous Andersonville Prison, officially Camp Sumter, was located just off an insignificant railroad station in a tiny hamlet of less than twenty people. It was constructed on twenty-six and a half acres over a six month period that began, ironically, about the time that Charlie Mosher was anguishing about reenlisting. Shortly after its construction there were approximately 5000 Union prisoners in confinement (one prisoner per 98.7 feet, or 11 square yards). By mid June there were twice the number of prisoners, allowing each less than 4 square yards, including land that was actually uninhabitable. By September, that space was reduced by two thirds. And a proportionate price was paid by the unlucky prisoners--over 13,000, or close to one-third of those who passed beyond the huge, imposing gates, perished.

Miraculously, Charlie Mosher, our diarist, survived. Thus, almost 30 years to the date of his parole, he was able to describe the stark reality of prison life.

This description was the result of at least three different factors--the diaries he so faithfully kept through the 315 days of imprisonment, the urging of his wife and a newspaper editor, and (probably unconsciously) the need to tell his story.

The letter may have been the most important, once it had surfaced. Increasingly, we are made aware of the aftereffects of war on veterans--the traumas, the need for recognition and the contrary need to assuage a gnawing feeling of guilt--"there but for the grace of God go I." This feeling was never so apparent as it was when Mosher revisited Andersonville a half century after his arrival there.

Although hereafter Mosher retains the spirit of a diarist--employing the present-tense with only occasional foreshadowing--he begins, a man at midlife, with an introduction to the most influential experience of his life.

1894

On March 1st, 1865, I reached union lines at Wilmington, N.C. after 315 days of prison life. Each recurring year I, with my family and a few friends, celebrate the event.

The last few days of this last month (this year) I did not work. So I wrote a short sketch of my last days in the Confederacy. I gave them to my friend Charles T. Andrews the editor of the *Seneca County Courier*. Thursday was publication day for the *Courier* so they appeared in to days issue. My wife put up a job on me. The week after the event - March 8, this clipping appeared.

The sketch of my last days took all night. Mr. Andrews and the business manager Mr. Costeto said, "give us some more of that stuff." "Do you mean it," I asked? They both said "yes." I had kept a diary all through my prison life, of which fact they both knew. My prison diary was so faded out that I took a magnifying glass to pick it out. Some evenings I picked a column or more I had never read through before this. I sat up night after night untill 11 o'clock reading and copying it, when I would get so nervous over it, I stopped. I had to go over my life there and see it all as I had lived it. My emotions over came me to such an extent at times that I cried. Could not help it. After some months I finished the copying of it. I was very glad for the opportunity of getting it in cold type. Then the *Courier* people cut me some bristin board[2] and I pasted a copy of it on and made a book of it as you see. Then they printed me an elaborate cover for it. I had more than I used at that time, so have used them for this occasion.

[Editor's Note: The remainder of the journal, as indicated by Mosher, first appeared in the *Seneca County Courier*, March 1, 1894, and was subsequently bound for Mosher in regular book binding. Also it appears the version in the *Courier* was distributed, though how widely is unknown, and was (and is) generally believed to be the entire journal. It repeats, for content, some parts of the journal previously read and is titled *A Story of Rebel Prison Life: Diary of Charles C. Mosher.*]

Plymouth, N.C., April 20, 1864. To-day about noon, after three days hard fighting, we had to surrender. We have been here since May 3, 1863.

Our forces here, in command of Brig.-Gen. Henry W. Wessells, on the morning of the 17th, reported for duty 1,800 men, consisting of the 103d Pa., 101st Pa., 85th N.Y. (my regiment)--these three regiments have been together since March, 1862--the 16th Conn. (who joined us here this last January), the 24th N.Y. Independent battery, two companies of the 2d Mass. H.A., and two companies of the 12th N.Y. Cav. Besides which there were being recruited two companies for the 2d North Carolina Inf. and two companies for a colored regiment.[3] Our gunboats in the river, Roanoke, were commanded by Lieut.-Com. Charles W. Flusser, U.S. navy. He was killed yesterday.

The rebels to whom we surrendered are commanded by Brig.-Gen. Robert F. Hoke--this makes him a major-general[4]--and consists of Hoke's, Ransom's and Kemper's brigades, the latter commanded by Col. Mercer--he was killed in a charge on the 85th redoubt Monday night--and are estimated at from 7,000 to 10,000 men, besides which they had the aid of the powerful iron-clad ram, *Albemarle*, in command of Com. James W. Cook, C.S. navy.[5] Yesterday morning the ram cleaned out our gunboats in the river. This morning we were cleaned out the land forces. It's tough, but we will have to stand it. It was an unequal contest from the first shot, but we showed the Rebs what we were made of, as they sent in the formal summons to surrender, which our general did not accede to. The old man is a fighter. One of the rebel officers said in my hearing that their loss was estimated at 1,700 in killed and wounded. Our loss is about 150 killed and wounded. Smith and Popple[6] of our company were killed. We had excellent shooting this morning; it was like shooting into a flock of black birds, with the exception that our shots were returned very hot.

On the first of last January the three regiments of our old brigade re-enlisted for three years or during the war. We are field veterans. Our first three years would have expired this coming fall. The terms of our re-enlistment were that we should have a thirty days' furlough as soon as troops could be sent to relieve us. On the first of this month the paymaster was here and paid us. All enlisted men received from two to three hundred dollars each, which exhausted the paymaster's money-drawer to such an extent that he could not pay the officers. The paymaster then made us this proposition: As our furloughs were expected daily would we keep enough money for our needs until we reached home, and take a paymaster check for the balance payable in Elmira, N.Y., then he could pay the officers and all would have money. To this we agreed. I have a check for $150, some money and a silver watch. I did have a revolver, but as I passed out of the works in town I dropped it in a well for fear the Rebs would take it from me. The rest of the boys are as well fixed financially as I am.

The clothes we have on are good. I have on a shirt made of ladies' cloth--a soft flannel--one of a pair which my mother made me last month when I was home on a furlough. And by the way, I had this same shirt on March 1, 1865, when I reached our lines. It was still a shirt, and showed more life than

I did. It was full of life, the botanical name of which is *Pendiculus vestimenti*.[7] I was granted a furlough in February, as my father was very sick and wished to see me. He died before I reached home. I think I was the only man in our regiment who received his veteran furlough.

Lieut.-Col. W. W. Clark, of our regiment, is in command of Roanoke Island, and has with him our Co. A, so they are not in this scrape. As soon as our flag was hauled down the officers and men of the 2d Loyal North Carolinians--Buffalos they were called--made a change, the officers doffed their uniforms and donned those of a private, as they did not wish to be recognized by the Rebs. The privates were very glad to change their names. They took the names of our men who were killed. Our little fellow, a drummer took the name of our Seymour Smith.

The officers who were recruiting for colored troops are a Captain Marvin and Lieut. Bascomb.[8] The captain reduced himself to the ranks without a hint of a court-martial. It was Private Martin in a private's uniform. He did not wish to be known as an officer of colored troops. The lieutenant kept his rank and his uniform, and said that he was an officer of colored troops, and told the rebel officers he would not deny it, and they could do as they d----d pleased with him. The last we heard of him was that he was breaking stone on the streets of Raleigh, N.C., along with darkies. He is a plucky fellow.

Plymouth, N.C., April 21, 1864. Yesterday, a short time before our surrender, our 85th color guard stripped the flag from its staff, tore it into pieces and distributed it among the boys. My share is a piece of the red stripe, six inches long by one inch wide.[9]

Last evening the Rebs went gunning for the colored troops, who, when the "jig was up" with us, broke over the works and took to the woods. They were shot down at sight. It was a massacre.

On Friday of last week a squad of recruits came in for our regiment. Among the number was Richard S. Sackett. He was the father of our townsman, Albert C. Sackett. This turn in our affairs will be very hard on them.

This morning we drew four days' rations, forty hard tack and about one pound of pork each. They were from our own commissary stores--small allowance for four days. I took my watch and hung it inside of my boot-top, making the chain fast to strap. All of us stowed our valuables out of sight for fear the Rebs would take them from us. But thus far none of us have lost anything, with the exception of a hat or canteen. There has not been any searching of our persons, no insulting language used to us; we have been treated in a soldierly manner, by men who are every inch soldiers, and very gentlemanly in their conduct toward us.[10]

Our guard to-day is the 35th North Carolina.

At 12:30 we were ordered into line, and with our backs to the North we began our march up the country. The roads are very bad, the creeks are swollen, some that we forded being knee-deep. We mingle freely with our guards, talk, laugh and blackguard with them, expressing our opinions on the war without any fear of offending any one.

After marching about fifteen miles we camped for the night--a tired lot of men. My feet are in poor shape.

Hamilton, April 23 [1864]. Yesterday was a very hard day's march. As we passed some of the houses the women brought us water to drink and were very kind to us. Others sang the Bonnie Blue Flag for us, to which we replied very happily by singing our Union songs. After a march of six miles this morning we reached this place. Here, some of the boys wrote home; I did not.[11]

The Rebs searched our ranks for deserters from their army. They were after the 2d Loyal North Carolina, and found a few, and, it is reported, they hanged their victims.

Our little Smith is safe with us yet.[12]

Sunday, April 24. We have had a good rest since yesterday. The Holcombe Legion of South Carolina are our guard now, and they are a jolly lot of fellows, pleasant in every way.[13] One of them is a curiosity, if not a genius. He carries the most of his person in front, and his mural decorations make him appear as if he was carrying a large brass kettle in front of him. He has a great passion for brass buttons, and if he finds a man with one different from his he must have it, and he has found a good many, for, beginning just under his chin and reaching down his whole front, it is nothing but brass buttons, and they are kept very bright.

After marching ten or twelve miles we camp to-night in a piece of woods. There is prospect of a rain.

April 25. No rain last night. We were up at sunrise this morning, and ate what little we had to eat, and then pulled out on the road again, reaching Tarboro, N.C., about noon. After a good deal of trouble we drew one day's rations, our first from the Rebs, which consisted of a little bacon and either a pint of corn meal or beans--not our old white army bean, but a small reddish kind, nearly round. The Rebs call them cow peas. These we had to cook for ourselves. It's very rank grub.[14]

The ladies of the place came out to see the "yanks," and said, "What did you'uns come down here to fight we'uns for? You'uns critter backs." As we are not up in the classics no reply was made. They are a snuff-dipping lot, and not very attractive. We camp here for the night.

April 26. Up early this morning, cooked our breakfast, then fell into line, when each man's name, company and regiment were taken down, after which we marched to the depot and were crowded into box cars like sardines in a box. At precisely noon we rolled out--bound for where?

At Rocky Mount we connected with the Weldon & Wilmington railroad, still going south, and reaching Goldboro[15] at sundown. We drew a ration of hard tack, which is very poor. We are very hungry. The railroad crosses the Neuse river here. Our brigade was with Maj.-Gen. Foster's expedition that burned the railroad bridge that crossed this river, December 17, 1862.

April 27 [1864]. We were so crowded [in boxcars] last night that sleep was impossible. We were stiff and sore when we arrived at Wilmington this morning at daylight. Orders came to change cars for [unreadable]. It was a restful change to put our feet on the ground again.

The following clipping needs no comment. It is truthful, and was written in Goldsboro, I think, as we did not pass through Raleigh:

The Prisoners

In consequence of some necssary delay on the route the Yankee prisoners captured at Plymouth by Gen. Hoke, did not reach here on Monday as expected. Yesterday evening, however, the first installment of them arrived, six hundred and eighty in number. Another lot will pass through to-day, to the number of about two thousand, two hundred and forty. The Yankees who passed through yesterday were an impudent set of well-dressed vagabonds, full of insolence and impertinence.[16]

Raleigh State Journal, April 30.

Then follows a list of the different commands.

Wilmington, N.C., April 27, 1864. We crossed Cape Fear river this morning on ferry boats. In the river we saw several large steamers being loaded with cotton from lighters. Our guards say they are blockade runners. Again taking the cars we have a very small ration of soft bread and meat given us; and on we go through a low, swampy country. The heat is very oppressive, as the cars have doors only at the sides, and with sixty men packed in each car fresh air is at a premium; there is not enough to go around. At Florence, S.C., we stop for a few hours. Change guards--the 19th Georgia now--and on again, through the heat and dust, we know not where as yet, only the farther south we go the hotter it gets.

Charleston, S.C., April 28. We reached here at midnight, tired and hungry. It was a very tedious journey yesterday. This city is where all this Hell began. In marching through the city we caught an occasional flash of our guns on Morris Island.[17] We are about five miles from our lines. Drew rations, boarded another train, and with the 18th S.C. regiment for guard, moved on. Just after we crossed the Ashley river the front end of our car jumped the track, which made us dance up and down very lively. "Nate" Wright was so frightened that he jumped out of the car, ran ahead and told the engineer to stop the train.

The Charleston and Savannah Railroad
(McElroy, *Andersonville, A Story of Rebel Military Prisons*)

We stopped [were] put on another car and [were on our] away through the swamps and over rivers, still south.

Savannah, Ga., April 29 [1864]. We reached here between three and four o'clock this afternoon. A great many people came to see the "Yanks." The ladies here are rather more attractive than their North Carolina sisters. We talked with one man who was from the State of Connecticut. How we did blackguard him. We made him leave the crowd. At one of the stations on our route we talked with a man who was born in Penn Yan, N.Y. He was a locomotive engineer. We turned our tongues loose on him. We have a new guard, a Georgia regiment, one that was in Fort Pulaski when it was taken by our men.[18] They have never been out of the State, put on a great many airs, and are very overbearing, while our other guards were men who had been to the front and knew how to treat men and men. At 7:30, all aboard and on our journey again.

April 30. To-day we passed through Macon, Ga. This is the only city we have seen that has a home look about it.

Andersonville, Sumter County, Ga. At four o'clock this afternoon our long and tedious journey ended here. Leaving the cars we pass large piles of lumber. Our guards tell us it is for barracks for prisoners. Marching into a large

Captain Henry Wirz

field, the rebel officers, wanting each man's name, rank, company and regiment, ordered us to stand up while they pass through our ranks for that purpose, but we being very tired from the effects of our long journey, prefer to lie down on the ground. After several ineffectual attempts to have us stand up, a small man, with a revolver in his hand, appeared on the scene and introduced himself to us in this startling manner: "Stand up, you Got tam Yankey sons of Got tam b-----, stand up, or I shoot you; you Got tam Yankeys, I vips you mit a broom stick." We stand. The man was Captain Henry Wirz, the commandant of the interior of the prison. (Wirz is a native of Switzerland, before the war was a citizen of Louisiana, by profession a physician, was seriously wounded at the battle of Seven Pines, Va., nearly losing the use of his right arm. Being unfit for field duty he was assigned to the command of a prison at Tuscalloosa, Ala. His health failing, he was granted a leave of absence, went to Europe, and on his return in February, 1864, was assigned to the command of this prison, on the recommendation of Gen. John H. Winder, who was and still is the commissary-general of prisoners, C.S.A., and assumed command here March 27, 1864.)

This is a prison for enlisted men only. Our officers are separated from us and go back to Macon, to a prison for officers. It is a sad parting for us all, as we have been together for so long a time. It's very hard. We shake hands and say good-bye; they march toward the railroad, we toward the prison.

This prison was located here on the 27th of November, 1863, by Captain William S. Winder, son of Gen. John H. Winder. In January, 1864, the stockade was built by slave labor. It is twenty feet high and encloses seventeen acres; is in the form of a parellelogram, facing the west, a small creek about six feet wide, running from west to east through it, dividing it into the north and south sides, the north side being twice as large as the south. There are two main gates on the west side, north and south they are called, and thirty-five sentry boxes on the outside of stockade reached by steps, which are covered to protect the guards from the sun, and high enough so they can look over into the prison and see what is going on at all times. Between the stockade and railroad are the camps for the rebel troops. To the north are earthworks, at the southeast angle of stockade is a fort, also one at the southwest. The graveyard is at the northwest. All around us are pine forests.[19] Lieut.-Col. A. W. Persons, of the 55th Georgia, is in command of the post.

Before entering the stockade we were divided into detachments of 270, which are in charge of rebel sergeants. Each detachment is divided into squads of 90, over which are placed our own sergeants. Sergeant C. J. Simmons is in charge of our squad.[20] The rebel troops with fixed bayonets form their lines on either side of the road way, through which we march into the prison, file left, move across the creek, up into the northwest corner and halt.[21] Our escort left us, and here we are, simply dumb at what we see around us. It seems as if we had been dumped into the infernal regions. As night is almost here, the boys select their chums as near as possible by their old homes and for neighborhood associations. I was a stranger in our company when I enlisted October 8, 1861. Emory P. Farrar was also a stranger (we had never chummed together in the field.)[22] He said to me, "You and I will keep together and let us keep clean." We are chums. After eating a bite of what little we had, and being very tired, we prepared for the night. Farrar and I each have an overcoat; I have two blankets and he one. We spread one blanket on the ground, then our overcoats, then ourselves, with the two blankets over us (the nights here are chilly), and go to sleep.

Sunday, May 1 [1864]. We awoke early this morning, feeling rather chilly, as some one during the night had stolen our blankets. Mary and Gregg[23] also lost two blankets. A company I man had a fight with a thief in the night, and put his knife into him. Rather a rough reception, and from our fellow prisoners, too.[24] There are about 10,000 prisoners here; men who have starved and frozen in the prisons in and around Richmond, Salisbury and Danville; many are without hats, coats, shoes, and have nothing on but an old shirt, all in rags, and a worse pair of pants; they scarcely look like human beings at all; whose countenances show that there has been a desperate fight between hope and despair, and that despair has won the day; men who a few months ago were the flower of the Union army; men who are patriots in the highest sense, and who prize the Old Flag above all else. If not, they would not be in this condition,

"Fresh Fish"
Members of the Eighty-Fifth N.Y. about to enter Andersonville Prison
(Original sketch by Benedict Maryniak)

but, long ago, would have taken the oath to the rebels and gone out. It makes my heart ache to see the poor fellows. Will I ever get to be in like condition? "Beware of the dead line," some one says to us. We look, and about twenty feet from the stockade are stakes driven in the ground, and poles are nailed to or laid on them, the whole about three feet high. We are told it's sure death to be near it, for the guards will shoot at the least provocation. The guard that shoots a Yank has a thirty days' furlough.

After what we called breakfast we took a stroll around. Down by the north gate are fifteen dead, placed in a row. They died during the night, and are a ghastly sight, with nothing on but old dirty shirts, on which is pinned a slip of paper with the man's name, rank, company and regiment written on it--a record of the dead is kept. The bodies of the dead, as well as the bodies of the living, are black and grimy from smoke and exposure, the skin looks like leather,[25] the bones almost prick through; they are simply skeletons.

There are a few stumps left that have not been grubbed out for fire wood. Near the south end of the stockade are three fine trees, which look to be more than one hundred feet high, and without a limb for nearly the whole height. They show the growth of the forests hereabouts, and that lumber might be very plenty for the use of us prisoners in the construction of some kind of protection from the sun and storm, if the rebels had a disposition to be human. Over in the northeast corner is what is called the hospital, and while there are seventeen acres enclosed here, six acres bordering on the creek are so low and wet as to be unfit for the men to camp on, and are used for evacuations. The water in the creek has a boggy taste, and we have to go up stream as near the dead line as we dare in order to have it anyways clear. Then it has the washings from the camps of the rebel guards, of which we get the full benefit. The men of the south side have dug a few shallow wells, which furnish water of a better quality. We Plymouth men are to have a place assigned to us, other than where we are at present. The watch I put in my boot top when we were captured is completely demoralized; one of the cases is off, and it won't go.

Our guards told us during our journey here that their money was as good as gold. Here the rate of exchange is five of theirs for one of ours--quite a drop in ten days. The Rebs take in all the greenbacks they can get at the price.

Our rations to-day consist of nearly one quart of corn meal, ground cob and all, and a small slice of bacon, which we have to cook for ourselves. To-night a lot of prisoners came in who were captured at Fort Pillow,[26] and are stripped of nearly everything, having on only shirts and drawers.

May 2 [1864]. This morning a guard shot a prisoner who just reached under the dead line for a few crumbs. After roll call and breakfast I went down to the creek and had an all-over wash, and then wrote home. A sheet of paper and envelope costs ten cents. (The letter never reached home.) The 101st Pa., 2nd Mass. H.A., and the 24th battery, our Plymouth men, just came in.

WHO EVER ENTERED HERE LEFT HOPE BEHIND

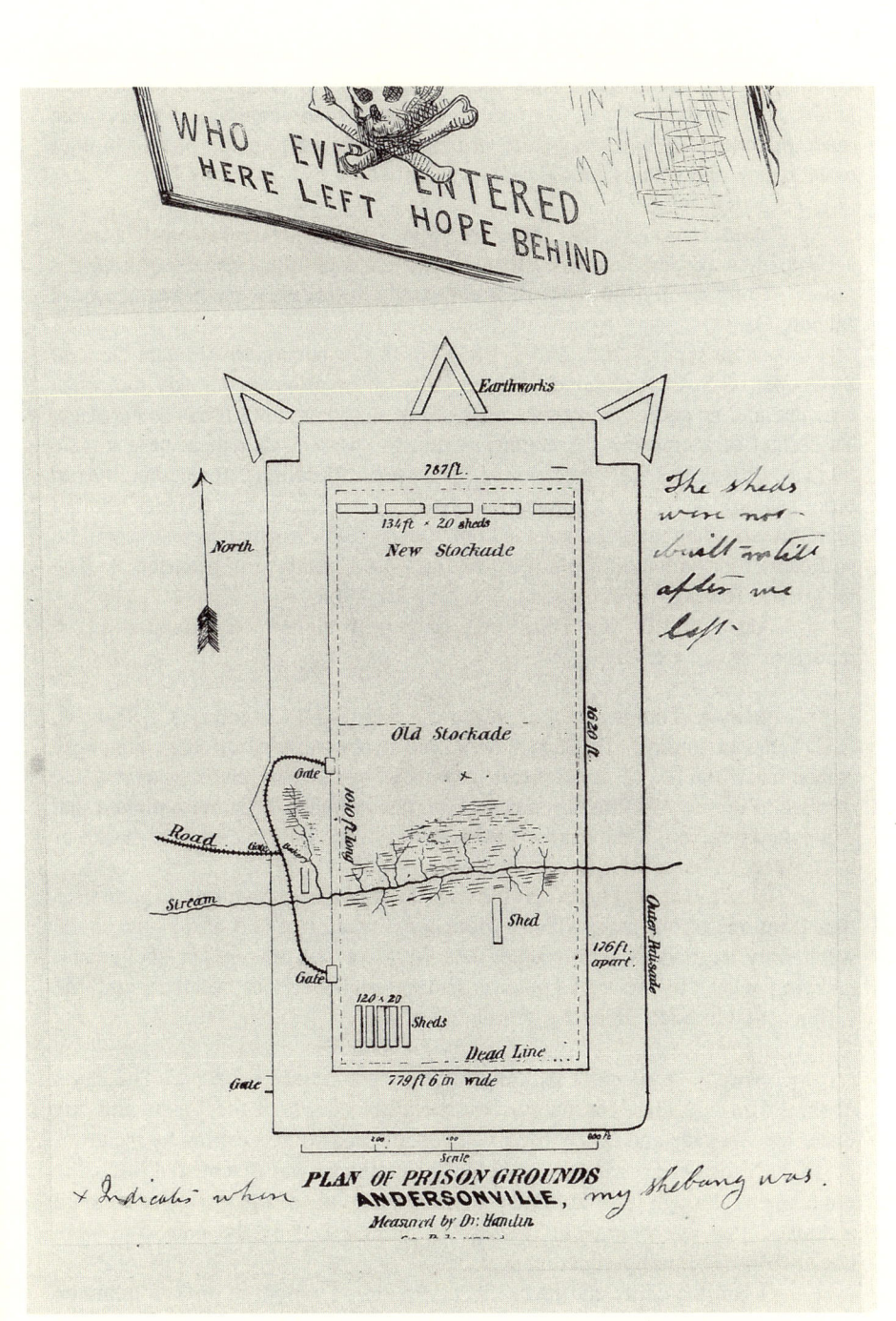

Earthworks

787 ft.
134 ft × 20 sheds
New Stockade

North

The sheds were not built until after we left.

1620 ft.

Road
Gate
Old Stockade
Long Joint
Stream
Gate
Shed
176 ft. apart
Outer Palisade
120 × 20 Sheds
Dead Line
Gate
779 ft 6 in wide

Scale

× Indicates where   **PLAN OF PRISON GROUNDS**   my shebang was.
                     ANDERSONVILLE,
                     Measured by Dr. Hamlin

213

[The association of ex-prisoners of war of Allegany county held a meeting at Friendship last Friday (April 20, 1894,) to commorate the thirtieth anniversary of the battle of Plymouth, N.C., in which engagement many were made prisoners. (Eight companies of our regiment were raised in the counties of Allegany and Cattaraugus.)]

Andersonville, Ga., May 3, 1864. Major-General Howell Cobb,[27] accompanied by Surgeon E. J. Elridge and Captain Wirz inspected prisoners today. Cobb is in command of the Georgia reserves, with headquarters at Macon, Ga.

In his report (dated May 5, 1864,) of this inspection to Adjutant-General S. Cooper, C.S.A., Richmond, Va., he says: "The prison is already too much crowded and no additional prisoners should be sent there until it can be enlarged. The effect of increasing the number within the present area must be a terrific increase of sickness and death during the summer months. I understand that an order has been given for enlarging the prison. It if was possible to make another prison it would be much better, for I doubt very much whether the water will be sufficient for the accomodation of the increased number of prisoners." The report was received in Richmond, Va. May 26, 1864.

The 103rd Pa. and 16th Conn. came in to-night.[28] The camp is full of reports as to our exchange.

May 4. Thomas Glenn,[29] of our company, who was left sick at Tarboro, N.C. came in to-day. He says they stayed in Charleston one day, and were placed under the fire of our General Gilmore's[30] guns when the Rebs sent a flag of truce to him saying "that he was shelling his own men." Gilmore replied that if his men were not removed by 3 P.M. he would tie their men to the mouth of his cannon. The result was our men were moved.

Chum [Emory] Farrar is sick with the diarrhea. I managed to get a hard tack from one of our men, which I toasted and made into coffee for him, as the water only aggravates this trouble. As we have not put up our shelter, not knowing where to locate, Chum has had to lie under this Southern sun and suffer. It's too bad. Hope he will be better soon.

May 5. Last night the long roll beat and bugles sounded. The cause of the alarm was the Rebs had discovered a tunnel, which the Yanks had dug under the stockade and nearly forty feet beyond, and were escaping by means of it. Eight Yanks had passed through, but the ninth one was discovered just as he put his head through ground. Bad for that Yank. One of the prisoners reported a tunnel[31] that was being dug, to-day. He was killed by the men who were engaged in the digging of it.

I had the chills and fever this afternoon. To-night at dusk, a quartette of the 16th Conn. sang several songs for us. One was a new one to us, called "Just before the battle mother." And the chorus--

"Farewell, mother, you may never, mother,
Press me to your heart again,
But, oh, you'll not forget me, mother,
If I'm numbered with the slain,"

as it floated over our prison pen, sent every one of our hearts away up North to its individual home and mother. (That scene, after the lapse of thirty years, is very vivid to my mind, and the old song when I hear it sung, still has the power to bring the moisture to my eyes.)

May 6 [1864]. Up very early this morning, ate our grub, had roll call and moved to our new quarters--that is, the spot of ground on which we are to stay, not live. We are located midway east and west of the stockade. Our street begins at the north wagon road and extends down the hillside. We are designated as 37-2, that is, we are the second squad in the thirty-seventh detachment. Chum Farrar and self buy a blanket for five dollars, and in company with John C. Boothe and Marcus M. Mead,[32] form a mess. We build a shebang by taking small poles--had to buy them--and drive the large ends in the ground, bring the tops together on a circle, spread two blankets over them, making them fast with wooden pins. We face the west; at our back some Cahawba boys have a shebang. Our shebang is seven feet wide, six feet high in the center and as deep as a blanket is long. We think we are fortunate in having so good a shelter.

The shebangs in here are of all shapes and sizes. Men having neither blankets nor money burrow into the hillside, or else lay out day and night. Twenty of us chip in fifty cents each and buy a Dutch oven,[33] minus a cover. It is fifteen inches in diameter and three inches deep, with legs one and a half inches long. We will find it very useful for baking our corn pones in, and we will have to watch our chances for turns. I have a quart pail with my steel watch chain for a bail, and a pint cup. [I still have it, with its pine smoke on, just a I used it in prison.] We have settled down now for how long? There are all sorts of rumors afloat about exchange.[34] One is that Wessell's brigade are exchanged. Hope so; but guess it's a "cod."[35]

May 7. As the cook house is completed we draw cooked rations, which are smaller than ever--a piece of corn bread six inches long, three inches wide and two inches thick; the rations of meat have also dwindled. This is for twenty-four hours.

May 8 (Sunday). My birthday. I am twenty-two years old. I washed out my shirt in the creek, and gave myself a cold water rinse--no soap. The Macon papers say there has been hard fighting on the Rapidan, that Longstreet is mortally wounded and Grant has driven Lee behind his works.[36] The Rebs feel a bit anxious. In a stroll around the prison to-day I saw some awful sights. (Last month the Rebs were afraid that the small-pox would get in here, and a

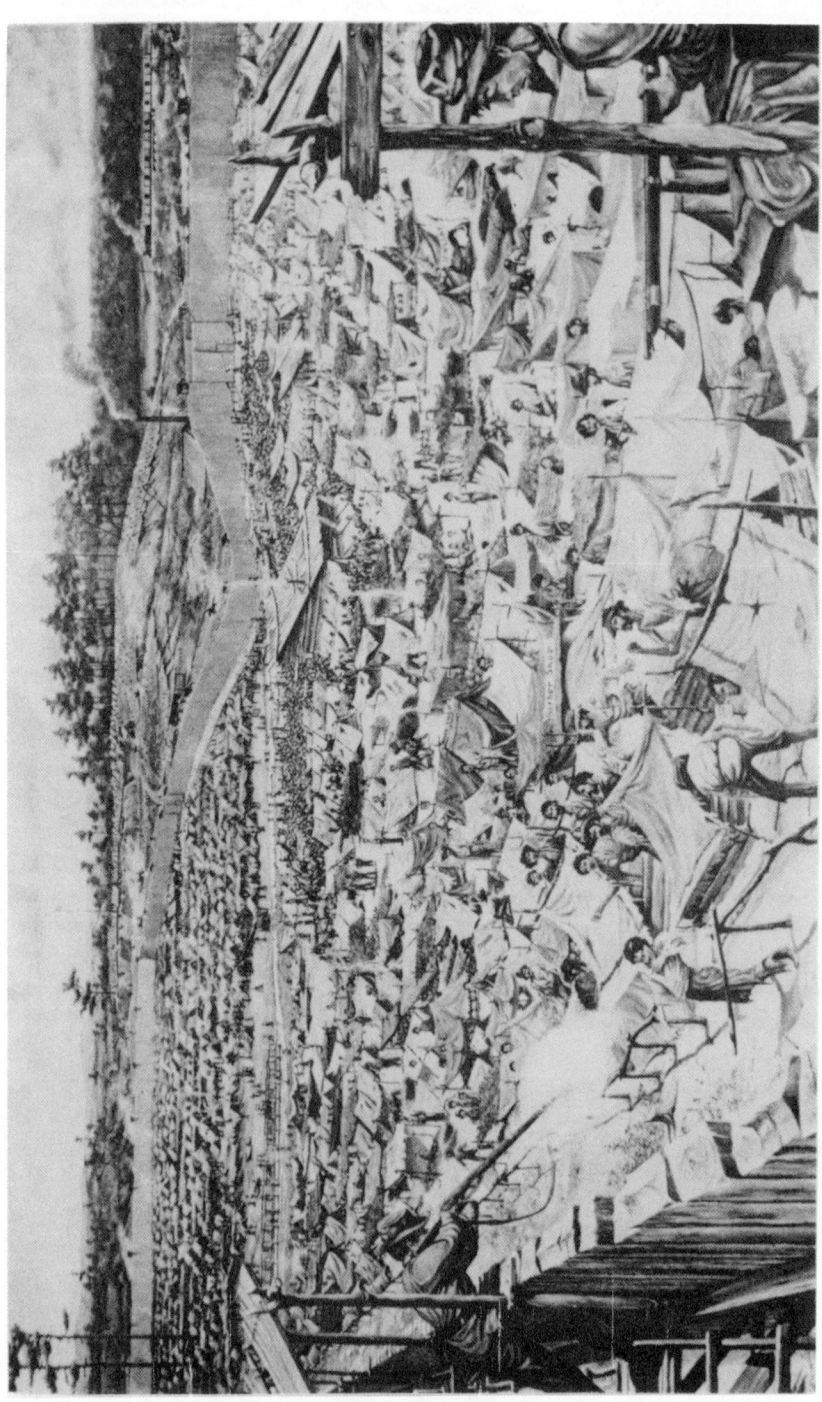

Artist's Conception of Andersonville in 1864
(from an 1884 painting)

great many of the prisoners were vaccinated.) I saw several men who had been vaccinated, and into their arms the gangrene had eaten a hole large enough to lay a half of an orange in. They will be dead men soon. In another place was a man sprawled out on the ground helpless and bleating like a sheep. The lice had eaten the scalp nearly off his head, and were still eating. Horrible, Hell! The lice are everywhere. Pick up a handful of earth from any place, blow out the finest dirt, and there will be from one to a dozen great body lice left as large as a grain of wheat. We have to take the skirmish line every day and go over our clothes carefully and pick the graybacks off. A healthy nit hatched to-day will be a grand-father tomorrow. Captain Wirz's report, dated to-day, contains the following:

Number of prisoners April 1	7,160
Number received to date	5,767
Number recaptured to date	7
Total	12,954
Deaths from April 1 to date	728
Escaped from April 1 to date	13
Total on hand to date	12,213

There is one man for every seven square yards of ground.

Andersonville, Ga., May 10, 1864. Quiet yesterday. The report is that Fort Darling on the James river is in our hands,[37] also Dalton in this State. The Rebs are getting nervous--they are afraid that a raid of our forces will come this way and release us. The officer of the day (Reb) told us there is to be a parole soon. A judge and three citizens came in this afternoon and told us it would be better for us to keep quiet and orderly in case we were paroled. We will wait and see how much truth there is in all this talk.

May 11. Roll call at seven this morning. The Reb sergeant who has charge of our detachment is named Smith; his eyes are on a twist--very clever though. Those who do not answer to their names must be accounted for, so our sergeants each take the Reb sergeants through the quarters and point out enough men to make his count good, whether they are in the right squad or not.

It has begun to rain this morning and has kept it up nearly all day.[38] The prison is the better for it, as it has washed the filth from the surface. A perfect windrow of lice, maggots and filth came rolling down on us from the hillside above--so much so we had to make little channels for it to run in to keep it out of our shebangs. To-night the air is quite chilly.

May 12. Clear this morning, but very cool. I have a touch of the diarrhea to-day; not very bad, but just enough to let me know what I may expect any time. Wrote home again. [This letter was not received.] Drew cooked rice to-night--queer stuff. It looks as if the cooks put in too much water for the quantity of rice, and when it was half cooked, it being too thin, more rice was added, and the result is we have a dish of rice half of which is well cooked and the rest is only half. In order to eat it we have to start a little fire--a very little too--and cook it till the whole is fit to eat, and there is not enough to fill up on.

May 13 [1864]. I feel some better to-day. A. H. Bancroft[39] is very sick. The Rebs have discovered another tunnel. The boys are great on tunneling. They first dig a well near a shebang which does not attract the attention of the Rebs, the earth from it being thrown out naturally, then at the proper depth they start a tunnel and the earth from it thrown down the well.[40] Yankee ingeunity is up to every thing, and it bothers the Rebs to keep up with it. We have been Yankees longer than they have been Rebs, and by the looks of things will continue to be. They are about busted.

May 14. Fifty prisoners came in who were captured below Newberne, N.C.[41] They say the Northern papers gave our brigade great praise for our defense of Plymouth, N.C. The report is that a transport loaded with prisoners is lying at Savannah, Ga., waiting to be exchanged. Hope it's true. The Rebs had a picnic outside to-day, and seemed to have a good time. The women went up into the sentry boxes and looked down on us poor miserables. I don't think they saw any thing very inviting in here. They must have lost all sense of common decency, for they staid some time in the boxes.

Sunday, May 15. This is a very pleasant morning, and if we were out of this place we could enjoy it. As it is we have a very poor show for life even, saying nothing about pleasure. The Rebs are getting cornered everywhere, according to their own accounts. A one-legged prisoner was shot this morning by the guard. He is the one who has been reporting tunnels being dug, so the men interested in the digging crowded around the poor fellow and pushed him over the dead line. It's awful. Breakfast only to-day, with hardly enough to break the fast.

May 16. The same as yesterday, with flying reports of exchange and parole. It looks as if this talk of exchange is just for our benefit and to keep us quiet.

May 17. Very pleasant to-day. Another regiment of rebel guards left for the front. A lot of prisoners came in who were captured ten miles this side of Dalton, Ga.[42] More Yanks made their escape last night and the guards went with them. Our whole talk is what we will have to eat when we reach our lines and betting on the time as to our release. This is the bet made to-day. T. W. Porter bet the oysters with T. W. Such that we would be released by a forces of our cavalry in one week.[43] I go halves with Porter and J. S. Carson goes halves with Such.[44] The bet includes Mead and Boothe. [The bet was lost.

Porter and Such both died in prison. I have had the pleasure of entertaining Carson at my home, and I tried to pay my proportion of the above bet.]

May 18 [1864]. Our men who were wounded at Plymouth came in this afternoon. Wilcox is wounded in the leg, Reed in the hand and Jacob Perkey in the under jaw.[45] (On the morning of our last day's fight our company was ordered by the colonel to charge a rebel brigade that was rushing through the town. As we neared them they gave us a volly. Perkey fell. The rest of us turned and made for the works. The Rebs kep on and swept the town.) The bullet entered his open mouth, knocked out a few teeth and bedded itself in his jaw. The skin of his face is not broken, but his head is as large as a big pumpkin. He can eat only liquids. As these men came through Macon they saw our officers, who were all right. Prisoners came in from Sherman's army; also some Colored ones, who were captured in Florida. Every Colored man was wounded. How the Rebs hate the black soldiers and their white officers. While this is a prison for enlisted men only, we have with us a uniformed commissioned officer, Major Archibald Bogle, of the 12th U.S. Colored troops. He was captured at Ocean Pond, Florida, February 20, 1864, and to punish him he was put in here with us instead of putting him in Macon, Ga., with the officers. The major is a very gentlemanly fellow, and true blue.

Andersonville, Ga., May 20, 1864. The Rebs told us yesterday that Grant was whipped. We have been prisoners a month. A squad of prisoners came in from Sherman's army to-day, with good reports of his work.

The water in the creek is very bad. In addition to the washings from the rebel camps, are the slops from the new bakery and cook house. Well digging is the order of the day among us. Our detachment has begun one. We use a half canteen to dig with. A canteen is a very useful article in here; it not only holds our drinking water, but when it is in halves we have plates, frying pans, sieves--by punching full of holes with a nail--to get the cob out of our corn meal, and bake pans for baking corn dodgers. We could not keep house without it; yet there are hundreds here who have not so much as a half canteen to cook in or eat out of. The earth from the well is drawn up in anything from a quart cup to a boot leg. It's a slow process, but it breaks up the monotony of prison life.

Our shebang is located so that we can look over the stockade where it crosses the creek, so we have a glimpse of what is going on outside of us. Every morning we can see a man called Harris start out with his pack of blood hounds, making the circuit of the prison to see if any prisoners had escaped during the night. If the dogs scent one, off they start, run him down and bring him in. Wirz says, "You tam Yankees I give twenty-four hours start of my dogs, then I catch you and bring you back." It is reported by the Rebs that the dogs were mustered into their service as horses. Our men at work in the cook house say that rations are issued to them from there. The dogs are of the same breed

Hounds Tearing a Prisoner
(McElroy, *Andersonville, A Story of Rebel Military Prisons*)

as are used to catch runaway slaves. It must have taken years of education for men who claim to be civilized and Christianized to have reached this high state of trying to capture prisoners of war with blood hounds. None but a slaveholding people could or would do such things.

May 21 [1864]. I saw a prisoner who belongs to the 126th N.Y., by the name of John Wilson.[46] He was on Belle Isle all last winter, and had a very hard time of it. He is a member of Captain Ira Munson's company. (Ira Munson was the son of the late Ebenezer Munson, of the town of Tyre, this county, and was killed at the Battle of the Wilderness, 1864. He was an old friend of mine.)

Prisoners came in to-day from Grant's army. They are from the 146th N.Y. They say they opened the fight of this campaign by a charge. They bring in a New York *Herald*, which says there will be an exchange made as soon as the spring campaign is over, and all men who had been prisoners eight months would be discharged.

Sunday, May 22. The hospital is being moved outside the stockade to-day--that is the men are being moved out, for there is no more shelter in the hospital enclosure than out of it. It's a horrible sight to see the poor fellows who cannot walk, dumped into an old blanket and carried by a man at each corner, bunching the sick man in a heap.[47] The sights in here are enough to kill us, even

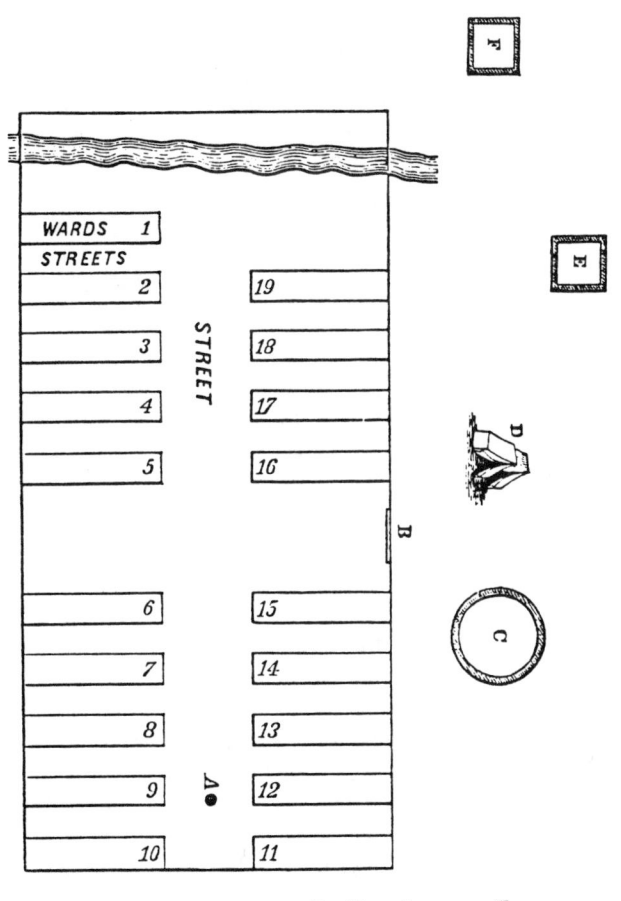

ANDERSONVILLE HOSPITAL.

A WELL.
B GATE.*
C FORT.
D HEAD-QUARTERS TENTS.
E DISPENSATORY.
F DISSECTING HOUSE.

*The other sides of the Hospital border upon Swamps.

Sketch of the Andersonville Hospital
(Robert Kellogg, *Life and Death in Rebel Prisons*)

The So-Called Hospital
(John McElroy, *Andersonville, A Story of Rebel Military Prisons*)

if we had plenty of grub. It's just hellish, the shape we are in, and not a sign of any change. A raider was caught last night. One-half of his head and face was shaved clean--he looks odd--then turned over to the Dutch captain.[48] More prisoners to-day.

May 23 [1864]. Up this morning at sunrise, had an early breakfast. The mornings are cool, but the heat in the middle of the day is intense. If we are in here in July and August it will be unbearable. More prisoners from Grant's army. Among the number is "Yankee Bill" Dillon, a member of the 146th N.Y.[49] He was a corporal in our company when we first entered the service, and was discharged from us in 1862. Prisoners from Sherman's army, who were captured within ten miles of Atlanta, Ga., report that the people there are moving their goods out of the city, expecting it will soon be in the hands of our men.

May 25. A notice was posted in here for the prisoners to be very quiet. Our Wilcox's brother came in yesterday. Two of Sherman's scouts came in to-day, who were captured five miles this side of Atlanta. They said the general ordered them to go on and not come back, and not be afraid of being captured, as he knew where the Bull pen was. Bull pen is one of the names of this summer resort. The Dutch captain has orders to parole us in case Atlanta is captured. I borrowed five dollars of one of the boys, as my money is all gone. A lot of prisoners were taken out for some purpose.

May 27 [1864]. We drew mush yesterday. As it was without salt it tasted flat. They caught another raider last night--(a raider is a thief)--and shaved half of his head, then marched him through the camp--(as an object lesson, we would say in these times). This afternoon the Rebs drew up a regiment before each gate, and the artillery was manned, when the Reb officers came in with a squad of darkies and searched for tunnels. They found three after a long search, and by driving a long crow bar into the ground at short intervals near the stockade. The Rebs are afraid we will break out, and have found out our plans, to wit: We have an organization of 8,000 or 9,000 men, who were to make a break for life to-morrow morning. The working squad, when they went out, were to capture the guns then fire a pistol as a signal for us inside, when we were to rush at the stockade, break it down, capture the guard, and make for the Union lines. It was a bold plan. Some would have been hurt; but anything for freedom. There are too many traitors in here for our good who would sell us out to the Rebs for an extra ration of corn meal. Good news to-night. The papers state that Atlanta has been captured with 5,000 prisoners, and Johns[t]on is falling back, part of his force to Mobile and part to Macon; and the report is Charleston is in our hands.[50] Drew buggy rice to-night--vile stuff.

Sunday, May 29. Pleasant and hot. 1,300 prisoners came in from Grant's army. The papers are full of lies--no truth in them.

Andersonville, Ga., May 31, 1864. Yesterday 900 men came in from Butler's army. This pen is filling up very fast, so we are a trifle crowded. Last week a strange thing happened in here. We saw a well-dressed gentleman moving in and out among the prisoners, talking as he passed along, and was here three or four hours. He is here again, and we learn that it is the Rev. John W. Hamilton, pastor of a Catholic church in Macon, Ga. This place is a mission attached to his church, and he is here to look after the members of that church. This time when he came in he had on a white linen coat, but inside of fifteen minutes it was covered with lice, when he took it off and ministered to his people in his shirt sleeves. He is not afraid nor careful of himself, but looks up every Catholic he heard of, and, if near to death, hears his confession and administers the sacrament to him. He found one poor fellow nearly dead in one of the burrows, when he got down on his hands and knees and crawled in along side the dying man, heard his confession and administered to him the rites of the church. He found one little fellow about sixteen years old, named Farrell, without hat, coat or shoes. His bare feet had been exposed to the hot sun so long that they were cracked open. Off came the Father's boots, and his socks were given to the boy to protect his poor feet, with a promise of clothing the next time he came from Macon. Farrell was happy in the thought that some one

Religious Services
(McElroy, *Andersonville, A Story of Rebel Military Prisons*)

cared for him. There is an awful sense of loneliness in here, even when one has his whole company and regiment around him, and how much more when one is alone and among strangers as is little Farrell. The last I heard from him his reason had left him, he got too near the dead line and the guard put a bullet through him. Happy release! (Father Hamilton made another visit here the week following, staying several days both in the stockade and hospital, administering to his own people. After him came Father Whelan. They both tried to impress on the mind of Gen. Cobb that something must be done for the relief of the prisoners, as the condition of the prison was known throughout Southwestern Georgia, and was a disgrace to the whole South. If nothing else could be done, they should parole them and send them to the Union lines. The Catholic church has priests here all the time to look up after their own.) It's corn bread and bacon for rations, and less every day. They are issued to us towards night; then we eat a little of it and try to save some for the next day. Hard work. One of the worst features of all is that we can buy anything we wish if we only had plenty of money. All kinds of vegetables can be had, warm biscuits and honey, ham and eggs, green peas, and even chicken can be had. Our brigade made this camp financially by the money we brought in. It's hard to keep money in my pocket when my stomach is empty. I had such an intolerable longing for something today, that out of my small amount of money I bought two oranges, for which I paid one dollar. They looked good, I wanted them, but they did not satisfy my longings only for a short time. We are feeling the pinch more and more each day.

June 1 [1864]. A touch of the diarrhea to-day again. More men from Butler's army, and a lot of wounded colored prisoners who were captured in Florida. Every darkie is crippled in some way.[51] A very heavy rain this afternoon, which brightened up the camp a good deal. No news--but for some reason the Rebs hang their under lip. We can detect a change in them very quick if anything is wrong.

June 2. I feel very bad this morning, so bad that I went out to sick call. The doctor gave me a little pine top whisky and some pills. If there is any way to keep this diarrhea from me I want to. The sights out at sick call are terrible. It rained torrents to-day. The lightning here is something terrific and the thunder sounds like the report of a rifle cannon.

June 3. Our mess put together and bought some green peas, which we had for breakfast. They were very good. More rain to-day.

Sunday, June 5. It rained hard yesterday, and three or four showers to-day. We do not have time to dry off between times. I am feeling quite well to-day. Hope it will continue. At dark to-night we drew uncooked grub--fresh beef and meal. Our wood is so wet we have hard work to make a fire, and have to go slow on wood--for all there are heavy woods all around us. After a fashion we manage to toast our meat on a stick, and with a crust of corn bread, eat our supper. The wood question is getting serious. While the Rebs issue wood in very small quantities, it is not enough for our use. The stumps are all grubbed out, even to the roots of any size. To-day I saw one poor fellow go down on the bog and fish out [of] the excrement small sticks and slivers, which had been used in lieu of toilet paper, with which to cook his grub. The sufferings of others, in addition to our own, has a very depressing effect on us, as we know unless relief comes soon we will be in a condition equal to the worst cases here.

June 7. Rainy yesterday. Pleasant this morning. More prisoners from Grant's army and a few from Belle Isle, who said that our men were throwing shells into Richmond. I saw a letter which was sent in here inside of a paper of pepper, which gave a description of things in and around Atlanta. They are in a bad way there. Our detachment has its well dug, and it affords us plenty of water of a good quality. No more creek water for us. The Rebs have begun to enlarge the stockade. They are to add six acres on the north end. On the first of this month there were 15,000 of us on this seventeen acres, with additions nearly every day, and it is very difficult for the Reb sergeants to call the roll, as our sergeants fool them so on the count. "Yank," is bound to keep his count

Two Views of Andersonville in August 1864
(U.S. Army Military History Institute)

good, even if he has to go in another detachment to count. The Rebs are great traders, and they want our brass regulation buttons which has the spread eagle on. They call them "buttons with hens on." The other day as one "Yank" was selling buttons to a Reb, another "Yank," with a sharp knife, was cutting the buttons off the back of his (Reb's) coat. Then he sauntered around in front of Mr. Reb and sold him more "buttons with hens on" at a fair margin.

Andersonville, Ga., June 10, 1864. It has rained for the past two days, not all the time, but frequent showers, which keep the camp in a muss. We are getting cooked rations now, cow peas this time, and corn bread. Each pea had a bug in it until the cooking released it from its shell, but not from the kettle; so we have a very unpalatable dish--peas and bugs. But we are hungry, so devour the mixture, and want more. Last night fifteen of the wood squad,[52] with their guards made their escape. Plesant, with showers to-day. The report is that Sherman has captured Atlanta.[53] The Northern papers state that the exchange will come off as soon as this campaign is over. Our whole talk is on the probabilities of an exchange or a parole, and what we will have to eat when we get to our lines. It sort o'keeps our spirits up.

June 12. Showers yesterday; cloudy and cool to-day. I don't feel very well this morning. The report that our officers at Macon are to be exchanged is all hoax, as Billy Bradley received a letter from his brother there (our 85th quartermaster),[54] which did not mention the matter of exchange at all.

June 13. Rainy to-day. I am feeling bad.

June 14. A number of our paroled men at work outside, left with their guards for parts unknown. Bully for them. I have the diarrhea sure enough now.

June 22. I have been in a wretched condition for the past week. Am feeling a trifle better to-day, but so very weak I can hardly crawl around. This disease needs a man with two legs to wait on it properly. I have not had but one for any purpose for several days past. My left leg has been shut up like a jackknife; my heel is drawn up to my hip.[55] It's not painful only as I try to straighten it. Hope it will let up soon, as it is very inconvenient at this time. As misery loves company, I have had plenty to add to my other trouble, in that I have been unable to take the skirmish line every day and keep the lice picked off. Its exquisite torture to have a million and a half of the gray devils feeding on you. My chum and comrades have done all in their power to assist me and make me comfortable. They make me coffee of toasted corn bread and gruel of corn meal. Those prisoners who are not able to go on the bog for their evacuations have a hole dug for them near their shebangs, which is used, then covered up another day, and so on. I am one of those in the above condition.

It makes the boys laugh to see the fix I am in. It is comical, and laughing helps to keep our spirits up. So we all laugh. It has been a very trying time for me; but the worst is over, and I am on the gain.

June 23 [1864]. Pleasant, and no rain. A few more prisoners from Grant's army to-day. They bring us nothing new, only the fighting is going on. I am still on the gain, and as soon as I can use my leg I will be around as usual. The raiders are getting to be very bold. They will rob a man in the day time as well as the night, and seem to have an organization with headquarters on the southside. One of our mess has to stay by the shebang all the time to watch our things. We have none to spare. Nights when I was so sick that I could not sleep, it helped to pass the time away to hear the guards on the stockade sing out the hour. The guard on post one would begin thus: "Post one, nine o'clock, and all is well." Post two would call his number, repeat the hour "and all is well." Thus it would go around the stockade. Some would jerk it out with a crack and ring to it. while the next guard would drawl it out one letter at a time. One night as they sung out twelve o'clock, one of the guards who was more of a prophet than a soldier, sung it, "Twelve o'clock and all is well, and the Southern Confederacy has gone to h-e-l-l." Some of them would sing, "Jeff Davis is a gentleman, Linkin is a fool; Jeff Davis rides a white horse, Linkin rides a m-u-l-e." I guess they will find that "Linkin's" mule has better staying qualities than Jeff Davis' white horse.

[The following letter from one of the guards will show up one item of our life here better than my diary does:

First Regiment Georgia Reserves
Camp Sumter, June 23, 1864

Respected Sir: Being but a private in the ranks at this place, consequently if I see anything to condemn (as I do) I have no power to correct it. Yet as a human being and one that believes that we should "do as we would be done by," I proceed to inform you of some things that I know you are ignorant of; and in the first place I will say I have no cause to love the Yankees, (they have driving myself and family from our home in New Orleans to seek our living among strangers,) yet I think prisoners should have some showing. Inside our prison walls all around there is a space about twelve feet, called the "dead line." If a prisoner crosses that line the sentinels are ordered to shoot him. Now, we have many thoughtless boys here who think the killing of a "Yank" will make them great men; as a consequence, every day or two there are prisoners shot. When the officer of the guard goes to the sentry's stand there is a dead or badly wounded men, invariably within their own lines. The sentry, of course, says he was across the "dead line" when he shot him. He is told he done exactly right, and is a good sentry. Last Sabbath there was two shot in their tents at one shot;

Shot at the Dead Line
(McElroy, *Andersonville, A Story of Rebel Military Prisons*)

the boy said that he shot at one across the "dead line." Night before last there was one shot near me (I being on guard). The sentry said that Yankee made one step across the line to avoid a mud hole. He shot him through the bowels, and when the officer of the guard got there he was lying inside of their own lines. He (the sentry) as usual, told him that he had stepped across but fell back inside. The officer told him it was exactly right. Now, my dear sir, I know you are opposed to such measures, and I make this statement to you knowing you to be a soldier, statesman and Christian, that if possible you may correct things, together with many others that exist here. And yet if you send an agent here he will, of course, go among the officers, tell him business, and be told that "all is well." But let a good man come here as a private citizen and mix with the privates, and stay one week, and if he don't find out things revolting to humanity, then I am deceived. I shall put my name to this believing that you will not let the officers over me see it, otherwise I would suffer, most probably.

Yours most respectfully,
JAMES E. ANDERSON

P.S. Excuse pencil.
President Jeff Davis.

Indorsements: James E. Anderson, First regiment Georgia reserves to Jeff Davis, Camp Sumter, Georgia, June 23, 1864, asks correction of the brutal shooting of prisoners (Yankees) in that camp without cause.

A.G.: Referred to Brigadier General Winder. By order,

J. A. CAMPBELL, A.S.W.

July 23, 1864.

[File.] Respectfully referred, by direction of the president, to the honorable secretary of war, July 23, 1864.

J. C. IVES, Col. and A.D.C.

Received July 23, 1864.

Received A. and I.G.O. July 25, 1894.]

Andersonville, Ga., June 26, 1864, (Sunday). Pleasant and warm. I have been on the gain for the last two days, and feel as if I would be all right in time. But my flesh has slipped out from between my skin and bones to a wonderful degree. It's too bad, for when I sit down the ground is nearer to me than ever. (We always sit on the ground.) Prisoners to-day from Gen. Sturgis' army.[56] The Macon papers confirm the report that 25,000 rebel prisoners left Fortress Monroe for Savannah, Ga., for exchange. It looks as if we might get out of this hole soon. The raiders are getting more bold every day. When the cry of "raider" is heard everyone is up and on the lookout for their "traps." It is whispered that there has been murder here by the organized gang.

June 27. Pleasant and warm. I am feeling better, and my leg is getting in shape again. I am able to hobble around a bit. More prisoners from the army of the Potomac. They were stripped of every thing, even to their clothes. What will the poor fellows do? The talk of an exchange is getting stronger; report says we will be out next month. Hope it's true. It's getting to be a question of endurance. Every day we have a chance to go out and work for the "Rebs," as they are after all kinds of mechanics. They want us to take the oath to their rotten government when we go. To-day they are after machinists to go to Selma, Ala., to work in the government shops, and offer every inducement--good grub and pay. They have poor success thus far, if any.

June 28. Another pleasant morning. More prisoners from Grant's army. This place is where a man shows his true nature. It's every man for himself. Heavy rain this afternoon and evening. John Barton[57] came in to-night. He is from near Shortsville, and an old acquaintance of several of our comppany. Sorry to see him here.

June 29. The prison is full of excitement to-day. The raiders are so bad, and there is so much violence done by them that Capt. Wirrz has issued an order that no more rations will be issued to us until they are pointed out, so he can take care of them. The prisoners have organized a band of regulators or

The Raiders in Action
(McElroy, *Andersonville, A Story of Rebel Military Prisons*)

police with "Big Pete" as chief--[58] Pete is one of the "Plymouth Pilgrims," as they call our brigade--who after a long search find fifteen or twenty suspects, who are turned over to the Dutch captain, but not without some hard fighting and broken heads.

June 30 [1864]. Cloudy and warm. If we were in the field this could be muster day (for pay). I have $170 coming to me, and if I only had it I could use it to good advantage. The report is that Sherman has whipped Johnston three times, and the "Rebs" will have to parole us or we will be released by our own forces. Captain Wirz has called out the sergeant of messes, to consult as to what means will be used for the punishment of the raiders. Two dead bodies have been found under the shebang of the raiders on the south side. They are a lot of murders and cut-throats.

July 1. Drew full rations last night. We had a place for them. Wirz's report for June is as follows: Whole number of prisoners, 22,291; number of deaths, 1,201. If the whole of the stockade was fit to camp on there would be just 33.2 square feet per man. We have been so crowded for a week or two past that the "Reb" sergeants did not call the roll; but as the addition to the stockade is completed, and the men are moving into it, we have more room and roll call. The prisoners are cutting up and carrying off that part of the stockade which separates the new from the old. We need the wood very much, and now is the time to get it. The report is that a train-load of sick left last night. No grub today at all. (Does the reader know what that means?)[59]

July 2 [1864]. Pleasant and hot. The boys have got to carry all that wood back, so the Dutch captain says. They are to try those raiders that were caught the other day, by court martial, and twelve sergeants of squads have been selected to act as a jury. They are men that have not being in here long. The air is full of reports. One man says he saw the Macon *Telegraph*, which said that 18,000 men were to be exchanged between the 7th and 15th of this month. Rations to-night.

Sunday, July 3. Hot to-day, and no rations.[60] We are hungry.

July 4. This is splendid morning for the Glorious Fourth. Only we have not much to eat. I tried to have my watch fixed so it would run, but it's played out. If it would run I could get a good price for it. Boothe sold his for $30, or its equivalent in Confederate scrip. He is in our shebang. There are all kinds of trades carried on here--watch tinkers, cobblers and tailors. Gambling flourishes at all times. Our detachment drew raw beef and meal this afternoon. The one next to us drew cooked beef, It was alive with maggots. The men devour it because they are starving to death. There is not enough grub issued in one day for a good meal. They have re-organized the detachments to-day. Our number now is 19-1. It looks as if there might be a chance of our getting out of here soon.

July 5. Pleasant, but very hot. Raw rations again. We like this, as we can cook it as we please. We are getting to be good cooks, considering. The report is that Richmond fell into our hands July 2. Richard D. Phillips of our company, is very low. Among those who were captured with our Plymouth men, was a Captain John Morris, of Utica, N.Y. He was down there on the coast of the Albemarle sound with a steamboat and barge buying corn, and had with him a quantity of Philadelphia stocks and bonds, which he has converted into Confederate money, and is buying up the paymaster's checks which our brigade was paid off in just before our capture. He pays one-third the face of the checks, which are as good as the gold. Several of our company have sold theirs. I have not. It is too big a discount.

Andersonville, Ga., July 7, 1864. The weather is very hot here now. Our old pen is in very bad shape--very filthy; and the stench which arises from the bog is enough to make us sick. To-day is the time for our release, if the reports are true. It's all talk. We have a new man at the head of this military post, Brigadier-General John H. Winder. When he left Richmond the Richmond *Examiner* exclaimed: "Thank God, that Richmond is at last rid of old Winder. God have mercy on those to whom he is sent." Since he came another pack of bloodhounds has been put on. They are in charge of Wesley W. Turner, a sergeant of Co. H, 1st regiment Georgia reserves, C.S.A. (Winder detailed him for this purpose without consulting the colonel of that regiment.) If there is any swear in a man these things make it bubble up to the surface. The devils are not satisfied to run the prisoners down with dogs, but they allow the dogs to bite and tear the man to such an extent that several have died. It's barbarous in the extreme. Will this thing ever let up? This evening one of the boys gave me a cold water rinse--that is, I stood up while he poured water over me and then rubbed me down. This is one way we have of helping one another here. (No soap.)

July 8 [1864]. I had a very hard time of it last night. A pain caught me in the right breast and shoulder, along towards midnight. It was so sharp that sleep was out of the question. It was more than human nature could stand, so tears came to my relief-hot, scalding tears. (My eyes fill now as I think of it.) It was a trifle easier this morning, but have to sit up all the time. One of the boys took a piece of board he had, and placed it up in the back of our shebang so I could lay back against it. So I rest a bit. What would I do without my comrades? To-night I am feeling better.

July 9. Had a poor night of it, and was very uncomfortable. This morning the pain has let up a little. Heavy rain this afternoon, which has relieved the camp. The boys say that there were twenty-one days of rain last month. More prisoners from Grant's army.[61]

July 10. I am quite like myself this morning. The pain has left me. I must have taken cold the other night when I had my rinse. It's very hot here now. Six hundred and forty prisoners came in. They say that Sherman is commissioner of exchange now, and that the exchange begins on the 15th. Also that Petersburg and Lynchburg are in our hands.[62] Bully. The court martial has founded six of the raiders guilty of murder, and they are to be hung to-morrow. Good. They are our fellow prisoners.

July 11. Cloudy and cool this morning. They are building the scaffold near the south gate. It is a crude affair, two uprights with a cross piece, from which dangle six ropes. The drop is a plank about three feet from the ground. This afternoon Capt. Wirz brought in the prisoners and turned them over to our police, saying, "Here, men, I bring you back the prisoners in as good condition as I received them; you can take them and do as you please with them, and may God help you." One of them broke loose from the police and made a dash for life--and a good one, too--but he had no friends to help him so was captured and

Execution of the Raiders
(McElroy, *Andersonville, A Story of Rebel Military Prisons*)

taken back and placed on the scaffold with the other five, their arms and legs pinioned, an old meal sack drawn over their heads, the noose adjusted, the drop fell, and five men danced on nothing. The sixth man broke his rope and fell to the ground. He thought he would get off because of this; but no, the rope was spliced, the poor fellow was placed on the end of a plank, the noose once more slipped over his head, the plank was jerked out from under him, and he, too, danced on nothing, along with the other five. It was a ghastly sight, and every one of us who could crawl out of his shebang or hole, saw it.[63] I guess this will put a stop to the raiding business, at least to the murders. "Limber Jim," a Kentuckian, was the executioner, and has gone outside to stay for fear the friends of the executed would put a knife into him.

July 12. Hot! It's just broiling. Was it Sydney Smith who said, "That he would like to take off his flesh and sit on his bones"? Well, if "Syd." were here about now, the old Dutch captain would see that his flesh was removed, then he could sit or stand as he felt inclined.

"For it's nothing but the ghost of Old John Brown
Then hoist up the flag, long may she wave

Over the Union, the noble and the brave.
Hoist up the flag, long may she wave
Over the Union, the noble and the brave."

This is the last line of each verse and the chorus of a song the Western boys, on the hillside above us, sung last night. We have great singing here. We make the echoes ring at times. Those of us who are alive (by spells) astonish the "Rebs" by the way we use our lungs. Occasionally we have a "response service." One fellow on the south side will jump up and shot, "Three cheers for Grant. Hip! Hip! Hurrah!" which receives a hearty response from all hands. Then one on the north side sends back "Three cheers for Lincoln!" and off we go with a rouser. South side again for Sherman, and so on, with a list of our generals. Then some bold spirit shouts out to be heard not only by us prisoners but by the guards as well. "Three cheers for h-e-l-l!" which is responded to by a yell. We have to do something to break up the monotony of this kind of life. All the exercise we have is to hunt our lice and tell stories.

This hot weather we take off every thing but our shirts and drawers, and some leave those off for the reason that they are so ragged that they will not hold together. "Just look up there on the hill above you," Farrar says. We look, and we see an object--is it a man?--naked as when born, as brown as a berry, a mere skeleton. It comes running and stumbling down towards us, part of the time on all fours, and helped along by a kick from some brute. We all shrink back out of the way. On it goes down to the creek, and tumbling in wallows like a hog. It was a Union soldier--some one's loved one--now a poor demented being, his condition caused by this prison life.

(By the way, some of you may have read the *Century Magazine* "How the rebel prisoners were treated at Camp Morton, Indianapolis, Ind."[64] The article claims that there was as much suffering there as in the Southern prisons. Do you think for a moment that the State of Indiana would have held together twenty-four hours if that camp had been like Andersonville? Not much. There would have been another rebellion against such damnable doings. It was not possible for any people north of Mason and Dixon's line to duplicate that place.)

Andersonville, Ga., July 14, 1864. Yesterday the same as usual. The heat is causing a great deal of suffering among us. It's very hard on the poor fellows without shelter and down with the diarrhea. The report is that Sherman has crossed the Chattahoochee river. General Winder had the sergeants of squads outside and told them that he had found out all of our plans for a break, and that we had better keep quiet. This afternoon a solid shot was fired over the prison. It was a general alarm for the "Rebs," and they made such a scramble to get into their positions that we set up a hoot and yell. It is very laughable to us.

One of Sherman's Veterans
(McElroy, *Andersonville, A Story of Rebel Military Prisons*)

July 15 [1864]. Hot, hotter, hottest! One of the boys says its hotter than--yesterday. Well, this is the fifteenth of July, and we are in here yet, with prospects of a continuation. Raw rations all the time now. I tried my hand at peddling to-day. I cooked up a lot of pancakes and hawked them about the prison, but every thing of that kind is overdone, so that I did not make any things out of trading. All over the prison men are trading, or trying to exchange one kind of grub for another. That is, a man that draws raw meal and has nothing to cook in, wants to trade it for corn bread. Another who has corn bread, wants to trade for rice. Another who wants a bit of tobacco, is singing out, "Who has tobacco for beans?" [To-day if two of the old prison boys meet the salutation is apt to be "tobacco for beans, old pard."] The prisoners will trade off half of their scant rations for tobacco, the habit of using the weed is so fixed. Well, there is a deal of comfort in here in a good smoke just after one of our hearty dinners. In all of our bets for the dinners, to be paid when we reach our lines, cigars are included, and none of your three-cent ones. The best of every thing we are to have. How our mouths do water as we go over the list of our good mother's cooking. One of our boys says he would like to be a Northern farmer's dog now, he would have one square meal sure.

Burying the Dead
(U.S. Army Military History Institute)

July 16 [1864]. Pleasant but hot. A lot of Sherman's men came in to-day. The papers of yesterday say that the "Rebs" are in Maryland, and both wings of Sherman's army are across the river. The report is that the rebel privateer *Alabama* has been sunk in French waters by one of our ships.[65] Good! Richard D. Philips died to-day. This is the first death in our company. He is one of the three of our company who did not re-enlist. His reason was that he was to be married this fall. His brother George is very sick. It's hard to stand by and see a comrade die in here, but to have one's brother die must be more so. A man that dies in the daytime is carried out to the dead-house which is between the outer and inner stockade now. This outer stockade has been built since we came here. Before it was built the dead-house was in the field, and when the men carried out a corpse they had a chance to bring in a back-load of wood. There used to be some savage fights over the question of who shall carry out the dead. There has been several cases where a "Yank" have [sic.] played dead, and his chums would tie a rag around his head to keep his jaw in place, tie his big toes together, pin a slip of paper to his clothing, with his name, company and regiment on it, and then, in a very solemn manner, carry the poor fellow out to the dead-house, which has nothing but crotches set in the ground with poles laid on and covered over with pine boughs. But the "Yank" had his weather eye open, and watching his opportunity when the guards are out of sight, steps quietly out of his dead surroundings and makes a break for the Union lines. But now this outer stackade has stopped all such things. Those who die during the night are carried to the main gates in the morning, then to the dead-house; here they are loaded on army wagons, just as wood is loaded, piled one on another, (simply skeletons, that's all) and hauled to the cemetery. The grave is a long trench, as wide as the length of a man. The bodies are laid in side by side, some poles are laid across, then some pine boughs; this is so that the earth will not come in contact with the bodies. A board at the head of each has the man's name, company and regiment (if known) and the number of his grave. A correct record is kept of all deaths. The prisoners keep this record and do all the burying.

Sunday, July 17. Pleasant. All days run together here. Reports of all sorts are afloat.

July 18. Cloudy and cool all day. The report is that Atlanta is ours with 20,000 prisoners,[66] and Rosecrans has Montgomery, Ala.[67] The "Rebs" say that instead of sending us away they are to parole us. We thought we were to have gone without grub to-day, but at dark it came around. The same wagons that haul the dead to the cemetery, haul our grub in here, and that, without being cleaned out.

July 19. Pleasant and hot. The "Rebs" are getting scared and are stopping all citizens that pass through this place, putting them in tents for duty.

More "Fresh Fish"
(McElroy, *Andersonville, A Story of Rebel Military Prisons*)

Rebel General Johnson has been superseded by Hood.[68] Our men are twenty miles this side of Atlanta, and three columns of them are moving this way. Bully! Two or three showers to-night.

July 20 [1864]. Very hot to-day. We have been prisoners three months. The "Rebs" have a large gang of darkies outside, throwing up fortifications. Hip, Hip, Hurrah! They are getting nervous, I should judge, by the way they act. There is a good deal of excitement in here now about getting up a petition to our government, asking help get us out of here. I think it shows a weak head and a cowardly crew. But I suppose they want to go home. Can't blame them for that. I want to go to, but I won't whine nor sign a paper.

July 21. Another hot day. The Macon papers of the 19th say Sherman has not taken Atlanta, but that his cavalry are near Columbus, Ga. A small squad of prisoners from Sherman's army came to-day, and they confirm the report that Atlanta is not in our hands. So all reports to that effect are bosh.

July 22. Pleasant. A lot of prisoners came in from Grant's army. They were taken in June, so have no late news. They are a lot of coffee coolers and blackberry pickers, and can't tell where they were captured nor the day. But they are here. I am sorry for them. The Dutch captain has taken the small boys outside and placed them by themselves, which is a kind act. There were about fifty little fellows in here, from twelve to fifteen years old--drummer boys. One little fellow was with the Western men near our shebang. They found him in one of their marches. His father was in our army somewhere; his mother was dead, and his home had been burned by the bushwackers. So he was given a horse to ride, but was captured with the squad he was with. He was very free with the prisoners. If he saw any one eating, and thought it looked good, he would help himself. None of us ever said nay to him. Couldn't. Our little Smith is all right, and outside with the rest.[69]

Andersonville, Ga., July 23, 1864. Cloudy to-day. I am not feeling well; am afraid I am going to be sick again. N. B. Carpenter died to-day.[70] Now Col. Clarke has escaped a whipping, for "Carp." said that if he ever got out of this he would whip the colonel. Clarke was our first captain, and when we were in the barracks at Elmira, N.Y., he said that those men who grumbled at the rations there did not have as good at home. "Carp." has always laid it up against the colonel. Our "little" Kern (C.L.) is in very bad shape.[71] He showed us the condition he is in--it is dreadful--and said, "Boys, I can't stand this much longer." There is no help for him. A good many of our boys are very sick, and it is not a pleasant thing to look in the face. The report is that the commissioners of exchange have agreed on terms.[72]

July 31. I have been very sick for the past week with the dyentery; so sick that it did not seem as if I could not hold together any longer. This is the worst sickness I have had. Hope it will be the last. The worst feature of it all is, there is nothing in here fit for a sick man to eat. Corn bread and cow peas, with a little rice, is all there is. And there are thousands who are as bad and worse than I have been, with not one-tenth of the care that I have. It's awful. Men are lying all around in the hot sun, face up, with their mouths wide. The fleas, lice and maggots are holding high carnival in here. Human nature is made of good stuff or it could not stand the strain. Just think of it. I saw a man with not only the lice and fleas feeding on him, but out of every aperture of his body the maggots were crawling.

[Order No. 13]

Headquarters
Confederate States' Military Prison
Andersonville, July 27, 1874

The officers on duty and in charge of the battery of "Florida Artillery" at the time will, upon receiving notice that the enemy have approached within seven miles of this post, open fire upon the stockade with grape shot without reference to the situation beyond these lines of defense. It is better that the 1st Federal be exterminated than be permitted to burn and pilage [sic.] the property of loyal citizens, as they will do if allowed to make their escape from prison. By order of John H. Winder, brigadier general.

W. S. WINDER, Adjutant General

Infested with Maggots
(McElroy, *Andersonville, A Story of Rebel Military Prisons*)

Our George A. Phillips (Dick's brother) died the 28th of last month. This is the second man out of six in the shebang across the alley from us. Charles J. Simmons and A. H. Bancroft are bad off. Bancroft is so low we have not told him of the death of his brother. Wirz's report for July is as follows:

Prisoners in camp July 1	25,005
" in hospital July 1	1,362
" received during month	7,064
" recaptured	12
Total	33,443
Died during the month	1,742
Escaped	20
Sent to other parts	3
Total on Hand	31,678
Of which there are in camp	29,998
" " " " " hospital	1,680
Averge number of prisoners each day	29,030
Average number of dead each day	56 1/2

August 2 [1864]. I am feeling better, with plenty of room for improvement. Four hundred prisoners came in to-day, who were captured near Macon on a raid. Major-General Stevenson and staff were captured also.[73] There is a deal of talk of a parole now. The petition they were talking about before I was sick, has turned out to be one from the sergeants from the State of Ohio to their governor, praying him to use his influence for their release. All right, it will be some time before our New York boys send in a petition, I reckon. Last night one of the boys told me he would give me a wash if I could stand it. I told him I thought I could. So I striped and stood up, with my feet wide apart so as to brace myself. Then I took a look down over myself, (I could do it easier than I can now,) which scared me so that my heart went almost out of me. Hope had almost died. But just then our Wetmore[74] cracked a joke on me, which made all the boys laugh; they fairly yelled, which took my mind off myself. My heart came back, and hope was alive again. (I shall never forget that night; and that joke makes me laugh every time I think of it.) I had my wash and feel better for it. I am alive yet.

August 3. Cool, with showers. Nearly 6,000 sick went out to-day for some place or other, report says to Hilton Head. I hope it's so, but am afraid it's not. We'll hope for the best.

August 4. Cool and pleasant. There are no sick to go out to-day; but they go to-morrow. A lot of prisoners from the Gulf department have been exchanged, and perhaps our turn will come next. Won't we be a jolly crew?

August 5. Hot, very. The sick of eleven detachments went out this afternoon, no one knows where. (Lieutenant-Colonel, D. T. Chandler, assistant adjutant and inspector general [Confederate State of America], in his report, after inspecting this prison, dated to-day, says: "My duty requires me respectfully to recommended a change in the officer in command of the post, Brigadier General J. H. Winder, and the substitution in his place of some one who unites both energy and good judgment, with some feeling of humanity and consideration for the welfare and comfort (so far as is consistent with their safe keeping) of the vast number of unfortunates placed under his control; some one who at least will not advocate deliberately and in cold blood the propriety of leaving them in their present condition until their number has been sufficiently reduced by death to make the present arrangement suffice for the accommodation; who will not consider it a matter of self-laudation and boasting that he has never been inside the stockade, a place the horrors of which it is difficult to describe, and which is a disgrace to civilization; the condition of which he might, by the exercise of a little energy and judgment, even with the limited means at his command, have considerably improved."

Andersonville, Ga., August 8, 1864. Every thing has been very quiet for the past two days. I am feeling better, but very weak, and do not recover my flesh; each attack leaves me worse than it found me. Now I am a mere skeleton, but able to be around. Charles B. Ingraham died the 3d and Parmer W. Lewis[75] to-day. We have a pet here in the shape of a toad. Where he keeps himself during during the day we can't find out; but every night at dusk he shows himself. He is a great fly-catcher, and we watch him by the hour as he takes in his supper. He will crawl up to a fly as a cat does to a mouse, until he gets within striking distance--then good-by fly. It's fun to watch the old fellow. Any thing for diversion. So the boys make a circle on the ground and put into it two or three lice, then bet as to which one will get out first. Rare sport, and no one hurt. Gambling flourishes here in many shapes from draw poker down to the sweat-board or chuck a luck[76] as some call it. My chum took a sweat-board to-day and went upon the main street to try his hand and see if he could not raise the wind. All he had in his bank was thirty-five cents. It was the extent of our pile. It would not buy much of any thing, so if we lost it, why, not much loss. He did not wait long before Denny (a well-known sport) and his friend came along. Denny says, "Let us stop here and break this fellow's bank." They stopped and played, and when they quit they left $11 with the bank. Then Farrar thought he would quit before any one else came along to play. Now we will live again for awhile. We can get all we want here for money. We need vegetables more than any thing else, as an antidote for the scurvy. This disease is very bad here now. Some have it in their mouth so that their teeth fall out. We do not let any one we do not know drink out of our tin cups. It's bad, but we have to protect ourselves. Others have it in their legs, so that they swell up and burst open and look like a link of sausage that has been fried brown and cracked open. It leaves running sores wherever it touches. [Three years ago I attended the Allegany County Association of the G.A.R. at Cuba, N.Y., and took dinner with some of our Co. C, 85th, boys in their tent. After dinner I saw John Holcombe[77] sitting down with the leg of his pants turned up. I asked him what he was doing. He said: "I left home so early this morning that my wife did not bandage my leg properly." Then he took off the bandages and showed me his leg below the knee. There was one running sore as long and as wide as my little finger, and half as deep; there were other smaller ones. He said he had nineteen running sores at one time between his knee and ankle. It was scurvy stil working, which he contracted in the rebel prisons. I said, "John, how much of a pension do you get on that?" "$4," John said. I told him he could get $12 under the new law. He said he would rot first rather than apply under that law. In other words, he would not swear he was a pauper. John was right. A man that was nearly four years in the army and one year of that in those rebel hells is no pauper--not much.] We are drawing fresh beef now, uncooked, and it is good for me, as there is life in beef.

Issuing Rations at Andersonville, August 1864
(U.S. Army Military History Institute)

Andersonville in August 1864
The "Dead Line" is on the Right
(U.S. Army Military History Institute)

**The Break in the Stockade
caused by the August 9, 1864 rainstorm**
(McElroy, *Andersonville, A Story of Rebel Military Prisons*)

August 9 [1864]. Hot. To-day we had the heaviest rain storm we have had in here. It washed out part of the stockade on the west side, also washed out three or four of our wells on the side hill--ours among the number. Now we can go down the hill and walk into the bottom of our well and dip up water. The well is sixteen feet deep, and the water very good. The stockade went out when the storm was the worst. It made the "Reb" guards fly around lively. A general alarm was given, and all the troops were out to prevent us poor miserables from trying to escape. The whole thing was very exciting, but soon over. These heavy rains are a blessing to our camp, as it cleanses the surface right good.

August 10. Hot and showery. After the storm yesterday, it was discovered that a spring had burst out between the dead line and the stockade, and midway between the north gate and the creek. But it is useless in its present shape. Some way will have to be provided to convey the water under the dead line so the men can get it. Clark L. Kern, Abram Vogt and Albert H. Bancroft, of our company, died to-day. Bancroft was one of the best of men, ready for any thing [sic.]. As we rehearse the good qualities of the boys, I tell them how Bancroft and myself captured a ham. It was at Harrison's Landing in 1862, after the seven days' fight. One day our sutler came in with a large wagon-load of supplies, and while he was putting up his team I climbed into his wagon to inspect the contents. Among other things I found a few hams (I always liked ham), so I went down to camp and tried to find one of the boys to go in with me and get a ham. Three of four of the boys refused. At least I found Bancroft, and he liked ham; so we started out. I went up to where the men were putting up the tent and hung around awhile; then I climbed into the wagon again and stayed there until Bancroft came up through the woods on the opposite side from where the men were at work. I dumped a nice plump ham into his arms, and away he went into the woods with it. I stayed in the wagon awhile, then got out and went where they were putting up the tent, hung around a short time, then sauntered down to camp. I never saw any thing more of that ham until my part was brought to me cooked. It was mighty good, and I wish I had some as good in here. Bancroft was a good comrade. But the poor fellow has gone, and more of us are bound to follow. Who will be next?

Andersonville, Ga., August 11, 1864. Heavy rain to-day and very hot. The men near where that spring burst out day before yesterday, have been allowed by the "Rebs" to dig it out, sink a barrel and to place a trough so as to convey the water under the dead line into the prison, so it can be used by the men. It will be a blessing to a great many. The water is said to be good, even better than the wells. [This is the so-called "Providence spring," about which so much has been said and sung--and also much rot. One celebrated temperance lecturer used it to illustrate the power of prayer. He said, "That the prisoners were without water fit to drink, so they gathered around a large stump and prayed the Lord to send water. And that while they were praying a terrific thunder storm burst upon the prison; when amid the roar of thunder and the flash of lightning out from under that stump a spring of water gushed forth, and enough to water the whole prison." All of which sounds very good. Now the storm was all right and the spring was all right; but when he tried to bring into his story a stump, he was stumped. Bless you, there was not a sign of a stump in that prison within three feet of the surfaced of the earth. They had all been grubbed out for wood weeks before. But the spring did burst out from under a stump. And if any of the boys had gathered around it for prayer they themselves would have been past praying for, as a rebel bullet would have plowed its way through them. As to its watering the whole prison, it could not be done. There were at that time 30,000 of us in there, and if there had been the best of discipline among us it would have been an impossibility. I never drank of the water. But one day I thought I would try and get a canteen of it so I went up and fell in line, and after waiting in the hot sun for over an hour, I gave up as a bad job, and went down and took a drink from our well. The spring was still flowing a few years ago. It was a good spring, and as it had to have a name "Providence" is as good as any.]

August 13. Heavy rains yesterday. No news to-day--only talk.

Another Comrade Gone
(McElroy, *Andersonville, A Story of Rebel Military Prisons*)

August 25 [1864]. I have made a long skip in my writing.[78] But there has been no news of any interest, only the dull monotony of prison life. We have been drawing better grub for a few days back--beef, beans, bread and a small quantity of rice. The beef and rice we use for soup. I am improving a bit, but weak in my knees. My spirits are up in good shape. As long as I don't go dead I won't worry. Some of the boys worry enough to kill them. The only way to do here is to take it easy, eat when we can and go without when we have to. Sergt. Charles J. Simmons, of our company, died day before yesterday. This is the fourth death out of the shebang opposite us. There are only two left in it-- Sergt. Joseph L. Cummings, and Corp. James S. Carson. [They both still live.] It's a strange feeling to have grim death staring you in the face day after day, week after week and month after month, with no chance to strike back at him. Over one hundred of our regiment have died thus far, and many others are edging along that way. A lot of officers who had smuggled in here as privates have been taken out for some reason. Report says all of our officers at Macon and Charleston have been exchanged. Our turn will come some time [sic.], at least it ought to.

August 26. I have been having the toothache for a few days back very bad. To-day, at sick call I went out to see what could be done for it. I found a dentist, a "Yank" cavalry sergeant, with a very neat office and outfit. Every thing [sic] was plain but durable. His chair was a pine stump of the right height. His instrument was of the latest pattern, adjustable. Every tooth in a man's head would fit it, or rather he made his one pair of forceps fit every tooth. They were a trifle rusty, as every time it rained they got wet. His manners and address showed that he was no country mechanic. After I had looked his shop over, he asked me what he could do for me. I told him. He asked me to be seated. I did so--the padding had gone out of myself or chair; it was very hard. He applied his instrument. The "Yank" gave a yank and a "Yank" was minus a tooth. It was a very slick operation. I asked him his charges. He said, "Nothing, it was all paid for by the C.S.A." [I hope he is alive with a good practice.] The "Rebs" have furnished picks and shovels to the prisoners who are camped close down to the bog, with which they are to dig down the bank and cover up the filth so as to make more room to camp on. And they have begun to build sinks[79] on the lower end of the creek, a much needed improvement. Also they are building barracks up on the north end, all of which looks as if we were to be here sometime yet. I makes the shivers run over me to think of being in here all winter. One of the boys who has been outside tells us of what he saw there: "Men who had tried to escape were strung up by the thumbs and left hanging until they were black in the face. Others were put into the chain gang-- that is a ball and chain were riveted to the ankle of the men, and then twelve or more were riveted to a long chain, so that they had to all go together. And others were placed in the stocks, which is so constructed as to make the victims lie on their back and exposed to the sun all day." All of this because a soldier is doing what is his duty to do, to-wit: trying to escape from the hands of the enemy.

Aug. 31 [1864]. Cool and cloudy. This is the last day of summer, and we have been in this Bull Pen four months, and there is still room for more. There seems to be a ray of hope of getting out next month. Perhaps it's all talk. Hope not. Some of the boys think we will surely be out before President election. We are drawing cooked rations--beans, beef and bread. The beans are not fit to eat, but the beef is very good.

September 1. Warm. A paper came in last night which stated that President Lincoln had agreed to an exchange, which was to take place immediately. Glorious news, if true.[80] The cooked rations we get now make a fellow go with a hungry belly the most of the time. To-night we drew a pint of half-cooked rice, a small piece of bread and meat. The whole would not make a good meal for us, we are so hungry. But we have to make it do for twenty-four hours. For if we eat it all at once--which we could do--it would be worse for us. So we eat a bit and fill up on the cold water to keep our shape!

Andersonville, Ga., September 2, 1864. Warm and pleasant. The nights are getting to be very cool. We can sleep better, but our beds are no softer. There is strong hopes of exchange.

Union Prisoners of War at Camp Sumpter, Andersonville, Georgia.
VIEW TAKEN FROM NORTH-EAST ANGLE OF THE STOCKADE.

Another view of the Andersonville Stockade in August, 1864
(U.S. Army Military History Institute)

Andersonville Cemetery
(U.S. Army Military History Institute)

September 3 [1864]. The report is that Sherman has drawn Hood out of Atlanta, and he (Hood) is falling back, and this place is all uncovered.

Sunday, September 4. Cool to-day. It looks as if fall weather was coming on. The lieutenant of the guard told us they would have to begin paroling this week, as they could not keep us here with Old Sherman raiding all through the country. He also said that General McClellan was nominated for President, and we would soon be out of here--in a horn. Of course, he will be pitted against Old Abe. It seems strange that Little Mac, the idol of our army in 1861 and 1862, should be nominated by the Democracy for President. I wonder if they think they can win with him.

September 5. Warm and pleasant to-day. A great deal of talk outside as well as in here of our getting out. [Read the following very carefully]: Consolidated return for Confederate States military prison, Camp Sumter, Andersonville, Ga., for the month of August 1864.

Prisoners on hand Aug. 1, 1864--in camp	29,985	
In hospital	1,693	
		31,678
Received from various places during August	3,078	
Recaptured	4	
		3,082
Total		34,760
Died during the month of August	2,993	
Sent to other parts	23	
Exchanged	21	
Escaped	30	
		3,067
Total on hand		31,693
Of which there are on the 31st of August--in camp	29,473	
In hospital	2,220	
	36,693	

The same complaint has been made again against the carelessness and inefficiency of the guard. Of the thirty prisoners eleven escaped while on parole of honor not to escape as long as they would be employed to work outside.

The balance of nineteen escaped, some on bribing the sentinel with greenbacks, some simply walking off from the guard while returning from the place where the tools are deposited at night, that are used in the stockade in day time. Perhaps twenty-five more escaped during the month, but were taken up by the dogs before the daily return was made out, and for that reason they are not on the list of escaped or recaptured.

That only four were recaptured is owing to the fact that the guard nor the officers of the guard reported a man escaped. The roll-call in the morning showed the man was missing, but he was too far gone to be tracked. As we have no general courtmartial here, all such offenses go unpunished, or nearly so.

The worthlessness of the guard forces is on the increase day by day.

H. WIRZ
Captain, Commanding Prison.

Indorsed: Consolidated return for Confederate States military prison for the month of August, 1864. Respectfully forwarded to General B. Cooper, adjutant and inspector-general.

JNO. H. WINDER
Brigadier General

September 5, 1864. [By way of compairson: The poplulation of our Seneca county in 1890, was 28,185, which is 1,638 less than Wirz's report for August. Now if all the people of this country were corrolled [corralled] in a twenty-three acre lot they would not be as crowded as we were in that pen. We outnumbered the city of Auburn by over 3,000. Our dead was nearly 100 each day. Can you comprehend what Andersonville meant for us? And still means? Can you?]

September 6. Hot. I slept all this forenoon. The "Reb" sergeants came in to-night and ordered the detachments from 1 to 18 to be ready to go out at a moment's notice. Such shouting and cheering all through the prison was never heard. We are fairly wild with excitement. It seems too good to be true.[81] Hope it's so. Our detachment is 19, and if from 1 to 18 go, will our turn come soon? There will be little sleep in here to-night. We are as excited as a good brother was in a protracted meeting in Canandaigua, N.Y., a few years ago, when he shouted, "Glory be to Beeman, brother God"; only we sing, "Yes, we'll rally around the flag, boys, rally once again, shouting the battle cry of freedom." This is our favorite song in here.

September 7. Hot again to-day. Not much sleep in here last night. We are going home. Glory. Orders came this morning for ten detachments to go out; and they went out, too, but they all came in again except three.[82] These three and the sick from the hospital went away on the cars. The others are to go at noon. We are all excitement now for fear something will happen. To-night orders came in for all up to the detachment 18 and from 103 to 108 to be ready. We are left, sure, now. It breaks us up bad, but we will have to stand it. No whining. Well, our Sergeant John Buell went out to-day. He died. John was one good man--good all through.

[Let the fathers and mothers of this generation try to realize this item: "The aged and honored. Died in East Bloomfield, N.Y., January 16, 1873, Timothy Buell, Esq., in the 82nd year of his age; and January 24, Mrs. Lucy Buell, his wife, in the 80th year of her age. * * It has been the intention of their children of whom eight were living, to come back to the old home and gather about them the many friends and relatives of the aged couple at their golden wedding in August 1864. But their youngest son, who early enlisted in the war to save his country, and who had made honorable record for himself, was at that time pining away in the Andersonville prison, where he subsequently died, and the afflicted mother could not consent to any festivities over which the thought of her suffering son would cast so deep at shadow."[83] *The Evangelist.* It was our John that home and mother mourned. There were thousands of such homes and others all over this land.]

September 8 [1864]. No sleep last night. Every one was up and on the move, and discussing the prospects of the exchange or whatever it is, and would we be among those who will go. A lot went out this morning, and more are waiting for transportation.

September 9. Our Franklin E. Wilcox died this morning. He is beyond all this trouble and wrong. All those who were ordered out last night have gone away. I hope will be on the list soon.

September 10. Our detachment had orders this morning to be ready at a moments notice to go out. Glory, Hallelujah! our turn next! It looks as if it were a sure thing this time, so we carefully take down our shebang and pack our things, what few we have, and wait in the hot sun all day until dark. Will we have to stay another night in this hell?

Chapter Seven

"OUT OF A FILTHY HOG PEN"

(September 11, 1864 - February 15, 1865)

Hope (and loyal friends) was the common denominator of the survivors of Andersonville. Persistent rumors of parole had been Mosher's mainstay throughout him painful experience at Andersonville. His diary, like others including John Ransom's, Robert Kellogg's and John McElroy's, was replete with references to rumors about release. Stories of the approach of Sherman's army fueled the rumors among these men whose physical health depended so much on their mental state.

And the stories of Sherman's presence were reinforced by the numbers of prisoners from his army entering already overcrowded Andersonville. Coupled with this was increased anxiety and vigilance by the guards and growing public concern over the conditions at Andersonville.

Prisoners, alert to every sign of change, reacted accordingly. And then the blessed day arrived--release from the "filthy hog pen." But another variable was to confound and frustrate the initial euphoria--Commander Grant's strategy, which recognized that it was now a war of attrition. Ultimate success would be based on the ability of the Union to stay the course and to press the Confederacy relentlessly. The releases of Mosher and his compatriots, based on the Dix-Hill Cartel, required exchanges. To obtain the release of Union prisoners, Grant would have to exchange Confederate prisoners, thereby working against the overall strategy. In short, Mosher's release would mean the release of at least one Southern counterpart.

Thus, Mosher was a pawn in this brutal chess game played with human lives. He could not know this and would therefore suffer even more. His existence depended upon hope of release. How many times could this hope be destroyed before he too would be destroyed like so many others who had perished?

But for now, he could feel free, could smell the "pure air again," exult at how "fresh and sweet" it was to his long deprived senses. Detachment 19 was out of Andersonville.

Andersonville, Ga., September 11, 1864. We are up early this morning after a sleepless night. We ate a little, pack our traps and wait in the hot sun all day until about six o'clock this afternoon, when we fall in line and march out of this hole by the same south gate through which we entered over four months ago. But what a change has come over us in that time. It seems a miracle that any of us have lived thus far. But we have; and a weak, flabby lot we are. Outside, in the pure air again! How fresh and sweet it is. It seems like getting out of a filthy hog pen, the change is so noticable. Here we are counted off in lots of sixty each, enough for a car-load, and at seven o'clock we are loaded into box cars, the whistle blows, and we are off for home. If there is any place on earth I want to see, it's home. But it makes us sad to think we have to leave some of our boys here who are too sick for the journey.

Savannah Junction, Ga., September 12, 1864. Well, we are out of that hell, called Andersonville, anyway. We arrived here at seven o'clock this morning after a very good night's rest on the car. We change cars, as well as exchange cars from box to flat, and on we go. We are going North sure enough, and home is up that way. These flat cars are very cool as well as very dusty. After an all day's ride we reach Charleston, S.C., at five o'clock this afternoon, but have to stay on the cars for nearly two hours. The Irish women gather around and give us plenty of good things to eat as well as words of sympathy but our guards drive them away; for why? Don't know, unless they are afraid we will eat too much. It would take a pile of grub to fill us up. We are hardly off the cars when John E. Blake[1] fell down dead. He was my tent mate on the Peninsula campaign. After a deal of bother we get in line and move out of the city to the race course. Our guards told us it was only a mile, but it seemed a mightly long one. The sick are brought out in wagons, after the women had fed them. This is a lovely place for a camp. There is a good green turf to lie on and a fresh sea breeze. It put life into me. The change is so great, it's like stepping out of hell into heaven as it were, but we are still prisoners of war, and the "Rebs" are as big devils as ever.

Charleston, S.C., September 13 [1864]. Had a good sleep last night and feel well this morning. We hear our guns at regular intervals all night, as they threw shells into the city. Gen. J. G. Foster is in command at Morris' Island. Our brigade was with him when he made the Goldsboro raid in December, 1862.[2] It seems good to think that our friends are so near, even if we cannot get to them. We can hear them talk with their swamp angel, as we call their big gun. This race course contains about forty acres. There are from 10,000 to 15,000 of us here.[3] Plenty of room. By digging four or five feet we get water, which is a trifle brackish. Our rations to-day are three large hard tack, fresh beef, a little salt and some soup. Very good grub. If it will only hold out I shall be content with this place as long as I have to be a prisoner of war.

September 14. Fifteen hundred prisoners left this morning, some say for Florence, S.C., to build another bull pen; which does not sound good to me. Here we have only a furrow turned for a dead line, which does not obstruct our view. I do not think as much of Charleston to day as I did yesterday. I have simply changed my mind, that is all, especially on the grub question, as all they gave us to-day was a small piece of raw beef, a pinch of salt and a bit of wood. At dark they gave us two hard tack. Take it all together it is a very small allowance for us. We are used to being hungry. But it's tough on us. Here we are organized into lots of one hundred. Farrar and I are still together as chums. Our shebang is not as good as it was in the other pen.

September 15. Cool and pleasant. Very good grub to-day. Three hundred prisoners went out last night to work on rebel fortifications. They are a miserable crew.

September 16. Cool, with prospects of rain. To-day another lot of pimps went out to work for the "Rebs." They are despised not only by us "Yanks" and "Rebs," but by the ladies also. Our rations to-day are beans, rice, hominey, meal, flour, beef and salt, and not a bit of wood to cook it with. The quality of the grub is good, but there is not enough of any one kind to make a dish, so we have to trade around until we got enough of a kind together.

September 17 [1864]. Very pleasant to-day. Last night we sat up a long time watching the shells from our guns on Morris Island, as they described their graceful curves in their flight into the city. We could hear them tear through the buildings and explode. It did our hearts good to hear them, as they are doing their missionary work. The shelling has kept up all day at intervals. But it did not stop the boys from flying their kites.

Sunday, September 18. Rainy to-day. The Line storm[4] is coming on by the appearance of things--if that is what they call it here. We had a variety of rations to-day, and very good, and to offset a good thing they gave us no wood. I scraped up some dried cow dung, with which chum [Farrar] and I cooked our grub. It made a very good fire.

September 19. Heavy rain last night, and we got very wet, as our roof leaked. The ground is so level that there is no chance for the water to run off, and the water has to stand until the run drys it up. Bacon and a bit of vinegar to-night. The Charleston papers state that the commissioners of exchange met to-day.

September 20. To-day begins our sixth month as prisoners. Things look kind o'blue for us at present. More rain to-day. Report says that the commissioners are trying to fix up an exchange for all prisoners at this point.

September 22. Another wetting yesterday. Pleasant to-day. We drew beef this morning, but the rest of the grub did not come in until dark, a trifle of flour, meal and beans, not enough of either to cook. The sutler and clerk of the 16th Conn. left to-night for our lines. Bully for them.

September 23. Pleasant to-day. The report says that the flag of truce boats met to-day. I believe that there is something in it, as our guns have been silent all day. The city has had a rest, and we have lost a day's sport. Will try and stand it if there is any prospect of our getting out of here. The days drag very slowly. Thomas W. Such died yesterday.

Sunday, September 25. Quiet yesterday. Pleasant this morning. The church bells in the city are ringing. My clothes not being in good shape, and a little off color, I guess I will not go to church this morning, as I do not want to appear odd. We had a great many visitors here to-day from the city. The Sisters of Mercy are good friends to us here. They are allowed to come on the grounds and minister to the sick. Our officers are in the city, Capt. C. S. Aldrich has sent money to some of our boys several times.[5] The papers state that Jeff Davis made a speech in Macon, in which he said, "He didn't know but he would have to come to Butler's terms before he could exchange." Our Sunday dinner was not served in very good style to-day. The older we get the less we care about style.

Charleston, S.C., September 26, 1864. We drew two days' rations this morning. That is what the "Rebs" call it, but we could eat it all at one meal. Things are looking good for an exchange just now. While we have more room here, we still have the same trouble we had in Andersonville, to wit: dysentery, diarrhea, scurvy, filth, misery, hell.

September 28. Nothing new yesterday. The "Rebs" want us to take the non-combatant's oath.[6] I can't see them for one. They want us to take the oath, then they would let us out. They are getting tired of keeping us. Their grub is short.

September 29. Two days' rations again to-day. The darkies came out to visit us to-day, droves of them. Just for fun, the "Reb" guards in charge of the artillery turned their guns on them, when the darks gave a yell and ran for the city. They made good time.

September 30. There is a deal of talk of our leaving here to-morrow for some place. Our stay here is to be short, it seems. Gen. Foster keeps up his firing on the city. We call it his morning report. The boys are still flying their kites. They are not afraid of his hurting them, or else they are out of range.

October 1. Rained last night. Fifteen hundred left this morning for Florence, they say. They were given hard tack and beans for one day only. I was around when they gave out the hard tack, and made a good breakfast of the pieces that were left. I am so much ahead.

Sunday, October 2. I sat up with our corporal, Thomas W. Porter, last night. He is very bad with the dysentery. We care for him as you would a baby, as he has lost all control of himself. During the night he said to me, "When you see I can't stand it any longer give me all the cold water I can drink." He knows that would end his case very quick. Poor Tom! how much he suffers, and we are powerless to help him. It's hard for us to witness such things, knowing that we are all on the same road, unless something is done for us. The "Rebs" have moved the hospital inside of the dead line.

October 3. Heavy rain last night. Two of our men had a paper to-day, but the officer of guard took it away from them. They were transporting troops through the city all night to the northward. We had to move our shebang to-day, to make room for the hospital. "Tom" Porter died late this afternoon. I had been with him nearly all day, and had started out to find some one of our boys who had some rice with which to make him some rice water; when I returned he was dead. "Tom" was one good boy--always ready for duty and generous to a fault.

October 4 [1864]. Fifteen hundred more left for Florence this morning. The report is we all leave here soon. Beef and rice to-day.

October 5. Two men were shot last night by the guard. We drew rations early this mornng. The report is that the yellow fever is in the city.[7] Orders are in for us to be ready to leave here to-morrow morning. We drew one day's raw rations of flour, meal, beans and molasses, not enough of one kind to be of any use to us. So we have to trade around in order to get it into shape for cooking. It's a small amount for us to move on, but we have learned not to kick, as it does no good.

October 6. Up early this morning, and ate what we call our breakfast. And still we fast with hardly a break in it worthy the name. We take down our shebang, pack up our traps, and at seven o'clock we march out of this prison. After laying around in the sun until nine o'clock we march down to the city, and are put on the cars. I am on a flat car. As we lay here we saw our officers leave on a train, our guards say for Colunbia, S.C. We recognize our Lieutenant Charles McHenry and Captain Allen of Co. F.[8] About ten o'clock our train started for Florence, S.C. It is very hot and dusty to-day on these open cars, and good water is hard for us to get. At one station where we stopped for the engine to water, the tank was overflowing so that it made quite a stream, so we jumped off to fill our cups, but the "Reb" colonel in command drove us back on the cars. We asked him if he did not believe in giving prisoners of war water. He said, "Yes, I believe in giving you all the water you want to drink, and then, G___ D___ you, I would kill you." As we did not get any water the rebel--did not have to kill us. We are very thirsty, and the water does look so good. But it's not for us poor miserables to have any. [This experience was one of the most cruel ones of my whole prison life.] Ira N. Deyo and Elam. B. Wetmore of our company swear that they will not go into another bull pen. They will die first. They are in a box car (our train is made up of box and flat cars), and the guards are all on top of the cars. Just as we are passing through a thick piece of woods Deyo jumped out of the car door, and did not make any noise to attract the guard, so he was all right. When Whetmore jumped he struck a dry scrub of a tree, which made such a restling noise that the guards heard it and fired a volley in that direction. The train was stopped. When the guards got off they found that they had riddled Wetmore through and through with bullets.[9] But they could not find any thing [sic] of Deyo. After leaving orders with some of the natives to bury Wetmore, our train starts on. We are filled with sadness over this event, at the same time we are glad that Deyo has made his escape.[10] We reach Florence, S.C., at seven o'clock to-night, and the rain is pouring down in torrents. It is dark when we leave the cars and march out into a large field,

Elam B. Wetmore
(Courtesy of Michael Nighan)

where we spread our blankets on the wet ground and lay ourselves down to rest and sleep.

Florence, S.C., October 7, 1864. We woke up this morning sore and stiff from lying out in the mud and wet all night. It was a most wretched night, as the storm kept up until nearly morning. All our clothing and blankets are thoroughly soaked. We had all the water we wanted last night if the "Reb" colonel did not give us any yesterday. The first thing we saw after we were fairly awake was a counterpart of the Andersonville stockade. It made me shiver. After standing around in the mud until nearly noon we are counted off into hundreds. Ours is the 33d hundred, 1st mess.[11] On our way into the stockade I saw a "Reb" guard with a lot of plug tobacco under his arm. I asked him if he would trade it for a watch. He said he would, and told me to come over and walk with him, I was not long in reaching him, and found he had twelve plugs, navy size. I told him I would give him my watch for the lot, but took up with his offer of ten plugs. A very good trade, as tobacco is as good as money. Here we are in another stockade. It is about the same size as the one at Andersonville, and has only one main gate. A creek runs through it, which divides it into two sections. A furrow turned by a plow is the dead line. The hospital is in the corner to the right of the gate. We are located just below the hospital and a few rods from the creek. Outside the stockade is a wide ditch; the earth from it has been thrown up against the stockade so to form a walk for the sentries. Chum Farrar and myself form a mess with our sergeant J. L. Cummins, and two of his home friends [Jepther]-- "Zade" Sabins of the 126th N.Y. and "Ben" Simons of the 1st Long Island. These three are from Naples, Ontario County, N.Y. Our cooking arrangements are all broken up since we left Andersonville. John J. Mary brought the Dutchbake oven from there, and therefore claims it. It leaves us short on our cooking utensils. This afternoon I traded some tobacco for a three-quart pail. This will help us out in good shape. To-night we drew a small ration of flour.

October 8. It was quite cold last night. This morning we began to build our shebang by going on the bog and, out of the black muck and clay, make up a quantity of brick, we call them, to build up the side and end walls with; then we put up a ridge pole, and draw two blankets over them for a roof. In front, on one side is the door, and on the other is our fireplace. We are in fair shape for cold weather as regards a shebang. The "Rebs" are in here getting recruits for their army and to work in the quartermaster's department at Charleston. To-day a large number went out for that purpose. They say they can't stay here and starve any longer. We call those who take the oath of allegiance to the Southern Confederacy "Galvanized Yanks."[12] One Colonel O'Neill is recruiting a regiment of them. The oath I took when I first enlisted and when I re-enlisted will not permit me to take any other, much less to this God-forsaken, rotten Confederacy. This prison is not different from the other

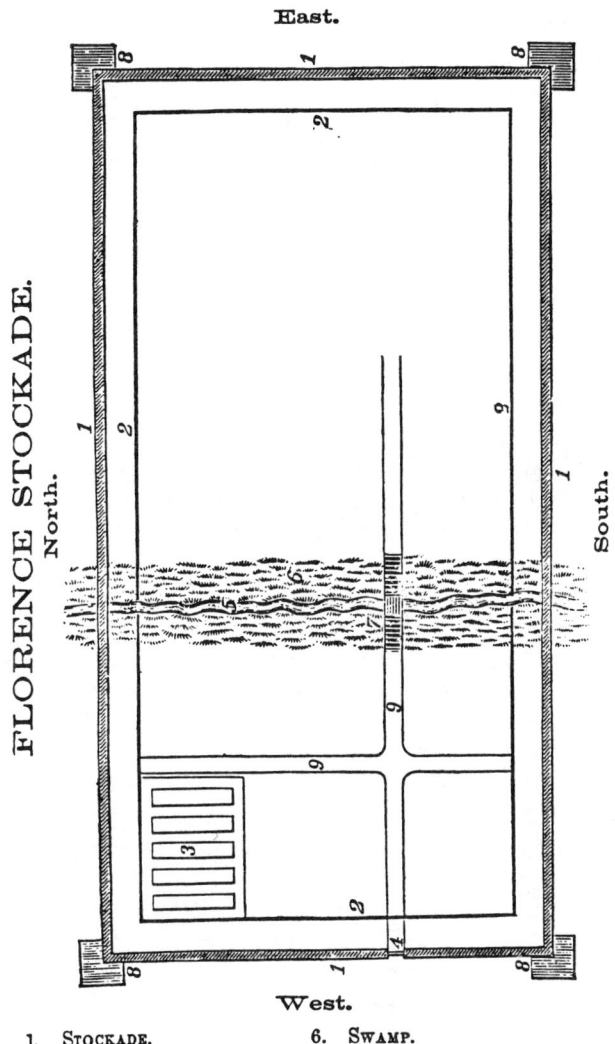

1. STOCKADE.
2. DEAD LINES.
3. HOSPITAL.
4. PRISON GATE.
5. BROOK.
6. SWAMP.
7. CAUSEWAY AND BRIDGE.
8. ELEVATED PLATFORM FOR ARTILLERY.
9. STREETS.

**Plan of the Florence Stockade
(Robert Kellogg, *Life and Death in Rebel Prisons*)**

two, only in this, we have more room and it is less filthy just now. Very good grub to-day.

Sunday, October 9 [1864]. It does not seem like Sunday to me. These cold nights drive our lice indoors to keep warm. That is they keep closer to our bodies. During the hot weather we could lay off our clothes part of the time and so get "shut" of our live stock.[13] Our sick came in to-day. Theodore Warner of our company is dead.[14] They keep dropping out one at a time. As long as I don't drop I won't kick; and if I do I won't. I am feeling very well now, as that stay in Charleston put life into me. It takes all there is of a fellow to keep up his spirits.

October 10. No excitement. We drew oat meal to-day. It's queer stuff, but we have to eat it. If there was more of it we would like it better. Anything to fill up. Will we ever get filled up again?

October 11. The weather is warmer than it has been for a few days past. The "Rebs" have re-organized us. We are into thousands and hundreds now. The eleventh thousand is not full. Drew beans, flour and meal, no salt. Just a pinch of each. I have been in the service three years to-day, and these last few months seem longer than all the rest.

Oct. 12. Our Ira N. Deyo came in today. (He is the one who made his escape when Wetmore was shot.) He says that he stayed around, but out of sight, until he saw where they buried Wetmore, and then started for the coast, with the thought that he might signal our men o'war. But being alone in his travels he became careless and discouraged and so exposing himself too much, was recaptured. We are glad to see him, but wish he had made good his escape. [In 1875 Deyo went down to Florence to have the remains of his comrade and chum interred in the National cemetery at that place. Deyo says he went to Florence and asked some of the oldest citizens if they remembered the circumstance of a Union prisoner being shot in 1864. They told him yes. And could they tell about where he was buried. O yes, they knew. But they didn't. After asking a good many people the same question, and not receiving any reply that met his ideas of the spot, he asked two old black women if they remembered the case. One said, "Yes, sah, I does." And where? "Come with us and I will show you, sah." He says they went along the railroad tracks for aways, which had been recently ballasted up, and the marks of the shovels could still be seen when the women stopped beside the track and said, "You will find his head down dah and his feet down dah." So he began to dig, and found the remains of Wetmore as they told him. He says how that black woman kept that exact spot in her mind all those years was a mystery to him, when there was not a sign of anything to mark it. He had the remains placed in the National cemetery, and Old Glory floats over his dust, which is fitting, as he gave three years of his

Ira N. Deyo
(Courtesy of Michael Nighan)

young life that Old Glory might float "over the land of the free and the home of the brave." Deyo still lives. His home is in Honeoye, Ontario county, N.Y.]

Florence, SC, October 14, 1864. There was some talk yesterday of an exchange. The sick and wounded are to go first. It was quite cold last night. It will be tough on us if we should have to stay in this hole all winter. All we drew for rations to-day was a few beans, and a bit of meal and hominy. Scant grub. We found the same police force here that we had in Andersonville, with "Big Peter" as chief. This prison was located early last month. There were about 3,000 prisoners here before the stockade was built. They had a sorry time of it. [Let the "Rebs" tell their own story.]

"Statebury, S.C., October 12, 1864. [15]

"Dear Sir: Inclosed you will find an account of the terrible sufferings of the Yankee prisoners at Florence, S.C.

"In the name of all that is holy is there nothing that can be done to relieve such dreadful sufferings?

"If such are allowed to continue they will most surely draw down some awful judgment upon our country. It is a most horrible national sin that cannot go unpunished. If we cannot give them food and shelter, for God's sake parole them and send them back to Yankeeland, but don't starve the miserable creatures to death.

"Don't think that I have any liking for the Yankee. I have none. Those near and dear to me have suffered too much from their tyranny for me to have anything but hatred to them; but we have not yet become quite brute enough to know of such suffering without trying to do something, even for a Yankee.

Yours, respectfully
SABINA DISMUKES

"Sabina Dismukes, Stateburg, S.C., October 12, 1864, forwards newspaper article on treatment of Yankee prisoners at Florence, S.C. Asks that they may be fed or paroled. Respectfully referred, by direction of the president, to the Hon. secretary of war.

BURTON N. HARRISON
Private Secretary"

"THE PRISONERS AT FLORENCE
FROM THE SUMTER WATCHMAN

"Mr. Editor: It may not be uninteresting to your numerous readers to hear something from the Yankee camp at Florence. Your correspondent went over upon the summons of one of those ominous O.B.'s which the times have made more familiar than agreeable, to take a drove of cattle to camp. Our party had in charge animals of all sizes, sexes and conditions, from the patriarch of the heard, whose scarred and wrinkled front bore the marks of many a bloody battle, to "auld Crumple," who had served her day at the milk pail, and whose constitution was evidently unable to stand the blasts of another March. We lost three on the way, two straggled and one fell down exhausted;the buzzards after all were not cheated out of their long-expected prey.

"The country through which we traveled is "flat, stale and unprofitable." The crops are poor, and every cotton field destroyed by the "army worm," as if in imitation of its more intelligent namesakes. No object of curiosity was encountered on the way, unless we take into account the "long bridge" over what the natives call "Spawa swamp." Most of the houses were uninhabited, with fences and outbuildings going to ruin.

"No product now the barren fields afford,
But men and steel, the soldier and his sword."

"The camp we found full of what were once human beings, but who would scarcely now be recognized as such. In an old field, with no inclosure but the living wall of sentinels who guard them night and day, are several thousand filthy, diseased, famished men, with no hope of relief except by death. A few dirty rags stretched on poles give them a protection from the hot sun and heavy dews. All were in rags and barefoot, and crawling with vermin. As we passed around the line of guards I saw one of them brought out from his miserable booth by two of his companions and laid upon the ground to die. He was nearly naked. His companions pulled his cap over his face and straightened out his limbs, and all was over. The captive was free.

"The commissary's tent was near one side of the square, and near it the beef was laid upon boards preparatory to its distribution. This sight seemed to excite the prisoners as the smell of blood does the beasts of a menagerie. They surged up as near the lines as they allowed and seemed, in their eagerness, about to break over. While we were on the grounds a heavy rain came up, and they seemed greatly to enjoy it, coming out of a puris naturalibus, opening their mouths to catch the drops, while one would wash off another with his hands, and then receive from him the like kind office. Numbers get out at night and wander the neighboring houses in quest of food.

"From the camp of the living we passed to the camp of the dead--the hospital--a transition which reminded me of Satan's soliloquy:

"Which way I fly is hell; myself am hell;
And in the lowest deeps, a lower deep,
Still threatening to devour me, opens wide,"

"A few tents, covered with pine tops, were crowded with the dying and the dead in every stage of corruption. Some lay in prostrate helplessness; some had crowded under the shelter of the bushes; some were rubbing their skeleton limbs. Twenty or thirty of them die daily--most of them, as I was informed, of the scurvy. The corpses lay by the roadside waiting for the dead cart, their glassy eyes turned to heaven, the flies swarming in their mouths, their big toes tied together with a cotton string and their skeleton arms folded on their breasts. You would hardly know them to be men, so sadly do hunger, disease and wrtched- ness change the "human face divine." Presently came the carts. They were carried a little distance to trenches dug for the purpose, and tumbled in like so many dogs a few pine tops thrown upon the bodies, a few shovelfuls of dirt, and then haste was made to open a new ditch for other victims. The burying party were Yankees detailed for the work, an appointment which, as the sergeant told me, they consider as a favor, for they get a little more to eat and enjoy fresh air.

"Thus we saw at one glance the three great scourges of mankind--war, famine and pestilence; and we turn from the spectacle sick at heart as we remember that some of our loved ones may be undergoing a similar misery. "Man's inhumanity to man makes countless millions mourn."

"Soon eight thousand more will be added to their number. Where the provisions are to come from to feed this multitude is a difficult problem. Five thousand pounds of bacon or ten thousand pounds of beef daily, seems, in addition to more urgent draughts upon her, far beyond the ability of South Carolina.

"The question is, are we not doing serious injury to our cause in keeping these prisoners to divide with us our scanty rations? Would it not be better at once to release them on parole?

HOWARD"

October 15 [1864]. I am not feeling well this morning. The sick get beef to-day. As I am sick I get a piece. I am beginning to feel weak for some reason or other. We drew molasses to-night. It's very poor stuff.

Sunday, October 16. Warm and pleasant. I could enjoy this day if I had my liberty and was in our lines. We did not expect any rations to-day, but just at night we were given a trifle--no salt. Mush and cold water with out salt is not very good eating. We use cold water in the place of milk. We have our little dish of water boiling when we get our corn meal, so that inside of fifteen minutes we have our mush cooked and devoured. We are worse off here in the matter of rations than we were in Andersonville.

October 17. Warm and pleasant. We managed to have a bit for breakfast by scraping up everything we had to eat. No rations to-day at all. We borrowed some beans, or we should have gone to bed very hungry. We are starving all the time with no prospects of any change for the better. Horace Z. Shepherd is dead.[16]

October 18. Cold and wet. Our clothing is so poor the cold goes through us easy. This morning we drew a little meal and flour, no salt, hardly enough for breakfast, but it stopped the hunger a bit. This afternoon we drew beef, rice, beans and salt, a very good ration of each. The prisoners are going out and taking the oath very fast.[17] Hunger is driving them to it, which just suits the "Rebs."

Florence, S.C., October 19, 1864. The report is there is to be an immediate exchange. Very good rations to-day. The weather is a bit warmer, but the nights are very cool.

October 20. Six months a prisoner. How many more? No one knows. Small rations.

October 22. Quiet yesterday. A cold northwest wind is blowing to-day, and it goes right through us. Our wood is getting scarce, for all there are heavy forests all about us.

Sunday, October 23. Cold last night; but it is warming up this morning. John Logan and Tobias Hadsell[18] of our company are dead. I heard to-day that Noah Turner died the 14th of this month. He was a member of the 148th N.Y., and was one of my home friends. This prison life did not seem to agree with him, as he worried too much. There is no place in here for worry. It kills every time. Very small rations to-day.

October 24. The report is around that an exchange is to take place soon. Hope so. Warm and pleasant to-day. We use these warm days to hand-pick our lice. All over the prison we see the men with their shirts off, and their backs to the sun, hunting the graybacks. Under the road seams of our trousers they are very thick, so we take and make one end of a leg fast, and then take our two thumbs and run over them. One of the boys says it reminds him of a company of infantry firing by file, they crack so. We have to kill 'em, as there is not grub for all of us. Drew rice meal and molasses to-day.

October 26. Quiet yesterday. Our hundred drew clothing to-day. They came from our sanitary commission. Chum Farrar got a rig throughout.

October 27. Cool, with rain.

October 28. No news to-day.

October 29. We drew a small piece of beef to-day. I was so meat hungry I ate mine raw.

Sunday, October 30. Pleasant to-day. The tobacco is gone which I got for my watch, and as I must have a smoke once in a while, I traded off my ration of molasses for a bit. The boys that both chew and smoke, dry their cud after chewing and then smoke it.

October 31 [1864]. The "Rebs" are very jubilant over the coming Presidential election. They tell us that McClellan will be elected, the war will end, and us "Yanks" will go home. Captain John Morris is in here and is trying to buy up our pay checks, as he did in Andersonville.[19] He offers me $45 for my $150 check. Farrar says he will stand half of it, and pay me when we get to our lines. It's too big a shave.[20] Some of the boys are selling.

November 1. Cool and cloudy to-day. Rainy to-night, and very cold.

November 2. It was a very disagreeable day yesterday. Cold and wet. It's very rough on us. It has cleared off to-day, but very cold. No news aloat.

November 5. Pleasant to-day. The papers state that 10,000 more are to be exchanged soon; also that Plymouth, N.C., has been recaptured by our men, and the ram *Albemarle* is sunk. Good news. That ram was the cause of our being captured last spring. Alexander Hussey died to-day.[21] This is the twentieth death in our company. The men are going out and taking the oath fast. N. H. Briggs of our company is among the number.[22] [A few days ago a number of our company met our captain, C. S. Aldrich, in Canandaigua, N.Y., and had a reunion on a small scale, but a very lively one. Briggs was there, but he did not have a good time with us, as he knew we were aware of the fact of his taking the oath to the Confederacy. "Cap." Aldrich asked me later what was the matter of Briggs. I told him he was a "Galvanized Yank," and explained the term. Aldrich was surprised and grieved to think that a member of our company would do such a thing. The plea that he took the oath to save his life does not go down with us.]

Sunday, November 6. There was a heavy frost last night. I was mighty cold. I don't know what we will do if we have to stay here all winter, with scarcely anything to eat and thinly clad. The prospect is very dark; but they say it's always darker just before day. Perhaps it will be so in our case. Hope so.

November 7. I am miserable to-day. I am so weak I can hardly get around. I disposed of my pay check to Captain John Morris to-day for $45--$20 down and the rest in thirty days, which is in the shape of a due bill. Farrar is to stand half when we reach our lines. I am running down so fast that I shiver to think of what next, and I have no notion of leaving my bones down here, nor taking the oath to this damable Confederacy. Money will buy anything here. Captain Morris was dining to-day on fried chicken, sweet potatoes and soft

Alexander Hussey, Co. B, 85th N.Y.
(Courtesy of Craig F. Senfield)

bread. Anything you want for money. Our money will help out our grub. We will have enough once more at least.

November 8 [1864]. Presidential election to-day. They vote in here by beans--red and white--red for Lincoln, white for McClellan. I don't vote, as it will do no good.[23] Last March, when I was home on my furlough, I walked about five miles through the mud and slush to vote at the town meeting, as that was the time when the question was to be decided as to the soldiers voting in the field. I voted yea and had to swear my vote in. It was my first vote. Here we are in this hold, so our votes don't count. Farrar and I had sweet potatoes and soft bread for breakfast this morning. We had our fill for once. We know how to eat yet. Had soup for supper to-night, which cost us twenty-five cents. I am feeling somewhat better to-day. With better grub and more of it, I hope to pick up. To-day's paper states that the exchange begins Thursday.

November 9. Warm and pleasant this morning. Nathan Wright died the 6th.[24] The night before he did he got into a fight with a fellow prisoner, and bit off his finger. When Farrar was sick in Andersonville last May, Wright would not lend him fifty cents for fear he (Farrar) would die and he would lose it. At that time Wright had $200 in money. It did him no good, as he gambled it away in a short time. Stormy to-night.

November 10. Pleasant to-day. The papers state that the first thousand will be exchanged to-morrow, and it will be kept up until 10,000 are exchanged. Also that Sherman is back to Atlanta, with four army corps, and is going to hunt Hood.

November 11. Cold and raw. Our rations to-day are rice and flour. Farrar and I have bought up two haversacks of rice and a quantity of flour. We are living very good now. No thanks to the rebels.

November 12. Hip, Hip, Hurrah! "Abe" Lincoln is elected. It makes the "Rebs" hang their under lip. I reckon the war won't end until the "Rebs" are whipped in good style, and they know it. This morning Farrar and I cooked our three-quart pail full of what we call flour gravy. We ate this up before we were aware of it. I said "I am still hungry." Farrar says, "I am too." so we cooked the same amount again, which we ate with a keen relish to the last bit. There is quite a bulge to us after we have put outselves outside of an eight-quart breakfast. To-night we are hungry as usual. So we cook our pail of rice and cup of gravy, which we dispose of without any trouble. When I went to school I was told that a man's stomach would not hold but a quart. That must have been a theory, as our practice to-day has proved to the contrary. I can go to bed to-night with the thought that I am full for the first time since I have been a prisoner. I feel very comfortable, and Farrar complains along the same line.

Sunday, November 13 [1864]. Beef and rice to-day. We traded until we got four or five extra rations of beef. We are trying to keep filled up for a while. Our "Joe" Cummings has sold his pay check of $180 to Capt. John Morris for $60. He divides with his two chums, Sabins [Sabin] and Simonds, and each is to stand one-third of the whole. Now our whle shebang has money.

November 14. Beefsteak and potatoes for breakfast. We have bought two bushels of sweet potatoes and to keep them from being stolen we have dug a hole under where we sleep to put them in. We know where they are now. A squad of seaman came in to-day, who say they were captured off the Jersey coast by the rebel privateer, *Tallahassee*.[25] They report that the exchange is going on bravely.

November 15. A lot of prisoners came in from Columbia, S.C., last night. No news to-day.

November 16. We have made our shebang more comfortable to-day. Beef to-day. Francis M. Francisco died to-day.[26] Our company is getting smaller. Too bad!

November 17. Beef to-day. A lot of the "Galvanized Yanks"[27] came back to-day. As they all tell a different story as to the way, we can't find out the true reason for it. They bring a report that 20,000 more are to be exchanged. It's most too good to be true.

November 18. Rice and molasses to-day. I am feeling very well now. I am not sorry I sold my check, for it was no good in my pocket.

Florence, S.C., Sunday, November 20, 1864. To-day begins my eighth month as a prisoner. How much longer no one knows. Beef and flour for rations. My piece of beef was as large as my three fingers, and the flour enough to make a pancake. The commandant of this prison is Lieutenant-Colonel John F. Iverson of the 5th Georgia.[28] Lieutenant Chatham is his adjutant. Lieutenant Barritt has charge of the prison interior, and is red-headed. We thought Wirz of Andersonville was the devil incarnate, but Barritt goes him one better. His prison name is the red-headed _____. Adjutant Chatham is a jolly good fellow, full of fun and frolic. They are both members of the 5th Georgia.

November 21. A nasty, drizzling rain. Our chimney fell down last night, which adds to our discomfort. No rations to-day. The "Rebs" say there is a tunnel in here somewhere, and there will be not rations until it's found.[29] Cold.

November 22 [1864]. Clear and cold this morning. Rebuilt our chimney. No rations to-day.

November 23. Last night was the coldest we have had. The report is that 150 died from the effects of the cold. Our money comes in good now, as we have had no rations for the past two days; but to-night we got rice and meal.

November 24. Thanksgiving up North. Farrar and I had beans for breakfast and rice for supper. We had all we could eat to-day, for which we were thankful.

November 25. A trifle warmer to-day. Our red-bearded Barritt is not as good an executive officer as Wirz was for he knew when a prisoner had escaped, but Barritt does not, and in order to find out how many of us there are in here we were run across the creek, and as we came back were counted.

November 26. This is a splendid morning. Great excitement to-day, as the sick in the hospital are being paroled.

Sunday, November 27. Another fine day. The first thousand were ordered outside this morning. The "Reb" surgeons passed through the ranks and picked out those they thought were the sickest and the least able to stand the hardships that they were putting upon us. The rest were sent in here again. It begins to look like as if there was something in the air, in the way of exchange. Nearly a thousand prisoners came in from Millen, Ga.[30] They have had a very sorry time of it. They were sent here to be out of Sherman's way. When we left Andersonville a large number were sent to Millen and also to Blackshear, Ga. The "Rebs" were afraid of Sherman then, and now they are very anxious to keep us "Yanks" out of his reach. A few of Sherman's men, who were captured only a week ago, came in to-night.

November 28. To-day they are picking out the sick from the second thousand, but stopped towards night for some reason or other. This has been a very pleasant day.

November 29. Splendid weather. Another lot of prisoners came in to-day. There were of the first that left Andersonville, and have been sent all over this blasted Confederacy to keep out of Old Sherman's way. "Uncle Billy" is making the "Rebs" hunt their various holes.

November 30. Another fine day for this time of the year. Sweet liberty, how I long for thee; and then the next thing on the list is a fill of meat. I am getting so meat hungry that I could eat a jackass and chase the rider, and then not be satisfied. We are getting mighty small rations now days, only a pint of meal or flour with the bit of salt every other day. No meat or molasses. But we do have plenty of wood to cook what little we have. The boys who were in Belle Island[31] last winter say it is as bad here now as it was there. Farrar and I have only one meal on hand. Our money is used up, but we have $25 due us the seventh of next month, which we look forward to with satisfaction. Adjutant Chatham is in to-day after clerks, so as to be in readiness for the next parole. We drew a half-pint of new beans to-night.

December 1 [1864]. Chilly this morning. We had to cross the creek again to-day, as the "Rebs" have forgotten how many there are in here, I reckon. Red-headed Barritt with a small guard of "Rebs" came in to superintend the count. He tried to jump across a small puddle of water, when his foot slipped and he went in the mud. We hooted and yelled at him, which made him so mad that he drew his revolver and leveled it at the crowd, but the old thing wouldn't work. He snapped it all around, but it was no good. This made us yell the more, when the grabbed a gun from one of the guards and fired it at the crowd. But the ball struck a mud shebang, so no one was hurt. We did not yell any more, not knowing what the red-head would do next. I would like to have him where I could cramp him. He is one of Morgan's raiders, and a bad lot.[32]

December 2. I had a hard time of it last night with a pain in my chest. I have caught cold someway. The pain is easier now. I'll come out right I think. Old Captain Morris[33] has his money, but will not pay us the amount of our due bill, as he says it is not due yet. We could use it just now to good advantage. It will be due the seventh, when we will be right.

December 3. Pleasant. The pain in my side has let up. The second lot who were paroled came back to-day. They say that they only reached Charleston, as General Foster had burned the bridge over the Black river, and Sherman was making it hot for the "Rebs" on all sides.

Sunday, December 4. Chilly. We were run over the creek again to be counted. They find it hard work to take care of us "Yanks." Adjutant Cheatham says, "You'ns Yanks' are the doggenest crew I ever saw." The "Rebs" think a "Yank" can do anything and make anything. One came in and wanted a "Yank" to make him a watch. "All right, being me in a piece of time and I'll make you one." "Yank" says. Anything to please. The guards here have orders not to trade with the "Yanks" who are outside at work; but they do. And the "Yank" has to smuggle his bargains in here the best he can. They used hollow logs at first, but the guards at the big gates put a stop to that. Now they take a log eight or ten inches in diameter and four feet long, split in halves, which they box out pig-trough fashion, then place their stuff inside, put on the upper half, and pin them together with a wooden pin. Strike the bit of their ax in, put all on their shoulder, and march by the "Reb" guard with a very clear conscience--for a

"Yank." In this way meat, beans and rice are brought in. No ordinary fool can fool a "Yank." The Red-headed Barrett has been relieved. Wonder what the devil could do with him if he had him below. Our rations to-day are a pint of rice and a little salt.

December 5 [1864]. They have begun taking out the paroled men this morning. And Captain Morris has gone out with them. This euchers Farrer and me out of $25.[34] It's too bad, as we have reckoned on this to help us out on grub. Day after tomorrow it would have been due. Well, I have played my last card and lost the trick. Old Morris stole the pot. Perhaps something else will turn up. As long as I don't turn my toes up I won't kick. But it's mighty tough for chum and me. When I was captured last April 1 had this check of $150, a good silver watch, a little money, and in here I have borrowed $15. It's all gone now. But what I received from it all has been a great help to me. We used to sing, "We'll never count the bubbles while there is water in the spring." But my spring has neither bubbles nor water in it now, so it's no good. [Say, now, I have that due bill for $25 in the pocket of my diary yet. If any one who reads this wants to buy a prison relic, this due bill is for sale with accrued interest. I don't know where Captain Morris is, as he passed in his checks long years ago.[35] He had our pay checks cashed as soon as he reached Elmira, N.Y.] We drew a pint of meal to-day. It's all we will have to eat for the next twenty-four hours. Starvation!

Florence, S.C., December 6. Pleasant to-day. General John H. Winder is in command of this military post.[36] Don't see how they could spare him from Andersonville. Meal, molasses, with a pinch of salt, and plenty of wood. Nothing new in the way of parole or exchange.

December 7. It rained last night. To-day they are paroling the sick again. Our thousand was in line this afternoon for the purpose of allowing the "Reb" surgeons to select those who in their judgment were sick enough to be exchanged or paroled, whichever it is. It was with a strange feeling that I stood there and kept my eyes on the surgeons as they began at the head of the line, and told one and another of the prisoners, "You can go," and watch the fortunate man step out of the line and make his way to the main gate and pass out. My heart showed more life than usual as the surgeons neared me; but when they passed me by it almost stopped--not quite. Marcus M. Mead of our company is one of the lucky ones.[37] Also Stephen B. Griggs, a bugler of the 8th N. Y. cavalry. He has messed with one of our company, and is a good comrade. Those that went out had to leave their blankets for those of us who are left. I was detailed by the sergeant of our thousand to help carry them to his shebang, when he would distribute them to those who were in the most need. Among the lot I had was one almost new. I told one of our boys to tell Farrar that I wanted to see him in a hurry. In due time he came to me. I told him to go to our shebang and get the worst blanket there, hurry back with it, when I would give him the good one in exchange, and turn in our old one to the sergeant. It worked to a charm. We have a good blanket, and will sleep warmer. The report is that there is to be an armistice of eighteen days at Charleston for the exchange of prisoners. The officer of the day told us to-night we would all be in Lincolndom before long. Drew rice and sweet potatoes. The confederacy has opened its black heart for once. Hope it will keep open.

December 8 [1864]. They finished examining the camp to-day, and the sick have all gone. That is, those the "Rebs" call sick. We are all sick of this kind of life; but not heart sick. Our orderly sergeant, James B. Robinson, was paroled.[38] He is not sick; but the "Rebs" let him go. Good for "Jim." He carries a note to my mother for me. I told her not to worry about me for she would see her baby in good time. I never said a word about how we live in this hell. It would not be good for her to know it, as she is an invalid. How I would like to see her once more.

December 9. It is getting to be very cold here. Ice formed last night. We have to lay close nights to keep warm. They are calling the first thousand again to-day for sick ones. One of the surgeons was drunk. He told one man that if he would whip another he would let him out. So the two went at it and had a fight. Then the surgeon told them both to go out. He passed out two others on a strength of that fight. Whisky did good work in this case. Wish all of the surgeons would get drunk and let all of us out. There are so many reports in circulation that we can't tell what to believe. Sweet potatoes and meal to-day. Hardly enough of either for a taste. It's a hard living.

December 10. Cold and stormy. The men who were paroled yesterday are still outside. Some of them froze to death last night. The report is that 20,000 more are to be paroled. A squad of prisoners came in to-day who flanked out of Salisbury, N.C., prison with a lot of "Galvanized Yanks" and went to Charleston with them, and from there to here. They report that there are 7,000 prisoners in Salisbury.[39] If the weather is cold and dreary the prospects are bright for exchange. I am bound to live in hopes if I die in despair. My father used to tell the story of a boy who in the early days was dancing round the house in the month of March, saying he was going to have some new trousers. His mother asked how he knew he was. He said he knew it because the flax seed was in the entry. The father of the boy had been to town that day and brought home the flax seed for the spring sowing. The boy could see a pair of trousers on the road even if he would have to wait for the flax to be sown, reaped, hatcheled, spun and woven into cloth. So I believe I am to see the end of this thing. My comrades laugh at me when I tell then I am going home. Home is the one thing uppermost in my mind. One of the boys was worrying about home and what his folks were doing, and how they were getting along.

I told him if we could get along down here they could up there, and the best thing they could do was not to worry on their account. Oh, for a good square meal once more! Drew meal and beans, a very fair ration of each.

Sunday, December 11. Heavy thunder storm last night. We had to cross the creek again to-day to be counted. This has been a very good day.

December 12. It was bitter cold last night. This morning is bright and clear. The last lot of the paroled are still outside, and more of them froze to death. Horrible! Oh, but it's hell! I went out this morning and brought in some boughs to help patch up our bed. A lot of those "Galvanized Yanks," who went out some time since, came in again this morning. I reckon they were so "ornery" the "Rebs" could not use them. They report that the exchange is surely going on, and they would not be surprised if we were all out of here in a short time. Bully! Hope it's so. "Joe" Cummings has a chance to work outside and Farrar is on the police force. Good for them! Rice only tonight.

December 13. Quite warm to-day. No news. Meal to-day.

December 14. Pleasant and warm this morning. They have been sorting out the sick again for parole. Bentley and Crosby[40] of our company were sent to the hospital this morning, and to-night they are paroled and off. Hunkey boys.

December 15. Pleasant. We had to cross the creek again to-day to be counted. It's very disagreeable to stand around on the damp ground for two or three hours for this kind of business.

December 16. The report is that 1,500 of our paroled prisoners on their way home were shipwrecked. It's too bad, that after all of their sufferings in these prisons they should be drowned when they were almost home. This Southern confederacy ought to be sunk in the lowest hell, and lower. Sherman has captured Savannah, Ga., with 8,000 prisoners, so it is reported.[41] Meal and beans to-night.

Florence, S. C., December 17, 1864. Pleasant this morning. The "Rebs" have a large number of darkies--slaves, I suppose,--at work on the fortifications outside. They are a happy lot, as they sing all the time while at work, and if they stop singing for a sort time the driver yells out, "Sing-dah." Our shebang is so located that we can see over the depression in the stockade where it crosses the creek. To-day the "darks" were carrying a heavy timber and their song was, "Go slow! Go slow! Go slow!" and they made a deal of music out of it. Their favorite songs are, "I want to go to heaben in de morning, I want to go to heaben in de morning, before de brake ob day." and "An eight-day furlough, an eight-day furlough, for I'se gwine home." They are as full of music as an egg is of meat. I told one of them who was inside doing some work, how little meat we had to eat, and his big eyes bunged way out of his head. They are a great lot of men, very active and supple. Meal and beans. No news.

Sunday, December 18 [1864]. This morning a lot of colored prisoners came in. They were guarded from Charleston by "Galvanized Yanks," While on the road the "Yanks" stole the "darks" blankets and stuff. The joke of it was that when all reached this place, the "Yanks" were disarmed and turned in here with the "darks." One of the "darks," a big fellow, reported how their blankets and stuff had been stolen from them, to Colonel Iverson. He told them to get them again if they could. Then the fun began, as the "Galvanized Yanks" had confederate uniforms on, there were easily spotted; but the "darks" had to fight to recover their stuff. I saw one "dark" strike one of them such a blow that the fellow changed ends in a twinkling. It is needless to say that the "darks" gained the day as well as their goods. Our N. H. Briggs[42] came in with the "Galvanized Yanks." He is quite fat from his venture. His story is that they were at work in the confederate quartermaster's department at Charleston, but do not know why they were sent back here. We are having beautiful weather now. I guess the exchange is played for a time at least. We got meal and beans again.

December 19. Another pleasant day. "Joe" Cummings and myself went in the creek and took a wash; the water was slightly cool. When in the water we saw a small eel, which we caught after a deal of work. It was about eight inches long and as large as my thumb. This has been a good day to take the skirmish line, and the boys have improved it, as the bare backs all over the stockade showed. The lice are very annoying [in] this cold weather.

December 20. To-day begins the ninth month as a prisoner. How much longer no one knows.

December 21. Stormy last night and this morning, but it has cleared up to-night. Very good rations to-day, beans and meal. No salt.

December 22. Pleasant. Meal and potatoes. As we were looking over the stockade to-day we saw a slave whipped. We were near enough to see the poor fellow as he lay across a log with his back bare, and could see the driver lay the blows on. This slave will play out some time.

Sunday, December 25. No news for the past few days. Cloudy this morning. Had beans and mush two days--two mushes to one bean. Farrar and self managed to have our fill such as it was. A very good Christmas. The boys sing one of our old songs to-night:

> Do they miss me at home, do they miss me?
> 'Twould be an assurance most dear,
> To know that this moment our loved ones
> Were saying, we wish he were here.[43]

As they sing the whole song we all seem to mellow a trifle, and our thoughts wander homeward. It's a blessed good thing our home friends are not here. One look would kill them. We are tough and can stand it. The air is full of rumors. One is that Sherman is making for Charleston, and another is that Kilpatrick[44] is making for this place. Hope it's true.

December 26 [1864]. Had a heavy rain last night, and drizzles this morning. It's cold and very disagreeable in here to-day.

December 27. Quite pleasant.

December 28. Cool and cloudy.

December 29. Beans and molasses.

December 30. No news.

December 31. Stormy. This is the last day of the year, month and week. Exchange news is very dull now.

Sunday, January 1, 1865. Clear and cold. It was very cold last night--one of the coldest. Water froze. This cold weather makes us think of home. The "Rebs" gave us to-day the same as they gave us Christmas--a trip across the creek, as they forgot in one week how many of us have died or escaped, so have to count us. If all the reports are true in regards to the position of our forces, we have reason to be hopeful. It helps to keep our sprits up. There is a passage in the Bible which reads like this: "The fool has said in his heart all men are liars." [By the way, I have never been able to find that passage. Have you?] The good folks up home are enjoying a good square meal of roast turkey and all the fixings, while we, poor fellows, have to eat our little pint of meal and molasses to-day. The meal is for a change only.

January 2. Clear this morning. Last night was very cold. As the old lot of wood carriers have run away, a new lot were put on to-day. They had to swear that they would not trade any with outsiders. But they did trade, as one smuggled in a pig that weighed eighty pounds, to-night. He used a log that had been bored out pig-trough fashion. A great deal of talk now of exchange.

January 3 [1865]. Pleasant. Fifteen of the new wood squad ran away to-day. The colonel says he will freeze the camp to pay for it. While I was up at the big gate this afternoon waiting to see what the prospect was for grub, one of the "Yanks" was playing on a three-stringed fiddle, and on the top of the gate post was the little "Reb" lieutenant, who has charge of the wood, who said, "Say, 'Yank,' can you play us 'Bonaparte's grand march!'" "Yank" says, "No; but I can play you 'Sherman's grand march.'" "Go to h--l," was the reply of the "Reb." We all gave a shout for Sherman. It corks the "Rebs" to hear anything about Sherman.

January 4. It rained a bit last night. Pleasant this morning. The boys who made their escape yesterday have had a good time to get off in. Hope they will succeed. The colonel says that if they are caught he will hang them. When a man gives his parole of honor he should keep it. We are to get molasses every other day, they say. Meal, hominy and beans to-night. Just a pinch of each. We get no wood on account of the wood carriers running away.

Florence, S. C., January 5, 1865. It froze very hard last night, and it's quite chilly this morning. I guess the colonel will be as good as his word and freeze the camp to death. Prisoners from Sherman's army came in to-day and report that Major Mulford, our commissioner of exchange has been to Richmond to make arrangements for an exchange. Hope so.[45] Meal and beans to-night.

January 6. Another wet and stormy day that has dawned on us poor creatures, with little or no wood on hand. Oh, but it's awful hard! The suffering here is very severe, more so than in Andersonville, but not so exposed. I traded some meal for salt to-day, as we are getting beans now and they require more. The "Reb" officers were in camp last night getting all the greenbacks they could find on the traders. They must think a great deal of themselves or nothing of their money. One of the officers said to one of our boys, "What is our money good for? We come in here to buy any thing and ask if you will take 'confederate' money; you say yes, ten for one or fifteen for one, just as it happens to sell." What is their money good for? It's as worthless as their rotten confederacy.

January 7. Cold and cloudy. I am on police to-day in Ben. Simon's place, as he is sick. I am to do his duty and take his extra ration, which will help out on the grub line. All prisoners who are on police or do any work, get an extra ration for it. Meal, molasses, salt and wood.

Sunday, January 8. Pleasant but cold. It was very cold on police last night; but I have an eye on that extra ration. They started to run us across the creek to-day, but the order was countermanded, which pleased us very much. "Billy" Bradley had a letter from his brother,[46] our 85th quartermaster, which said that our company B, C, E and F officers had gone North; also that our commissioner had gone to see the rebel Commissioner Ould[47] in regard to an exchange. The Catholic priest who comes in here to look after his own people, tells us that it won't be long before we will all be out of here.

January 9 [1865]. Warm and pleasant. The exchange is talked of stronger than ever. They are making out the description list of the first and second thousand to-day. Meal and molasses; no salt. Adjutant Chatham was in trying to find a "Yank" who could tune pianos. He promises such an one that every time a piano is tuned the tuner shall dine on roast turkey. I don't know if he found his man or not.

January 10. Quite warm. I am on police this afternoon, and was out in a heavy thunder shower. To-night we got meal, potatoes and salt.

January 11. Pleasant to-day. No excitement of any kind. Meal, potatoes and salt.

January 12. Another fine day. the report is that there is to be no exchange during the war. And that our government is to clothe and feed us. Big thing. Meal, potatoes, salt; no wood.

January 13. It was so cold last night that a prisoner froze to death. Too bad. Traded my old blouse for a "Reb" jacket. Meal, beans, salt and wood.

January 14. Warm and pleasant. I played a joke on my lice to-day--a practical joke--as they were getting most too numerous to be cared for properly. They were so thick on my shirt that a pin would prick one wherever it was stuck in. There was little red ones as well as the old linebacks. I took our three-quart pail and crammed my shirt in it, then filled it up with water--there was not much room for water--and hung it over the fire in the fireplace and awaited results. There being so little water in the pail it was not long in coming to a boil, and then I smelled something burning. Sure enough, as the water had boiled out of the pail, my shirt was burning. I took the pail and contents from off the fire. On examination I found one to two holes in my shirt. But the lice were done for. They were thoroughly cooked, and rattled off like grains of wheat. As it was nearly time for our supper I took the pail down to the creek and gave it a cold water rinse and then filled it up with water to cook our mush in. I thought the mush had a meaty flavor to it, but as Farrar did not detect it I kept mum. I think I shall have quiet now for a time, at least, until a new generation arrives, which will not be long. The prisoners are taking the oath to this Confederacy again, and going out. Well, let them go. I won't as long as I am alive.

Sunday, January 15 [1865]. This is beautiful weather for this time of year. We took our trip across the creek this morning to be counted. Exchange news is on the rise. The report is that 20,000 are to be exchanged, and 5,000 from this camp, and the tenth of next month is the time fixed. More men take the oath and go out. Meal and molasses to-night for a change.

January 16. Warm and pleasant. There is a good deal of sickness in here, in the shape of camp fever. And scurvy is taking hold of us in a bad way.

January 17. Pleasant. The report is that Wilmington is taken, but as it has been taken once before, I reckon it is a lie. Trading is down fine now. One chew of tobacco for one spoonful of meal, and five grains of pepper for the same.

January 18. Pleasant. We get our little meal and molasses as usual. I traded my boots for a pair of shoes and a pair of socks, as the fellow said his shoes did not keep his ankles warm. I think I have made a good trade.

January 19. Lowering and looks like a storm. The report is confirmed about the capture of Wilmington, N. C., with 4,000 prisoners. The 2d N. C. and the 2d S. C. regiments laid down their arms and would not go into a fight. Also that Branchville is ours. To-day one of our boys got a part of a beef's head, and in the top of it was clotted blood, which I shook out into my hand--there was a handful of it--and ate it down. It was as sweet a morsel as I ever ate. Then I dug out the eye ball, stuck it on a stick and roasted it over the fire, then ate it. I am so hungry all the time. Meal and molasses to-night.

January 20. Rained last night. Cloudy and cool this morning. Nine months put in as a prisoner. Who would have thought we could have lived nine months in this style on a pint of meal a day. To-night we get a half-pint of meal and the same of beans. Just enough for supper, at least I made it do. I thought I would not make two bites of a cherry, but eat all to-night and let to-morrow take care of itself. The report is that France and England have recognized this Confederacy. (In a horn.)[48] The "Reb" officers went through the working squad to-night and took $1,300 Confederate money from one "Yank," and then put him in the dungeon.

January 21. Cold rain last night, and it's not over yet. This weather is what makes a man think of home and its comforts. Oh, for the crumbs that fall from the table, would be all I ask. I go to bed hungry, and then dream of something good to eat. We are getting plenty of wood now. My ration to-day was a stick of hickory, four feet long and as large as my wrist--the first piece I have seen in here. I took it and, with the help of an old axe and knife, I haggled our a walking stick, as my knees are getting kind o' shaky now days. [By the way, I brought it out of prison with me, and it still serves me as a walking stick.]⁴⁹ We get a little better ration of beans and meal to-day. The report is there is to be a general exchange the first of next month. I traded my knife for meal and beans to-night. All quiet.

Florence, S. C., Sunday, January 22, 1865. Cloudy, with prospects of fair weather. I did not sleep a wink last night as I had a pain in my side. I am feeling better this morning. Room for improvement.

January 24. A fine morning. Had breakfast of boiled corn. It was not very good, as it was old corn, and we could not boil it soft; but it was all we had. The times are getting very hard for us poor miserables.

Sunday, January 29. Another cold night. These nights are hard for us. I have a bad cough to deal with, as well as a touch of the dysentery. We had to cross the creek again to-day. They have reorganized the camp again. No news.

January 30. Very cold last night; but the weather is fine today. The peace question is all the rage outside now.

January 31. Pleasant. News is dull. Meal, beans and molasses.

February 1. Fine weather. Had a hair cut and a clean shave today, by one of our boys. I heard one of the surgeons say that we would all be out of here by the first of April, as the peace commissioners have gone to Washington to see what they can do.⁵⁰ It is warm enough to-day to sit outside and hunt lice. It's very good hunting, as we can always find'em. A little better rations. We can dispose of all we get.

February 2. Warm and pleasant. The latest is, there is to be an exchange immediately, if not sooner.

February 3. Stormy and disagreeable. I am feeling a little better; but I have a fever hanging around me, I am afraid. My feet are beginning to swell. If I could have meat all the time I could get some strength. The report is that Branchville is taken again. Hope so. This is the third or fourth time it has been taken.

February 4. Warm and pleasant. This is too fine weather to be cooped up in this Confederate Bull Pen.

Sunday, Februray 5. Pleasant. The camp is afloat with rumors. One is we are to get a half pound of meat a day. Bully! Another is we are going to

Southwest Georgia. Another, we are to be paroled in four days. And there are 7,000 to be exchanged at Charleston. Also that Grant has had a big battle before Richmond and got whipped--as usual. Eleven of the wood carriers run away to-day. Our James S. Carson[51] is among the number. [He and four others reached the Pedee river, where they found a boat, by which they reached the coast, where they were picked up by one of our men-o'-war. His home is in Mertensia, N.Y. A good man.]

February 6. Colder to-day. The wood squad do not go out to-day. No news.

February 7. Stormy and disagreeable. The report is that General John H. Winder is dead.[52] Good for him! Meal and molasses.

February 8. Pleasant, but cool. The camp is alive with news. There is now communication between here and Charleston, also here and Columbia. there was strong talk of moving us, but it's played out now.

Florence, S. C., February 12, 1865. I have been very sick for a few days back. The men in the wood squad bring me in some wild cherry bark, which I put into a bottle--one that has had Plantation Bitters [in] it--and put cold water on, then drink it. I think it helps my cough, which is very bad now. I raise a great deal [of phlegm]. Nights I cough and raise so much that I have to use my pint cup to spit in. My feet have swelled so that I have to cut my shoes open to the toe in order to get them on. Added to it all, is a bad case of dysentery and a touch of camp fever. I am in a bad way; but I'll come out of it some way, I hope.

February 15. I am still under the weather. The first thousand have left, for where no one knows.

MAP OF WILMINGTON AND NEIGHBORHOOD.

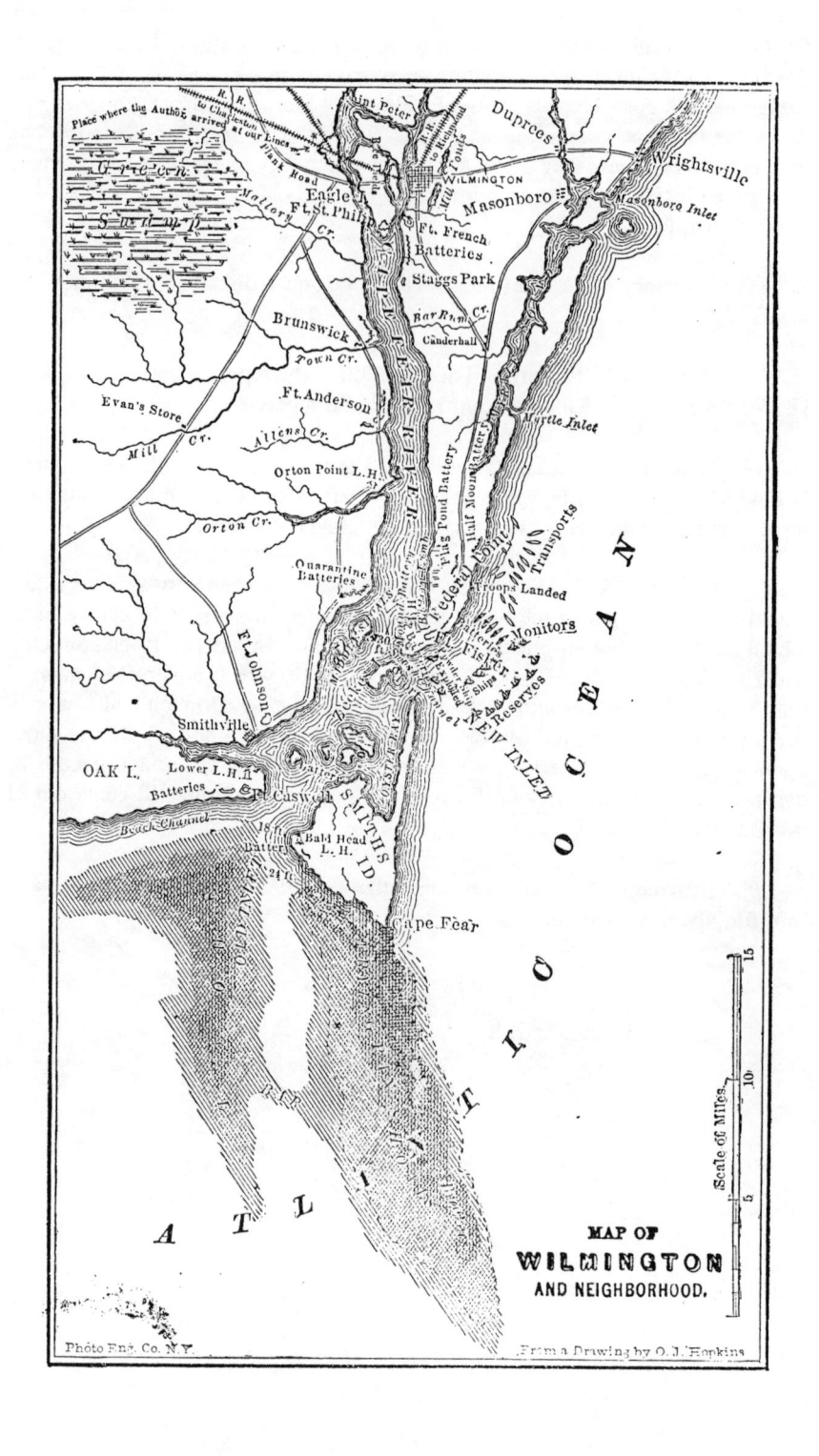

Chapter Eight

"Still Alive . . . Tears Flowed Freely"

(February 20, 1865-June 27, 1865)

"Parole," "release," "exchange." Whatever the term, Private Mosher was to be freed. He knew it as sure as that the knew he was "still alive;" the questions were when and whether there was enough of him left to make it "home."

Contrary to Mosher's gloomy assessment on February 5, Grant had not been "whipped--as usual." Grant's vise grip on the South had tightened. Sherman's "March to the Sea" was wreaking havoc. General John Bell Hood's confrontational strategy before Atlanta had failed. And the siege of Petersburg would shortly drive the Confederate troops out of their capital as well.

The end of the Confederacy--and the war--was near. Indeed, that day Grant's Second and Fifth Corps were headed toward the Boydton Plank Road and Hatcher's Run thereby extending the lines of battle and further straining Lee's sparse defenses. Only two days earlier, aboard the *River Queen* in Hampton Roads President Lincoln, Secretary of State Seward and three Confederate peace commissioners, Alexander Stephens, John A. Campbell, and R.M.T. Hunter had unsuccessfully met to hammer out terms.

Shortly Columbia, South Carolina would be in flames and prideful Charleston would be evacuated. Then on February 22 Wilmington, North Carolina, the last major Southern port would fall to the inexorable march of the Union troops. Inevitably--and shortly--they would reach Florence, South Carolina. The prison there would be emptied no matter the guards or wardens.

Though Mosher would not know it, he could feel his release was imminent. If only his body, wracked by a "graveyard cough," could match his indomitable spirit.

February 20, 1865. I am in bad shape, so bad, that I have not written any for the last few days. I am having all I can do to hold myself together. The prisoners have been leaving every day, the boys tell me--report says for exchange. This morning our thousand was ordered to move, those who are able. Those who are not are to go to the hospital. I am booked for the hospital, as my feet are swollen so I can hardly walk, which, with my cough, dysentery, and a touch of camp fever, renders me a fit subject. It's too bad. I wish I was home. It seems a long way off now. I shake hands with "Joe" Cummings.[1] [He still lives, and is proprietor of a hotel in LaPorte, Ind., and is one of the very best of comrdes. We have met several times since those dark days.] And then my chum, Farrar, and I exchange the addresses of our home people.[2] I give him the address of my mother, and take the address of his grandmother. Mrs. Pirses Farrar, Fort Wayne, Ind., care of W. B. Farrar (his uncle. He is an orphan, and has always lived with his grandparents.) Then we shake hands and say goodbye. [We have never met since.] He moves off for--where? I go to the hospital. Well, we have kept the compact me made last May as we entered Andersonville, close. We have shared and shared alike; to-day is the first break, and no fault of ours. [Emery P. Farrar was a royal as well as a loyal chum. It would do me all sorts of good to see the old boy once more. Perhaps I shall. Perhaps I shan't. Who knows?] This hospital is a rude building, with the bare ground for a floor. The bunks are made by driving stakes into the ground, on which are placed poles, then pine boughs, then ourselves. The rebel flag which floats over us, we call the sanitary sheet, as it was made from sheets sent by our sanitary commission for the benefit of us prisoners, and from which we received no benefit. While the prison was horrible this hospital is hell. It is the essence of the whole camp simmered down and dumped in here, men in all stages of disease. The man on the bunk next to mine is being literally eaten up with lice, unable to help himself and no one to care for him. It is just awful in here. Outside, with my own comrades, I had some care by those who had some regard for me. In here no one has any special regard for me, or any one else for that matter, as there is not much one can do, even with the disposition to do it.

February 24. Still alive. To-day we were ordered to move out; but, as we reached the cars, orders came to send us back, as the road near Wilmington, N. C., is out.[3] We returned a weary and disheartened lot of miserables.

February 28. This time it's a sure go. I have a piece of corn bread in my haversack, two inches by four inches square and two inches thick, and Augustus Gregg of our company, who is in the cook-house, gave me what they call a loaf of wheat bread. It is most as large as one of mother's tea biscuit. I place this in my haversack also, but not the one I carry over my shoulder. We were a wretched lot of men as we straggled across the fields to the cars, which were box cars, and into which we were helped by the guards. It was nearly dark before we were all stowed away, or rather packed in. We leave this prison about

"Off for God's Country"
(McElroy, *Andersonville, A Story of Rebel Military Prisons*)

sundown. Our guards tell us we are to go to Wilmington, N. C. As we have been fooled so many times, we will wait and see.

March 1 [1865]. We had a hard ride last night, as the road is very rough and with nothing but the bottom of a box car to lie on, and in our weak condition it was all we could to do hold together; but we did. Had to. Being a trifle hungry this morning, I would try a bit of the brown bread I drew yesterday; but some one more hungry than I had stolen a march on my haversack, so I have no breakfast. I reckon my dinner will be short, too. I have been this way many times during the past months; I will wait. Our guards did not lie to us this time, for after a long, tedious ride, at three o'clock this afternoon, we reached our Union lines on the opposite side of the river from Wilmington, N. C. My tears flowed freely, couldn't help it. We were helped out of the cars by the men of the 24th Michigan,[4] who, with the 25th Michigan, are doing duty here. It was a grand sight to see our old flag once more, and to be among our own people again, or, as the boys say, in "God's country," which means something to eat and plenty of it. [I wish I could put it in words just how I felt at that time.] As I was sauntering along I saw coming towards me a surgeon, and under each arm he had a bottle, which I quickly recognized was whiskey. Asking for some I received a "thimble" full. In a few minutes I met another surgeon with bottles. I took another "thimble" full. After I had my third "thimble" full of whiskey, the "boys," "our boys," "Yanks"--how slick they looked--came among us with coffee hard tack and meat. I took coffee and hard tack, it was so good--the first I have had in nearly a year. It seems strange, this change--yesterday starvation, to-day among one's own people and under "Old Glory," with everything to eat for the asking, and with the thought that if we are careful in our eating we will have some chance of seeing "home and friends once more." After eating all we want we dispose of ourselves on the ground under the trees for the night. Safe! Glory Hallelujah! This ends the three hundred and fifteenth day of prison life. [I keep March 1 as a sort of saint day.]

March 2. This morning we crossed the river to Wilmington. I was so weak I was placed in an ambulance, and taken with others to the Wright House hospital and placed on the upper floor of the brick barn, as the hospital proper was full. I have plenty of straw to lie on, and am very comfortable as an ex-prisoner of war.

Wilmington, N. C., Sunday, March 3, 1865. Slept well hast night. It seems good this living under a roof, even if we have nothing but straw between us and the floor. Every thing here is in a hubbub, as the city has been in our hands but a short time. The main building being full of sick and wounded, is why us ex-prisoners are in this barn. It's good quarters to what we have been having. Elegant. I had my hair cut short and saturated with alcohol, which had the effect of killing off the numerous winter boarders who came with me from Florence. Report says that Sherman's bummers went through the old pen the day after we left. After a while I found a clean shirt, which, after a bath, I put on in the place of the one I have worn since April 17, 1864. It is quite a shirt vet--old, but lively. I dropped it over the fence into the next yard without regret. I am feeling quite well myself, but my poor body is so badly racked I will have to be very careful how I feed it or it will go back on me yet, which would be bad for both of us. Think of it! We are in "God's country," where every one eats three times a day, and all they want. Hope I will be in a condition to do so soon. Now, a little too much puts me in misery. It's hard work not to overeat, after being starved so long. But we know it's here for us when we can stand it.

March 16. I have been so contented for the last two weeks with my quarters that I have not written any thing in order. My cough is quite bad yet. So is my bowel trouble. Otherwise my condition is improving. My food does not distress me as it did, for which I am thankful. I am still hungry all the while. I was down town the other day for the first time. On my way down I was coughing hard, as I passed two old "Sesech." One said to the other, "There goes a man with a graveyard cough." I replied to him in words more expressive than polite, and passed on. In my walk around I strayed into an alley in the rear of a grocery store, the back door of which was open. I walked in and found several barrels of clams and oysters in the shell. Taking all I could carry in my arms, and a weight from the platform scales, I went and sat on the stone doorstep and cracked and ate my catch with a good relish. Returning the weight to its place, I walked out a fuller man. I did not know enough to step on the sales and weigh myself. [Wish I had.] The weather here is very pleasant. Spring is here, as the peach trees are in blossom. Today I saw a darkey driving in with a mule and cart. I asked him if I might ride. "Yes, sah, git right in, sah." Which I did, and found he had a quantity of oysters which he was peddling along the way. I assisted him to pay for my ride. I was his clerk. He dished up the oysters, and I took the money. When we reached the business part of the city I bid the old fellow good-day, thanking him for my ride. The ride was a real help to me--in this way. I went into a restaurant and had a chicken dinner, with pie. I brought a good lump of butter back with me, to help out on my rations. Uncle Sam does not give us any such article. The surgeons do not give us much attention, as they are to[o] busy with the sick. Occasionally the hospital steward comes around and gives us a sip of milk punch,[5] and sometimes a nip of the raw. It's bracing. We seem to need something of the sort. I have not written to my friends up home, as yet, as to my whereabouts. I am all right. Hope they are. I shall try and go on the first steamer, if I can. But I am in no hurry, as it will be very rough in passing Cape Hatteras. The longer I stay here the better condition I will be in for the journey.

Wilmington, N. C., Sunday, March 19, 1865. Small-pox has broken out in the city. We had a case here in our barn, which was very bad before it was discovered and removed. The weather is very pleasant here to-day. The ladies are out on the street in style. Especially those who have a tinge of black in their complexion, as well as those who have a tinge of white. I have been thinking that some more chicken would be good for me, but as I have no money and cannot get a position as clerk to a colored oyster dealer, I think I shall have to try my old-time army tactics, just to see if I have forgotten them--that is all. I thought of chicken so much this forenoon that this afternoon I started out to see where and how they lived. In my travels I saw four. Three of them took pity on me because of my dilapidated appearance and followed me into camp. Clever chickens! One of the cooks in the hospital kitchen, who saw them following me, told me that if I would turn them over to him I could take my meals with the cooks as long as I stayed here. I turned them over sat down to the table and ate my supper, which was very good. I can eat all I want without its [sic.] distressing me very much.

March 25. I have had good living with the cooks this week. For breakfast this morning we had coffee, fried potatoes, hot biscuit. This forenoon the surgeon came around and said that those of us who thought they would be able to stand the journey north, to get ready as a vessel would sail in the afternoon. After dinner I, with others, made our way down to the wharf. Here we waited for over two hours, when we were told that the steamer would not leave until to-morrow. Tired and disappointed we came back to our old quarters here in the barn. Supper with the cooks.

Sunday, March 26 [1865]. Pleasant this morning. I am feeling tiptop now. A good breakfast and dinner with the cooks. Just as we were through dinner orders came to go down to the wharf, as the steamer was to leave sure. We reached the wharf none too soon, and went on board the hospital steamer, *S. R. Spaulding*, a very large vessel. At 3 p.m. the whistle blew, lines were cast off and we are homeward bound. I am getting interested for the first time since my release, in the idea that I am going home. I was so contented in the old barn that I hardly thought of home, at least not enough to write to my friends. I am located on the main deck, starboard side, upper birth. There are three tiers of berths. I brought a clean shirt on board with me, which I put on throwing my other overboard, as I do not want to carry any old prison friends [lice] north with me. On deck a barrel of onions and boxes of hard tack stand open for us to help ourselves as we wish. We all wish. I ate before supper as well as after, and still hungry. I shall turn into my berth early to-night, as I like to sleep on board ship.

Morehead City, N. C., March 27. We arrived here early this morning. As we have to coal up, shall be here for some time. Just after dinner, Dr. J. M. Palmer,[6] assistant surgeon of our regiment came on board. He looks as good as ever, and seemed pleased to see Ward of Co. E[7] and myself-the only two of our 85th on board. We had a good visit together. As he left he gave each of us a dollar. Our quarters on board are good, as well as our fare--all we can eat at meal time with a continuous lunch of hard tack and onions between. We are still here at dark.

March 28. We left here at daylight this morning. Our meals are served to us in our berths. For breakfast to-day we had coffee, soft bread, meat and potatoes. The potatoes fell short before the waiter reached me. He said he could give me some sauer krout, if I would like it. I said I would. "How much do you want?" I told him a quart. In a few minutes he came back with a large plate heaping full. I put myself outside of it in due time, with the rest of the good things. A charming breakfast! The sea was very smooth as we passed Cape Hatteras. We could see the coast line for a long way. The wind gets a little cooler as we go north.

March 29. Nothing of any moment transpired to-day. Eating and sleeping takes up the most of my time. I am not sea sick in the least, and enjoy the trip.

New York Harbor, March 30. We arrived here some time during the night. About noon we were transferred to another boat and taken up the sound.

Between three and four o'clock we reached Willett's Point on Long Island.[8] Here we landed, and walked about a quarter of a mile to the Great General Hospital. We are most home, at least it seems so to me. After we had rested we were given clean white underclothing only. I threw my old clothes away. Everything is lovely here in our ward. Clean and sweet.

Willett's Point, March 31, 1865. The last time I wrote home was April 17, 1864. I told my people we were going to have some fun. To-day I wrote, telling them we have had our fun, that I am here alive and quite well. A number of ladies from the city were here to-day. Our squad of prisoners was the center of attraction. We are a strange lot of beings, and look like so many ghosts with our white clothing. The ladies gave us apples, oranges, eggs and a piece of cake and cookies. One lady had quite a chat with me, asking about my home and friends. She asked me if I did not want to see my mother. I told her, laughingly, "No, of course not." She told me that I should have another cookie for that answer. Of course we all had a package of tobacco given us. This afternoon I drew a blouse, pair of pants and shoes.

Sunday, April 2. We are having a good time here, eating and sleeping. I am gaining slowly.

April 4. Drew an overcoat, dress coat, pants, two pairs of drawers and two pairs of socks. Now I am well fixed.

April 5. Had a good dinner. My first letter from home, which stated that all were well. It did me good.

April 7. The ladies from the city were up again. They gave each of us old fellows a bag containing tobacco, pipe, sopa, pen, paper, envelopes, comb, needles and thread. Then they passed around some blackberry wine, cakes, apples, oranges, lemons, eggs. One gave me a pair of cloth slippers and promised me a pair of woolen shirts the next time she came up. Some of the younger ladies of the party sang for us. I begin to think I am almost home.

April 9. The same old story, eating and sleeping, and all we want.

April 11. Some ladies from Flushing visited us to-day. They gave the sick some wine and jellies, and us prisoners each a piece of heavy cake. The papers they left us to read were three or four years old. Small favors thankfully received.

April 12. Letter from home. Cousin Augustus Mosher and wife from New York were here to see me--I had written to him, stating that I was here--and asked what I needed. I told them nothing, only I wanted to see some one who was related to me. Wrote home.

April 14 [1865]. This is a lovely day. I am feeling quite well.

April 15. I have a severe pain in my side. I am recommended for a furlough. A letter from the American Express Co. in New York stated that a box was there for me, and either come for it or send an order. I wrote my cousin to forward it to me. This afternoon I looked out of the window and saw a file of soldiers march by with a man in citizen's clothes. I asked what it meant, and was told that he had said that he was glad that Lincoln was shot. The man was a citizen nurse, and they were drumming him out of camp. [This incident is the only recollection I have of the assassination of Abraham Lincoln or anything connected with it.][9]

Sunday, April 16. Stormy. My side is very lame yet. Had eggs for breakfast. I ate three.

April 21. I am feeling miserable. Very. My express box came tonight. It's from home.

April 22. I had a bad night. Pleurisy pain in both sides. The boys say I screamed in agony. The doctor gave me a little relief, so that I am able to be around. As I was opening my box the hospital steward came in with my furlough. I told the boys to take the contents and pay me what they liked, as I was going home. They all told me I would not live to get there. I knew better. Gathered up my traps, walked to the wharf and boarded the steamer for New York. I reached the transportation office at the Battery just after 4 o'clock--too late to get my papers. I asked a policeman to direct me to the railroad station, which he did. On my way up one street a Jew clothier tried to pull me in, as he would sell me something very cheap. I drew up my stick and told him I would knock him down if he did not let me alone. (I could not have knocked one of our old line backs, such as we had in prison, over.)[10] Taking the street car I reached the station just as the 6 o'clock express had started. I managed to pull myself on board and crawl into a seat. I paid my fare to Albany like a little man, and had twenty-four cents left. The car was full of men and tobacco smoke. During the night I was feeling very bad, and had a severe headache. Across the car from me were four Germans having a good time, rather noisy. They made my head worse. I asked them if they would not be more quiet, telling them my condition and the cause of it. They looked me over, and were as quiet as kittens. They were gentlemen. At Albany we came round by the way of Troy Bridge, so I did not have to change cars. This side of Albany the conductor came along and asked me for my ticket. I told him I had none. He then asked for my money. I told him I had none. "Where are you going?" was the next question. I told him I was going home. That settled it. He gave me a good looking over and passed on.

Sunday, April 23 [1865]. Early this morning we reached St. Johnsville. Ten minutes for refreshments. I got off and crawled up the high steps to the dining rooms, and called for a cup of coffee and a piece of custard pie. Twenty-five cents the wait said. I laid down my twenty-four, and said I would not bother for the other. All right! After we left Syracuse a gentleman became interested in me. We had a long talk together. He told me that he came up from New York on the same train I did, and if he had seen me I would not have had to pay my fare. When the conductor passed through our car a few words explained the situation to him, so I was not molested. The gentleman gave me his card, which I placed in the pocket of my diary. [I still keep it there, a pleasant rememberance of him and of his kindness to me.] It reads:

Edward Burt

With
    G. Ahrens & Co.
255 Washington Street,
    Corner of Murray,   New York.

I reached Seneca Falls a little after 9 o'clock this morning. On getting off the cars I asked a young man if he could direct me to Mrs. Mosher's on Troy street. He said yes, as he was going by there on his way home. (His name was John Phillips.) As I reached the house my sister came out on her way to the post office. A shout went up, "Charlie has come! Charlie has come!" This was the point I had had in my mind for over a year, and next to my allegiance to Old glory, all there was of me was my bones with my skin drawn on over them, and an appetite which was simply enormous. Since then I have placed between my skin and bones a small amount of tissue, with room for more. My appetite has modified slightly. I was confined to the house for weeks with pleuro-pneumonia, which was overcome by the skillful treatment of William A. Swaby, M.D., and the good nursing of my sister. My furlough had to be extended another thirty days. Before its expiration I was ordered to report to the hospital the first week in June. I reported to DeCamp General Hospital, David's Island, New York harbor--the hospital at Willett's Point had been discontinued--where I was mustered out of the United States army June 27, as per telegram from the war department, dated May 4, 1865: "To muster out all prisoners of war."

Out of the nine companies of our regiment captured April 20, 1864, at Plymouth, N.C., two hundred and forty-five died in prison. It was no fault of the so-called Southern Confederacy that the rest of us did not die. In conclusion, I would say that I had never read my diary, except to find the dates as to my whereabouts, until I began to copy it. I had not the least idea as to its contents.

I found statements of facts of which I have no recollection, some of which made me almost sick a I read them, and which I did not copy. If the reader has been interested in my story of prison life I am content.

"In treason's prison hold
Their martyr spirits grew
To stature like the saints of old,
While amid agonies untold,
They starved for me and you!
Good friend, for me and you."

-Round Table

THE END.

Mosher shortly after his release from Florence Prison, June 1865 (Wayne Mahood Collection. Reproduction by Ronald Pretzer.)

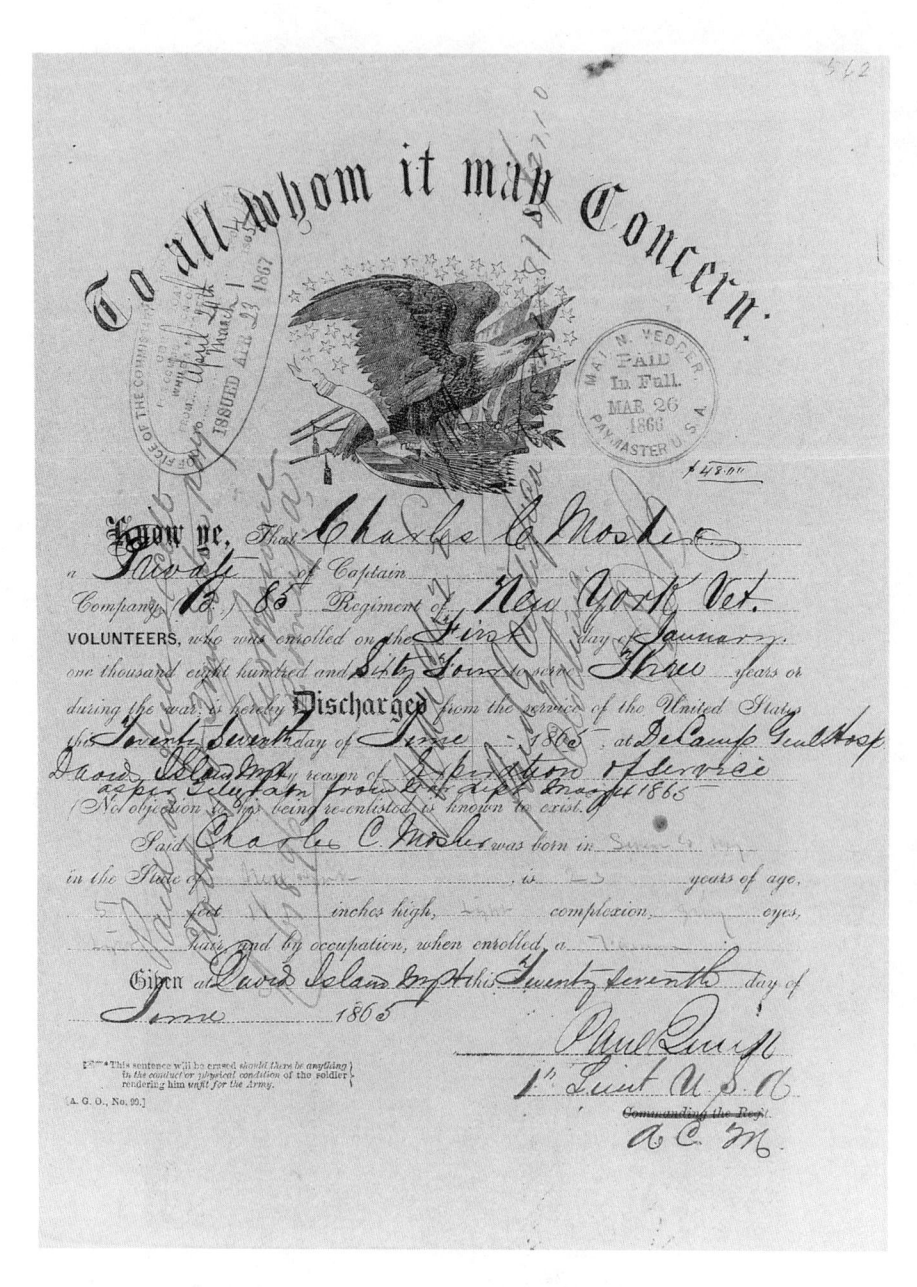

Charles Mosher's Discharge Certificate
(Wayne Mahood Collection)

Post Script
"Completely Overcome By My Emotions"

Charles Condit Mosher, Private, Company B, Eighty-fifth Volunteer Infantry, became civilian Charles Mosher June 27, 1865 upon his regiment's mustering out. He would return "home," not to his late father's Chapinville farm, but to this own Seneca Falls home, purchased with his reenlistment bounty.

Two months later, his pneumonia only a memory, Mosher would resume his machinist's job at the Steam Fire Engine Work in Seneca Falls, New York, and less than four years later he would marry Maria Antoinette Badgley with whom he raised an adopted daughter, Louise. He was getting on with his life, so rudely interrupted, as it had been for millions of Americans in 1861. But, he had been changed forever. His army experience would stay with him forever, and he would relive parts of it. Indeed, he even took on leadership roles so foreign to him while on active duty, becoming successfully chaplain, adjutant and commander of the Seneca Falls G.A.R. And on May 30, 1889, at 4 p.m. as chairman of the Soldiers' Monument Committee, he took his reserved seat for the unveiling of the monument.

Later Mosher was four-term commander of the Swift Post #94 in Geneva, where he had moved in 1899 and where he was employed first at the American Can Company and later the American Optical Company. He played the role of ex-soldier so seriously that his old friend, Ira Deyo of Naples called him a "bit of a windbag," a description that apparently was applied to Deyo himself.

Meantime he also became a family "genealogist," a "frequent contributor" to the *Geneva (New York) Times* on various historical topics, and an elder of the Presbyterian churches in Seneca Falls and Geneva.

Mosher apparently attended at least one reunion of the Eighty-fifth Regiment in Allegany County, getting reacquainted.

His most memorial post-war experience, however, was an emotional return to Andersonville in later April 1916. On the 29th of that month he spent ten hours at the dedication of twenty-one foot high mounument to New York State soldiers who died there. Flooded with memories, he broke down despite his resolve not to.

The lasting memories of that trip and his retirement, April 1, 1916, at age 74 led to more time to reflect on America's Civil War and his experience in it. Once more he reminisced; this time for the benefit of readers of the *Geneva Times*.

Six and a half years later, on December 31, 1920, a few months shy of Mosher's seventy-ninth birthday, that same *Geneva Times* ran a two-column obituary reporting the unexpected death of "one of the well-known older residents of the city" the previous day. His strong body--the one that had held up over almost four years of war, including 315 days of captivity--simply gave out. The pencil of the farm boy cum soldier was finally stilled.

But his memory is preserved in his journal: just as his artifacts (his cane made of wood at Andersonville, a piece of the regimental flag, and his tin cup) are guarded by his niece and her niece.

Charlie Mosher was a hero despite himself.

The New York State Monument at Andersonville

**Union Ex-P.O.W. Badge of Private Charles C. Mosher
(Photograph by Ronald Pretzer)**

Charles Mosher at age 74 in July 1916.
(Wayne Mahood Collection)

Appendix A

Charles C. Mosher's Obituary, Geneva (N.Y.) *Daily Times,* December 31, 1920

C. C. MOSHER DIES SUDDENLY

Victim of Cerebral Hemorrhage Last Evening

Was Well Known Citizen and a Veteran of the Civil War

The death of Charles Condit Mosher, aged 78 years, one of the well known older residents of the city, occurred suddenly last evening at about 3:20 o'clock at his home in the Pulteney Apartments. Mr. Mosher was seated conversing with friends who were calling when suddenly he was observed to collapse and almost before medical assistance could reach him he had died. The bursting of a blood vessel over the brain is believed to have been the direct cause of death. Mr. Mosher had been in his usual health for the past few days, and while for some few months it had been observed by his friends that he had been growing more and more feeble his immediate death was entirely unexpected.

Mr. Mosher was born in the village of Waterloo May 8, 1842, and had spent his entire life in this vicinity, living in Seneca Falls many years before coming to Geneva. For many years he was employed by the Silsby Manufacturing Company at Seneca Falls, and, after coming to Geneva, was employed by the American Can Company, and later, previous to his retirement from active work, by the Standard Optical Company.

When a young man of about twenty years the Civil War broke out and in October 8, 1861, he joined the ranks of the Union Army, serving with the 85th New York Volunteers. His discharge from the army came June 27th, 1865. In the meantime Mr. Mosher had been captured by the Confederates at Plymouth, North Carolia, and was taken to Andersonville Prison at Andersonville, Ga., where he lived through all the sufferings and horrors of that notorious prison pen. He was captured April 20, 1864 and was not released until March 1st of the following year.

His reminiscences of the Civil War and especially of Andersonville were always clearly in his mind, refreshed from time to time by a very accurate diary of happenings which he kept all through his war experience. A few years ago portions of this diary relating to Andersonville were reprinted in *The Times*, the copy being carefully prelared by Mr. Mosher himself, who since then has been a frequent contributor to the columns of *The Times*, generally on some matter of historical interest, but also quite frequently on up-to-date topics was well. Only recently he contributed an article on the history of the old Free Bridge Road, which meant considerable research, and since then he had been engaged collecting material for another article dealing with a community colony that formerly flourished at Shortsville.

Mr. Mosher's mind was always keenly active and his memory relative. Events of half a century or more ago were still quite fresh in his memory and he was a reliable source of information. He also took a most active interest in up-to-date matters and was thoroughly posted on all modern events and had deep-seated convictions which he was always prepared to defend. His mind never failed him and it may be truthfully said that he died possessed of all his mental faculties.

For practically his entire life Mr. Mosher had been connected with the Presbyterian church, being a member of the Seneca Falls church during his residence there and joining the First Presbyterian church in this city in 1899 shortly after coming here to live. At the time of his death he was one of the elders of the church, having served in that capacity over a period of a great many years. While in Seneca Falls he was also an elder in the church there. One of his pastors was the Rev. E. H. Dickinson, now pastor of the church here, who will conduct the funeral services for Mr. Mosher Sunday afternoon.

Mr. Mosher is survived by his wife; a daughter, Mrs. A. M. Seekel of Fargo, North Dakota; a sister, Miss Sarah Mosher of Easthampton, Mass.; a brother, David Mosher, of Buffalo; and by several nieces and nephews.

The funeral will take place from the First Presbyterian church Sunday afternoon at 2:30 o'clock.

The family makes the request that flowers be omitted.

Appendix B

Company B Roster

NAME	RANK	AGE	DATE	DISPOSITION
Clark, Will W.	Captain[1]	34	Aug. 26, 1861	Must. Out w/Co., June 27, 1865
Aldrich, Chauncey S.	1st Lt.[2]	27	"	Disch. Dec. 16, 1864
Brunson, Amos	2nd Lt.	21	"	Died, Disease, May 24, 1862
Martin, Spencer	1st Sgt.[3]	23	"	Disch., Disability, Aug. 17, 1863
Cummings, Joseph L.	Sgt.	25	"	Disch., June 17, 1865
Buell, John	"	27	Sept. 27, 1861	Died, Andersonville, Sept. 8, 1864
McHenry, Charles	"[4]	25	Sept. 28, 1861	Must. Out w/Co., June 27, 1865
Robinson, James B.	"	21	Sept. 17, 1861	Must. Out w/Co., June 27, 1865
Carson, James S.	Corporal	23	Aug. 26, 1861	Disch. June 15, 1865
Crandall, Sheridan	"	19	Oct. 1, 1861	Died, Richmond Prison, May 3, 1862
Dillon, William H.	"	24	"	Disch. Disability, July 27, 1862
Gooding, Zephaniah W.	"	21	Oct. 8, 1861	Disch. Aug. 18, 1865
Humphrey, Charles	"[5]	22	Sept. 14, 1861	Must. Out w/Co., June 27, 1865

Name	Rank	Age	Enlisted	Status
Munson, Charles H.	"	23	Sept. 25, 1861	Disch. Disability, Sept. 2, 1862
Stillman, Ellicott R.	"6	18	Aug. 26, 1861	Disch. June 7, 1865
Warner, Theodore	"	24		Died, Florence Prison, Oct. 8, 1864
Phillips, George A.	Musician	24	Oct. 1, 1861	Died, Andersonville, July 29, 1864
Simmons, Charles J.	"7	21	Sept. 26, 1861	Died, Andersonville, Aug. 21, 1864
Sherman, Daniel	Wagoner	29	Sept. 17, 1861	Disch. June 7, 1865
Ackley, Edmund	Private	27	Sept. 18, 1861	Died, Disease, Aug. 11, 1862
Bancroft, Albert	"	18	Sept. 26, 1861	Died, Andersonville, Aug. 11, 1864
Bennett, Amos	"	22	Sept. 30, 1861	Must. Out w/Co., June 27, 1865
Bentley, Edgar F.	"	21	Sept. 30, 1861	Died, Disease, Jan. 12, 1865
Blake, John E.	"	22	Oct. 7, 1861	Died, Charleston Prison, Sept. 12, 1864
Boothe, John E.	"	24	Sept. 17, 1861	Disch. June 5, 1865
Briggs, Nathan H.	"	21	Aug. 26, 1861	Disch. June 7, 1865
Brogan, James	"	18	Sept. 7, 1861	Died, Andersonville, Nov. 11, 1864
Burlington, Charles H.	"	20	Aug. 26, 1861	Disch. Aug. 10, 1862
Carpenter, Napoleon B.	"	24	Aug. 26, 1861	Died, Andersonville, July 26, 1864

Name		Age	Enlisted	Remarks
Chamberlin, Oliver W.	"	29	Sept. 25, 1861	Disch., Disability, May 27, 1864
Chamberlin, Rensaler G.	"	27	Sept. 25, 1861	Disch., Disability, May 28, 1862
Cone, Linus	"	21	Sept. 25, 1861	Disch., Disability, March 11, 1862
Crane, Henry	"	40	Aug. 26, 1861	Died, parole, Sept. 20, 1864
Crosby, Reuben	"	18	Aug. 26, 1861	Died, parole, Jan. 4, 1865
Culver, Lyman W.	"	22	Sept. 13, 1861	Disch. Mar. 1, 1862
Demeritt, John	"	22	Sept. 21, 1861	Died, Disability, May 14, 1862
Depant, Henry	"	19	Aug. 26, 1861	Paroled, Feb. 26, 1865. No further word.
Deyo, Ira S.	"	18	Sept. 25, 1861	Disch. June 9, 1865, NYC
Dunlap, James	"	31	Aug. 26, 1861	Died, Andersonville, Sept. 18, 1864
Farrar, Emory	"	21	Oct. 1, 1861	Disch. July 3, 1865
Francis, John H.	"	25	Sept. 26, 1861	Disch., Disability, Sept. 29, 1862
Francisco, Francis M.	"	20	Aug. 21, 1861	Died, Andersonville, Nov. 16, 1865
Gilbert, Joseph	"	35	Sept. 13, 1861	Disch., Disability, Jan. 25, 1863
Gipple, Henry	"	29	October 1, 1861	Disch., Disease, May 15, 1862
Glenn, Thomas J.	"	23	Aug. 26, 1861	Must. Out w/Co., June 27, 1865

Graham, William C.	"	18	Oct. 3, 1861	Disch., Disability, Aug. 15, 1862
Green, Stephen L.	"	22	Sept. 13, 1861	Must. Out w/Co., June 27, 1865
Gregg, Augustus	"	18	Sept. 5, 1861	Died on steamer, Mar. 20, 1865
Gooding, Chester A.	"	21	Oct. 8, 1861	Disch., Disability, June 1, 1863
Hadsell, Tobias	"	23	Aug. 26, 1861	Died, Florence, Oct. 6, 1864
Hall, William	"	24	Sept. 10, 1861	Disch., June 7, 1865
Hart, Calvin B.	"	28	Aug. 26, 1861	Disch., Disability, May 18, 1862
Hussey, Alexander	"	18	Aug. 26, 1861	Died, Florence, Nov. 11, 1864
Ingraham, Andrew S.	"	32	Aug. 26, 1861	Disch., Disability, June 7, 1864
Ingraham, Charles B.	"	21	Sept. 13, 1861	Died, Andersonville, Aug. 4, 1864
Insse, Boswell	"	18	Sept. 19, 1861	Disch., Disability, Oct. 2, 1862
Jones, Edward R.	"	20	Sept. 19, 1861	Disch., Disability, Aug. 14, 1864
Kern, Clark L.	"	21	Sept. 1, 1861	Died, Andersonville, Aug. 11, 1864
Kern, Jared	"	22	Sept. 13, 1861	Disch., Disability, Dec. 13, 1862
Knapp, Edwin A.	"	21	Sept. 1, 1861	Must. Out, June 27, 1865 New Bern
Leach, Silas	"	18	Sept. 13, 1861	Died, parole, Feb. 28, 1865

Lewis, Parmer W.	"	24	Aug. 24, 1861	Died, Andersonville, Aug. 9, 1864
Logan, John, Jr.	"	21	Sept. 26, 1861	Died, Florence, Oct. 18, 1864
Macumber, Andrew J.	"	23	Sept. 19, 1861	Died, Disease, Sept. 17, 186?
Marra, John	"	20	Aug. 26, 1861	Must. Out, Sept. 3, 1864, New Bern
Mary, John J.	"	19	Aug. 26, 1861	Disch., Sept. 22, 1865, Annapolis
McNinch, Charles B.	"	21	Sept. 13, 1861	Disch., Disability, June 1, 1863
Meade, Marcus	"	19	Sept. 25, 1861	Must. Out w/Co., June 27, 1865
Morris, Lyman K.	"	25	Sept. 15, 1861	Died, Andersonville, Sept. 20, 1864
Mosher, Charles C.	"	19	Oct. 8, 1861	Must. Out w/Co., June 27, 1865
Parks, Joel E.	"	25	Sept. 17, 1861	Disch., Disability, Feb. 7, 1863
Peck, Benjamin W.	"	19	Aug. 26, 1861	Died, Disease, June 8, 1862, D.C.
Phillips, Alvah	"	18	Oct. 14, 1861	Killed Jan. 21, 1864, Harrellsville, N.C.
Phillips, Richard D.	"	22	Sept. 26, 1861	Died, Andersonville, July 14, 1864
Plimpton, William	"	24	Sept. 26, 1861	Died, Disease, Mar. 28, 1862, D.C.
Popple, Barber G.	"	19	Sept. 13, 1861	Killed, Plymouth, Apr. 20, 1864

Porter, Thomas W.	"	19	Sept. 24, 1861	Died, Charleston Prison, Oct. 3, 1864
Purkey, Daniel	"	24	Aug. 26, 1861	Died, Andersonville, Aug. 31, 1864
Purkey, Jacob, Jr.	"	19	Aug. 26, 1861	Must. Out w/Co., June 27, 1865
Reed, Daniel L.	"	22	Aug. 26, 1861	Died, parole, Feb. 2, 1865, Annapolis
Richardson, William L.	"	19	Sept. 13, 1861	Must. Out, July 18, 1865
Rose, Lansing H.	"	18	Sept. 5, 1861	Must. Out, May 31, 1865, NYC
Ross, Albert C.	"	24	Oct. 4, 1861	Died, parole, Apr. 21, 1865
Spears, James	"	21	Sept. 23, 1861[8]	Died, D.C., May 18, 1862
Steele, Edgar H.	"	19	Sept. 30, 1861[9]	Killed, May 31, 1862, Fair Oaks, Va.
Such, Thomas W.	"	19	Sept. 25, 1861[10]	Died, Charleston, Sept. 22, 1864
Tanner, George B.	"	18	Aug. 16, 1862	Died, Andersonville, June 17, 1864

NOTES

PREFACE

1. Subsequently included in Wayne Mahood, *The Plymouth Pilgrims: A History of the Eighty-Fifth New York Volunteer Infantry* (Hightstown, New Jersey: Longstreet House, 1989).
2. Unless otherwise noted, all quotes are from Mosher's handwritten *Civil War Journal*. Two volumes, no date, no publisher. Permission to edit and annotate given by Mr. & Mrs. William Harvey and the Seneca Falls Historical Society.
3. "The Diary of Asa W. Root, A Northern Soldier, 1861-1862"; #734, D. R. Barker Library, Fredonia, New York.
4. C. Vann Woodward, Ed., *Mary's Chestnut's Civil War* (New Haven: yale University Press, 1981), page xvi.
5. Wayne Mahood, *The Plymouth Pilgrims* (Hightstown, New Jersey: Longstreet House, 1989).

INTRODUCTION

1. "The Congress of the Colony of Massachusetts," May 15, 1775; and Congressional Commission, January 1, 1777. Copies in Mosher's original diary.
2. All quotes are from Mosher's handwritten journal unless identified otherwise.
3. An inconsistency appears in his pension statement signed and filed February 27, 1907, wherein he declared he was five feet eleven inches tall with <u>grey</u> eyes, light hair, light complexion, and a <u>farmer</u>. With age he might well have shrunk a half inch and bred white hair, but how his eye color changed over forty years is less understandable. The change in occupation probably is explained by the fact that he was retired.
4. Captain, later lieutenant colonel, William ("Will") W. Clark from Naples is interesting in a number of respects. Certainly, Mosher's obvious affection for him appears throughout the diary. He also clipped and pasted Clark's obituary. Later, Mosher may have been influenced by his friend, Ira Deyo, to whom Clark was distantly related.

    Even the spelling of Clark's surname is curious, for others in his family, including his parents and eleven siblings, spelled the name Clarke. A widower at 34, Clark became the eldest of four brothers to serve in the Union Army, leaving in the care of his aged mother, twin sons.

Introduction

5. Apparently Mosher thoroughly enjoyed his leadership roles and opportunities to speak to various groups, for the great-grandson of Mosher's good friend, Ira Deyo, recalls family anecdotes and letters about Mosher (and Deyo) suggesting he became a "bit of a windbag" in his later years. (Conversation with Michael Nighan, June 18, 1986.)

6. Named for Brevet Brigadier General Joseph Gardner Swift, a member of West Point's first graduating class and later Chief Engineer, U.S. Army 1812, who died in Geneva, New York, July 23, 1865. *Dictionary of American Biography* (New York: Charles Scribner's Sons, 1936), Vol. XVIII, page 247.

CHAPTER ONE

1. Mosher appended his grandfather's military career in the original.
2. William W. Clark, whose surname was alternately spelled Clarke, was the fourth of twelve children of Lorenzo and Laura Turner Clarke, of Naples, New York. In 1861, a thirty-four year old widower with two children, Clark recruited what was to become Company B and was mustered captain December 12, 1861. He became lieutenant colonel May 1, 1863, mustering out June 27, 1865. Later he was a custom-house officer in New York City for twenty years, dying in Brooklyn City Hospital September 26, 1897.
3. James M. Bull, 37, a Geneva lawyer, was mustered lieutenant colonel, August 15, 1862 and colonel October 25, 1863, in the 126th N.Y. Vols. A more extensive biography is provided by Arabella Willson, *Disaster, Struggle, Triumph: 1000 Boys in Blue* (Albany: The Argus Co., Printers, 1870).
4. Spencer Martin, 23, was mustered first sergeant of Company B, August 30, 1861, was promoted to first lieutenant March 1, 1862 with rank from January 30 and was discharged August 17, 1863.
5. Later; probably after 1894, Mosher added, "George W. Caton was the neighbor and afterward fife major of the 148 N.Y."
6. George Otis Mosher, born March 4, 1833, was married to Anna Mann Mosher and at the time had one daughter, Carrie C., born June 26, 1861. Mosher also had an unmarried sister, Sarah E., a year younger than George and another brother, David Brainerd Mosher, born February 27, 1838.
7. Twenty-seven year old Chauncey Aldrich enrolled at Canandaigua, September 16, 1861, was mustered first lieutenant, Company B, December 2, 1861, and promoted to captain August 21, 1863. Aldrich's escape from a Southern prison with four others was the subject of a monograph by one of the escapees. Captain Daniel A. Langworthy,

Chapter One

Reminiscences of a Prisoner of War and His Escape (Minneapolis: Byron Printing Co., 1915). A photograph of escapee Aldrich appears in Bertram Groene, *Tracing Your Civil War Ancestor,* (Winston-Salem, North Carolina: John F. Blair Publ., 1981), page 85.

8. See drawings which show location and arrangement in Elmira on pages 11 and 20. By contrast, a fellow member of Company B, Corporal Albert H. Bancroft, recalls moving "to South Point from No. 2 barracks" on October 8, 1861. "Diary of Albert H. Bancroft of Co. B, Eighty-Fifth N.Y.S.V." (Albany: Bureau of Military Statistics, Annual Report, 1868), page 675.
9. Private Augustus C. Gregg, from Manchester, north of Canandaigua, a nineteen year old who had been mustered September 9, 1861 into Company E.
10. Captain Reuben V. King, 23, enrolled at Olean, was mustered as captain of Company A, November 25, 1861 and was mustered as major, March 14, 1862.
11. Underage at nineteen, Mosher needed permission from a parent or guardian to enlist and had written home for it.
12. Robert B. Van Valkenburg, brigadier general in the New York State Militia, was commander of the Elmira depot, one of three in the state until it became a federal depot January 1, 1862. Van Valkenburg subsequently became colonel of the 107th N.Y.S. Vols. while serving in the 37th and 38th U.S. Congress.
13. Amos Brunson, 21, from East Bloomfield, enrolled at Canandaigua, August 26, 1861, and was mustered second lieutenant of Company B, December 12, 1861.
14. In modern lingo, "K.P.," or kitchen police, not a very honorific duty, but Mosher could make sport of virtually everything.
15. Bancroft recalled the date as November 5. Albert H. Bancroft, *Diary of Albert H. Bancroft of Co. B, Eighty-Fifth Regiment, N.Y.S.V.* (Albany: Bureau of Military Statistics, Annual Report, 1868), page 575.
16. A regiment was normally composed of ten companies lettered "A" to "K," traditionally omitting "J".
17. Probably written subsequent to this entry, possibly after 1894, and names are corrected by editor to correspond to spellings in *N.Y.S. Adjutant General's Report of 1902.*
18. To whom this refers is uncertain.
19. Phillips was from Bristol, southwest of Canandaigua and enrolled October 14, 1861, at age 18.
20. Parmer W. Lewis, a twenty-four year old from Canadice, southwest of Canandaigua who mustered as a private in Company B August 30, 1861.

Chapter One

21. Named the "Steuben Rangers," for the county from which most of the regiment was drawn, it was mustered November 20-23, 1861, at Elmira and subsequently saw duty in the Peninsula Campaign with the Eighty-Fifth N.Y. and later were part of the Third and Second Army Corps.
22. The dried purgative tuberous root of or powdered drug from a Mexican plant containing resinous glycosides. The purpose, of course, was to assure regular bowel movements among the soldiers.
23. The .57 caliber Enfield rifle, manufactured in Enfield, England, and generally accurate to 700 yards was issued to almost half of all New York regiments. It was considered far superior to the Belgian which had a "fearful" recall, uneven caliber and crooked barrels. Francis A. Lord, *They Fought for the Union* (New York: Bonanza Books, 1960), pages 140, 141.
24. Knapsacks, of flannel and sole leather, carried clothes, photos, cards, pens, paper, ink and virtually anything the soldiers could get in before strapping them to their backs.
25. Haversacks were light bags slung over the shoulder and typically stank of a mixture "of bacon, pork, salt, junk, sugar, coffee, tea, desiccated vegetables, rice and bits of yesterday's dinner," according to Abner R. Small (Harry A. Small, Ed.), *The Road to Richmond* (Berkeley, California: University of California Press, 1939), page 193.
26. William H. Dillon from Canandaigua, who was discharged for disability July 27, 1862.
27. The Sixth Massachusetts Volunteers en route to Washington, riding horse-drawn railroad cars between stations, were obstructed by Southern sympathizers throwing bricks and a few wielding pistols. Militia were called in and dispersed the crowd by firing indiscriminately. Four militiamen and twelve civilians were killed. Mark M. Boatner III, *Civil War Dictionary* (New York: David McKay Co., Inc., 1959), page 42.
28. Charles McHenry, a twenty-six year old from West Bloomfield, who was mustered October 7, 1861 and was promoted to first sergeant of Company B on March 1, 1862 and second lieutenant May 25. He was made captain April 11, 1865.
29. Probably referring to the brigade commanded by Lincoln's friend, the late Major General Edward Dickinson Baker, killed at Balls Bluff (Leesburg, Virginia) October 21, 1861. Baker, born in London in 1811, had an illustrious, if peripatetic, career as a soldier in the Black Hawk and Mexican Wars, a congressman from Illinois, and a senator from Oregon.
30. Brigadier, later Major General, Silas Casey, 54, a West Pointer and veteran of the Mexican War who had resigned from the regular army prior to the Civil War. When the war began he had recruited a

Chapter One

31. Sixty-Seventh N.Y. Vols.
32. Between what is now 14th and 16th Streets just north of W Street and near the Fourteenth Street Bridge and so named because it was the seventy-seventh meridian, reckoned from Greenwich, England. On it was the old Columbia College.
33. Invented by West Pointer '38, Henry Hopkins Sibley, it was "conical, light, easily pitched, erected on a tripod holding a single pole and will comfortably accommodate twelve soldiers with accoutrements ... A fire can be made in the center of this tent and all soldiers sleep with their feet toward the fire. This tent is hardly ever used." Boatner, *Civil War Dictionary*, page 760.
34. Likely, this is a letter saved by his sister, Sarah, and copied later, sometime after 1894.
35. Referring to the type of ammunition: the round being a solid shot used against a concentration of troops and the explosive shell which had a black powder-bursting charge.
36. Lieutenant Colonel Jonathan S. Belknap, 40, who enrolled at Elmira and was commissioned November 7. He was promoted to colonel February 9, 1862 and was discharged March 24, 1863.
37. Referring to muffs, a tubular covering used by women to warm their hands.
38. Captain Will W. Clark.
39. What would be referred to today as a poncho.
40. Sometime after 1894 Mosher added, "Russell Wright: He was color corporal of the 148th Co. K, killed at Fair Oaks, 1864." It is unclear to what Mosher was referring here, though.
41. Assistant Surgeon James D. Lewis, 33, who was mustered November 11, 1861 had a rather checkered army career. He was dismissed September 18, 1862, but the order was revoked later (no date given), then was mustered as surgeon July 1, 1863 after Surgeon William Smith's resignation only to be suspended and remustered September 2, 1863, finally being discharged December 29, 1864.
42. Skirmish drills were simulated battles in which companies played "the enemy" while the others in the regiment played "friendly" troops. Skirmishing would prove especially difficult and deadly in time. See Francis A. Walker, *Second Army Corps* (New York: Charles Scribner's Sons, 1887), pages 450-451.
43. The ambitious expedition proposed by Brigadier General Ambrose P. Burnside whereby he sailed 65 vessels to Pamlico Sound, captured

Chapter One

	Roanoke Island February 8, 1862, then New Bern, North Carolina, March 14, 1862, thereby securing the North Carolina coast.
44.	Corporal Zephaniah W. Gooding, 21, from Bristol, southwest of Canandaigua; John E. Blake, 23, from West Bloomfield mustered as a private, October 16, 1861; Private George A. Phillips, 24, from Bristol, mustered as a musician in Company B, October 7, 1861, but returned to ranks, no date; Charles J. Simmons, a twenty-one year old, mustered as a musician in Company B, October 16, 1861; Henry C. Simmons, 21, enlisted as a private in Company D from Bristol and was transferred to Company B, January 1, 1862; Private Chester A. Gooding from Bristol was mustered at age 21 October 16, 1861; Henry Crane, a forty-year old from Shortsville, just southeast of Canandaigua, who was mustered August 30, 1861, transferred to Company A and transferred back to Company B, September 1, 1864; Albert H. Bancroft, 21, from Bristol, was mustered as a private October 7, 1861, and was discharged for disability, September 29, 1862, at Fort Monroe, Virginia; Richard D. Phillips, 22, from Bristol, was mustered as a private, Company B, October 7, 1861 and was promoted to corporal, September 1, 1862; Seymour A. Smith, an eighteen-year old from Bristol was mustered as a wagoner in Company K, October 7, 1861, but his grade was changed to private and transferred to Company B, January 1, 1862; Private Henry P. Seymour, 19, from East Bloomfield who was mustered in Company D, October 25, 1861, transferred to Company B, January 1, 1862, and died of disease May 15, 1862.
45.	Obviously added subsequent to the actual writing of his diary were the statements, "My name has never left me. If one of Co. B. should meet me now after 30 years, 'How are you, Mose!'" and "This summer - 1896 - Deyo wrote me and began his letter with 'My Dear Mose.'"
46.	Left blank in the original.
47.	Captain Will Clark and Spencer Martin.
48.	A muzzle-loading weapon firing .54, .55, and .58 caliber cartridges, which had been disposed of as obsolete in Austria. Francis Lord, *They Fought for the Union* (New York: Bonanza Books, 1960), page 141.
49.	Not identified in "Muster Rolls," Vol. I, 1864.
50.	Not identified in "Muster Rolls," Vol. I, 1864.
51.	Part of the old Columbian College.
52.	Seventy-seventh meridian from Greenwich, England.
53.	Sixth Pennsylvania Cavalry Regiment.
54.	Twenty-three year old Glenn from Manchester, northeast of Canandaigua, was mustered private in Company B, August 30, 1861, and, despite his rheumatism, survived imprisonment at Andersonville, being mustered out June 27, 1865.

Chapter One

55. Corporal James S. Carson, 23, Company B, from Manchester.
56. Nineteen-year old Private Boswell Insse, Company B, who enrolled from Bristol, September 19, 1861.
57. Major Charles H. Young, who was mustered May 17, 1861, in Albany.
58. Capture of Fort Henry, Tennessee by Commodore Andrew Foote and seven Union gunboats before General U.S. Grant could arrive with his troops, February 6, 1862. See also note 64.
59. Private Edwin A. Knapp from East Bloomfield, just west of Canandaigua.
60. Thirty-five year old Major General George Brinton McClellan, West Pointer, '46, had a meteoric career before leaving the army to serve as Chief Engineer of the Illinois Central Railroad and in 1860 as President of the Ohio & Mississippi Railroad. Shortly after Fort Sumter fell, McClellan was appointed major general of the Ohio volunteers, and July 1861 he replaced the aged and inform Winfield Scott as Commander of the Army of the Potomac.
61. Private James Dunlap, 34, Company B, mustered private August 30, 1861.
62. Gatling gun, a forerunner of the machine gun. See Lord, *They Fought for the Union*, page 160.
63. Kate Dean (also Deane), an Ithaca native, was a lesser known soprano who had performed locally before heading for New York and Washington. Her first appearance in New York City was in 1858. George C. D. Odell, *Annals of the New York Stage* (New York: Columbia University Press, 1931), Vols. VII, IX, X, pages 106, 192, 262.
64. The battle that made Grant famous for his "Unconditional Surrender" message was the second phase of the expedition to free a large portion of Tennessee and abandonment by Confederates of a foothold in Kentucky. The combined Union naval and army operation captured 11,000 Confederates, a serious blow to Southern morale.
65. Jonathan Belknap.
66. In fact, on February 28, 1862, Van Valkenburgh declined Colonel Davis's offer of a commission as colonel of the Eighty-Fifth N.Y.
67. The nipple is the short, perforated piece which fits on the breech of a muzzle-loading gun and on which the percussion cap is fixed and exploded.
68. Brigadier General John J. Peck, 41, West Point, '43, a classmate of U. S. Grant, brevetted captain then major for gallantry in the Mexican War, resigned from the army in 1853 for a business career in Syracuse, New York near his native Manlius. August 9, 1861 he was appointed by Lincoln brigadier general of volunteers to command the Second Division, Fourth Corps. July 7, 1862 he was promoted to Major

Chapter One

69. General. At Suffolk, Virginia the next spring he was badly injured beating off Confederate divisions of John B. Hood and George E. Pickett under James Longstreet, but returned to command in North Carolina. Peck resigned from the army in 1865 and died thirteen years later in Syracuse of illness and war injuries.
69. Northwest corner of the District of Columbia near where the Potomac branches west and north of Georgetown on the Rockville Road.
70. Reuben V. King, Co. A, who was mustered major March 12, 1862.
71. Major General Nathaniel P. Banks, from Waltham, Massachusetts, lawyer, editor, politician and actor, was commanding the Fifth Corps, Army of the Potomac and had been ordered into the Shenandoah Valley to secure the region, including Harpers Ferry and Charlestown, West Virginia.
72. mottle, or courage.
73. The 103rd Pennsylvania Infantry, commanded by German-born, fifty-nine year old Theodore Lehman, was largely from western Pennsylvania and would be brigaded with the 85th N.Y. throughout their active service.
74. Twenty-two year old John Raines, a Geneva lawyer and Canandaigua native who had recruited volunteers primarily from Seneca County to form Company G. Raines resigned in 1863 to resume his law practice, later becoming a prominent New York State politician from Canandaigua.
75. This refers to regimental staff officers. Aldrich had been a member of Mosher's Company B.
76. Twenty-three year old Spencer Martin was mustered First Sergeant, Company B, August 30, 1861, and Amos Brunson, 21, from East Bloomfield, later died of disease at Rose Cottage Hospital near Bottom Bridge, Virginia, May 24, 1862.
77. Typically the Union army was made up of a corps, which consisted of two or more, usually three, divisions. A division had two or more, normally three, brigades, which had two to five regiments.
78. Brigadier General, later brevetted Major General, Innis N. Palmer, graduated from West Point in 1846, with such distinguished classmates as McClellan, Darius Couch, Thomas (Stonewall) Jackson and George E. Pickett. He saw service in the Mexican War, after which he served under Albert S. Johnston and Robert E. Lee. He was now brigade commander of the Fourth Corps under General Erasmus Keyes.
79. The Fourth Corps under Major General Erasmus D. Keyes, West Point '32, who served four years as Commander of the Army Winfield Scott's aide until incurring Scott's wrath. Made colonel May 1861 and brigade commander of Tyler's division at the first Bull Run, Keyes was

Chapter One

appointed Fourth Commander in the Peninsula Campaign. Reactions to Keyes differ, but generally are unfavorable.

80. William W. Corcoran (1798-1888), a prominent Washington merchant, banker and philanthropist, who began the famous Corcoran Gallery before his southern loyalties led him to live abroad during the war. *Dictionary of American Biography* (New York: Charles Scribner's Sons, 1930), Vol. IV, page 440.

81. Cf. another, more bitter description. "[We] bivouacked in the streets and on the sidewalks, without tents, camp or garrison equipage of any kind. The following night we were subjected to a violent snow storm while in this destitute condition. The men walked around or lay on the ground all night without cover or shelter of any kind, and in the morning were covered with six to eight inches of snow. This sorry piece of business was the result of Gen. Casey's orders and cost [one] regiment over seventy men sick and disabled." David A. King, A. Judson Gibbs and Jay Northrup, Comp., *History of the Ninety-Third Regiment, New York Volunteer Infantry, 1861-1865* (Milwaukee, Wisconsin: Swain and Tate, 1895), page 31.

82. Colonel William Dutton, who enrolled at Albany, was mustered colonel January 23, 1862 and died, July 4, 1862, at New York City.

83. Reuben V. King.

84. Private Henry Gipple, 29, from West Bloomfield died only a few months later, May 15, 1862. Crandall is probably Sheridan Crandall, who too was from West Bloomfield, a corporal in Company B, and John Marra, 20, also a private in Company B from West Bloomfield.

85. An hour had passed.

CHAPTER TWO

1. Warren Goss, "Campaigning to No Purpose," in Robert U. Johnson & Clarence C. Buel, *Battles and Leaders of the Civil War*. New York: Century Co., 1884, 1887, 1888, Vol. 2, 153-159.

2. The Union ironclad *Monitor* dueled with the 50-gun Confederate ironclad *Merrimack* off Hampton Roads, Virginia, March 9, 1862.

3. The Union gunboat, *Cumberland*, a sloop-of-war, which March 8, 1862 was, with the *Congress*, fired on and battered by the *Merrimack*. Its commander, William Radford, was sitting on a Board of Inquiry and ran out in time to see the *Cumberland* sinking off Sewells Point near Norfolk with the loss of 121 men killed outright or drowned. There was an ironic footnote to this battle. The *Merrimack* was commanded by Commodore Franklin Buchanan. His *Merrimack* also sank the *Congress* on board which was Buchanan's brother Paymaster McKean

317

Chapter Two

      Buchanan. David D. Porter, *The Naval History of the Civil War* (New York: Sherman Publishing Co., 1887), pages 44 et seg., 122.

4. Man-made shoals created by dumping large stones in the water off Fort Monroe.

5. Sewell's Point was on Chesapeake Bay, downriver from Norfolk and across the bay from Newport News at the mouth of the James River.

6. Confederate Major General John Bankhead Magruder, West Point 1830, served in Texas, Florida and Mexico and was brevetted colonel just prior to the Civil War. In May 1861, he accepted appointment as a colonel and June 1861 as a brigadier general in the Confederate State of America. Called "Prince John" because of his dress and manner, he showed occasional brilliance as an officer, becoming a major general fall 1861.

7. "Learning the ropes," or getting used to military life.

8. Largely from Seneca County, recruited in April 1861 for two years.

9. Pickets, posted in three lines 30-300 yards apart, were spread around camps to prevent surprise and to repel, if possible, an attack. Shifts were two hours on, four off. See Mosher's description in letter to sister Sarah, April 28, 1862.

10. Private Horace Sheppard from Canadice, southwest of Canandaigua, who had enlisted as first sergeant of Company K but who had been returned to the ranks as a private and transferred to Company B, January 1, 1862. Augustus Gregg; James S. Carson; and Private Calvin B. Hart. Nine years older than Mosher, Hart, a Canandaiguan, mustered August 30, 1861, died of disease May 18, 1862 at Chesapeake Hospital in Virginia.

11. See note 29 below.

12. Leeks are an edible garden herb with pungent leaves.

13. Either Private Chester A. Gooding or Corporal Zephaniah Gooding; Corporal Charles Humphrey, a twenty-two year old from Springwater in Livingston County; Corporal William Dillon and Private Edwin A. Knapp. All were members of Company B.

14. Written some time after 1894.

15. To spike the guns was to place a pin in the porthole rendering it inoperable. More precisely "to drive into the vent a jagged and hardened steel spike with a soft point or nail without a head; break it off flush with the other surface, and clinch the point inside by means of a rammer . . .," Boatner, *Civil War Dictionary*, page 782 quoting the *Confederate Ordnance Manual*.

16. John Wynn Davidson, a thirty-seven year old from Fairfax County, Virginia, West Point class of 1845, who saw duty in Kansas and Wisconsin before being promoted captain of the First Dragoons in 1855.

Chapter Two

At the beginning of the war he was near Los Angeles. February 3, 1862 he was appointed brigadier general of volunteers and in this campaign commanded a brigade of W. F. Smith's division of Keyes's Corps. Davidson died June 25, 1881 from an injury falling from a horse near St. Paul, Minnesota.

17. An unsubstantiated rumor.
18. In modern terns, a "fox hole."
19. First U.S. Sharpshooters created by Colonel, later Brigadier General, Hiram Berdan, a prewar New York City mechanical engineer and "top rifle shot," Boatner, *Civil War Dictionary*, page 61.
20. This refers to the "Siege of Yorktown," whereby General McClellan, fooled by Confederate General Magruder's marching of troops to different locations at Yorktown, brought in huge 200 pound Parrott guns, mortars and howitzers to drive the Confederates out. In fact, General Joseph Johnston had already evacuated, moving his thinly dispersed troops ten miles northeast to Williamsburg, closer to Richmond.
21. Minie ball from muskets.
22. Lee's Mill. Water was dammed up for water power in more peaceful times. Here it was released with the result indicated. The Vermont soldiers were probably the 2nd Vt. Infy., according to Frederick Dyer, *A Compendium of the War of the Rebellion*.
23. "Light marching order," given on a moment's notice, meant carrying only absolute necessities, musket, ammunition, haversack and canteen and moving at double time. On the other hand a "heavy marching order" entailed bearing fifty-eight pounds of what the army felt was necessary - the above items plus full cartridge box, belt, crossbelt, knapsack, double wool blanket, shelter half, wool coat, extra shirt, pants and socks.
24. "February 1898. Our flag has been called 'Old Glory' for a number of years back. The first time I ever heard the term, was in a letter I received from my father while we lay in front of Yorktown. That is why I used it in my diary which I have just copied." [C.C.M.]
25. Burke Davis, *The Civil War: Strange and Fascinating Facts* (New York: Fairfax Press, 1982) pages 105, 106, claims these land mines were the invention of fifty-eight year old Confederate Brigadier General Gabriel J. Rains, the elder son of a New Bern, North Carolina cabinet maker, a West Pointer. Mines were distributed all over the terrain, causing extensive bloodshed until Rain's commander, James Longstreet, called a halt to their use. However, Longstreet's order was countermanded by C.S.A. Secretary of War, George Randolph, though mining

Chapter Two

was limited strictly to combatants. See also *O.R.*, Ser. I, Vol. XI, Part III, pp. 509-511.

26. Zephaniah Gooding.
27. Twenty-one year old James Spears from Springwater had been transferred from Company K to Company B January 1, 1862. Spears's name was also spelled Spurs. [He died here after we left. C.C.M.]
28. Founded in 1693, making it second oldest to Harvard, founded in 1636.
29. Hardtack (or hard bread) was a plain flour and water biscuit 3 1/8" x 2 7/8" x 1/2" thick. A normal day's ration was nine to ten hardtack per day. John Billings, "Hardtack and Coffee," in Henry Commager, *The Blue and The Gray* (Columbus, Ohio: Bobbs-Merrill, 1950), page 291. Soldiers normally were less clinical, describing hardtack, often stale, wormy and hard, as "worm castles," "tooth dullers," and "sheetiron crackers." Bell, I. Wiley, *The Life of Billy Yank* (Indianapolis: Bobbs-Merrill, 1952), pp. 237, 238.
30. Probably Henry Simmons and Albert Bancroft.
31. White House was the home of Martha Curtis when she married George Washington. In 1862 it was owned by Robert E. Lee's wife, the daughter of Martha Curtis's son, who also was heir to Arlington. Lee, after resigning his commission in the U.S. Army, had moved his family from Arlington to White House, reportedly a beautiful place on a commodious plantation.
32. "He dies May 24. He was a good man, and officer." [C.C.M.]
33. Traps was a term used rather generically for what might be called "gear" that would be accumulated in their knapsacks until, periodically, items would be shipped home, if not lost, stolen, or dumped en route to new assignments. (Help for this definition was Benedict R. Maryniak, President, Buffalo, New York Civil War Round Table.)
34. Reconnaissance is the process of obtaining information about an enemy position.
35. "He died from it." [C.C.M.]
36. This is called alternately the Battle of Seven Pines or Fair Oaks. In fact, there were two battles fought over two days, the first at Seven Pines, named for the tall pine trees at the intersection of the Williamsburg Stage Road and Nine-Mile Road. The subsequent battle was at Fair Oaks Station less than a mile away. As evident in the next footnote, men in the 85th N.Y. Vols. lumped both battles together as the Battle of Fair Oaks.
37. "The great battle of Fair Oaks was on." [C.C.M.]
38. Will Clark.

Chapter Two

39. Private William F. Young, a thirty-one year old private from Almond, in Allegany County. August 27, 1862 Young was discharged due to wounds suffered.
40. Probably Abram Voad (also spelled Vogde), 25, from West Bloomfield, mustered as a musician in Company D, but returned to ranks and transferred to Company B, January 1, 1862; Private Emory Farrer, a twenty-two year old Company B private from Elmira.
41. Samuel Peter Heintzelman, born in Manheim, Pennsylvania, September 30, 1805, West Point class of 1826, brevetted major for gallantry in the Mexican War and lieutenant colonel in 1851 for services in the Southwest. May 14, 1861 he was commissioned colonel of the 17th Infantry, brigadier general three days later and major general May 5, 1862. He retired in 1869, died in Washington May 1, 1880 and was buried in Buffalo's Forest Lawn Cemetery.
42. Unsubstantiated and incorrect (see June 1 entry).
43. Private Sheridan Crandall from West Bloomfield; Private Elam B. Wetmore from Richmond, outside Honeoye, southwest of Canandaigua; Private John J. Mary, from Canandaigua, and Corporal Charles H. Munson, East Bloomfield; and Private Edgar H. Steele, 20, from East Bloomfield; were captured, as Mosher reported. Private Edgar H. Steele, 20, of East Bloomfield, was called. All were from Company B.
44. Authorized regimental strength was 1000.
45. Wellman was severely wounded, but was not discharged until March 24, 1863.
46. He was not.
47. William G. Graham, a nineteen-year old private in Company B from West Bloomfield. Graham's illness continued, and he was discharged for disability August 15, 1862.
48. Insse's wounds proved serious enough to lead to his discharge for disability, October 2, 1862.
49. Charles H. Van Wyck, 37, joined in Newburgh, July 1861. Most of the 56th were from Newburgh.
50. Approximately seven miles. In fact, from a good observation point Richmond could be seen.
51. Referring to Mosher's having as a joke, given his name as "Moses" to a pedlar, January 10.
52. This reflects a reorganization of Casey's division, necessitated partly by heavy losses suffered at Fair Oaks, whereby Casey's three brigades were consolidated into two and the entire division was renumbered the second division, replacing Smith's division, now Sixth Corps, with Brigadier General John J. Peck, a New York State native and West Pointer, class of 1843, commanding this new second division. This also

Chapter Two

reflects a criticism of the conduct of Casey's division at Fair Oaks. The first is illustrated by the fact that the division lost 1429 men (or one-third of the division's strength). In Palmer's brigade, 34 were reported killed, 27 wounded and 55 captured or missing. Nor was the Eighty Fifth N.Y. Vols., Mosher's regiment, spared, losing a sergeant, two corporals, and seven privates, two from Mosher's Company B. Of the 45 reported wounded, one sergeant and two privates died later. The 81st and 98th N.Y. Vols. suffered similar losses. Thus, the charge that Casey's division had not conducted itself well was greatly resented by its members.

53. Brigadier General Henry W. Wessells, 53, a Connecticut native and West Pointer, class of 1833, fought in the Seminole War of 1837-40 and the Mexican War. In the latter, though wounded, Captain Wessells bravely bore the colors, for which the state of Connecticut presented him a jeweled sword. Later he served on the Pacific Coast and participated against the Sioux in 1855.

   On June 6, 1861, he was promoted major and two months later colonel of the 8th Kansas Infantry. February 15, 1862, Wessells was commissioned a U.S. regular and in March transferred to the Army of the Potomac, where he was assigned command of the Second Brigade, Second Division of the Fourth Corps. On the death of General Keim, Wessells was assigned to command the Second Brigade of Casey's division just before the battle of Seven Pines. Wessells retired January 1, 1871 at age 62 and died in Dover, Delaware January 12, 1889.

54. Palmer was assigned to Brigadier General Charles Devens's brigade of the first division commanded by Brigadier General Darius Couch.

55. Meaning, of course, that a Confederate had picked up his gun left by Adjutant Aldrich when Mosher was too sick to fight.

56. Augustus Gregg who would meet a worse misfortune. Captured at the Battle of Plymouth, he was imprisoned at Andersonville, paroled, and perished March 30, 1865 when the boiler of the steamer *General Lyon*, taking him and others home, exploded causing it to sink, with close to 1000 Union parolees losing their lives.

57. Indeed, that is a fairly accurate description, for the symptoms were malarial and best treated by quinine, which, however, was in short supply. Regimental surgeon William M. Smith diagnosed it as "Billious Remittent Fever" the remedy for which, in the absence of quinine, was the bark of "Corinis Floridae" or, more commonly, whiskey and brandy. William M. Smith, *Report of the Sanitary Conditions, Marches, Battles and Other Data in Relation to the 85th N.Y. Vols.* New Berne, North Carolina, February 22, 1863, page 4. Unpublished. Fevers and diarrhea

Chapter Two

58. Brigadier General Darius Couch, born in Putnam County January 23, 1822, West Pointer '46, brevetted for duty in the Mexican War, but resigned in 1855 to join his wife's family business. At the time of First Manassas he was colonel of the 7th Massachusetts Vols. in Washington and was promoted brigadier general of volunteers August 9, 1861. Ill during the Peninsula Campaign, he tendered his resignation, but was appointed major general July 4, 1862. His regular army career ended after a dispute with General Joseph Hooker at Chancellorsville. Then he commanded a Pennsylvania militia during the Battle of Gettysburg. Couch resigned this commission May 26, 1865. Later he served in a variety of state positions, including Connecticut Quartermaster General and Adjutant General. He died February 12, 1897.

were frequent and fatal. Scurvy became the scourge in late June and early July due to inadequate supply of vegetables.

59. Fitz John Porter, 40, from a distinguished naval family including his uncle, Commodore David Porter and his cousin, David Dixon Porter. Graduated from West Point 1845 eighth in his class and was brevetted captain and major in the Mexican War. From 1849-1855 he served as assistant instructor at West Point, then 1857-60 in Utah after which he was commissioned colonel of the 15th Regular. August 7, 1861, he was appointed brigadier general of volunteers assuming command of the First Division, Third Corps in the Peninsula Campaign. After Malvern Hill Porter was made major general, but he was dismissed after Sharpsburg for being critical of General Pope. He was finally exonerated in 1879 and restored to the rank of colonel in 1886. Porter died in Morristown, New Jersey, May 21, 1901.

60. Henry Faurot, 28, from Canandaigua, who enlisted May 7, 1861 and formed a company in the 18th New York Vols., mustering in Albany.

61. William Henry Ellis, a thirty-one year old was second lieutenant in Faurot's company, having mustered in Albany May 7, 1861 along with his brother a sergeant, four years younger.

62. Private Gardiner King, 23, also in Henry Farout's company of the 18th N. Y. Vols.

63. Probably Private William Hall, 25, from Springwater, Livingston County, who was mustered in Company B, September 28, 1861.

64. As the name implies, this was a rise of land above a flat terrain accessible only by a narrow road with swamp and woods on both sides. On the hill Fitz John Porter commanded divisions by Generals Sykes, Morell and Truman Seymour. To the right were Kearny, Hooker, Sickles, and Couch's Division with Sumner in reserve. Artillery fire proved murderous to the Confederates. The battle of Malvern Hill is part of the Seven Days' battle.

Chapter Two

65. That is, in battle position, prepared to fight.
66. Privates William C. Graham, who enlisted October 3, 1861 and was discharged for disability August 15, 1862, and Edward R. Jones, 21, from Bristol who mustered October 16, 1861, in Company B and was discharged August 14, 1862.
67. So called because it was land that once belonged to President William Henry Harrison.
68. Brigadier General William F. ("Baldy") Smith, West Point '45, commanded the Second Division, Fourth Corps. Smith's contentiousness apparently made him subject to criticism, repeated moves to have him relieved and "special duty" after June 1864. Boatner, *Civil War Dictionary*, pages 775-776.
69. Faurot, see note 60, and Lt. Isaac S. Green, 26, who was mustered as a private in Co. G, 18th N.Y. Vols. and was promoted to 1st. Lt. September 30, 1861.
70. Talked back; made smart remarks.
71. Aide, or assistant.
72. Apparently some time after 1894 Mosher edited his diary for June 13 through July 27, 1862.
73. A field howitzer firing a solid shot shell, weighing 32 pounds, out of a rifled barrel which had a longer striking velocity than the old smooth bores.
74. Mosher's sister.
75. Colonel Jonathan S. Belknap, 41, from Elmira, was discharged June 13, 1863, but Mosher's report seems unproven.
76. A battalion, composed of four or more companies, "was not an organic component of the regiment as is the case today." Benedict R. Maryniak, "Military Organizations," *Newsletter*, Buffalo, New York Civil War Round Table. Undated.
77. An inflammation of the lingual tonsil.
78. Sergeant John Buell, 28, who enlisted September 27, 1861, at East Bloomfield; Edwin Knapp, a 22-year old private from East Bloomfield, was mustered October 7, 1861; Private John Van Wie, 21, from Canandaigua, was transferred from Company D, January 1, 1862; William L. Richardson, 20, from Springwater, was mustered private, September 28, 1861. All were in Company B.
79. Apparently Chapinville.
80. Henry C. Simmon's rheumatism led to his discharge for disability, October 22, 1862 at Philadelphia, Pennsylvania.
81. "A great many lives lost." [C.C.M., after 1894.]
82. Jonathan Belknap.

Chapter Two

83. "At one of our regimental reunions in Allegheny County a few years since [ago] the above report was confirmed. [Inasmuch] as Col. Belknap showed the colors from his house. Our boys saw them February 15, 1898." [C.C.M.]

CHAPTER THREE

1. Alfred M. Waddell, *An Address Before the Associated Army of Northern Virginia* (Richmond: William Ellis Jones, Book and Job Printer, 1888), p. 11, quoted in Wayne Mahood, *The Plymouth Pilgrims* (Hightstown, New Jersey: Longstreet House, 1989), pp. 109-114, wherein there is a fuller treatment of the significance of coastal North Carolina.
2. In fact, it was now only two brigades: Wessells's and Brigadier General Orris S. Ferry's, effective August 23, 1862.
3. Major General John Sedgwick, West Point, 1837, another Connecticut native, who saw service in the Mexican War. With the outbreak of the war, Sedgwick was promoted to brigadier general and was assigned a division in the Second Corps. He was wounded at the battle of Frayser's Farm June 30, 1862 after which he was promoted to major general. He was killed at Spotsylvania May 19, 1864 while serving as Sixth Corps commander.
4. Lucien A. Butts, a thirty-six year old Elmiran, who was mustered second lieutenant, Company K, December 3, 1861 and promoted to first lieutenant, March 11, 1862. Butts served as regimental quarter master from September to January 1, 1863.
5. That is, army rations.
6. Joseph L. Cummings, from Naples, who was mustered as sergeant in Company B, August 30, 1861.
7. "Joe and I have met many times since the war, to talk over old times. We always have to discuss that supper." [C.C.M., some time after 1894.]
8. "It has been a reflection on my army life all these years since. It's now 1898." [C.C.M.] Note, however, no remorse for Black-American.
9. Master's house.
10. Poncho.
11. Pup tent, or shelter half.
12. John J. Peck, recently promoted to major general.
13. Private John Marra.
14. See Fn. 30 for May 11, 1862 entry. Apparently Marra was also involved but was not caught.
15. Fresh baked bread, as opposed to hardtack.
16. Cleaning up around the camp.

Chapter Three

17. The sloop-of-war sunk by the *Merrimack*, March 8, 1862. See March 31 entry.
18. Courage, or spirits.
19. Letter inserted, likely some time after 1894.
20. Early in the war a common practice was to exchange prisoners as both a humane act and to avoid having to guard, feed and shelter them while on the march. However, on April 17, 1864, General Grant realized this humane policy, carefully worked out by Major Generals John A. Dix for the Union and Daniel H. Hill for the Confederates in July 1862, and known as the Dix-Hill Cartel, was a faulty strategy. The Union was exchanging two Confederates for every Federal soldier, a circumstance sure to jeopardize Sherman's march through Georgia. Louis A. Brown, *The Salisbury Prison: A Case Study of Confederate Military Prisons, 1861-1865* (Wendell, North Carolina: Broadfoot's Bookmark, 1980), pp. 3-7; *O.R.*, Ser. II, Vol. IV, pages 220, 230, 265.
21. That is, divide it within the family.
22. Older brother, David Mosher.
23. Private Daniel L. Reed, a twenty-four old in Company B from Gorham, southeast of Canandaigua, who died of wounds February 2, 1865 at Camp Parole, near Annapolis.
24. Again, Mosher's description of foraging, or stealing.
25. A tropical American tree of the bean-caper family sometimes called Guayacan, it has a resin once used to treat rheumatism and is an extremely hard wood. *World Book Encyclopedia.*
26. Sounding the alarm for battle.
27. Given a demerit, resulting in some punishment; in this case, police duty.
28. George M. Munger, a Penn Yan native, was mustered as First Lieutenant, Company G, December 2, 1861, and was discharged April 24, 1863.
29. From Company B, privates Elam B. Wetmore, John J. Mary, a nineteen-year old from Canandaigua, Nathan H. Briggs and Alvah Phillips would suffer far more serious calamities before the war was over.
30. A reference to the fact that the new recruits received bounties intended to encourage enlistments. Volunteers were highly critical of those who enlisted for bounties. Witness the letter from Lafayette Maxson to his brother-in-law, September 27, 1864: " . . . if you are drafted get in as a volunteer, for a sub or drafted man is made as much of as a little child just running alone, for they have a guard for almost every man." Allegany County Historical Society, Courtesy of Craig Braack, Allegany County Historian.

Chapter Three

31. The 148th N.Y. Vols. were organized in Geneva, New York by Colonel William Johnson, mustered September 4, 1862, and left the state September 22, 1862.
32. Twenty-two year old Francis M. Francisco from Canadice, southwest of Canandaigua, and Henry Crane, a forty-two year old private from Shortsville, south of Canandaigua, both of Company B. Both Francisco and Crane were to die from disease later, Crane at New Bern, September 20, 1864, and Francisco at Florence, South Carolina, November 16, 1864.
33. More likely Brigadier General Orris Ferry, a prewar U.S. Congressman from Connecticut. See note 2.
34. Private Lendall Rowley from Candice, New York.
35. Francis Francisco.
36. For officers' horses and horses used to pull wagons.
37. Refers to gubernatorial election between Unionist Party candidate Brigadier James S. Wadsworth and Democrat Horatio Seymour which illustrated the deep division in New York State over Lincoln's conduct of the war and general policies. However, Wadsworth did little campaigning, instead serving until late September as Military Governor of Washington. See Henry G. Pearson, *James S. Wadsworth of Geneseo* (New York, Scribner's Sons, 1913).
38. Joshua B. Howell, a fifty-six year old lawyer from Uniontown, Pennsylvania, had been a brigadier general in the state militia before the war and before forming the 85th Pa. Infantry.
39. Apparently "Kate" was the object of Mosher's attention at the time. Later, probably after 1894, Mosher added "(Mrs. Thomas Rhodes.)"
40. "The above is supposed to be a parody on Joe Bowers," [C.M.M.] was apparently added later.
41. Chaplain Darwin E. Maxson had served from December 2, 1861, to June 23, 1862. Indeed, by early 1864 newly arrived Chaplain A. S. Billingsley of the 101st Pa. Vols. found the soldiers at Plymouth, N.C., including the Eighty-Fifth N.Y., "were almost destitute of preaching." A. S. Billingsley, *From the Flag to the Cross* (Philadelphia: New World Publishing Company, 1872), page 19.
42. A brand of popular cookies.
43. "The above is a copy of one of my home letters," a note which Mosher apparently added after 1894.
44. Joyners Bridge (or Ferry), Virginia, on the Blackwater River about five miles north of Franklin, Virginia, twenty miles west of Suffolk, Virginia, and fifteen miles north of the North Carolina border.
45. Pontoon bridge.
46. Loghouse described on page 78.

Chapter Three

47. Felling trees.
48. At the time, virtually any protected position made by piling up dirt and digging trenches behind the dirt was called a fort.
49. Apparently a reference to the move by the Army of the Potomac now commanded by Major General Ambrose Burnside toward Fredericksburg, though no significant battle had occurred yet.
50. Private Edgar F. Bentley, a twenty-three year old East Bloomfield native who was to die while on parole in Richmond, New York, near Honeoye January 1, 1865.
51. According to General John J. Peck, this expedition, led by Col. Samuel F. Spears of the 11th Pa. Cav., was a "great success" with the capture of the "famous Petersburg Rocket Battery." *O.R.*, Ser. I, Vol. XVIII, page 37.
52. Given on a moment's notice and soldiers were to carry only absolute necessities. See note 23, Chapter Two.
53. Forty-two year old Henry Crane.
54. Referring to General Orders to disrupt railroads in the vicinity of Goldsboro, North Carolina, noted at the beginning of this chapter. *O.R.*, Ser. I, Vol. XVIII, page 41, with General Foster commanding.
55. Hard cider made from fermented apple juice and referring to the 85th Pa. Infantry.
56. Ellicott R. Stillman, who on August 26, 1861 at age eighteen enlisted as corporal in Company B and was promoted to sergeant September 1, 1862 and sergeant major approximately a year later.
57. See note 43, Chapter One.
58. See map page 90.
59. See map page 93.
60. Thirty-nine year old John Gray Foster, a New Hampshire native, classmate of General McClellan, and engineer, who was brevetted twice in the Mexican War where he was severely wounded. Foster was chief engineer at Charleston, S.C. when Fort Sumter was fired on, and in October 1861 was promoted brigadier general of volunteers. Toward the end of the war he was brevetted in the regular service and later became an underwater demolitions expert. He died in 1874 and was buried in Nashua, New Hampshire at age 51.
61. Near Trenton, North Carolina.
62. Ironically, Chapin was fifty-two years old, only two years older than General Wessells, called familiarly "the old man" or "Dad," but who received considerable respect.
63. Colonel Radcliffe's Sixty-First North Carolina.

Chapter Three

64. 3rd Regiment of Artillery (Light), organized and commanded by Colonel James Ledlie in Union Springs, New York, it consolidated Companies B, C and E into Battery B.
65. Forty year old Charles Adam Heckman, who had served in the Mexican War, was commissioned lieutenant colonel of the 9th New Jersey Volunteers October 8, 1861 and was promoted colonel February 10, 1862. Under command of General Burnside, Heckman was wounded at New Bern March 14, 1862 and Youngs Crossroads July 26, 1862, subsequently promoted to brigadier general U.S.V. in November. General Heckman resigned March 25, 1865 and died thirty-one years later.
66. Lt. Col. S. D. Pool's 40th Heavy Artillery was firing grape (layers of shot) and canister (iron or lead balls in a tin case).
67. The reference appears to be Private George W. Crump, who had enlisted at Elmira August 21, 1861. This injury led to his discharge for disability, June 1, 1863.
68. Twenty-five year old Charles O. Gray, who was mustered as lieutenant colonel March 5, 1862 at Plattsburg, New York.
69. "Through all the years of service this saying of Tom's never left him. 'I can't skirmish' was his torment." [C.C.M.]
70. Radcliffe's 61st N.C.
71. See note 52, Chapter Two.
72. Almost directly west of New Bern about twenty-five miles on the North Carolina railroad line.
73. Zephaniah W. Gooding.
74. Horace Z. Sheppard (also spelled Shepherd) from Candace, was mustered is as first sergeant, Company K, August 30, 1861, and returned to ranks then transferred to Company B, January 1, 1862. Ironically, a detail had to bury Sheppard October 18, 1864 when he died of disease as a prisoner of war.
75. Private Albert Bancroft.
76. Lieutenant Charles McHenry.
77. As opposed to Mosher and others who enlisted for three years, the nine month men were the 45th Massachusetts Infy., another source of friction.
78. Sgt. Joseph Kittinger from Niagara County, New York, a member of the 23rd Ind. Light Artillery, reported that at one point a "fierce cannonade was kept up for an hour" with some guns shooting up all their ammunition. Joseph Kittinger, *Diary 1861-1865* (Buffalo: Kittinger & Co., Inc., 1963), page 90.
79. Colonel (later Brigadier General) Clement A. Evans, *Confederate Military History* (New York: Thomas Yoseloff, 1962), page 146

Chapter Three

recalled that Lt. George A. Graham of the 23rd Ind. Light Artillery "dashed gallantly forward, in spite of the efforts of [Col.] Pool's men to reach him with their rifles, set fire to the bridge."

80. He did not, suffering losses of approximately 13,000 men killed, wounded and missing in a series of assaults against the impregnable Confederate position.

81. Probably South Carolinian Brigadier General Nathan G. Evan's command, which included the 7th, 22nd, 23rd and Holcomb legion, all from South Carolina. Joseph Kittinger, *Diary 1861-1865*, page 92, wrote that three Confederate regiments after the Union infantry had left the field crossed the bridge as if to surrender. Then, within 500-600 years "gave a yell and started on a charge . . . The slaughter was terrible. The rebels fell in windrows . . ." from the Federal guns.

82. A reference to their clothing privately procured rather than government issue.

83. Again, Mosher is distinguishing the short term volunteers with those, like himself, who had enlisted for three years.

84. The drumfish, which in salt water can weigh up to 100 pounds, derives its name from the drumming sound made by throat teeth. *The World Book Encyclopedia*, Vol. 5 (1972).

85. Referring to the practice of Roman Catholics who did not eat meat on Fridays, which typically meant no meat was served on Fridays.

86. James B. Robinson, 23, from Springwater in Livingston County, was mustered in as fourth sergeant, Company B, October 7, 1861 and was promoted first sergeant, July 10, 1862.

87. According to Luther S. Dickey, *The History of the Eighty-Fifth Pennsylvania Volunteer Infantry* (New York: J. C. & W. E. Powers), 1915, pp. 207-209, Mosher was correct. That is, Wessells' brigade "was merely loaned to Gen. Foster for ten days, but the exigencies of the service prevented it from returning to the command of Gen. Peck." The key was Wessells, the only "general graduate of West Point" whose general services General Foster had requested from General Dix and whose assignment was subsequently approved by Gen. Halleck, *O.R.*, Vol. XVIII, p. 473, as "temporary."

88. Lewis Cass Hunt, brother of General Henry J. Hunt and son of a regular army man and son-in-law of General Silas Casey, was born at Fort Howard, Green Bay, Wisconsin February 23, 1824 and was orphaned at age five. Raised in Missouri, he graduated from West Point in 1847, and eight years later he was made captain of the 4th Infantry. May 1852 at Seven Pines newly promoted Colonel Hunt was badly wounded. Six months later he was promoted brigadier general of volunteers and brevetted lieutenant colonel, regular army for service at Kinston and

Chapter Three

Goldsboro, North Carolina. In 1865 Hunt was brevetted brigadier general, regular army, dying in service at Fort Union, New Mexico September 6, 1886.

89. "The above letter was written on paper, and enclosed in an envelope, which I picked up on the field at Kinston, N.C.," was added later, probably after 1894.

CHAPTER FOUR

1. This introduction borrows heavily upon Wayne Mahood, *The Plymouth Pilgrims* (Hightstown, New Jersey: Longstreet House, 1989).
2. While a fairly large town of 8000 with five churches (two for colored), several halls, an academy, hotel, court house, post office, printing office, small cotton mill, lumber mill, turpentine distillery, tannery, gas works, and two banks, the town appeared almost deserted, for many residents stayed inside as much as possible to avoid the pillaging that was going on despite being forbidden. Mary L. Thornton, *New Bern, N.C.: 1862-1865* (unpublished, dated December 1959), page 20, a collection of letters from David L. Day, *My Diary of Rambles With the 25th Mass.* The produce markets were special favorites, but the only cheap items were fish: drum, sheepshead, trout, and herring.
3. That is, accepted by the baker.
4. Which explains how Mosher could pass for an officer when burying items in town.
5. That is, one's front side was warmed by the fireplace made of dirt but the back side remained cold.
6. Joshua Blackwood Howell, a New Jersey native, studied law in Philadelphia and practiced in Uniontown, Fayette County, from which the bulk of the regiment he raised in November 1861 came. Howell, brevetted brigadier general, died September 14, 1864, at age fifty-eight near Petersburg, Virginia, from injuries received in a fall from his horse.
7. Brigadier General David Hunter, whose maternal grandfather was signer of the Declaration of Independence, Richard Stockton, was particularly favored by his early relationship with president-elect Lincoln, leading to his appointment as fourth ranking volunteer general in February 1861. A West Point graduate (1822) Hunter's career was mainly political--presiding over the court-martial of Fitz John Porter and acting as presiding judge of the trial of the Lincoln assassination conspirators. He retired in 1866 as colonel of cavalry and lived in Washington, D.C. until his death in February 1886 at age 83.

Chapter Four

8. From Springwater, Theodore Warner was mustered as a corporal in Company B, October 7, 1861, while twenty-one year old Franklin Wilcox from West Bloomfield had transferred from Company K to Company B, January 1, 1862. Both were to die as prisoners of war.
9. A redoubt was a small, often temporary, defensive position set up by piling dirt around pits dug in the ground.
10. Private Marcus M. Meade, a twenty-one year old enlistee from East Bloomfield.
11. "It kept good until long after the war." [C.C.M. some time after 1894.]
12. A common practice at the time to show respect and affection for a superior officer. Joseph Kittinger, *Diary 1861-1865*, page 95, noted that his battery had bought an $80 sword for his captain, a $50 saber sash and belt for one of the lieutenants and a saddle and bridle for another lieutenant in the 23rd Light Artillery at New Bern.
13. Mosher's two brothers.
14. A present of a friend, William Cullistes, just after Mosher enlisted, not army issue. See November 20, 1861 entry.
15. Joseph Kittinger, *Diary 1861-1865*, page 104, recalled that the review included the brigades of brigadier generals Wessells, Francis B. Spinola, and Lewis C. Hunt and Col. T. J. C. Armory (four regiments each) and a scattering of batteries including the 1st R.I., 3rd N.Y. Light Artillery, and 23rd N.Y. Light Artillery. Kittinger also noted with obvious interest that Foster "wore a cocked hat ornamented with plumes [and] an abundance of gold lace and showy tinsel . . . altogether I think out of keeping for a man of his age, rank, and position," page 105. Foster was 39. Kittinger was comparing him with "plain noble old chieftain General Burnside when he reviewed the troops of this place last June." It is surprising that Mosher, who usually took note of such ostentation, failed to comment on the review.
16. Probably Lieutenant Colonel Gerard L. McKenzie.
17. Martin was discharged August 17, 1863, but the reason may have been due to dissatisfaction with promotion of Chauncey Aldrich, see August 22, 1863 entry.
18. That is, reporting to sick call to avoid duty.
19. This is added some time after 1894.
20. The 3rd N.Y. Cav. on March 4 near Swan Quarters, N.C., suffered three enlisted men killed and two mortally wounded, one officer and ten enlisted men wounded, as well as one officer and ten enlisted men wounded, but recovered. Fred. Phisterer, *New York in the Rebellion* (Albany: J. B. Lyon, 1912), Vol. I, page 780.
21. A hanging. An interesting description of Southern civilian prisoner's attitudes toward the Union appears in an unpublished journal written in

Chapter Four

1864 by Henry Morris, a Dutch Reformed minister and agent of the Christian Commission of North Carolina (New Bern, Plymouth and Roanoke Island). Collection of Christopher Densmore, Associate Archivist, State University of New York at Buffalo.

22. This is uncharacteristic bravado on Mosher's part and may be for the benefit of his father, a veteran of the War of 1812 and an antislavery advocate. Of course, this is also from a young man close to the sources of war, but not yet seriously threatened by it.

23. John E. Blake, a twenty-four old private in Company B, was from East Bloomfield.

24. Thirty-five year old James J. Pettigrew, a North Carolina native who had opposed the 85th N.Y. in the Peninsula Campaign, was on February 28, ordered by General Longstreet to cut the New Bern garrison off from the seacoast. Bogged down by swampy roads and broken bridges and dragging 2 rifled guns, four "worthless" 20-pound Parrotts and a Whitworth gun, Pettigrew took the blame for this failed expedition, which cost him two killed, 21 wounded (2 mortally). *O.R.*, Ser. I, Vol. XVIII, 900, 192-195.

25. Hiram Anderson, who at age thirty-four was mustered captain of Company A, 92nd N.Y.V. at Camp Union, Potsdam, on October 30, 1861.

26. To Joseph Kittinger, *Diary 1861-1865*, page 111, it seemed "almost miraculous that the 92nd escaped with so small a loss."

27. Pivoting artillery guns to fire right or left at an enemy.

28. Raking, lengthwise.

29. Parrot guns, rifled and muzzle loading cannon ranging in size from the 3-inch (10-pound shell) to the 10-inch (250-pound shell) with a range of up to 4400 yards, or nearly two and one-half miles, were designed and manufactured by Robert Parker Parrott, West Point, class of 1824, at his West Point Iron and Cannon factory. Considered more accurate with twice the range of smoothbores, the Parrott guns played decisive roles for both sides. Mark Mayo Boatner III, *The Civil War Dictionary* (New York: David McKay, 1959), page 621. But compare Pettigrew's description, *O.R.*, Ser. I, Vol. XVIII, p. 194.

30. See April 2, 1864 entry.

31. Truman A. Merriman, was mustered captain, Company B, 92nd N.Y.V. at Potsdam October 30, 1861, age twenty-two.

32. "In talking with Capt. Allen of Co. F our regiment twenty-five years after the above event. He said that trip across the river was the hottest place we were ever in. I agreed with him." [C.C.M. sometimes after 1894.]

33. Fort Gaston on the Trent River south of New Bern.

Chapter Four

34. General Pettigrew may have had extra incentive, having been born not far from here.
35. A force commanded by Brigadier General Henry Prince, with Generals Spinola's and Jordan's brigades, near Pollocksville, successfully drove off Confederate Beverly H. Robertson's six squadrons of cavalry of 500 men intent on cutting the railroad between Sheppardsville and New Bern.
36. The 85th, 92nd, and 96th New York Volunteers and the 85th, 101st and 103rd Pennsylvania.
37. Companies B, C and D reconnoitered. Albert Bancroft, *Diary of Albert H. Bancroft of Company B* . . . (Albany, NY: NYS Bureau of Military Statistics, 1868), page 584.
38. Of course, referring to Confederate State of America president, Jefferson Davis.
39. "Little Washington," on the Pamlico River, lay almost exactly midway between New Bern and Plymouth to the north. This refers to the beginning of the siege of Washington, part of a revised, three-pronged attack on New Bern ordered by Major General D. H. Hill with Brigadier General James J. Pettigrew's brigade of North Carolinians doing the shelling.
40. Privates Barber G. Popple, a twenty-one year old private from Bristol and Ira S. Deyo, from Honeoye, a distant cousin of Captain Clark.
41. Virginia, capital of the Confederacy; an obviously false rumor.
42. Private Henry Mosure, 34, from Olean was mustered in Company D, October 16, 1862, had, indeed, deserted April 3.
43. Incorrect. See note 17 to February 28, 1864 entry.
44. George A. Snooke, a twenty year old from Manchester, was mustered in as sergeant in Company K, August 30, 1861, but was returned to the ranks and on January 1, 1862 was transferred to Company B. He was discharged for disability, March 16, 1864 at Plymouth, North Carolina. Reuben R. Crosby from West Bloomfield was mustered as a private in Company B August 30, 1861 at age 18.
45. Apparently an affection, for the forty-one year old Spinola was a Long Island born politician who had served variously as a Brooklyn alderman, New York State assemblyman, and delegate to the Democratic National Convention in 1860. He was appointed brigadier general October 2, 1862, later was wounded near Manassas after Gettysburg and was court-martialled for fraud. He resigned June 18, 1865 and later served three terms as a Democratic congressman from New York, dying in office in 1891.
46. See map on page ---- FILL IN.
47. James Belger, Battery F, 1st Rhode Island Light Artillery.

Chapter Four

48. At New Hope School House, Bancroft, *Diary of Albert Bancroft . . .*, page 535.
49. By contrast, Joseph Kittinger was more upset by the church service he attended in New Bern which featured "Secesh Southern Methodism [with] too much wind [and] long prayers." Kittinger, *Diary, 1861-1865*, page 122, April 13 entry.
50. Either Edward, 20, or Jesse C., 27, from Angelica in Allegany County. Neither was listed as a sergeant, nor does the Adjutant General's Report of 1901 note any confinement of either.
51. Lieutenant Morris C. Foote, 92nd New York. For an account of Foote's and Captain Hiram Coates's escape from a Confederate prison, see *American Heritage*, June 1960, pages 66-75. Foote would eventually become a brigadier general in the regular army.
52. This refers to the fact enlisted men were given a $52.00 yearly clothing allowance, against which they were to draw for any needed clothing.
53. Brig. General Spinola's report to General Wessells mentions only the capture of two pickets from the 7th North Carolina Cavalry Battalion commanded by Colonel W. C. Claiborne. *O.R.*, Ser. I, Vol. XVIII, pp. 247-249.
54. Regiments rotated duty as lead outfits, usually allowing those who had been in the lead earlier to march toward the rear of the column.
55. Earthworks built up to protect from artillery shelling.
56. The Whitworth was an "English rifled cannon of various calibers" which fired a solid shot that was effective. Boatner, *Civil War Dictionary*, page 917.
57. Pamlico River.
58. The First Brigade, Fifth Division, Eighteenth Army Corps consisted of the 171st, 158th and 175th Pennsylvania Infantries. *O.R.*, Ser. I, Vol. XVIII, page 254.
59. Either Alva C., 23, or George C. Peckham, 20, from Clarksville in Allegany County, privates in Company I.
60. Paper money.
61. Thomas W. Such (also called Sulch), a twenty-one year old native of Naples, New York was mustered in as sergeant, Company K, but was returned to the ranks and transferred January 1, 1862 to Company B. He died a prisoner of war September 22, 1864.
62. Colonel Theodore Lehmann, a native of Eystrup, Germany, graduated from a military academy as a second lieutenant in 1829, but resigned 1833 to begin the study of drawing and painting, coming to New York City in 1837. Later he served as an engineer and school superintendent before being appointed as lieutenant colonel in the 62nd Pennsylvania Vol. Infantry in 1861. In October 1861 he was transferred to command

Chapter Four

of the 103rd Pennsylvania which lasted until his discharge June 25, 1865. Luther S. Dickey, *History of the 103rd Regiment, 1861-1865* (Chicago: L. S. Dickey, 1910), pages 67, 68.

63. See map on page 90.
64. Like so many villages suffering from war, the business section and finer homes had been burned less than six months earlier when Lieutenant Colonel John C. Lamb had ordered a cavalry charge and "Moore's battery" attack.
65. Probably Seymour Smith from Bristol who originally had been a wagoner, Company K, but was transferred to Company B, January 1, 1862.
66. The Roanoke River which flows into Albemarle Sound.
67. Performing various duties around camp.
68. "Fort Wessells," or 85th Redoubt, see May 25, 1863 entry.
69. That is, hand carried, rather than wheel barrows.
70. Privates Ellicott R. Stillman, George A. Snooke, and Horace A. Sheppard.
71. Dismal Swamp Canal, see map on page 90.
72. That is, in the burned out village of Plymouth.
73. See map on page 94.
74. See top northwest corner of map on page 90.
75. That is, unloaded the *Commodore Perry* to lighten it.
76. Lieutenant Commander Charles W. Flusser.
77. "In copying this from my diary today I found a copy of one of those papers, the *Richmond Whit* dated Monday morning, May 18, 1863. it is in a good state of preservation and reads very funny for these times. It records the death and burial of 'Stonewall' Jackson." [C.C.M., July 18, 1916.]
78. See note 21 on March 7, 1863 entry.
79. Horace Sheppard.
80. Thomas W. Porter, corporal, Company B, from Naples, New York.
81. Southern deserters who terrorized loyal North Carolinians.
82. Both twenty-three year old Gooding from Bristol and McNinch, the same age, from Springwater, were discharged June 1.
83. That is, let them pass through the post manned by Mosher, as picket.
84. Mosher, as most soldiers, was assuring that he would get his share of the eggs, even at the expense of the middleman.
85. A three year war (1853-1856) between Russia and allied armies of England, France, Turkey, and Sardinia over control of the Holy Land in Jerusalem. Russian forces were driven out of Turkish territory into the Crimean Peninsula, jutting out from southern Russia into the Black Sea and the Sea of Azov.

Chapter Four

86. See map on page 169.
87. Meaning, killed or died from disease.
88. Or vedette, cavalry pickets or sentries, in advance of army outposts.
89. Meaning Mosher and others on picket who carry muskets and had the previous night partaken of more than their fill of whiskey.
90. See map on page 169.
91. Vicksburg, on the Mississippi River at the Arkansas-Mississippi border, finally fell to Union troops under General Ulysses Grant after a two and one-half month siege, capturing 27,000 Confederates and opening the Mississippi River to the Gulf of Mexico.
92. A false rumor.
93. A Massachusetts native and West Pointer class of 1837, his leadership and bravery in the Mexican War and in the early part of the Civil War earned him the sobriquet "Fighting Joe Hooker," but his carping about others and possible failure to prosecute the war led to his being relieved after Chancellorsville. He retired in 1868 as major general and died in Garden City, New York October 31, 1879.
94. Brigadier General of Volunteers George Gordon Meade was born in Cadiz, Spain, December 31, 1815 of a wealthy but soon to be impoverished American merchant and graduated from West Point 1835. After serving a year, Meade resigned, but sought and was granted reappointment in 1842. August 1861 Meade was promoted from captain to brigadier general of volunteers at the instance of Pennsylvania governor Curtin and was severely wounded in the Seven Days Battle of the Peninsula Campaign. Meade was given command of the army only days before the battle of Gettysburg after which he was promoted brigadier general in the regular army July 7, 1863 and served as Grant's subordinate to the end of the war. He died nine years later of pneumonia.
95. Large fishing nets with weights at the bottom and floats at the top to catch quantities of fish.
96. Twenty-seven year old Hiram A. Coats from Wellesville near the Pennsylvania border who had been mustered in as first lieutenant, Company H, December 2, 1861 and as captain, Company G, July 1, 1863, replacing Captain John Raines, from Geneva, who had resigned.
97. John C. Welch, 24, mustered in as private, Company F, September 11, 1861; transferred to Company E, September 20, 1861; promoted sergeant, Company D, September 25, 1861; commissary sergeant, Special 28, 1861; second lieutenant, Company A, December 25, 1862; transferred to Company C, September 28, 1863.
98. The battle of Gettysburg, July 1-3, which was the Confederate's farthest north penetration and, to many, proved the turning point of the war.

Chapter Four

99. A cake made in the Southern United States with corn bread and originally baked on a hoe. *Random House Dictionary*, revised edition.
100. Riots in New York City to protest the drafting of men to fill the ranks being depleted by war and illness.
101. See map on page 194.
102. Wessells.
103. Draftees.
104. See note 109 on August 17, 1863 entry, Enrico Fardella.
105. From Companies F, H and K.
106. Private Stephen L. Green, Company B, from Springwater.
107. Private Marcus Meade.
108. Probably Charles J. Simmons.
109. The forty-four year old Fardella enrolled in New York City and was mustered in as colonel, June 26, 1863. He enlisted the 101st New York Volunteers in the Hancock area, east of Binghamton.
110. It remains unclear as to the circumstances, but Martin was discharged August 17, 1863.
111. A Soldiers Memorial is a large poster, often with the capitol of Washington at the top left, a red, white and blue bunting on the top right, photographs of the three company officers, and a listing of the non-commissioned officers and enlisted men. None has been found for Company B yet.
112. Complement.
113. Bancroft, *Diary of Albert H. Bancroft . . .*, reported three vedettes were shot, one mortally, page 594.
114. Private Noel H. Burlingame, 20, from Black Creek, was mustered September 7, 1861.
115. See map on page 90.
116. Stephen T. Andrews from Olean who was mustered in as first sergeant of Company F, September 7, 1861 and promoted to second lieutenant May 2, 1862.
117. Ira Deyo from Honeoye.
118. Elizabeth City, North Carolina. See map on page 90.
119. George A. Snooke.
120. Charles H. Humphrey, 24, from Springwater, who was mustered in as a corporal, Company B, September 28, 1861.
121. Twenty-six year old Parmer W. Lewis from Canadice who was mustered in as a private in Company B, August 31, 1861.
122. Named for the area along the Scuppernong River across Albemarle Sound from Plymouth.
123. Major General William Stark Rosecrans, West Point 1842, had served under McClellan in western Virginia and Grant in Mississippi.

Chapter Four

Rosecrans forced Confederate General Bragg out of Chattanooga, Tennessee earlier in the summer, but in September his army was badly crushed at Chickamauga just prior to this entry and he was relieved of command.

124. A twenty-two year old in Company F, from Black Creek.
125. The 152 foot long *Albemarle*, which had been designed and was being built by nineteen-year old engineer-inventor Lieutenant Gilbert Elliott 17th North Carolina from Elizabeth City, would have a frame of yellow pine timbers 45 feet at the beam and two 200 horsepower engines. The iron plating, of course, made it a ram.
126. James Dunlap, a thirty-six-year-old from Canandaigua.
127. A bit of sarcasm, of course.
128. Unauthorized absence from duty.
129. Samuel B. Adams from Friendship who was mustered in as first sergeant, Company C, September 28, 186, as second lieutenant, July 13, 1862, and as captain, May 3, 1863.
130. Twenty-six year old native of Granger in Allegany County, George W. Pitt was mustered in as sergeant, Company E, October 10, 1861. He was promoted to first sergeant, November 1, 1862, and second lieutenant, January 17, 1863.
131. Alexander Hussey, a nineteen-year old West Bloomfield native who was mustered in as a private in Company B, August 20, 1861.
132. That is, he had been exchanged for Confederate prisoners.
133. Thomas Porter.
134. Italian Enrico Farella.
135. Twenty-six year old private Albert C. Ross from Gorham, southeast of Canandaigua.
136. That is, still had its skills and spirit.
137. Rioting in opposition to the conscription of men into the army.
138. Pounders.
139. However, Bancroft, "Diary of Albert H. Bancroft . . ." page 597, recalled "an election," probably a state election in which Lt. Col. Clark issued mock ballots for the soldiers to choose between candidates for secretary of state. *New York Times*, November 13, 1863.
140. When the surgeon on horseback kept barging through the ranks of tired men. See December 15, 1862 entry.
141. Stephen L. Green.
142. Major General Benjamin F. Butler did, indeed, succeed Foster as commander of the Department of Virginia and North Carolina on November 11, 1863.
143. From furlough.

Chapter Four

144. Twenty-four year old Samuel J. White from Friendship, who had been promoted sergeant, August 28, 1862.
145. And a dance that night. *Diary of Albert A. Bancraft* . . ., page 599.
146. That is, too ill to stand inspection.
147. There is an unconfirmed story that this change was made because of "slack discipline" among soldiers in Company I. Allen W. Howe, in a letter to surgeon William Smith, February 19, 1885, claims he interceded . . . "and got our company [A] send down . . ." Letter in Friendship, New York Historical Society.
148. See note 125, October 5, 1863 entry.
149. Norman J. Maxwell.
150. Twenty-three year old Black Creek native, Francis R. Wilson, was mustered as a sergeant Company D, September 10, 1861, but was returned to the ranks and transferred to Company F, New Years Day 1862.
151. Hertford, North Carolina, across Albemarle Sound from Plymouth. See map page 90.
152. See map after lower right quadrant, north shore of Pamlico Sound on page 90.
153. See map on page 90.
154. Second Lieutenant Spencer S. Peake, from Hinsdale, New York, mustered in Company K, October 10, 1861.
155. See September 13, 1863 entry.
156. About whom the legend of the Scythe Tree developed. See Wayne Mahood, "Until I Return: The Legend of the Scythe Tree," *Civil War Times Illustrated*, Vol. XXV, No. 9 (January 1987), pp. 38-43 and Wayne Mahood, *The Plymouth Pilgrims* (Hightstown, New Jersey: Longstreet House, 1989).
157. See note 111, August 29, 1863 entry.
158. A form of money order.
159. Horse race, a sport among officers, referred to periodically.
160. From Springwater, John E. Boothe, who mustered in as a private in Company B, October 7, 1861.

CHAPTER FIVE

1. See map on page 194.
2. Private John S. VanWie, a twenty-two year old who enlisted at Canandaigua, was mustered in Company D, October 7, 1861, and was transferred to Company B January 1, 1862.
3. "All three of the above died in prison." [C.C.M., added later.]

Chapter Five

4. "I have placed the above [re-enlistment papers] in here for safe keeping. It was given to me in Plymouth, N.C. so that I could get my $300.00 from Ontario County. I got it all right." [C.C.M., added later.]
5. Harrelsville, along the Chowan River, southeast of Gatesville on detail map on page 123.
6. Theodore Warner, who had enlisted from Springwater September 17, 1861 and was mustered in as a corporal in Company B, October 7, 1861.
7. Approximately 63 U.S. gallons measure.
8. That is, North Carolinians who remained loyal to the Union and served in specially designated outfits.
9. Vedettes, advance guards.
10. Phillips, from Bristol, was not yet old enough to vote.
11. That is, reenlisted as veteran volunteers.
12. That is, room for a team of yoked oxen to walk along the canal.
13. Meaning, of course, Brigadier General James J. Pettigrew, fatally shot at Falling Water Virginia July 14, 1863.
14. Dutch Reformed minister Henry Morris, a Christian Commission agent in North Carolina at this time reported similar atrocities committed by Confederates on this expedition, including a cavalryman killing a young Black woman and stomping to death her infant child. *Journal of Henry Morris*, Feb. 3, 1864 (unpublished). Collection of Christopher Densmore.
15. Non commissioned, meaning sergeants or below in rank.
16. Apparently Marion R. Mosher from Wethersfield, New York, who had enlisted in what became the 24th N.Y. Battery September 7, 1861 and served in the Third Detachment. F. M. Crocker, *Boys in Blue* (unpublished, 1938), Genesee Valley Collection, Milne Library, SUNY-Geneseo.
17. Samuel Tolles.
18. Windsor, just northeast of Plymouth on the Cashie River. See detailed map on page 123.
19. Refer to the introduction to this chapter and Lee's plans to recapture New Bern.
20. Harrelsville.
21. "I have never seen that pipe since. I have seen the Lt. Col. Clarke many times since then, he still kept that pipe, much to my regret." [C.C.M.-added later.]
22. This refers to recurring reports of a force of Confederates under Brigadier General Robert Hoke and the construction of the ironclad, *Albemarle*, being built upriver. Christian Commissioner Morris reported being awakened at 3 a.m. February 3 by the ringing of alarm bells and

Chapter Five

the sounds of marching troops. But, in fact, it was a salute to the successful defense of New Bern. *Journal of Henry Morris.* Collection of Christopher Densmore.

23. Twenty-seven year old Sylvanus Fay from Olean, who was mustered in as Company F first lieutenant, December 2, 1861; and George W. Buckingham, who enlisted in Brooklyn, was mustered in as a private in Company I, April 1, 1862 and was promoted to sergeant just over a month later.
24. Ellicott R. Stillman, from Canadice, who had been mustered in as a corporal in Company B, August 30, 1861 and at age 20 was made sergeant major September 16, 1863.
25. "The above is the pass I had." [C.C.M. - written later.]
26. Alanson L. Fairbanks, who was mustered in as a sergeant, Company A, at Olean, August 30, 1861.
27. "His son Fred Bucklin is a member of the Sons of Veterans, Geneva, N.Y. this September 2, 1916." [C.C.M.]
28. "The same troupe and same play, was in Fords theater, Washington, D.C., April 14, 1865 when Abraham Lincoln was shot." [C.C.M. - 1916]
29. While Mosher was gone, rumors of a Confederate attack were reinforced by Lt. Charles McHenry's reading of the Articles of War.
30. Second Lieutenant Benjamin F. Jones, who enlisted at Sharon, Pennsylvania, September 7, 1861. He was promoted sergeant in Company D January 1, 1862 and was mustered lieutenant June 6, 1863.
31. A black woman who occasionally prepared and delivered baked goods to the soldiers.
32. While referring to recurring rumors of the ironclad *Albemarle* being built upriver on the Chowan, this specific reference is unclear.
33. Dover's powder, named after English doctor, Thomas Dover, was a compound of ipecac, opium and lactose and was used as a pain killer and inducement to profuse perspiration.
34. Augustus G. Gregg.
35. Thirty-one year old Walter C. Crandall, who was mustered in at Elmira as a first lieutenant, Company C, December 7, 1861, then as captain almost exactly a year later and as major, July 1, 1863.
36. Alonzo G. Cartwright, from Ward in Allegany County, who at age 22 had been mustered as first lieutenant, Company I, December 2, 1861 and was mustered as Captain, November 10, 1863.
37. Bancroft noted only thirty-seven recruits. *Diary of Albert H. Bancroft . . .,* page 610.
38. Apparently Lt. Robert J. H. Russell of the 12th N.Y. Cavalry.
39. See map on page 194.

Chapter Five

40. Leonard H. Marvin, from Friendship, was mustered in as private, Company C, September 28,. 1861, was promoted sergeant-major, April 9, 1862 and was discharged October 5, 1863, for promotion to second lieutenant of the Thirty-Seventh U.S. Colored Troops. *Annual Report of the Adjutant General of the State of New York* (Albany: J. B. Lyon, State Printer, 1902), page 1057. When he was promoted captain is uncertain. See also note 8, Chapter Six for information about Bascombe.

41. Confederate Brigadier General Robert F. Hoke, a twenty-seven year old native of Linconton, North Carolina, employed approximately 12,000 troops in a flanking movement. Moving Major General Matt Ransom, another native North Carolinian and later U.S. Senator from North Carolina, with fourteen artillery pieces and four regiments around the Union left to approach Fort Comfort on the river side of the Columbia Road, Hoke directed the main body toward Fort Wessells (the 85th Redoubt) lying between Jamesville Road on the north, Washington Road on the east and Welch's Creek on the west. Simultaneously, the ironclad *Albemarle* was to ply its way down the Roanoke River past Fort Gray and neutralize the Union gunboats, *Miami* and *Southfield*, thereby trapping Wessells's Union troops on all sides. The key was the ability of Confederate Commander James W. Cooke to free the *Albemarle* from the trap set by Union Captain Charles W. Flusser. (See March 27 entry).

42. Compher and Conaby, named for Conaby Creek.

43. There are numerous accounts of the ram *Albemarle*. One is James Dinkins, "The Confederate Ram *Albemarle*," in R. A. Brock (ed.), *Southern Historical Society Papers* (Richmond, Virginia, 1902), pages 205-214.

44. Sylvanus A. Fay, from Olean.

45. A woody marsh along Welch's Creek.

46. See map on page 194 (a road running parallel to the Roanoke River).

47. Killing Captain Nelson Chapin and Sergeant James L. Sheldon, who had enrolled as a private at Cuba, New York, September 17, 1861. The Adjutant General's report lists Chapin and Sheldon as dying April 20. See Appendix.

48. Cascabel - a projection behind the base ring or breech of a muzzle-loading cannon.

49. For more details of the killing of Commander Flusser and of the ram *Albemarle's* operations, see Wayne Mahood, *The Plymouth Pilgrims*, pages 177-180.

50. Courage.

51. Abatis, a barricade of felled trees.

Chapter Five

52. Privates Barber G. Popple, 22, from Springwater, and twenty-one year old Smith from Bristol.
53. Often simply piling dirt to afford some protection. Similar action was being taken by the 16th Connecticut Vols. who early afternoon of the 19th had been furnished entrenching tools to build "bombproofs" as their only hope to escape being killed or captured. Robert Kellogg, *Life in Rebel Prisons* (Freeport, New York: Books for Libraries Press, 1971).
54. Annie Laurie?
55. Bancroft reported the time to be "at 4:30 a.m.," *Diary of Albert H. Bancroft* . . ., page 610.
56. Twenty-two year old Jacob Purkey, Jr., from Gorham, who had mustered as a private, August 30, 1861, was captured and later paroled. He subsequently rejoined his company, B, May 8, 1865 and was mustered out, June 27, 1865 at New Bern, North Carolina.
57. "I still have it to this 10th day of Sept. 1916. I carried it through the southern prisons in the pocket of my diary for nearly a year. I am very proud of that bit of 'Old Glory'." [C.C.M.]
58. "It was a four inch Colts and was given to me in 1861 by my Sunday School teacher Mr. William Calister of the Methodist Church in Chapinville, N.Y. (now Chapin). I wonder if it is in that well yet." [C.C.M., 1916]
59. The end was inevitable, for four North Carolina regiments, including the 24th and 56th, had charged down Columbia Road (now Second Street) and marched through the 101st Pa. and into the 16th Connecticut, "pouring terrible fire into [the latter's] rear." Robert Kellogg, *Life and Death in Rebel Prisons*, page 32. For an account of the Confederate movement, John W. Graham, "The Capture of Plymouth," in Walter Clark, (ed.), *North Carolina Troops, 1861-1865* (Wendell, N.C.: Avers Press, 1962, 175-195.).
60. This circumstance and the fact they were captured at Plymouth led them to be called "The Plymouth Pilgrims," made popular by MacKinlay Kantor's *Andersonville* (Cleveland: World Publishing Co., 1955).
61. In 1885 I wrote to the General, reciting the facts in this case and that I still wished his "photo." Then I asked him this question, "Was there any formal demand for the surrender of Plymouth?" He replied yes. Col. Dearing a confederate field officer came in under a flag of truce, and demanded surrender of the town, or there would be no quarter shown. "His request was not granted, and you know the results. It is not a pleasant thing to think about." He sent his "photo." I sent it with the letter to comrade Ira N. Deyo of our Company B. [C.C.M.]

Chapter Five

62. "My prison experience is bound in this Volume, which will tell of our getting ready for our trip up country." [C.C.M.]
63. *O.R.*, I, Vol. XXXIII, page 295.
64. Newly promoted Major General Robert F. Hoke and Commander James Cooke.
65. *O.R.*, Ser I, Vol. XXXIII, page 305.

CHAPTER SIX

1. John McElroy, *Andersonville, A Story of Rebel Military Prisons* (Toledo: D. R. Locke, 1879), p. 168.
2. Bristol board, or cardboard with a smooth surface suitable for writing or printing.
3. Thirty-Seventh U.S. Colored Troops. See April 17, 1864 entry.
4. In fact, Hoke was promoted major general, effective the date of the surrender, by Jefferson Davis who praised Hoke's "brilliant success." *O.R.*, Ser. I, Vol. LI, page 874.
5. "This is the ram that Lieut. Cushing, U.S. Navy, destroyed in the October following." [C.C.M.]
6. Privates Seymour A. Smith, Company B, from Bristol, Ontario County and Barber G. Popple, also Company B, from Springwater, Livingston County.
7. Body lice, literally louse (Pendiculus) living on clothing (vestimenti).
8. Thirty-nine year old Richard Bascombe was mustered in as private at Rome, New York, August 26, 1862, Company C, 50th N.Y. Engineers. He was promoted corporal December 27, 1862 and sergeant March 16, 1864. On March 26, 1864 he was mustered in as second lieutenant, Thirty-seventh Colored Infantry, captured at Plymouth, paroled March 1, 1865 at North East Ferry, North Carolina and mustered out June 14, 1865. Fred Phisterer, *New York in the Rebellion* (Albany: J. B. Lyon, 1912), Vol. 5, page 4126.
9. "I still have it." [C.C.M.]
10. This is seconded by Kellogg, *Life and Death in Rebel Prisons*, though Kellogg, pages 33, 34, recalled that one intoxicated officer rode up to a member of the 16th Connecticut, "drew his sword and demanded his watch, using threatening and insulting language, and declaring he would split open his head if he refused. Of course, there was no way but to yield."
11. Kellogg recalls the postmaster at Williamston offering to mail the prisoner's letters, Kellog, *Life and Death in Rebel Prisons*, page 37.
12. The drummer who took the name of the dead Seymour Smith.
13. Seventeenth South Carolina Infantry.

Chapter Six

14. That is, offensive food.
15. Goldsboro.
16. Giving rise to the sobriquet, "Plymouth Pilgrims," which was used with sarcasm in the Charleston papers. Kellogg, *Life and Death in Rebel Prisons*, page 51.
17. Just outside the harbor of Charleston from which Major General Quincy A. Gilmore (West Point 1849) is said to have ushered in a "new era of engineering and gunnery" which led to the capture of Batteries Wagner and Gregg and the shelling and eventual capture of Charleston. Ezra J. Warner, *Generals in Blue* (Baton Rouge, Louisiana: Louisiana University Press, 1964), pp. 176. 177.
18. Also attributed to General Gilmore. Fort Pulaski, which was defending the water approach to Savannah, was reduced by massed mortar batteries on Taylee Island. *Ibid.* The guards were the 1st Georgia, according to Bancroft, *Diary of Albert H. Bancroft . . .*, page 612.
19. See drawing on page 213.
20. Charles J. Simmons, from Bristol, who was mustered in as a musician, Company B, October 16, 1861, wounded at Fair Oaks and promoted sergeant, February 11, 1863. Simmons, 24, was to die of disease August 21, 1864.
21. Kellogg, *Life and Death in Rebel Prisons*, recalls especially the suffocating smell coming from the swamp which prisoners used as a latrine, page 58.
22. Farrar enlisted in Elmira, October 1, 1861, escaped February 20, 1865, and was mustered out July 3, 1865, at Annapolis, Maryland.
23. John J. Mary, 22, mustered in as a private August 30, 1861 at Canandaigua and paroled February 26, 1865 at Wilmington, North Carolina; and Private Augustus Gregg, Company E (see note 56, Chapter Two).
24. A common practice among suffering prisoners, though some prisoners were crueler than others--the "Raiders," about whom Mosher writer later, pages, 308, 311, 312, 313, 316, 137. See David L. Mallison, "The Andersonville Raiders," *Andersonville* (Jamestown, Virginia: Eastern Acorn Press, 1983), pp. 7-11. Reprinted from *Civil War Times Illustrated*, 1971.
25. A classic sign of starvation. See "Case Studies: Persecution/Genocide," *The Human Rights Series*, Volume III (Albany, New York: The State Education Department, 1986), page 8.
26. Known as the "Fort Pillow Massacre," a Tennessee garrison of approximately 550 Union infantry soldiers in almost equal numbers of whites and blacks was overcome on April 12, 1864 by Confederates led by General Nathan Bedford Forrest.

Chapter Six

27. Native Georgian Cobb, born September 7, 1815, was in turn after graduation from the University of Georgia in 1834, a lawyer, Congressman, Speaker of the House (1849-51), Georgia Governor, and Secretary of the Treasury (1857-60). He advocated secession after Lincoln's election and was appointed brigadier general C.S.A. February 2, 1862 and major general September 9, 1863. His service consisted primarily of trying to resolve differences between President Jefferson Davis and Georgia Governor Joseph E. Brown. Ezra J. Warner, *Generals in Gray* (Baton Rouge: Louisiana State University Press, 1959), pp. 55-56.
28. The two outfits were with the Eighty-Fifth at Plymouth.
29. Private Thomas J. Glenn, a twenty-six year old from Manchester, Company B, who was paroled, rejoined his company March 26, 1865 and was mustered out June 27, 1865 at New Bern, North Carolina.
30. See note 17.
31. That is, reported to the Confederate guards, likely to secure some favor, possibly food.
32. Twenty-seven year old Corporal John E. Boothe, a Springwater native, and Private Marcus M. Meade, Company B, who enlisted at East Bloomfield, September 25, 1861.
33. A metal shield for roasting or baking over an open fire.
34. See note 20, page 74. For a fuller account of exchange policies, see Louis A. Brown, *The Salisbury Prison: A Case Study of Confederate Military Prisons, 1861-1865* (Wendell, North Carolina: Broadfoots Bookmark, 1980), pp. 3-6, 171, 172 and footnote 4, July 23, 1864 entry.
35. A "cod" was slang referring to a codger, so the meaning here would be that the rumor was designed to fool or trick someone. *Webster's New International Dictionary*, Second Edition.
36. Likely a reference to the Battles of the Wilderness, Virginia, wherein superior numbers of Union troops (101, 895) fought Confederates at two-thirds of the strength and, because of the disadvantageous woods, suffered an estimated 17,666 losses (2,264 killed, 12,073 wounded). Longstreet was wounded, but not mortally.
37. This preliminary report was accurate, for on May 5, 1864 General Benjamin Butler started up the James River with a Union force that was initially successful. But Confederate General Beauregard's troops repulsed the Federals around May 16. The battle resumed May 19 with better results. Two days later General Gilmore's batteries and Union gunboats secured Union control of the fort.
38. Kellogg, *Life and Death in Rebel Prisons*, page 82, called it "a pitiless storm," but in time they would become more immune.

Chapter Six

39. Corporal Albert Bancroft, Company B, from Bristol, who died of disease, August 11, 1864. See also "Diary of Albert H. Bancroft . . .," which ends May 5, apparently corresponding to the onset of his illness.

40. An interesting description of tunnelling is found in Kellogg, *Life and Death in Rebel Prisons*, pages 118-120.

41. Probably from the May 4 and 5 operations at Deep Gully and Brice's Creek, North Carolina by General Hoke to wrest control of New Bern from Union general Innis Palmer. General Beauregard's order "to repair to Petersburg," Virginia, cut short his operation. See also Lee's request to Major General George E. Pickett to forward Hoke's troops to the Rapidan River in anticipation of a Union movement. *O.R.*, Ser. I, Vol. XXXIII, pages 1273, 1320, 1326, 1330.

42. Dalton, Georgia, near the Georgia-Tennessee border, was the opening action of the Atlanta campaign of General William Sherman, May 5-11, 1864. By splitting his armies Sherman was able to dislodge Confederates from Rocky Face Ridge covering Dalton before moving to Resaca, May 13-16. Mark M. Boatner, *The Civil War Dictionary* (New York: David McKay Co., Inc., 1959), pp. 220-221.

43. Corporals Thomas W. Porter, Company B, enlisted from Naples, September 24, 1861 and died of disease October 3, 1864 at Charleston, South Carolina; and Thomas W. Such, a twenty-two year old, who died from disease only ten days earlier than his Napolitan friend Porter.

44. Corporal James S. Carson, a Manchester, New York native who was mustered out June 15, 1865 at Elmira.

45. Probably Private Franklin E. Wilcox from East Bloomfield, who had mustered originally in Company K, but transferred to Company B with friends the first of January 1862 and died of disease, September 10, 1864 at Andersonville; Private Daniel L. Reed of Gorham, southeast of Canandaigua who died at age twenty-five at Camp Parole, near Annapolis, February 2, 1865; and Private Jacob Purkey, Jr., also from Gorham, who miraculously was mustered out with Company B June 27, 1865 at New Bern, North Carolina. Purkey's older brother Daniel was not as fortunate, succumbing to disease at Andersonville, August 31, 1864.

46. Private John M. Wilson from Seneca, New York was recruited by Isaac Shimer, subsequently elected captain, and was mustered July 2, 1862 to serve in Company F.

47. The gruesome hospital conditions are detailed by Quarter-Master Sergeant Hiram Buckingham of the 16th Connecticut Vols. in Kellogg, *Life and Death in Rebel Prisons*, pages 247-282. It was the "last [place] on earth" for the really ill (page 247). Assessments of doctors varied, giving real credit to a Georgia doctor who was "a fine fellow"

Chapter Six

48. and Union man who had been conscripted, as had most, at $11 per month, of $1 "greenbacks" (page 256).

48. A reference to Captain Henry Wirz. Predations by "raiders" were a real concern: "Man killed by the raiders near where we slept. Head all pounded to pieces with a club. Murders are an every day occurrence," *John Ransom's Andersonville Diary* (New York: Berkley Books, 1988), page 83.

49. Twenty-seven year old William H. Dillon, who enlisted at Canandaigua August 26, 1861 and was discharged for disability, July 27, 1862, Washington.

50. A false rumor. Charleston was not occupied by Union forces under General Gilmore until February 18, 1865.

51. Ransom reported that on June 3 wounded black soldiers from the 54th Massachusetts Infantry, made famous by the 1989 movie *Glory*, were brought in. *John Ransom's Andersonville Diary*, page 86. Kellogg, *Life and Death in Rebel Prisons*, pages 124, 125, too recalled their arrival, but contrary to other reports, stated that they "were universally treated better than we white soldiers."

52. Prisoners selected to go outside the stockade to draw wood for fires primarily.

53. False. It would be almost three months before Atlanta will fall, though Sherman's army had been successful at Dalton, Georgia on May 8 and Resaca, Georgia a week later. See July 21, 1864 entry.

54. Referring to First Lieutenant Alfred B. Bradley from Friendship, who had mustered in as a private in Company C, September 28, 1861.

55. Typical signs of scurvy, as are swelling of different parts of the body or decaying gums and loosening of the teeth.

56. Brigadier General Samuel Davis Sturges, a Pennsylvanian who graduated from West Point 1846 and who as a second lieutenant of dragoons was captured during the Mexican War, had performed well at Second Manassas, Fredericksburg, and Sharpsburg before being routed by Confederate Nathan Bedford Forrest at Brice's Cross Roads, Mississippi, which virtually terminated his Civil War service. After the war he reverted to his regular rank of lieutenant colonel, later colonel of the Seventh Cavalry, the lieutenant colonel of which was George A. Custer.

57. Barton was a member of the 146th N.Y.V. which was mustered October 10, 1862 and had fought at Gettysburg, defending Little Round Top.

58. "Big Pete" apparently was a member of the 12th Cavalry, according to Ransom. Both Kellogg, *Life and Death in Rebel Prisons*, page 157, and Ransom, recalled that "a big strapping fellow called Limber Jim" headed the "police," *John Ransom's Andersonville Diary*, page 106.

Chapter Six

McElroy, *This Was Andersonville* (New York: McDowell, Obolensky, Inc., 1957), page 77 recalled that he was from the 67th Illinois and was lithe like a "young Sioux brave."

59. No doubt added some time after 1894.
60. Apparently on orders from Wirz until the leaders of the rebels were arrested and tried. *John Ransom's Andersonville Diary*, page 105.
61. The 9th Michigan Infantry according to *John Ransom's Andersonville Diary*, page 110. Ransom had checked them out, under the impression they were from his outfit, the 9th Michigan Cavalry.
62. Both rumors untrue. In fact, Grant would lay siege to Petersburg after being repelled later in the month. Lynchburg too had been safely defended.
63. Ransom's account is particularly detailed. *John Ransom's Andersonville Diary*, pages 112-116. For a fuller, more recent treatment see Brian Bennett, "The Most Horrible Barbarism," *Civil War*, Vol. X, No. 1 (January-February, 1992), pages 16-20, 54.
64. Written after 1891 and referring to W. R. Holloway & J. A. Wyeth, "Treatment of Prisoners at Camp Morton," *Century*, Vol. 42 (1891), 20 New Series, page 757. This is Holloway's rejoinder to Weyeth's critical account as a prisoner.
65. June 19, 1864 in the port of Cherbourg, France, the Confederate ship *Alabama* was sunk by the U.S.S. *Kearsage*, commanded by then Captain John A. Winslow, in a naval battle in which the Confederate Commander Semmes could have declined to participate. The battle, which lasted almost four hours, resulted not only in the loss of the notorious *Alabama*, but the loss of forty lives, ten from drowning. David D. Porter, *Naval History of the Civil War* (New York: The Sherman Publishing Company, 1887), page 650.
66. False. See note 53, June 10, 1864 entry.
67. To what this refers is somewhat unclear, for Major General William Rosecrans, who had earlier succeeded General Pope and had by means of a "brilliant maneuver forced Confederates from Chattanooga," was not commanding the Department of Missouri after the disastrous Chickamauga loss to Confederate General Bragg. Ezra J. Warner, *Generals in Blue* (Baton Rouge: Louisiana State Press, 1964), pp. 410-411.
68. Lieutenant General John Bell Hood, West Point 1853, who had suffered severe injury to his arm at Gettysburg and the loss of his leg at Chickamauga, superseded the controversial Joseph E. Johnston, who had displeased C.S.A. President Davis by his plans to withdraw strategically before Sherman in the Atlanta campaign.

Chapter Six

69. Unclear, but probably a reference to the drummer from the 2nd North Carolina (Union), April 20 and 21, 1864 entries.
70. Private Napolean B. Carpenter, 27, Company B, from Naples.
71. Indeed, twenty-four old Private Clark Kern, Company B, from Springwater, Livingston County, succumbed to disease August 11, 1864.
72. This reference is unclear, but the South, feeling burdened by the number of prisoners to guard and feed, was desirous of exchanging prisoners and had made overtures. Grant's policy, however, was to reduce further the Confederate troop strength. Possibly to this end he made General Benjamin Butler "Commissioner for exchange of prisoners." Butler was outlawed by the South. Nonetheless, by November 1864 the South had begun sending prisoners north from Andersonville and elsewhere "without man-to-man exchange." Mark M. Boatner, *The Civil War Dictionary* (New York: David McKay Co., Inc., 1959), pp. 270-271.
73. Probably a reference to John Dunlap Stevenson, but, if so, rumor was untrue.
74. See October 12, 1864 entry.
75. *The Annual Report of the Adjutant General of the State of New York* (Albany, New York: J. B. Lyon Company, State Printers, 1902), Serial No. 30, pages 1039 and 1053 lists Private Charles B. Ingraham, from Springwater as having died from disease August 4 and Private Parmer W. Lewis, a Canadice native, as having succumbed August 9, 1864.
76. A "banking game played with three dice, the players betting that a certain number will appear on one or more of the dice or that a sum of the three dice will make a certain number or that all three dice will turn up alike." *Webster's New International Dictionary*, Second Edition. The reference to bank, then also becomes clearer.
77. John C. Holcomb, who enlisted at Friendship, October 18, 1861 served in Company C, escaped March 1, 1865 and was mustered out March 7, 1865 at New Bern, North Carolina.
78. Coincidentally, Ransom was strangely silent too, entering only phrases, not his thoughtful reflections. *John Ransom's Andersonville Diary*, pages 129-130. By contrast, Kellogg, *Life and Death in Rebel Prisons*, recalled on August 15, "photographic artists" from Macon, Georgia taking positions in various sentry boxes to make engravings (page 223) and the release of "quite a number of" sergeants who held officers' commissions but had not been mustered, including two men from Plymouth (page 230).
79. Latrines.
80. False.
81. While true, there was a caveat: "All who cannot walk must stay behind," *John Ransom's Andersonville Diary*, page 131.

Chapter Six

82. Kellogg, *Life and Death in Rebel Prisons*, pages 241, 242, recalled 7 detachments, or over 1800 men, were released on September 7 with more being released at 1 a.m. on the Eighth, a number of whom were from the 2d Loyal Regiment of N.C. who claimed they were from New York, Pennsylvania and Connecticut. Some apparently were successful.
83. Sergeant John Buell, age 27, enlisted at East Bloomfield, September 27, 1861 and was mustered in Company B, October 7, 1861. Like virtually all others, he had reenlisted January 1, 1864.
84. Sergeant John Buell, age 27, enlisted at East Bloomfield, September 27, 1861 and was mustered in Company B, October 7, 1861. Like virtually all others, he had reenlisted January 1, 1864.

CHAPTER SEVEN

1. John E. Blake, also from East Bloomfield, was mustered in October 16, 1861.
2. See entries December 11-19, 1862.
3. Kellogg, *Life and Death in Rebel Prisoners*, pages 292-293, recalled there being 6000 prisoners, divided into "hundreds" and "thousands" in contrast with the organization into squads of 90 ("nineties") at Andersonville.
4. "An equinoctial [seasonal] storm." *Webster's Seventh New Collegiate Dictionary.*
5. Similarly, June 22, Captain Samuel Adams sent $200 to Sergeant Edgar Irish to buy vegetables for members of his Company C, as well as the admonition "exercise, cleanliness and courage." Letter in Collection of Susan Nahas, a distant relative of Irish's. See photograph of Irish in Mahood, *The Plymouth Pilgrims*, page 258. Adams' photograph is on page 157 above.
6. See also Ellsworth Eliot, "A Civil War Diary," The Yale University Library *Gazette*, Vol. 16, No. 1 (July 1941), page 11.
7. Kellogg reinforces this report, though there were only two cases in the camp--hospital attendants. Kellogg, *Life and Death in Rebel Prisons*, page 312.
8. First Lieutenant, later Captain Charles McHenry, Company B, was mustered out with his company, June 27, 1865, at New Bern, North Carolina; and Seneca Allen, 24, from Black Creek, Allegany County, was mustered captain, Company F, October 20, 1861, and was mustered out April 7, 1865.
9. Wetmore, who has served approximately 100 days in prison after Fair Oaks had vowed to escape when given a chance.
10. Deyo was recaptured almost immediately. See October 12, 1864 entry.

Chapter Seven

11. Kellogg estimated that 12,000 prisoners were there. Robert Kellogg, *Life and Death in Rebel Prisons*, page 320.
12. See also September 28, 1864 entry.
13. Lice and ticks.
14. Twenty-seven year old Warner was mustered in as a corporal, Company B, October 7, 1861. He was from Springwater, Livingston County. The Adjutant General's Report lists the death as October 8, 1864.
15. Reprinted in *O.R.*, Ser. II, Vol. VII, page 976, along with an account of conditions at Andersonville by Surgeon Joseph Jones, Provisional Army, C.S. to C.S.A. Surgeon General S. P. Moore, October 19, 1864, including "hospital gangrene" to remarkable degree and with such fatal effects . . ., page 1012.
16. Also spelled Sheppard, from Canadice, Ontario County, was mustered in as first sergeant, Company K, August 30, 1861, but was returned to the ranks and transferred to Company B, January 1, 1862. Death was recorded officially as October 18, 1864.
17. See September 28, 1864 entry.
18. Twenty-four year old Logan from Bristol, Ontario County, mustered in as a private in Company B, October 7, 1861; and Corporal Tobias Hadsell, 26, enlisted August 26, 1861 at Manchester, Ontario County and is listed as having died October 9, 1865. *Annual Report of the Adjutant General of the State of New York* (Albany, New York: J. B. Lyon Company, State Printers, 1902), Serial No. 30, pages 1054 and 1027 respectively.
19. See entry July 5, 1864.
20. That is, Morris's discount is too high.
21. Private Alexander Hussey, Company B, who enlisted at West Bloomfield, August 26, 1861, left a widower father who had been dependent on Hussey's wages. Hussey would be memorialized with his fellows from Company B on a monument set up in the cemetery in West Bloomfield, N.Y.
22. Nathan S. Briggs, a Richmond, Ontario County native, served in Company B until paroled, no date, and discharged June 7, 1865 at Elmira, New York.
23. Kellogg recalled black and white beans and 2 1/2 to 1' margin for Lincoln. Robert Kellogg, *Life and Death in Rebel Prisons*, pages 289, 330.
24. Thirty-eight year old Private Wright enlisted at Springwater, Livingston County, September 23, 1861 and was mustered in September 28, 1861, Company K, but was transferred to Company B, January 1, 1862.
25. Referring to a converted Confederate cruiser which had sailed from Wilmington, North Carolina to get coal and other supplies on the Cape

Chapter Seven

Fear River. This ship, ultimately and appropriately named the *Chameleon*, also had been called the *Atlanta* and *Olustee* and had been a merchant ship and blockade runner, as well as a cruiser. Unable to return to port in 1865, it was captured by the U.S. government. David D. Porter, *The Naval History of the Civil War* (New York: The Sherman Publishing Company, 1887), page 820.

26. Twenty-three year old Corporal Francisco from Canadice, west of Canandaigua, had mustered into Company B, August 30, 1861.
27. Union prisoners who had taken the Confederate oath.
28. Iverson had been mustered as captain of Company I, 5th Georgia Volunteers, May 11, 1861. His adjutant was R. S. Cheatham. The regiment saw duty at Pensacola, Florida before serving the Army of Tennessee and finally C.S.A. General Joseph Johnston on the Georgia coast and Carolinas.
29. Punishment for the offender took the form of hanging him by the thumbs with the feet off the ground, "thus bringing the entire weight of the body upon the thumbs." Robert Kellogg, *Life and Death in Rebel Prisons*, page 331.
30. Millen, with forty-two acres may have been the largest prison tract in the Confederacy. E. Merton Coulter, *Confederate States of America 1861-1865* (Baton Rouge: Louisiana State Press, 1952), page 471.
31. Belle Isle in the James River near Richmond, which held only enlisted men, was occupied continuously from Bull Run until the Kilpatrick-Dahlgren Raid in February 1864 when prisoners were moved to Andersonville.
32. Named for the commander, C.S.A. Brigadier General John Hunt Morgan, and 2nd Kentucky Cavalry's raids in Tennessee, Kentucky, Indiana and Ohio rank with those of the famous Jeb Stuart. Their exploits came to an end when Morgan was surprised and killed by Union cavalry September 3, 1864.
33. Trader Morris's activities as the money changer were described earlier.
34. A reference to a card game, wherein if the bidder does not make the bid, he is considered "euchered."
35. Died.
36. Commissary General John Henry Winder, a Maryland native and West Pointer 1820 had gained possibly an unearned opprobrium for his alleged treatment of prisoners earlier in Richmond and later at Andersonville. He died allegedly from fatigue and anxiety over his duties February 7, 1865.
37. Private Marcus M. Meade from East Bloomfield was mustered out with his company, June 27, 1865 at New Bern, North Carolina.

Chapter Seven

38. First Sergeant Robinson of Company B was mustered out with Company B, June 27, 1865 at New Bern, North Carolina.
39. For an extended treatment of prison life at Salisbury prison see Louis A. Brown, *The Salisbury Prison: A Case Study of Confederate Military Prisons, 1861-1865* (Wendell, North Carolina: Avera Press, 1980).
40. Unfortunately Private Edgar F. Bentley, 24, from East Bloomfield died January 12, 1865 at Richmond near Honeoye on furlough while Private Reuben R. Crosby, 21, of West Bloomfield, died January 4, 1865 at the First Division Hospital in Annapolis, Maryland.
41. The capture and burning of Atlanta occurred a month earlier.
42. Twenty-four year old Private Nathan S. Briggs from Richmond, near Honeoye, New York, Company B. See November 5, 1864 entry.
43. "Do They Miss Me At Home," words by Caroline Atherton Mason, music by S. M. Grannis.
44. Brigadier General (Hugh) Johnson Kilpatrick, a New Jersey native and West Point graduate, was the first regular army officer wounded in action at Big Bethel, Virginia, June 1861. The controversial Kilpatrick's attack on Richmond in February 1864 led to Union prisoners being transferred from Belle Isle to Andersonville. Later Minister to Chile, he died in Santiago in 1881.
45. This rumor was true and within a month there was the "general resumption of exchange; with the sick being sent out first." E. Merton Coulter, *Confederate States of America 1861-1865* (Baton Rouge: Louisiana State University Press, 1952), page 479.
46. First Lieutenant and Quartermaster, Alfred B. Bradley, from Friendship, who had mustered in as a private, Company C, September 28, 1861. He was promoted, but not mustered, captain August 19, 1865.
47. Forty-five year old Robert Ould, a Washington, DC native and agent for exchange of Confederate prisoners beginning in July 1862 had an interesting career. He was a Washington lawyer from 1842-1861, when he volunteered for government duties with CSA. As district attorney in 1859 he had prosecuted Congressman (later general) Daniel E. Sickles for the murder of Philip Barton Key, the son of Francis Scott Key, who Sickles suspected of having an affair with Sickles's wife. Jon L. Wakelyn, *Biographical Dictionary of the Confederacy* (Westport, Connecticut: Greenwood Press, 1977), page 336 and C. Vann Woodward, Ed., *Mary Chestnut's Civil War* (New Haven: Yale University Press, 1981), page 92.
48. Today's equivalent might be "stick it in your ear."
49. At last report this cane is owned by William Harvey, Elmira, New York, husband of Mosher's niece. It has a metal head inscribed with Mosher's name.

Chapter Seven

50. A rumor proved true, see January 1 and 8, 1865.
51. Twenty-six year old Corporal Carson from Manchester, northwest of Canandaigua, was listed as paroled and mustered out June 15, 1865 at Elmira.
52. Winder indeed was dead.

CHAPTER EIGHT

1. Sergeant Cummings, 28, from Naples, New York, was mustered out June 7, 1865 at Elmira.
2. Farrar escaped that day and was mustered out July 3, 1865 at Annapolis, Maryland.
3. For a more extended treatment of the frustration see Wayne Mahood, *The Plymouth Pilgrims* (Hightstown, New Jersey: Longstreet House, 1989).
4. Mosher recorded that he was rescued by the 24th and 25th Michigan infantries, but the 24th was at Springfield, Illinois at this time. The 25th Michigan Infantry was part of the recreated Department of North Carolina that had captured Wilmington, February 22, 1865 before its advance on Goldsboro, North Carolina, March 6, Frederick H. Dyer, *A Compendium of the War of the Rebellion*, New York: Yoseloff, 1959, pages 359, 360, 1292.
5. An alcoholic drink (whiskey or rum) with milk and sugar often served iced and flavored with nutmeg.
6. John M. Palmer, 40, who was mustered in August 12, 1862. He was discharged April 5, 1865, by promotion to surgeon, Third Infantry.
7. Twenty-one year old LeRoy S. Ward, from Clarkesville, who enlisted as a private in Company I, November 18, 1861. He was mustered out June 17, 1865 at Elmira.
8. Near Flushing in the present Borough of Queens.
9. Lincoln, the victim of a bullet wound inflicted by John Wilkes Booth the evening before, had died early on April 15, shocking a war-weary nation.
10. That is, he was too weak even to strike a louse.

Appendix B

1. Promoted Lt. Colonel, May 1, 1863
2. Promoted Captain, Aug, 21, 1863
3. Promoted 1st Lt., Mar. 1, 1862
4. Promoted Captain, April 11, 1865
5. Promoted QM Sgt. Major

Appendix B

6. Promoted Sgt. Major
7. Promoted Sgt. Feb. 11, 1863
8. Transferred from Co. K, Jan. 1, 1862
9. Transferred from Co. D, Jan. 1, 1862
10. Transferred from CO. K, Jan. 1, 1862

BIBLIOGRAPHY

Public Documents

A Record of the Commissioned Officers, Non-commissioned Officers and Privates of the Regiments which were Organized in the State of New York and Called into service of the United States to assist in suppressing the Rebellion. Albany, New York: Comstock & Cassiday, Printers, 1864, Vol. 3, "Muster Rolls."

Annual Report of the Adjutant-General of the State of New York, Vols, 30, 36. Albany: Oliver A. Quayle, 1902.

Phisterer, Frederick (comp.) *New York in the War of the Rebellion.* Third ed. Albany: J. B. Lyon Company, 1912, Five Volumes.

The War of the Rebellion: A Compilation of the Official Records of the Union and Confederate Armies. Washington: 1880-1891, 128 Volumes. "O.R."

Diaries, Manuscripts, Letters, Addresses.

Bancroft, Albert H. "Diary of Albert H. Bancroft of Co. B, Eighty-fifth N.Y.S.V." Albany, New York: Bureau of Military Statistics, Annual Report, 1868.

Crocker, R. M. *The Boys in Blue: Perry in the Civil War.* Mss. Genesee Valley Collection, SUNY - Geneseo.

Day, David. *My Diary of Rambles With the 25th Mass.*, in Mary L. Thornton, *New Bern N. C., 1862-1865.* Unpublished manuscript, dated December 1959, in Craven County Library, New Bern, North Carolina.

Howe, Allen W. Letter. February 19, 1885, to Dr. William M. Smith, Friendship (New York) Town Historical Society and Museum.

Irish, Edgar. Letter. Collection of Susan Nahas.

Kittinger, Joseph. *Diary, 1861-1865.* Buffalo, New York: Kittinger & Co., Inc., 1863.

Langworthy, Daniel A., *Reminiscences of a Prisoner of War and His Escape.* Minneapolis: Byron Printing Co., 1915.

Maxson, Lafayette. Letter. Allegany Historical Society, Belmont, New York.

Morris, Henry. *Journal of Henry Morris.* Unpublished journal in collection of Christopher Densmore.

Root, Asa W. "The Diary of Asa W. Root, A Northern Soldier, 1861-1864," #734, D. R. Barker Library, Fredonia, New York.

Smith, William M. "Report of the Sanitary Conditions, Marches, Battles and other data in Relation to the 85th N.Y. Vols., New Berne, N.C., Feb. 22,1863." Papers of Abijah Wellman, Friendship (New York) Town Historical Society and Museum.

Waddell, Alfred M. *An Address Before the Associated Army of Northern Virginia.* Richmond: William Ellis Jones Book and Job Printer, 1888.

Articles and Periodicals

Bennett, Brian. "The Most Horrible Barbarism," *Civil War Magazine*, Vol. X, No. 1 (January/February, 1992), 16-20, 54.

Billings, John D. "Hardtack and Coffee" in Henry S. Commager, *The Blue and the Gray.* Indianapolis, Indiana: Bobbs-Merrill, 1950, Vol. 1, 290-295.

Dinkins, James. "The Confederate Ram *Albemarle*," in R. A. Brock (ed.) *Southern Historical Society Papers.* (Richmond, Virginia, 1902), 205-214.

Eliot, Ellsworth. "A Civil War Diary." *The Yale University Library GAZETTE*, Vol. 16. No. 1 (July 1941), 3-13.

Goss, Warren. "Campaigning to No Purpose," in Robert U. Johnson & Clarence C. Buel, *Battles and Leaders of the Civil War.* New York: Century Co., 1884, 1887, 1888, Vol. 2, 153-159.

Graham, John W. "The Capture of Plymouth," in Walter Clark (ed.) *North Carolina Troops, 1861-1865.* Wendell, North Carolina: Avera Press, 1962, 175-195.

Holloway, W. R. & J. A. Wyeth. "Treatment of Prisoners at Camp Morton," *Century*, Vol. 42 (1981), 20. New Series.

Mahood, Wayne. "Until I Return: The Legend of the Scythe Tree," *Civil War Times Illustrated.* Vol. XXV, No. 9 (January 1987), 38-43.

Mallison, David L. "The Andersonville Raiders," *Andersonville.* Jamestown, Virginia: Eastern Acorn Press, 1983, 7-11.

Maryniak, Benedict R. "Military Organizations," *Newsletter* of Buffalo Civil War Round Table, undated.

Regimental Histories

Dickey, Luther S. *History of the 103rd [PA.] Regiment, 1861-1865.* Chicago: L. S. Dickey, 1910.

―――――. *History of the Eighty-Fifth Regiment Pennsylvania Volunteers Infantry, 1861-1865.* New York: J. C. & W. E. Powers, 1915.

King, David A., A. Judson Gibbs and Jay Northrup, Comp. *History of the Ninety-Third Regiment, New York Volunteer Infantry, 1861-1865.* Milwaukee, Wisconsin: Swain & Tate, 1895.

Mahood, Wayne. *The Plymouth Pilgrims: A History of the Eighty-fifth New York Infantry in the Civil War.* Hightstown, New Jersey: Longstreet House, 1989.

Willson, Arabella M. *Disaster, Struggle, Triumph: 1000 "Boys in Blue".* Albany: Argus Company, Printers, 1870.

Books

Billingsley, A. S. *From the Flag to the Cross.* Philadelphia: New World Publishing Co., 1872.

Boatner, Mark M. *The Civil War Dictionary.* New York: David McKay Co., 1959.

Brown, Louis A. *The Salisbury Prison: A Case Study of Confederate Military Prisons, 1861-1865.* Wendell, North Carolina: Broadfoot's Bookmark, 1980.

Coulter, E. Merton. *Confederate States of America, 1861-1865.* Baton Rouge: Louisiana State Press, 1952.

Davis, Burke. *The Civil War: Strange and Fascinating Facts.* New York: Crown Publishers, 1982.

Dictionary of American Biography, Vols. IV, XVII. New York: Charles Scribner's Sons, 1930, 1936.

Dyer, Frederick. *A Compendium of the War of the Rebellion.* Dayton, Ohio: Morningside Press, 1978. Reprint.

Evans, Clement A. *Confederate Military History.* New York: Thomas Yoseloff, 1962.

Groene, Bertram. *Tracing Your Civil War Ancestor.* Winston-Salem, North Carolina: John F. Blair Publ., 1981.

Hill, Thomas E. *Hill's Manual of Social and Business Forms.* Chicago: Hill Standard Book Company, 1885.

Kantor, MacKinlay. *Andersonville.* Cleveland: World Publishing Co., 1955.

Kellogg, Robert N. *Life and Death in Rebel Prisons.* Hartford, Connecticut: L. Stebbins, 1865. Reprinted by Books for Libraries Press, 1971.

Lord, Francis A. *They Fought for the Union.* New York: Bonanza Books, 1960.

McElroy, John. *Andersonville. A Story of Rebel Military Prisons.* Toledo: D. R. Locke, 1879.

New York State Education Department. "Case Studies: Persecution/Genocide," *The Human Rights Series,* Vol. III. Albany, New York: author, 1986.

Odell, George C. D. *Annals of the New York Stage.* New York: Columbia University Press, 1931, Vols. VII, IX, X.

Pearson, Henry Greenleaf. *James S. Wadsworth of Geneseo.* New York: Charles Scribner's Sons, 1913.

Porter, David D. *The Naval History of the Civil War.* New York: Sherman Publishing Co., 1887.

Ransom, John. *John Ransom's Andersonville Diary.* New York: Berkley Books, 1988.

Small, Abner R. (Harry A. Small, ed.). *The Road to Richmond.* Berkeley, California: University of California Press, 1939.

Wakelyn, Jon L. *Biographical Dictionary of the Confederacy.* Westport, Connecticut: Greenwood Press, 1977.

Walker, Francis A. *History of the Second Army Corps of the Army of the Potomac.* New York: Charles Scribner's Sons, 1891.

Warner, Ezra J. *Generals in Gray.* Baton Rouge: Louisiana State University Press, 1959.

———. *Generals in Blue.* Baton Rouge: Louisiana State University Press, 1964.

Wiley, Bell I. *The Life of Billy Yank.* Indianapolis: Bobbs-Merrill, 1952.

Woodward, C. Vann, ed. *Mary Chestnut's Civil War.* New Haven: Yale University Press, 1981.

Wyeth, John A. *That Devil Forrest.* New York: Harper, 1959.

GENERAL INDEX

Alabama, 236
Albany, N.Y., 87, 160, 188, 292
Albemarle, 196, 197, 198 (ill.), 200, 204, 268
Alexandria, Va., 37, 38
Allegany County, N.Y., 214, 243, 297
Anderson, James E., 229
Andersonville, Ga., 201, 208-254, 260, 264, 266, 268, 269, 271, 272, 274, 279, 286, 297, 298, 299, 301, 303, 304
    Bloodhounds, 219, 220, 233
    Dead Line, 212, 228, 229, 244, 245, 255
    Providence Spring, 245, 246
    Raiders, 222, 223, 228, 230, 231, 232, 233
    Regulators, 230
Andrews, Charles T., 203
Annapolis, Md., 158, 308
Atlanta, Ga., 222, 223, 225, 227, 238, 239, 250, 270
Auburn, N.Y., 251

Badgley, Maria, xiii, 297
Baltimore, Md., 21, 183, 184, 188
Baritt, Lt. (C.S.), 271, 272, 273, 274
Barrows, Emily, 77
Barstow, ---, 176
Barton, Gen. (C.S.), 71
Bascomb, Lt., 205
Baseball, 87
Beach, Col. Francis, 193
Beagle, Lt., 158
Belle Island Prison, Va., 220, 225, 273
Black Creek, N.Y., 12
Blackshear, Ga., 272
Bloom, N.Y., 7
Bloomfield, N.Y., 17, 60, 88
Blounts Creek Mills, N.C., 124, 126
Bogle, Maj. Archibald, 219
Bombshell, 163, 165, 174, 180, 182
Bristol, N.Y., 7
Buell, Lucy, 252
Buell, Timothy, 252
Buffalo, N.Y., 302
Burnside, Gen. Ambrose, 88, 91, 92, 115
Burt, Edward, 293

Cady, Capt. Lester, 193
Callister, William, 186
Camp Morton, Ind., 235
Camp Shepherd, 23
Camp Warren, 24
Camp Winfield Scott, 46
Campbell, John A., 285
Canandaigua, N.Y., xi, 7, 12, 15, 36, 44, 184, 186, 188, 189, 251, 268
Cape Hatteras, N.C., 289, 290
Casey, Gen. Silas, 22 (ill.), 23, 24, 27, 29, 33, 36, 37
Caton, G. W., 79
Cattaraugus County, N.Y., 214
Cedar Landing, N.C., 180
Chandler, Lt. Col., 242
Chapin, Frank, 30, 36, 79, 129, 137, 139
Chapin (Chapinville), N.Y., xi, 7, 15, 61, 79, 85, 139, 184, 186, 188, 297
Charles City Courthouse, Va., 70
Charleston, 165, 166, 170
Charleston, S.C., 109, 110, 142, 207, 214, 223, 247, 254, 255, 256, 257, 260, 262, 272, 275, 277, 278, 283, 285, 304, 308
Charleston & Savannah Railroad, 208
Chattannooga, Tenn., 152
Cheatham, Lt. (C.S.), 271, 273, 280
CHerry Ridge Landing, N.C., 167
Cobb, Gen. Howell (C.S.), 214, 244
Colored Troops, 205
Col. Rucker, 149, 182, 191
Columbia, S.C., 146, 161, 258, 271, 283, 285
Columbus, Ga., 239
Commodore Hull, 165
Connecticut Troops:
    1st Heavy Art., 65
    10th Inf., 103
    15th Inf., 179, 181, 190
    16th Inf., 179, 180, 190, 191, 192, 193, 204, 214, 256
Congress, 43
Cooke, Capt. James (C.S.), 200, 204
Cooper, Gen. Seth (C.S.), 214, 251
Costelo, Mr., 203
Cotton Plant, 200
Counterfeiting, 150, 167
Cuba, N.Y., 243
Cullistes, William, 18
Cumberland, 43

Dalton, Ga., 217, 218
Daniel, Gen. Junius (C.S.), 107
Danville, Va., 210
David's Island, N.Y., 293
Davis, Jefferson, 171, 228, 229, 256
Dentist, 247, 248
Dickenson, Rev. E. H., 302
Dillon, Capt., 156
Dismal Swamp, N.C., 183
Dismukes, Sabina, 264
Dix, Gen., 86
Dix-Hill Cartel, 253
Dollie, 149, 158
Donelson, Judge, 166
Drummer Boys, 239
Dutton, Col. William, 319

East Bloomfield, N.Y., 252
Easthampton, Mass., 302
Edenten, N.C., 149, 152, 155, 156, 161
Elizabeth City, N.C., 149, 150, 167
Ellis, Henry, 61, 64
Elm City, 38
Elmira, N.Y., 3, 7, 8, 9, 17, 31, 37, 44, 176, 184, 188, 204, 240, 274
Elridge, S. J., 214
Express, 78

Fair Oaks, Va., 41, 59, 60, 62, 67, 78, 79, 91, 96, 97, 113, 119, 135, 308
Fargo, N.D., 302
Farrar, Mrs. Pirses, 286
Farrar, W. B., 286
Farrell, ---, 223, 224
Farrut, Capt., 64
Fawn, 183, 188
Florence, S.C., 207, 255, 258, 260-287, 288, 295, 304, 306, 307
Flushing, N.Y., 291
Flusser, Capt. C. W., 134, 180, 181, 182, 193, 197, 200, 204
Fort Darling, Va., 59, 217
Fort Donelson, Tenn., 31, 32
Fort Gray, N.C., 193, 195
Fort Hamilton, Va., 38
Fort Munroe, Va., 41, 42 (ill.), 43, 48, 69, 73, 173, 183, 188, 230
Fort Pillow, Tenn., 212
Fort Pulaski, Ga., 208

Fort Wayne, Ind., 286
Fort Wessells, N.C., 193, 195, 196, 197
Fort Williams, N.C., 193, 195, 197, 199
Fort Worth, N.C., 182, 193, 195, 197
Foster, Gen. John, 69, 92, 99, 100 (ill.), 101, 113, 114, 117, 118, 119, 121, 122, 125, 126, 127, 143, 161, 207, 255, 257, 272
Fosters Mills, N.Y., 158
Friendship, N.Y., 12, 214

Galena, 75
Galvanized Yankess, 260, 271, 275, 276, 277
Gatesville, N.C., 89
Gatling Gun, 31
General Berry, 165, 166, 167, 182, 183, 189, 191
Genesee, 75
Geneva, N.Y., 12, 192, 297, 301
Georgetown, D.C., 33, 34, 36
Georgia Troops:
    5th Inf., 271
    19th Inf., 207
    55th Inf., 210
    1st Reserves, 228, 229, 233
Gettysburg, Pa., 171
Gilmore, Gen. Quincy, 214
Goldsboro, N.C., 69, 101, 114, 171, 207, 255
Grant, Gen. U. S., 171, 235, 253, 283, 285
Gray, Col., 97
Griggs, Stephen, 274
Gum Neck, N.C., 167

Haggard, Calvin, 193
Halifax, N.C., 165, 171
Hamilton, Rev. John, 223, 224
Hamilton, N.C., 155
Hampton, Va., 43, 71, 72, 73
Harp, Sgt., 29
Harper's Ferry, W.Va., 33
Harrelville, N.C., 174, 307
Harrison, Burton, 264
Harrison's Landing, Va., 62, 245
Harroldsville, N.C., 82
Hatcher's Run, Va., 285
Heintzelman, Gen. Samuel, 41
Hertford, N.C., 165

Hickman, Col., 96
Hildreth, Mrs., 36
Hill, Gen, D. H. (C.S.), 107
Hilton Head, S.C., 242
Hinsdale, N.Y., 12
Hodges, Capt., 149
Hoke, Gen., (C.S.), 171, 200, 204, 207
Honeoye, N.Y., 264
Hood, Gen. John (C.S.), 238, 250, 269
Hooker, Gen. Joe, 141
Hopewell, N.Y., 174, 186
Hoskins, Charles, 186
Hunt, Gen., 109
Hunter, R. M. T., 285

Indianapolis, Ind., 235
Iverson, Lt. Col. John (C.S.), 271, 277
Ives, J. C., 230

James, G. P. B., 179
Jamesville, N.C., 143, 151
Jessup, Frank, 30, 186
Jessup, W. L., 86
Johnson, Capt. Thomas, 175, 193
Johnston, Gen. Joe (C.S.), 223, 231, 238

Keene, Laura, 188
Kellogg, Robert, 253
Kemper, Gen. James (C.S.), 171, 204
Keyes, Gen. Erasmus, 36, 37, 41, 69
King, Gardner, 61
Kingston, N.C., 97
Kinston, N.C., 69, 102, 125, 160, 171
Knapp, Cash, 79

Lake Phelps, N.C., 182
Lancer, 190
LaPorte, Ind., 286
Lee, Admiral, 162
Lee, Robert E., 171
Lee's Mills, Va., 46, 48, 190
Lehman, Col. Theodore, 160, 161, 169, 193
Lima, N.Y., 77
Lincoln, Abraham, 228, 235, 248, 270, 285, 292

Little Dismal Swamp, N.C., 167
Little Genessee, N.Y., 12
Little Washington, N.C., 121, 122, 124, 126, 127, 151
Longstreet, Gen. James (C.S.), 107, 215
Long Island, N.Y., 291
Lynchburg, Va., 233

Mackey's Ferry, N.C., 156, 172
Macon, Ga., 208, 209, 214, 215, 219, 227, 230, 232, 239, 242, 247, 256
Malvern Hill, Va., 62
Manson, Mrs. James, 186
Martin, Capt., 205
Massachusetts Troops:
    2nd Heavy Art., 183, 193, 197, 204, 212
    6th Inf., 19, 89
    23rd Inf., 103
    24th Inf., 103
    25th Inf., 103, 130
    26th Inf., 130
    27th Inf., 103, 127, 130, 183, 188
    44th Inf., 115, 127
Massasoit, 149, 153, 155, 156, 158, 159, 164, 172, 177, 180, 182, 191, 192
Mattamusket Lake, N.C., 166
Maxwell, Lt. Col., 165, 176
McClellan, Gen. George, 3, 31, 35, 36, 40 (ill.), 41, 64, 69, 70, 250, 268, 270
McElroy, John, 201, 253
Meade, Gen. George, 141, 142
Mercer, Col. (C.S.), 204
Meridian Hill, Va., 23, 24, 29, 37
Merrimac, 43, 75
Miami, 182, 190, 193, 195, 196, 197
Michigan Troops:
    24th Inf., 287
    25th Inf., 287
Millen, Ga., 272
Mobile, Ala., 223
Monitor, 43, 75
Montgomery, Ala., 238
Morris Island, S.C., 207, 255, 256
Mosher, Abel, 180
Mosher, Abijah, xii, 3, 7, 10, 184, 186
Mosher, Amelia, 186
Mosher, Augustus, 291, 292
Mosher, Carlone, xi, 184, 186

Mosher, David, xi, 15, 30, 32, 35, 36, 43, 83, 108, 112, 113, 115, 128, 145, 148, 149, 155, 162, 168, 186, 191, 193, 302
Mosher, Frank, 179, 180, 181
Mosher, George, xi, 7, 27, 32, 36, 66, 84, 112, 113, 148, 184, 188, 192
Mosher, John, xi, 7
Mosher, Sarah, xi, 10, 21, 27, 28, 32, 35, 65, 76, 85, 105, 129, 143, 168, 184, 185 (ill.), 188, 192, 302
Mosher, William, 186
Mulford, Major, 279
Munson, Ebenezer, 220
Munson, Ira, 220
Murfreesboro, N.C., 133, 134

Naples, N.Y., 260, 297
New Bern, N.C., 69, 92, 97, 98, 102, 104, 107, 108, 114, 116, 119, 121, 124, 127, 128, 140, 152, 153, 159, 171, 176, 182, 183, 189, 193, 218, 306, 307
New Ironsides, 27
New Jersey Troops:
    9th Inf., 23, 25, 92, 96, 103
New Kent Court House, Va., 51
Newport News, Va., 74, 114
New York City, N.Y., 159, 290, 292, 293, 305, 308
New York Draft Riots, 143
New York Troops:
    Bat. B, 1st Art., 96, 101
    24th Bat., 172, 178, 179, 180, 193, 204, 212
    3rd Cav., 92, 103, 114, 122, 126, 128, 151
    8th Cav., 274
    12th Cav., 139, 151, 193, 204
    24th Cav., 186
    50th Engineers, 70
    13th Inf., 19, 191
    14th Brooklyn, 30
    18th Inf., 29, 61, 64
    33rd Inf., 43
    44th Inf., 189
    53rd Inf., 35
    56th Inf., 57
    64th Inf., 23
    67th Inf., 29
    75th Inf., 186, 188
    76th Inf., 30, 31
    77th Inf., 32, 260

New York Troops (cont.):
- 87th Inf., 32
- 89th Inf., 23
- 92nd Inf., 103, 117, 118, 119, 124
- 93rd Inf., 47, 48
- 96th Inf., 70, 110
- 98th Inf., 35, 37, 62
- 101st Inf., 145
- 103rd Inf., 35
- 126th Inf., 75, 220, 260
- 139th Inf., 77
- 146th Inf., 220, 222
- 148th Inf., 79, 86, 132, 137, 267, 310

New Orleans, La., 228
Nixonton, N.C., 153, 159
Norfolk, Va., 16, 78, 79, 183, 188
North Carolina Troops (C.S.):
- 2nd Inf., 281
- 17th Inf., 148, 155
- 35th Inf., 205

North Carolina Troops (U.S.):
- 1st Cav., 114, 151
- 2nd Inf., 132, 175, 193, 204, 205, 206

Ocean Pond, Fla., 219
Olean, N.Y., 12
O'Neill, Col. (C.S.), 260
Ontario County, N.Y., 161, 164, 174, 179, 181, 186, 189, 260, 264
Ould, Commissioner, 280

Page, Dr., 153
Palmer, Gen. Innis, 36, 53, 59, 122
Pautuket, 189
Peck, Gen. John, 162, 200
Pennsylvania Troops:
- 11th Cav., 87
- 11th Inf., 74
- 57th Inf., 23
- 85th Inf., 84, 94, 99, 109
- 87th Inf., 21
- 101st Inf., 132, 136, 139, 141, 147, 148, 149, 166, 193, 204, 212
- 103rd Inf., 35, 55, 96, 98, 108, 112, 122, 129, 139, 141, 143, 147, 160, 161, 165, 166, 169, 176, 193, 204, 214

Penn Yan, N.Y., 208

Pensions, 243
Persons, Lt. Col. A. W. (C.S.), 210
Petersburg, Va., 233
Pettigrew, Charles, 177
Pettigrew, Gen. J. J., 107, 117, 118, 119, 178
Pettigrew, Mary, 178
Phillips, John, 293
Pickett, Gen. Edward (C.S.), 171, 178
Pilot Bay, 83
Plymouth, N.C., 107, 129, 130, 132, 135, 142, 144, 149, 150, 153, 155, 156, 158, 159, 168, 169, 171, 175, 176, 178, 179, 180, 188, 189, 193, 195, 199, 200, 207, 214, 218, 219, 268, 293, 301, 307
Porter, Gen. Fitz John, 41
Portsmouth, Va., 137, 139

Quinlan, Jack, 133, 196, 197

Rainbow, N.C., 190
Raines, Rev., 37
Raleigh, N.C., 171, 205, 207
Ransom, Gen. John (C.S.), 171, 204, 253
Richburg, N.Y., 12
Richmond, Va., 41, 59, 122, 171, 210, 214, 225, 232, 279, 283
River Queen, 285
Roach, Capt., 193
Roanoke Island, N.C., 144, 159, 164, 165, 166, 167, 168, 183, 189, 192, 193, 205
RObertson, Gen. (C.S.), 107
Rochester, N.Y., 191
Rocky Mount, N.C., 207
Rosecrans, Gen. W. S., 152
Rush, Dr., 174

Sabins, Zade, 260, 270
Sackett, Albert, 215
Salisbury, N.C., 210, 275
Sampson, Capt., 193
Savage Station, Va., 53-57, 60
Savannah, Ga., 208, 218, 230, 254, 276
Scuppernong Grapes, 151
Scurvy, 243
Seekel, Mrs., 302
Selma, Ala., 230
Seneca County, N.Y., 251

Seneca Falls, N.Y., 44, 186, 192, 293, 297, 301, 302
Seven Pines, Va., 53
Seward, William, 285
Seymour, 149, 150
SHerman, Gen. W. T., 227, 231, 235, 239, 250, 270, 272, 276, 277, 279
Shortsville, N.Y., 230
Sibley Tent, 23
Simons, Ben, 260, 270
Skull, Mrs., 175
Smith, Sydney, 234
South Carolina Troops:
    2nd Inf., 281
    18th Inf., 207
    Holcombe Legion, 206
Southfield, 149, 155, 196 (ill.)
Spinola, Gen., 122, 124, 125
S. R. Spaulding, 290
Statebury, S.C., 264
Stephens, Alexander, 285
Stevenson, Gen., 242
St. Johnsville, N.Y., 293
Suffolk, Va., 69, 74, 78, 79, 82, 83, 103, 105, 108, 133
Swaby, Dr. William, 293
Swamp Angel, 255
Swan Quarter Bay, N.C., 166
Syracuse, N.Y., 293

Tacoma, 192
Tallahassee, 271
Tarboro, N.C., 206, 214
Taylor, Col. A. W., 193
The Brothers, 183
Thos. Collyer, 181, 189
Troy, N.Y., 158
Trumpeter, 164, 166
Turner, Noah, 267
Turner, Wesley, 233
Tuscaloosa, Ala., 209
Tyre, N.Y., 220

Underwriter, 149, 181
United States Troops:
    12th U.S.C.T., 219
Utica, N.Y., 7, 232

Van Valkenburg, Gen., 10, 31, 32
Van Wyck, Col., 57
Veteran Reserve Corps, 172
Vicksburg, Miss., 141, 142

Wadsworth, Gen., 84
Warwick Court House, Va., 46
Washington, D.C., 3, 4, 21, 33, 34, 41, 69, 183
Washington, George, 34, 38, 46
Washington, 78
Washington Irving, 151
Waterloo, N.Y., 168, 186, 301
Weldon, N.C., 171, 182, 207
Wellsville, N.Y., 12
Wessells, Gen. Henry, 3, 59, 74, 80, 81 (ill.), 84, 87, 96, 99, 101, 102, 103, 109, 110, 118, 120, 122, 124, 125, 126, 135, 146, 149, 159, 171, 176, 182, 193, 199, 200, 204
Whelan, Father, 224
Whitehead, 191
White House Landing, Va., 57
Wight, Elizabeth, 168
Wilderness, Va., 220
Willet's Point, N.Y., 291, 293
Williamsburg, Va., 49, 50, 70
Wilmington, N.C., 107, 171, 203, 207, 281, 285, 286, 287, 288, 289
Wilson, John, 220
Winder, Gen. John (C.S.), 209, 210, 230, 232, 233, 235, 240, 242, 251, 274, 283
Winder, Capt. William (C.S.), 210, 240
Winfield, N.C., 134
Winsor, N.C., 180
Winton, N.C., 161
Wirz, Capt. Henry (C.S.), 201, 209, 214, 217, 219, 222, 230, 231, 232, 233, 234, 239, 241, 251, 271, 272
Wright, Russ, 129

Yaro, Jack, 29
Yorktown, Va., 46, 47, 48, 71, 72, 73

INDEX TO MEMBERS OF THE 85TH NEW YORK

Ackley, Edmund, 14, 304
Adams, Samuel, 156, 157 (ill.)
Aldrich, C. S., 7, 9, 10, 13, 17, 29, 31, 32, 35, 36, 57, 60, 91, 112, 142, 146,
    147, 148, 151, 152, 160, 162, 164, 176, 180, 181, 182, 183, 186,
    190, 191, 192, 198, 256, 268, 303
Allen, Capt., 258
Andrews, Lt., 149
Avery, Lt. Col., 25

Bancroft, Albert H., 14, 27, 29, 30, 33, 51, 64, 65, 98, 99, 128, 139, 178, 179,
    180, 218, 241, 245, 246, 304
Barton, John, 230
Bascom, Lt., 193
Beeman, Elam, 189
Belknap, Jonathan, 12, 23, 29, 31, 36, 57, 114, 118, 125, 137, 139
Bennett, Amos, 14, 304
Bentley, Edgar, 14, 88, 276, 304
Blake, John, 27, 55, 59, 115, 255, 304
Booth (Boothe), John, 14, 25, 169, 215, 218, 232
Bradley, Billy, 227, 229
Briggs, N. H., 14, 268, 277
Brogan, James, 14, 304
Brunson (Bronson), Amos, 10, 12, 29, 30, 36, 53, 54 (ill.), 60, 191, 303
Buckingham, Sgt., 182, 183
Bucklin, Ambrose, 183
Buell, John, 12, 66, 91, 136, 147, 192, 247, 251, 303
Burlingame, Pvt., 148
Burlington, Charles, 304

Carpenter, Napollon, 14, 240, 304
Carson, James, 12, 30, 44, 218, 219, 247, 283, 303
Cartwright, Capt., 192
Chamberlin, Oliver, 14, 305
Chamberlin, Rensaler, 14, 305
Chapin, Capt., 88, 94, 108, 159, 197
Clark (Clarke), Capt. William, 3, 7, 10, 11 (ill.), 12, 21, 24, 25, 28, 32, 38,
    43, 46, 51, 55, 57, 58, 60, 64, 65, 74, 75, 80, 87, 115, 122, 128, 140,
    144, 146, 149, 159, 160, 164, 172, 182, 192, 205, 240, 303
Clum, Pvt., 96
Coates, Capt., 145, 147, 150, 172, 182, 192
Cone, Linus, 14, 305
Corning, Edward, 12

Crandall, Sheridan, 14, 38, 57, 303
Crane, Henry, 14, 27, 80, 89, 163, 305
Crane, Walter, 168, 188, 192
Crosby, Reuben, 14, 122, 276, 305
Culver, Lyman, 14, 305
Cummings, Joe, 12, 71, 162, 247, 271, 276, 277, 286, 303

Davis, Col. Uriah, 12, 30, 31, 32
Demeritt, John, 14, 305
Depant, Henry, 14, 305
Deyo, Ira, 14, 121, 149, 150, 172, 258, 262, 263 (ill.), 297, 305
Dillon, Bill, 9, 12, 46, 222, 303
Dix, John, 83, 84
Dunlop, James, 14, 31, 155, 305
Dutton, Col., 38, 43

Evarts, Ed, 66

Fairbanks, Sgt., 183
Fardella, Col. Enrico, 145, 160, 191, 192, 193, 196
Farrar (Ferrar), Emory, 14, 55, 210, 214, 215, 235, 242, 256, 260, 267, 270, 271, 272, 274, 276, 277, 280, 286, 305
Fay, Pvt., 182, 183, 192, 195
Francis, John, 27, 305
Francisco, Francis, 14, 80, 98, 109, 148, 155, 271, 305

Gilbert, Joseph, 14, 305
Gilbert, William, 14
Gipple, Henry, 38, 84, 305
Glenn, Tom, 14, 29, 152, 214, 305
Gooding, Chester, 14, 27, 46, 49, 58, 59, 63, 66, 78, 97, 136, 173, 306
Gooding, Zephaniah, 13, 27, 37, 125, 137, 303
Goodrich, Lt., 12, 291, 147
Graham, William, 57, 58, 62, 306
Green, Stpehen, 14, 144, 161, 306
Gregg, Augustus, 9, 14, 44, 60, 192, 210, 286, 306
Griffin, Henry, 14

Hadsell, Tobias, 14, 267, 306
Hall, William, 14, 62, 182, 306
Hamilton, Capt., 147, 160
Hart, Calvin, 14, 44, 306
Hodges, Quartermaster, 177, 178, 180
Holcombe, John, 243

Humphreys, Charles, 12, 46, 147, 149, 303
Huntington, Rev., 172
Hussey, Alexander, 14, 158, 268, 269 (ill.), 306

Ingraham, Andrew, 14, 306
Ingraham, Charles, 14, 35, 78, 243, 306
Insse, Boswell, 14, 30, 57, 113, 306

Jessup, Frank, 32
Johnson, Wyman, 168
Jones, Edward, 14, 62, 190, 306

Kern, Charles, 14, 245
Kern, Clark, 14, 173, 306
Kern, Jared, 46, 306
King, Charles, 108, 127, 145
King, Reuben, 9, 33, 36, 57, 74, 98, 164
Knapp, Edward, 14, 30, 46, 66, 80, 82, 83, 88, 98, 103, 109, 163, 306

Leach, Silas, 14, 306
Lewis, James, 12, 24
Lewis, Parmer, 14, 18, 151, 243, 307
Lindsay, Samuel, 152
Logan, John, 14, 267, 307

Macumber, Andrew, 14, 307
Marra, John, 14, 38, 73, 114, 151, 152, 158, 307
Martin, Spencer, 10, 17, 27, 28, 29, 35, 36, 49, 51, 58, 59, 60, 62, 63, 83, 85, 88, 112, 113, 122, 128, 136, 145, 146, 147, 160, 303
Marvin, Capt. Spencer, 12, 193
Mary, John, 14, 57, 79, 210, 260, 307
McHenry, Charles, 12, 19, 27, 44, 58, 60, 64, 67, 89, 91, 94, 96, 98, 103, 108, 112, 118, 134, 143, 144, 147, 160, 163, 173, 190, 191, 193, 258, 303
McNinch, Charles, 136
McNinch, John, 307
Meade, Marcus, 14, 110, 111 (ill.), 145, 215, 218, 274, 307
Morris, John, 232, 268, 271, 273, 274
Morris, Lyman, 14, 307
Munger, Lt., 78
Munson, Charles, 12, 37, 304

Oliver, Pvt., 92

Parke, Charles, 307
Parks, Joel, 14
Peak, Lt., 94
Peck, Benjamin, 14, 317
Peckham, Pvt., 4
Perkey, Jake, 198, 219
Phillips, Alvah, 14, 15, 57, 79, 176, 307
Phillips, George, 14, 27, 92, 115, 173, 238, 241, 304
Phillips, Richard, 14, 27, 62, 173, 232, 238, 244
Pieke, Lt., 166
Pitt, Lt., 156
Plimpton, William, 14, 307
Poppel, Barber, 14, 179, 197, 204, 307
Poppo, Pvt., 121
Porter, Thomas, 14, 132, 135, 158, 159, 177, 179, 218, 257, 308
Purkey, Daniel, 14, 308
Purkey, Jacob, 14, 308

Raines, John, 35, 37
Reed, Daniel, 14, 77, 219, 308
Richardson, William, 14, 66, 308
Robinson, James, 12, 77, 103, 104 (ill.), 132, 144, 147, 150, 160, 173, 193, 275, 303
Rose, Lansing, 308
Ross, Albert, 14, 158, 308
Rowley, Len, 14, 82

Sackett, Richard, 205
Sage, Oscar, 15, 31
Seymour, Henry, 14, 27, 28, 29
Shepherd (Sheppard), Horace, 14, 44, 131, 135, 266, 278, 297
Sherman, Daniel, 14, 304
Simmons, Charles, 14, 27, 34, 43, 51, 55, 57, 78, 147, 210, 241, 247, 304
Simmons, Henry, 14, 27, 34, 61, 66, 145
Simons, Ben, 279
SMith, Seymour, 14, 27, 130, 140, 161, 163, 173, 197, 204, 205
SMith, Dr. William, 12, 137
Snook, George, 14, 122, 131, 150, 172, 179
Spears, James, 14, 49, 308
Steele, Edgar, 14, 57, 308
Stillman, Ellicott, 14, 91, 131, 183, 304
Straight, John, 15
Such, Tom, 14, 140

Tanner, George, 308

Underhill, Sgt., 125

Van Wie, Pvt., 15, 66, 172, 173
Vogt (Voad, Vogde), Abram, 15, 55, 245

Warner, Theodore, 12, 110, 175, 176, 262, 304
Watrous, Myron, 15
Welch, Lt., 142
Wellman, Major Alijah, 12, 36, 57, 91, 97, 98
Wetmore, Elam, 57, 79, 156, 179, 242, 258, 259 (ill.), 262
Wheeler, Milton, 15
White, Sam, 162
Whitney, Lt., 77, 139
Wilcox, Franklin, 15, 252
Wilson, Frank, 165
Wright, Nathan, 15, 91, 92, 146, 207, 270
Wright, Russ, 32

Young, Charles, 31
Young, William, 55

BRIEF BIOGRAPHY OF THE AUTHOR

The author, Professor of Social Studies Education at the State University of New York - Geneseo since 1969, grew up in Illinois and received his B.A., M.A., and Ph.D. degrees at Hamilton College, the University of Illinois, and Syracuse University respectively. He has served as a public school teacher in Illinois, Chairman of Elementary and Secondary Education at SUNY-Geneseo, President of the Geneseo Central School Board, and President of the New York State Council for the Social Studies.

Dr. Mahood has authored or co-authored five books: *The Market Place; The Human Dynamo; Government, USA: Teaching Social Studies in Middle and Senior High Schools; Decisions! Decisions!;* and *The Plymouth Pilgrims: A History of the Eighty Fifth New York Infantry in the Civil War.* He has also written articles in such journals as *Social Education, The Social Studies, The Clearing House, Civil War Times Illustrated* and *Civil War Regiments.*

Recognition Dr. Mahood has received include a SUNY Chancellor's Award for Excellence in Teaching (1976), the Distinguished Social Studies Educator from the New York State Council for the Social Studies (1984), *Who's Who in American Education* and *Who's Who in the East.*

MORE FINE BOOKS ON NEW JERSEY IN THE CIVIL WAR

BY LONGSTREET HOUSE, PO BOX 730, HIGHTSTOWN, NEW JERSEY 08520

JERSEY CAVALIERS: A HISTORY OF THE FIRST NEW JERSEY VOLUNTEER CAVALRY, by Edward G. Longacre. An all-new history by the award winning author of *The Cavalry at Gettysburg*. 423 pages, roster, 15 maps, over 90 illustrations including 50 individual portraits. $35 plus $3 postage.

HEXAMER'S FIRST NEW JERSEY BATTERY IN THE CIVIL WAR, edited by Dr. David Martin. 36 page pamphlet. Roster. $6 plus $1 postage.

HISTORY OF BATTERY B, FIRST NEW JERSEY LIGHT ARTILLERY, by Michael Hanifen. Reprint of 1905 edition (D-NJ-1). One of the scarcest of all New Jersey regimentals. The only monograph memoir on any of the state's five batteries in the war. 200 pages, roster, 44 illustrations, new indices. $25 plus $3 postage.

HISTORY OF THE ELEVENTH NEW JERSEY VOLUNTEERS, by Thomas B. Marbaker. Reprint of 1898 edition (D-NJ-46) with new introduction by John Kuhl. 490 pages, over 90 illustrations, 10 maps, roster, index. $32 plus $3 postage.

TO GETTYSBURG AND BEYOND: THE TWELFTH NEW JERSEY VOLUNTEER INFANTRY, II CORPS, ARMY OF THE POTOMAC, 1862-1865, by Edward G. Longacre. 467 pages, roster, index, 15 maps, over 90 illustrations, including 53 portraits of members of the regiment. $36 plus $3 postage.

THE MONOCACY REGIMENT: A COMMEMORATIVE HISTORY OF THE 14TH NEW JERSEY INFANTRY IN THE CIVIL WAR, edited by Dr. David Martin. Contains an exact reprint of Terrill's *Campaign of the Fourteenth New Jersey Volunteers* (1884); reset text of *Letters of Major Peter Vredenburgh of the Battles and Marches of the Old Fourteenth Regiment* (1870's); and new material by Joe Bilby and David Martin. 352 pages, 3 maps, 48 photographs of regiment members, indices. $30 plus $3 postage.

THREE ROUSING CHEERS: A HISTORY OF THE FIFTEENTH NEW JERSEY INFANTRY FROM FLEMINGTON TO APPOMATTOX, by Joseph G. Bilby. An all-new history. 462 pages, roster, 12 maps, over 100 illustrations including 60 individual portraits. $36 plus $3 postage.

FIFTY YEARS AGO: A BRIEF HISTORY OF THE 29TH NEW JERSEY VOLUNTEERS, by T.C. Morford. Reset text of 1912 edition (not in Dornbusch). Introduction, roster and index by David Martin. 54 page booklet. $8 plus $1 postage.

NEW JERSEY TROOPS IN THE GETTYSBURG CAMPAIGN, by Samuel Toombs. Reprint of 1888 edition, with new index and introduction by Dr. David Martin. 440 pages. $30 plus $3 postage.

ADDRESS DELIVERED AT THE REDEDICATION OF THE MONUMENT TO THE FIRST NEW JERSEY BRIGADE AT GETTYSBURG, OCTOBER 9, 1982, by Dr. David Martin. 12 page booklet. $3.50 plus $1 postage.

CAMP VREDENBURG IN THE CIVIL WAR, by Dr. David Martin. 28 page booklet on the camp's location and history near Freehold. 3 maps, 4 illustrations. $6 plus $1 postage.

FORGOTTEN WARRIORS; NEW JERSEY'S AFRICAN AMERICAN SOLDIERS IN THE CIVIL WAR. The first study to present the experience of Black troops from a single state. 80 page booklet, 11 illustrations, $7.95 plus $1 postage.

MEN OF COLOR AT THE BATTLE OF MONMOUTH, JUNE 28, 1778: THE ROLE OF AFRICAN AMERICANS AND NATIVE AMERICANS AT MONMOUTH, by Richard S. Walling. Includes a list of nearly 200 names and identifications. 2nd edition. 40 pages. $4.95 plus $1 postage. Available February 1994.

MORE FINE BOOKS FROM LONGSTREET HOUSE

REGIMENTAL STRENGTHS AND LOSSES AT GETTYSBURG, by John Busey and David Martin. An absolute must for all serious students of the battle. Contains order of battle and strength data not available elsewhere. Detailed comparative strength and loss tables. 351 pages, indices. $20 plus $3 postage.

THESE HONORED DEAD: THE UNION CASUALTIES AT GETTYSBURG, by John Busey. Full list of 5097 killed and mortally wounded, listed by state and regiment, plus complete index. A definitive study that gives age, enlistment date, nature of wound, and burial data. 404 pages, 30 illustrations. $24 plus $3 postage.

THE LAST FULL MEASURE: BURIALS IN THE SOLDIERS' NATIONAL CEMETERY AT GETTYSBURG, by John Busey. The only published index to the cemetery, with corrected name listings. 277 pages, 7 illustrations, map. $20 plus $3 postage.

HOLDING THE LEFT AT GETTYSBURG, THE 20TH N.Y.S.M. ON JULY 1, 1863. by Seward Osborne. A well received original pamphlet. 36 pages, 2 maps, 6 photographs. $6 plus $1 postage.

A CASUALTY AT GETTYSBURG AND ANDERSONVILLE: SELECTIONS FROM THE CIVIL WAR DIARY OF PRIVATE AUSTIN A. CARR OF THE 82ND NEW YORK INFANTRY, edited by Dr. David Martin. 22 page booklet. $6 plus $1 postage.

CLARA BARTON AND HIGHTSTOWN, by Grace Norton Rogers, Maurice P. Shuman Jr., and Dr. David G. Martin tells of Clara Barton's year teaching in East Windsor, NJ, in 1851-52, and her close relationship with Mary Norton. 36 pages, 5 illustrations. $6 plus $1 postage.